Step Forward
Language for Everyday Life

Step-By-Step Lesson Plans

SERIES DIRECTOR
Jayme Adelson-Goldstein

4

Jenni Currie Santamaria

OXFORD
UNIVERSITY PRESS

OXFORD
UNIVERSITY PRESS

198 Madison Avenue
New York, NY 10016 USA

Great Clarendon Street, Oxford OX2 6DP UK

Oxford University Press is a department of the University of Oxford.
It furthers the University's objective of excellence in research,
scholarship, and education by publishing worldwide in

Oxford New York

Auckland Cape Town Dar es Salaam Hong Kong Karachi
Kuala Lumpur Madrid Melbourne Mexico City Nairobi
New Delhi Shanghai Taipei Toronto

With offices in

Argentina Austria Brazil Chile Czech Republic France Greece
Guatemala Hungary Italy Japan Poland Portugal Singapore
South Korea Switzerland Thailand Turkey Ukraine Vietnam

OXFORD and OXFORD ENGLISH are registered trademarks of
Oxford University Press

Executive Publisher: Janet Aitchison
Editorial Manager: Stephanie Karras
Senior Editor: Sharon Sargent
Art Director: Maj-Britt Hagsted
Senior Designer: Claudia Carlson
Layout Artist: Colleen Ho
Production Manager: Shanta Persaud
Production Controller: Zainaltu Jawat Ali

Printed in China

10 9 8 7 6

ISBN: 978 0 19 439231 0 STEP-BY-STEP LESSON PLANS
ISBN: 978 0 19 439841 1 STEP-BY-STEP LESSON PLANS WITH CD-ROM (PACK)
ISBN: 978 0 19 439842 8 CD-ROM

Many thanks to Sharon Sargent for her guidance
and encouragement; Jayme Adelson-Goldstein
for her insight and leadership; and Stacey Hunter
and Meg Araneo, who made my writing look
good. I am also grateful to Jean Rose and my
colleagues and students at ABC Adult School for
their constant inspiration.

Special thanks to Tony and Amaya, whose love
and laughter keep me going.

Jenni Currie Santamaria

I gratefully acknowledge the dedication and
expertise of Jenni Santamaria, Barbara Denman,
Stephanie Karras, Sharon Sargent, Stacey Hunter,
Meg Araneo, Nicoletta Barolini, Colleen Ho,
Maj-Britt Hagsted, Shanta Persaud, and Zai Jawat Ali.
Special thanks to Jenni for bringing her exceptional
"multilevel" talents to all four books.

For Norma, who always taught that the best
lessons come from the learner.

Jayme Adelson-Goldstein

Acknowledgments

The publishers would like to thank the following for their permission to adapt copyright material:

p. 14-15 "Test Anxiety" used with permission of www.hsc.edu

p. 14-15 "Managing Test Anxiety" used with permission of SDS's Learning Skills Services, The University of Western Ontario web site, www.sdc.uwo.ca

p. 28-29 "News Audiences Increasingly Politicized: Where Americans Go for News" used with permission of http://people-press.org

p. 42-43 "Background on CTIA's Semi-Annual Wireless Industry Survey" used with permission of CTIA - The Wireless Association®

p. 56 "Career Exploration" used with permission of www.acinet.org

p. 168-169 Copyright © 2002 by The New York Times Co. Adapted from "She has a Knife and She Knows How to Use it", by Elaine Louie, originally published June 5, 2002 by The New York Times

Cover photograph: Corbis/Punchstock
Back cover photograph: Brian Rose

Illustrations by: Jane Spencer, p.2, p.8, p.36, p.101, p.134; Bill Dickson, p.3, p.25, p.34, p.53, p.67, p.107, p.138, p.165,;Tom Newscom, p.4, p.116, p.158; Karen Minot, p.5, p.19, p.61, pg.102 (#'s 2, 3, and 4), p.144; John Batten, p.6, p.13 (top), p.55, p.64, p.78, p.110, p.111, p.123, p.148, p.151; Geo Parkin, p.11, p.23, p.40, p.74, p.96, p.112, p.124, p.130, p.154, p.155; Annie Bissett, p.13, (bottom), p.28, p.69 (bottom), p.139 (top), p.162; Arlene Boehm, p.17, p.20, p.24, 39, p.125; Barb Bastian, p.18, p.47, p.70, p.81, p.89, p.109, p.117, p.125, p.137, p.145, p.159; Laurie Conley, p.31, p.45, p.46, p.92, pg.102 (#'s 5, 6, 7, 8, and 9), p.120, p.143, p.157; Uldis Klavins, p.32, p.60; Mark Hannon, p.33, p.75; Shawn Banner, p.50; Terry Paczko, p.88, p.95; Ken Dewar, p.103; Kevin Brown, p.106, p.126, Mike Hortens, p. 75, p.83, p.131, p.139, p.153.

We would like to thank the following for their permission to reproduce photographs: Photo Edit Inc.: Spencer Grant, p.10; Index Stock: HIRB, p.14; Getty Images: Don Emmert, p.18 (General Assembly); Punch Stock: p.19 (bus); Photo Edit Inc.: Michael Newman, p.19 (traffic); Age Fotostock: Grantpix p.22; Age Fotostock: Andy Goodwin, p.38; Punch Stock/Digital Vision: p.42 (man); Punch Stock: p.42 (woman); Getty Images: Mecky, p.52 (american sights); Punch Stock/Visions of American.com: Joseph Sohm, p.52 (football game); Photo Edit Inc.: Kayte M. Deioma: p.59; Reuters: p.66; Photo Edit Inc.: Spencer Grant, p.69 (teacher); Age Fotostock: Michael N. Paras, p.69 (hotel worker); Masterfile: Dana Hursey, p.69 (computer technician); Photo Edit Inc.: Barbara Stitzer, p.73; Masterfile: p.84; Superstock/BrandX: p.87; Superstock: Nicholas Eveleigh, p.94 (computer); Superstock/SSC: p.94 (books); The Image Works: Lauren Goodsmith, p.98; Punch Stock: p.102; Masterfile: Jeremy Maude, p.108; Masterfile: p.115 (left); Getty Images: Marc Romanelli, p.115 (right); Photo Edit Inc.: Dana White, p.129; Photo Edit Inc.: Tony Freeman, p.136 (top); Photo Edit Inc.: Cindy Charles, p.136 (bottom); Masterfile: Tim Mantoani, p.144; Dennis Kitchen: p.150; Masterfile: Steven Puetzer, p.153; Superstock/Banana Stock: p.159; Photo Edit Inc.: p.164 (top); Masterfile: p.164 (bottom); Photo Edit Inc.: Sonda Dawes, p.168; Getty Images: Ryan McVay, p.171.

Contents

Introduction to *Step Forward Step-By-Step Lesson Plans* ....T-v
    What is *Step Forward*? .... T-v
    What's in this book? .... T-v
    How does *Step Forward* meet learners' needs? ....T-viii
    What are *Step Forward's* principles of effective lesson-plan design? ....T-ix
    How do I use this book? .... T-x
    How does *Step Forward* address the multilevel classroom? ....T-x
    How do I use the Multilevel Strategies to plan multilevel lessons? ....T-xi
    How is *Step Forward* a complete program? ....T-xi

Pre-unit The First Step T-2

Unit 1 It Takes All Kinds! T-4

Unit 2 Keeping Current T-18

Unit 3 Going Places T-32

Unit 4 Get the Job T-46

Unit 5 Safe and Sound T-60

Unit 6 Getting Ahead T-74

Unit 7 Buy Now, Pay Later T-88

Unit 8 Satisfaction Guaranteed T-102

Unit 9 Take Care T-116

Unit 10 Get Involved! T-130

Unit 11 Find It on the Net T-144

Unit 12 How did I do? T-158

Listening Scripts 172

Grammar Charts 183

Vocabulary List 193

Index 196

Reproducible Answer Cards T-199

Learning Logs T-200

Multilevel Troubleshooting Chart T-204

Introduction to *Step Forward Step-By-Step Lesson Plans*

Welcome to *Step Forward Step-by-Step Lesson Plans.* These lesson plans are your guide to *Step Forward,* the adult English language course designed to work in single-level and multilevel classes. In addition to being a step-by-step lesson-planning tool, this book is also a rich collection of tips, strategies, and activities that complement the lessons in the *Step Forward Student Book.* In keeping with current, scientifically based research on language acquisition and instruction, these lesson plans provide a variety of instructional strategies and techniques that work across methodologies and learner populations.

What is *Step Forward?*

The *Step Forward* series is

- the instructional backbone for any standards-based, integrated skills, English language course;
- a program that teaches the skills needed for everyday life, the workplace, the community, and academic pursuits;

- a ready-made framework for learner-centered instruction within a single-level or multilevel environment; and
- a four-skills program that develops students' listening, speaking, reading, and writing skills, as well as their grammar, pronunciation, math, cooperative, and critical-thinking skills.

Step Forward's communication objectives are authentic and taught in conjunction with contextualized language forms. Research shows that when lessons are based on authentic communication and there is a focus on form within that context, learners incorporate new and correct structures into their language use.[1]

What's in this book?

The *Step Forward Step-By-Step Lesson Plans,* a comprehensive instructional planning resource, contains detailed lesson plans interleaved with *Step Forward Student Book* pages.

Each unit in the *Step-By-Step Lesson Plans* follows this format.

Student Book pages are next to lesson plan pages for easy reference.

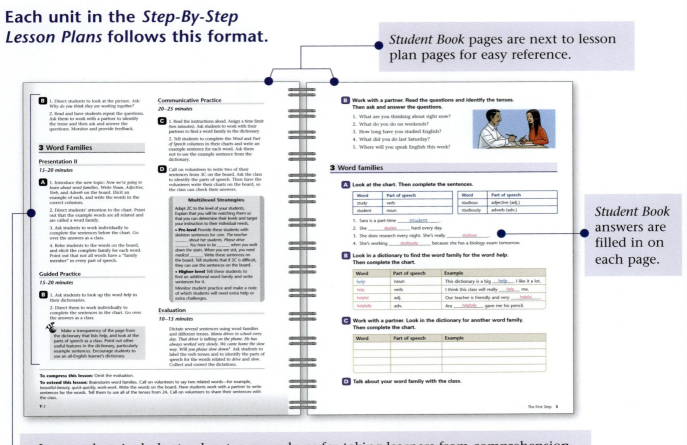

Student Book answers are filled in on each page.

Lesson plans include step-by-step procedures for taking learners from comprehension to accurate production to meaningful and fluent interaction.

---

[1] Rod Ellis, et al., "Doing focus on form," *Systems,* 30 (2002): 419-432.

Each lesson references related *Oxford Picture Dictionary* topics for vocabulary support.

Every lesson in *Step Forward* is correlated to CASAS competencies, Florida's Standardized Student Syllabi (LCPs), Equipped for the Future (EFF) standards, and the Secretary's Commission on Achieving Necessary Skills (SCANS).

A general lesson information chart provides multilevel objectives, support-skill focus, and correlations.

Unit 1 Lesson 5

Objectives	Grammar	Vocabulary	Correlations
On- , Pre-, and Higher-level: Read about and discuss test anxiety	Simple-past and simple-present tense (*I took the driving test. I think children take too many tests.*)	*Challenge, college-entrance exam, faint, manageable* For vocabulary support for pre-level students, see this **Oxford Picture Dictionary** topic: Feelings	**CASAS:** 0.1.2, 0.1.5, 0.2.1, 2.5.6, 7.4.4, 7.4.7, 7.4.9 **LCPs:** 39.01, 49.06, 49.16, 49.17 **SCANS:** Acquires and evaluates information, Uses computers to process information **EFF:** Listen actively, Read with understanding, Speak so others can understand, Take responsibility for learning

Warm-up and Review

10–15 minutes (books closed)

Draw a happy face and sad face on the board as column heads. Elicit words that describe feelings, and ask students which column they belong in. Write the words. If students run out of ideas, describe situations to elicit more "feeling" words. *How do you feel at the doctor's office? On a roller coaster? When you can't understand what someone is saying?*

Introduction

5 minutes

1. Add the word *anxiety* to the board. Tell students that it means extreme nervousness. If most of the words on the board are adjectives, point out that *anxious* is the adjective form of *anxiety*.

2. State the objective: *Today we're going to read and write about test anxiety.*

1 Get ready to read

Presentation

15–20 minutes

A Read the question aloud. Circle any words on the board that students use to describe their feelings about taking tests.

B Read the words and definitions. Elicit sample sentences from students using the words.

Pre-Reading

C 1. Direct students to look at the title, the picture, and the section headings. Call on a volunteer to say what the article is about.

2. Ask students to guess what strategies the article will recommend for dealing with test anxiety.

2 Read and respond

Guided Practice I

25–30 minutes

A 1. Ask students to read the article silently.

2. Direct students to underline unfamiliar words they would like to know. Elicit the words and encourage other students to provide definitions or examples.

3. Check comprehension. Ask: *What are some symptoms of anxiety?* [headaches, nausea, crying easily, feeling annoyed and frustrated, difficulty concentrating]

Multilevel Strategies

Adapt 2A to the level of your students.

• **Pre-level** Provide these students with a summary of the ideas in the reading. *1. Many people experience test anxiety. Test anxiety can cause headaches, nausea, and emotional symptoms. Test anxiety makes it difficult to concentrate. 2. You can control test anxiety. Prepare for the test. Take care of your health. Come to the test early. When you feel nervous, take deep breaths.*

Direct these students to read the summary while other students are reading 2A.

T-14

Lesson plans are organized into seven stages.

Multilevel Strategies help meet the varying needs of all learners in the classroom.

Time guidelines help you pace the class.

Guided Practice II

15–20 minutes

B 1. Play the audio. Have students read along silently.

2. Elicit and discuss any additional questions about the reading.

C Have students work individually to circle the correct answers. Go over the answers as a class. Write them on the board.

Multilevel Strategies

For 2C, work with pre-level students.

• **Pre-level** Ask these students questions about the summary while other students are completing 2C. *What are some symptoms of test anxiety? How can you control test anxiety?* Give students time to copy the answers to 2C from the board.

3 Talk it over

Communicative Practice

15–20 minutes

1. Read the questions aloud. Set a time limit (three minutes). Have students work independently to think about the questions and write their answers in note form.

2. Call on individuals to share their ideas and experiences.

Application

5–10 minutes

BRING IT TO LIFE

Read the instructions aloud. Provide students with URLs where they can find free learning-style tests.

 Before students do the *Bring It to Life* assignment, type *learning-style test* into a search engine on the Internet to find a number of free learning-style test sites. Test formats vary from multiple choice, a *one-to-four* ranking system, and *never/seldom/often* choices. Print and make a transparency of the first page from several different tests. Go over them in class to familiarize your students with different ways of answering tests and to demonstrate the importance of following directions.

Tips provide insights and ideas to make lessons even more successful.

To compress this lesson: Conduct 2C as a whole-class activity.

To extend this lesson: Set up a debate about question 2 in *Talk it over.*

1. After students have discussed the question, elicit arguments and write them on the board under *Pros* and *Cons.*

2. Choose eight students (two groups of four) to be the debaters. Tell one side they are going to argue in favor of frequent testing in schools and the other that they are going to argue against it. Tell them to choose a role: 1, 2, 3, or 4. Number 1s will present the team's argument. Number 2s will respond to what the first team said. Number 3s will conclude. Number 4s will take notes and help teammates. Give students five minutes to talk with their teammates, choose their roles, and prepare their best arguments.

3. While the teams are preparing, explain to the rest of the class that they will be judges. Tell them they need to judge on how clear and convincing the arguments are, not on whether they agree or not.

4. Toss a coin to decide which team will go first. Have the Number 1s speak, then the Number 2s and Number 3s. Ask the class to choose a winning team. Applaud everyone for the effort.

And/Or have students complete **Workbook 4 page 7** and **Multilevel Activity Book 4 pages 24–25**.

Tips on how to compress or extend a lesson aid time and classroom management.

Unit 1 Learning Log for _____ (name) **Date:** _____

I can
- ❑ use words for personality and learning styles.
- ❑ write a paragraph about learning styles.
- ❑ use action and non-action verbs. *(I like books. I'm reading right now.)*
- ❑ express opinions about education.
- ❑ ask *Yes/No* and information questions.
- ❑ understand information about test anxiety.

My favorite exercise was _____

I need to practice _____

I want to learn more about _____

Unit 2 Learning Log for _____ (name) **Date:** _____

I can
- ❑ use words for news and newspapers.
- ❑ write about a news story.
- ❑ use the past passive. *(The accident was caused by the fog.)*
- ❑ talk about current events.
- ❑ use reflexive pronouns. *(I saw myself on TV.)*
- ❑ understand an article about reading the news.

My favorite exercise was _____

I need to practice _____

I want to learn more about _____

Unit 3 Learning Log for _____ (name) **Date:** _____

I can
- ❑ use words for travel emergencies and problems.
- ❑ write a story about using the phone.
- ❑ use reported speech. *(He said that he was stuck in traffic.)*
- ❑ talk about travel plans.
- ❑ use reported speech with instructions. *(She told me to look at the map.)*
- ❑ understand an article about cell phones.

My favorite exercise was _____

I need to practice _____

I want to learn more about _____

T-200 © Oxford University Press • Permission granted to reproduce for classroom use.

O
Unit 9
Exercise 56

Name: _____

Date: _____

Complete the conversations with the gerund or infinitive form of the words in parentheses. Sometimes there are two correct answers.

Meg: Hi, Tony. Have you decided (1) *to apply* (apply) for a home loan?

Tony: I'm not sure. I'm considering (2)_____ (get) one, but I need (3)_____ (find) out more information first.

Meg: Do you plan (4)_____ (go) to the bank?

Tony: Yes. I like (5)_____ (work) with my loan officer. She always answers my questions.

Ms. Jones: Hello, Tony. I've continued (6)_____ (research) your situation. I just have one question.

Tony: OK. I plan (7)_____ (make) a decision soon.

Ms. Jones: Good. Do you have many debts?

Tony: No. I avoid (8)_____ (use) credit cards, and I don't have any other loans.

Ms. Jones: Perfect. You shouldn't have a problem getting a loan. You can start (9)_____ (fill) out the application today.

Tony: Thank you, but I feel like (10)_____ (take) the application home and reading it first.

Ms. Jones: No problem. Call me if you have any questions.

Oxford University Press © 2006 • Permission granted to reproduce for classroom use.
Step Forward Multilevel Grammar Exercises CD-ROM 4
Verbs with gerunds and infinitives

How does *Step Forward* meet learners' needs?

Step Forward's framework supports the creation of effective, learner-centered classes. Researchers and teachers alike know that learners have a variety of learning styles and preferences; therefore the activities in the *Step Forward* program derive from a number of approaches and techniques.[2] Each lesson includes the visual and aural material, practice exercises, communication tasks, and evaluation activities that are key elements of an effective lesson. No matter what your teaching style, *Step Forward* will make it easier to respond to your learners' language needs.

The Step Forward Framework

Step Forward Student Book 4 has 12 thematic units based on these life-skill topics:

1. Learning Styles
2. News Sources
3. Travel
4. Job Search
5. Safety
6. Interpersonal Skills
7. Money
8. Shopping
9. Health
10. Community
11. Internet
12. Goal Setting

2. C. Van Duzer and M. Florez Cunningham, *Adult English Language Instruction in the 21st Century* (Washington, D.C.: National Center for ESL Literacy Education/Center for Applied Linguistics, 2003):13.

Each unit is divided into six lessons. The first five lessons focus on objectives related to the unit theme and develop specific language skills within the context of the topic. The sixth lesson provides opportunities to review and expand upon the previous lessons' language and information.

In addition to its main objective, each lesson works with the support skills students will need in order to achieve the objective (vocabulary, grammar, pronunciation, computation, etc.) In each of the lessons, learners accomplish the following general objectives:

Lesson 1 Vocabulary: express thoughts and opinions about a topic using thematically linked vocabulary.

Lesson 2 Real-life writing: use model letters, memos, or essays related to the unit topic as the basis for communicating needs or expressing ideas and opinions in writing.

Lesson 3 Grammar: learn and accurately use grammar in order to effectively interact and write on the lesson topic.

Lesson 4 Everyday conversation: use an authentic exchange as the basis for conversations on the lesson topic while developing listening and pronunciation skills and fluency.

Lesson 5 Real-life reading: increase comprehension of narrative reading materials while developing the vocabulary and skills required for both academic and non-academic reading.

Review and expand: integrate the language learned in the previous five lessons in order to accomplish a variety of communication tasks.

What are *Step Forward's* principles of effective lesson-plan design?

Lessons in the *Student Book* follow four principles of effective lesson-plan design:

- Successful learning is anchored to objectives that connect to learners' needs outside the classroom;
- Learners need listening, speaking, reading, and writing, plus math and critical-thinking skill development within each lesson. The lesson's skill focus always relates to the skills that support the objective;
- A staged and sequential lesson helps learners move from knowing about and understanding new language and concepts to putting the new language and concepts to use in their daily lives; and
- A variety of processing and practice activities help learners integrate new information with their prior knowledge in order to achieve the lesson objectives.

Step-by-Step Lesson Plans employs these principles in the easy-access, detailed lesson-teaching notes and multilevel strategies for each of the 72 lessons in the *Student Book*.

The Stages of the *Step Forward* Lesson

A typical *Step Forward* lesson includes seven basic stages, as shown in the chart below. Multiple presentation and practice stages may occur in a lesson, depending on the complexity of the objectives.

Math Extension, Pronunciation Extension, and Problem Solving are self-contained mini-lessons that occur throughout the book. Each provides presentation and practice activities.

STEP FORWARD LESSON STAGES	
Warm-up and Review	Learners typically engage with the whole class and prepare for the upcoming lesson. Missing this stage does not penalize learners who have arrived late.
Introduction	The instructor focuses learners' attention on the lesson objective, relating it to their lives outside the classroom.
Presentation	New information, language, and content is presented and developed to ensure comprehension. Comprehension is carefully checked before proceeding to the next stage.
Guided Practice (controlled practice)	Learners work on developing their accuracy through various exercises and activities, which may be interactive. The activities are tightly structured to support learners' use of the lesson's grammar and vocabulary.
Communicative Practice (less-controlled practice)	Learners apply their skills to build their fluency. Team tasks, pair interviews, and role-plays are all examples of communicative practice.
Application	This stage is often merged with the communicative practice stage. In Lesson 5, however, learners "Bring It To Life" by finding print materials on the life skill or narrative reading topic outside of the classroom.
Evaluation	This stage assesses learners' achievement of the objective. Instructors use informal assessments, such as observations, and more formal evaluation tasks or tests.

How do I use this book?

Planning daily lessons with *Step Forward* and the *Step-by-Step Lesson Plans* is as easy as opening this book, making a couple of notes, and heading to class. Before you begin your daily planning though, it's wise to do a bit of "big picture" planning.

Step One

Reflect

The first step in planning effective lessons is to determine which learning objectives match the needs of your learners. Because the objectives in *Step Forward* are based on the CASAS competencies and the curriculum of some of the best adult programs across the country, it's a pretty safe bet that most of the objectives will match your students' communication needs. Nevertheless, it's important to determine what experience learners already have with the lesson topic, and what they already know. Before starting a unit, read through the topics (labeled *Focus on*) on the first *Student Book* page in the unit and ask yourself the following questions:

- What level of experience do my learners have with each of these topics?
- What is their command of the support skills needed to communicate about these topics?
- How will I determine what my learners already know about this topic? (Possible answers include using the opening exercises in each lesson, using the warm-up activity from the *Lesson Plans*, and using the Picture Differences activity from the *Multilevel Activity Book*.)

Step Two

Preview

Once you have an overview of the unit, preview the *Student Book* page of the first lesson and read through the lesson plan objectives. If you have a single-level class, you may choose to work from the on-level objective, or (as is so often the case) if you have an unidentified multilevel class, you may want to identify which learners will be working toward which objectives.

Step Three

Scan

Next, read through each stage of the lesson plan and the matching sections of the *Student Book* page. The lettered and numbered sections in the lesson plan correlate to the lettered and numbered exercises on the *Student Book* page.

Step Four

Gather

Be sure you have the tools you need. Ask yourself:

- Would any authentic materials help with the presentation of any of the lesson content? (For example, are coins needed for a lesson on money?)
- Will I use the audio CD or cassette tapes for the listening practice or read from the audio script (pages 172–182)?
- Which pages of *The Oxford Picture Dictionary* will be helpful in building comprehension?
- Which *Workbook* pages can learners use while waiting for other learners to complete a lesson task?

Step Five

Calculate

As you read through each stage of the lesson, be sure to notice the suggested time frames and use the compression and extension tips to adjust the lesson to your instructional time period.

Planning for Closing

Many teachers, new and experienced alike, commonly forget to provide a closing activity. Formally bringing the class back together to emphasize what has been accomplished gives learners a chance to assess what they liked and learned in the lesson. Closing activities can be as simple as a class brainstorm of all the words and ideas covered in the lesson or a chain drill that completes the sentence, "Today, I learned …." The closing is also an opportunity for you to share your positive reflections on the lesson and send everyone out into the world a little more lighthearted.

How does *Step Forward* address the multilevel classroom?

Step Forward's multilevel framework addresses a common classroom reality that most instructors face: Even though learners share a classroom and an instructor, they may be working at different competency levels.

Two of the key concepts of successful multilevel instruction are:

1) learners need to feel that they are all part of the same class community; and
2) learners at different levels can work in the same general topic area while achieving different objectives.[3]

---

3. Jill Bell, *Teaching Multilevel Classes in ESL* (San Diego: Dominie Press, 1991): 36–38.

Using *Step Forward's* Multilevel Framework

Multilevel experts recommend that instructors begin their lesson planning by identifying a common theme for students at all levels. Instructors can then create level-specific objectives that relate to that theme. All the lessons within a *Step Forward* unit link to a common theme, with each lesson exploring a facet of that theme. In addition, each lesson plan in *Step-by-Step Lesson Plans* has a set of objectives for three sequenced levels:

Pre-level objectives are for those students who place below the level of the selected student book.

On-level objectives are for those learners who place at the level of the selected student book.

Higher-level objectives are for those learners who place above the level of the selected student book.

By planning a lesson around these three objectives, the teacher can use the *Student Book* and ancillary materials to support instruction across three sequential levels of learners.

Working with Broad Spectrum Multilevel Classes

Experts in multilevel instruction suggest that even broad spectrum classes, those with learners ranging from low-beginning to advanced and having a wide array of skill levels, can be divided into three general groups during each lesson. Because not all learners have the same proficiency level in the same skill areas, learners in multilevel classes may be placed in different groups depending on the skill focus. For example, a student may be in the beginning group in speaking but the intermediate group in writing. Also, depending on the span of levels, an instructor may want to use two levels of *Step Forward* to help meet the needs of learners at either end of the spectrum. (For more information, see the *Step Forward Professional Development Program*).

Learners may move between groups based on the type of lesson being taught. In a lesson where learners' listening and speaking skills are the focus, you might create one group of beginners, a second group of intermediate learners, and a third group of advanced learners. Of course, the formation of these groups would also depend on the number of learners at each level.

For more information, see the Multilevel Troubleshooting Chart on pg T-204 for more tips and resources for resolving multilevel instruction challenges.

How do I use the Multilevel Strategies to plan multilevel lessons?

Planning a multilevel lesson incorporates the same five steps from page T-x with three variations:

1. Base the lesson on two or three of the multilevel objectives (identified at the top of the lesson page), depending on the abilities of students in your class.
2. In preparing for the presentation stage, consider correlating materials from the *Basic Oxford Picture Dictionary* program for your pre-literacy learners.
3. Incorporate the multilevel grouping and instructional strategies in each lesson.

Grouping students in the multilevel classroom maximizes learner involvement and minimizes teacher stress. Putting learners in same-level groups during guided practice activities allows them to move at the right pace for their level. Creating different-level groups for communicative practice allows learners to increase their fluency. Assigning roles and tasks based on learners' proficiency level allows all learners to participate and succeed. The multilevel instructional strategies in this book are fairly consistent within each lesson type. Once a strategy is mastered, it can easily be applied to future lessons or activities.

How is *Step Forward* a complete program?

In addition to the *Student Book* and the *Step-by-Step Lesson Plans*, the *Step Forward* program also includes ancillary materials that support communicative language instruction. Each of the following ancillary materials is correlated to the units and topics of each *Student Book:*

- *Audio Program*
- *Workbook*.
- *Multilevel Activity Book*
- *Test Generator*

In addition, the *Step Forward Professional Development Program* provides opportunities to learn about, reflect upon, and refine instructional strategies.

We created these materials with one goal in mind: to help *you* help *your learners*. Please write to us at **Stepforwardteam.us@oup.com** with your comments, questions, and ideas.

Jayme Adelson-Goldstein, Series Director

TABLE OF CONTENTS

Unit	Life Skills & Civics Competencies	Vocabulary	Grammar	Critical Thinking & Math Concepts	Reading & Writing
Pre-unit **The First Step** **page 2**	• Greet others • Talk about personal information	• Verb tenses • Word families	• Review various verb tenses • Identify word families	• Distinguish between verb tenses • Create word family chart	• Write sentences about classmates • Write word families
Unit 1 **It Takes All Kinds!** **page 4**	• Identify personality traits, talents, and learning styles • Describe yourself and your learning style • Express agreement and disagreement about educational topics • Ask and answer questions about school and studying • Read and reflect on an article about controlling test anxiety	• Personality traits • Talents • Learning styles • Test anxiety terms **In other words:** • Disagreeing politely	• Action verbs in the simple present and the present continuous • Non-action verbs in the simple present • Review *Yes/No*, information, and *or* questions	• Reflect on personality traits, talents, and learning styles • Compare learning styles • Examine personal feelings about learning English **Real-life math:** • Calculate an average using a graph **Problem solving:** • Find solutions to a problem with roommates	• Read about different types of learning styles • Read and write about learning styles **Writer's note:** • Introducing examples
Unit 2 **Keeping Current** **page 18**	• Identify news habits • Interpret a news website • Summarize a news story or current event • Discuss, clarify, and give opinions about a current event • Use previewing skills to predict the content of a magazine article • Identify a variety of sources for news	• Newspaper sections • News terms • News sources **In other words:** • Expressing agreement **Idiom note:** • *to make a long story short*	• The past passive • Past passive questions • Reflexive pronouns	• Reflect on news habits • Analyze a news website • Speculate on dangers of reporting news • Reflect on favorite source for news • Discuss bad news and decide if there is too much on TV **Real-life math:** • Calculate the number of people evacuated from their homes **Problem solving:** • Determine new ways to get news	• Read and write a news story • Read an article about news habits • Write sentences in the past passive **Writer's note:** • Information that a news story provides
Unit 3 **Going Places** **page 32**	• State travel problems and give advice • Describe experiences using the phone • Make travel arrangements using the Internet • Make suggestions related to planning a trip • Interpret a magazine article on tele-communication • Scan an article for numbers	• Travel emergencies • Travel problems • Telecom-munication **In other words:** • Making suggestions **Idiom note:** • *I'll bet*	• Reported speech with statements • Reported speech with *told* + noun or pronoun • Reported speech with instructions • The suffix *-less*	• Reflect on favorite ways to travel • Compare and contrast speaking on the phone to speaking in person • Analyze a travel ad website • Interpret a confirmation email for a hotel reservation **Real-life math:** • Calculate cost of a hotel reservation **Problem solving:** • Resolve conflicts regarding traveling with an old car	• Read and write about using the phone • Read an article about cell phone usage **Writer's note:** • Using quotation marks

Listening & Speaking	CASAS Life Skills Competencies	Standardized Student Syllabi/ LCPs	SCANS Competencies	EFF Content Standards
• Listen for and give personal information • Talk about a variety of topics with a partner	0.1.2, 0.1.4, 0.1.5, 0.2.1, 7.4.5	39.01, 49.09, 49.10, 50.02	• Listening • Speaking • Sociability	• Listening actively • Speaking so others can understand
• Talk about personality traits • Discuss personal learning styles • Discuss issues about learning English • Listen to a conversation about educational topics • Discuss test-taking issues **Grammar listening:** • Listen for action or non-action verbs **Pronunciation:** • "t" sound	L1: 0.1.2, 0.1.5, 0.2.1, 4.8.1, 7.4.5 L2: 0.1.2, 0.1.5, 0.2.1, 0.2.3, 7.4.7, 7.4.9 L3: 0.1.2, 0.2.1, 7.4.7 L4: 0.1.2, 0.1.5, 0.2.1, 1.1.3, 1.1.8, 6.0.3, 6.0.4, 6.1.4, 6.7.2 L5: 0.1.2, 0.1.5, 0.2.1, 2.5.6, 7.4.4, 7.4.9 RE: 0.1.2, 0.1.5, 0.2.1, 4.8.1, 7.3.1, 7.3.2, 7.3.4, 7.4.9	L1: 39.01, 49.02, 49.10, 49.16 L2: 39.01, 49.02, 49.13, 49.16, 49.17 L3: 49.16, 49.17, 50.02 L4: 39.01, 49.02, 49.03, 49.09 L5: 39.01, 49.06, 49.16, 49.17 RE: 39.01, 49.01, 49.13, 49.16, 49.17, 50.02	Most SCANS are incorporated into this unit, with an emphasis on: • Knowing how to learn • Participating as a member of a team • Seeing in the mind's eye	Most EFFs are incorporated into this unit, with an emphasis on: • Conveying ideas in writing • Reading with understanding • Reflecting and evaluating
• Talk about news habits • Discuss a current event from the news • Listen to a conversation about a current event • Listen to a news story • Discuss issues related to controversial news **Grammar listening:** • Listen for sentences with the same meaning **Pronunciation:** • Stressing words to clarify meaning	L1: 0.1.2, 0.1.5, 0.2.1, 4.8.1, 7.4.4 L2: 0.1.2, 0.1.5, 7.2.1, 7.4.4 L3: 0.1.2, 0.1.5, 7.2.1, 7.4.4 L4: 0.1.2, 0.1.5, 0.2.1, 6.0.3, 6.0.4, 6.1.2, 7.4.4 L5: 0.1.2, 0.1.5, 0.2.1, 7.4.4 RE: 0.1.2, 0.1.5, 0.2.1, 4.8.1, 7.2.4, 7.3.1, 7.3.2, 7.3.4	L1:38.01, 39.01, 49.02, 49.09 L2: 49.02, 49.03, 49.13, 49.16 L3: 0.1.2, 0.1.5, 7.2.1, 7.4.4 L4: 39.01, 49.02, 49.09, 49.16, 49.17 L5: 39.01, 49.02, 49.16, 49.17 RE: 39.01, 49.02, 49.16	Most SCANS are incorporated into this unit, with and emphasis on: • Knowing how to learn • Participating as member of a team • Speaking	Most EFFs are incorporated into this unit, with an emphasis on: • Convey ideas in writing • Listen actively • Read with understanding
• Talk about traveling and travel emergencies • Discuss feelings about speaking English on the phone • Listen to an automated message • Talk about cell phones **Grammar listening:** • Listen and complete sentences with reported speech **Pronunciation:** • The letter "s"	L1: 0.1.2, 0.1.5, 0.2.1, 2.5.1, 4.8.1, 7.2.5, 7.4.5, 7.4.7 L2: 0.1.2, 0.1.5, 0.2.1, 7.4.7, 7.5.6 L3: 0.1.2, 0.1.5, 0.2.1 L4: 0.1.2, 0.1.5, 0.2.1, 2.2.1, 6.0.3, 6.0.4, 6.2.1, 6.2.3, 6.2.5 L5: 0.1.2, 0.1.5, 0.2.1, 2.1.4, 7.4.4, 7.4.7 RE: 0.1.2, 0.1.5, 0.2.1, 4.8.1, 7.3.1, 7.3.2, 7.3.4	L1: 39.01, 44.01, 49.02, 49.03, 49.10, 49.17 L2: 39.01, 49.01, 49.02, 49.03, 49.16, 49.17 L3: 39.01, 49.09, 49.13, 50.07 L4: 39.01, 40.02, 43.02, 43.04, 49.02, 49.09, 51.03 L5: 39.01, 49.02, 49.04, 49.09, 49.16, 49.17 RE: 39.01, 49.01, 49.02, 49.16	Most SCANS are incorporated into this unit, with and emphasis on: • Creative thinking • Reading • Speaking	Most EFFs are incorporated into this unit, with an emphasis on: • Conveying ideas in writing • Observing critically • Speaking so others can understand

Table of contents **v**

Unit	Life Skills & Civics Competencies	Vocabulary	Grammar	Critical Thinking & Math Concepts	Reading & Writing
Unit 4 **Get the Job** **page 46**	• Discuss job training opportunities • Write a cover letter to a potential employer • Interpret classified ads • Ask and answer questions at a job interview • Clarify meaning • Make a career plan	• Job training terms • Career planning • Job interview terms **In other words:** • Checking understanding	• The past perfect • Past perfect questions • Compare the simple past, the past perfect and the present perfect • Suffixes -er and -ee	• Analyze a job training flyer • Speculate about necessary training for careers • Reflect on career advice • Evaluate personal work skills **Real-life math:** • Analyze resume to determine time worked at jobs **Problem solving:** • Prioritize preparatory steps for job interview	• Read and write a cover letter • Read classified ads • Read an article about career planning **Writer's note:** • Information to include in a business letter
Unit 5 **Safe and Sound** **page 60**	• Identify safety hazards • Interpret a safety poster • Outline steps to take in common emergencies • Warn against unsafe situations • Scan for numeric information • Identify types of injuries on the job and at home	• Safety hazards and warnings • Safety procedures • Weather emergencies • Accidents and injuries **In other words:** • Reporting a problem **Idiom note:** • *take care of it*	• *Have to, have got to,* and *must* for necessity and prohibition • Necessity in the past • The past of *should have* • The suffix *-ous*	• Speculate on ways to prevent accidents • Interpret a safety plan • Compare and contrast safety of different jobs • Speculate on types of safety training that employers should give workers **Real-life math:** • Analyze a pie chart **Problem solving:** • Find ways to report a safety problem	• Read a safety poster • Read about emergency preparedness • Write an emergency plan • Read an article about safety statistics **Writer's note:** • Writing an outline
Unit 6 **Getting Ahead** **page 74**	• Identify interpersonal skills and personal qualities • Describe job applicants' experience and skills • Identify workplace hierarchy • Problem-solve workplace issues • Ask for information • Use a company's phone directory • Use previewing strategies to better understand a reading passage on teamwork	• Interpersonal skills • Personal qualities • Recommendation terms • Skills training **In other words:** • Asking for information	• Adjective clauses after main clauses • Adjective clauses inside main clauses • Adjective clauses with *whose* • Prefixes for negative forms of adjectives	• Analyze an employee's evaluation • Interpret a recommendation • Interpret a company's organizational chart • Speculate on ways that diverse groups can work together **Real-life math:** • Calculate net pay **Problem solving:** • Resolve interpersonal difficulties within a group	• Read an evaluation • Read and write a memo to make a recommendation • Read an article on skills **Writer's note:** • Subject lines and paragraphs in a workplace memo

Listening & Speaking	CASAS Life Skills Competencies	Standardized Student Syllabi/ LCPs	SCANS Competencies	EFF Content Standards
• Talk about future work plans • Discuss career centers and job preparation • Talk about resumes • Listen to a conversation about a resume • Discuss best ways to find jobs **Grammar listening:** • Listen for information using the past perfect **Pronunciation:** • Use rising intonation to check understanding	**L1:** 0.1.2, 0.1.5, 0.2.1, 4.1.4, 4.4.2, 4.4.5, 4.8.1, 7.4.5 **L2:** 0.1.2, 0.1.5, 0.2.3, 4.1.2, 7.4.7 **L3:** 0.1.2, 0.1.5, 0.2.1, 7.4.7 **L4:** 0.1.2, 0.1.5, 0.2.1, 4.1.5, 6.0.3, 6.0.4, 6.1.1, 6.6.6, 7.4.7, 7.5.6 **L5:** 0.1.2, 0.1.5, 2.5.6, 4.1.9, 7.4.4, 7.4.7 **RE:** 0.1.2, 0.1.5, 0.2.1, 4.8.1, 7.2.4, 7.3.1, 7.3.2, 7.3.4	**L1:** 37.01, 39.01, 35.03, 49.10 **L2:** 49.02, 49.13, 49.16, 49.17 **L3:** 39.01, 49.01, 49.02, 49.16, 49.17, 50.02 **L4:** 39.01, 49.02, 49.09, 49.16, 49.17, 51.05 **L5:** 35.04, 38.01, 49.04, 49.09, 49.16, 49.17 **RE:** 35.03, 39.01, 49.01, 49.02, 49.13	Most SCANS are incorporated into this unit, with and emphasis on: • Arithmetic/Mathematics • Decision making • Interpreting and communicating information	Most EFFs are incorporated into this unit, with an emphasis on: • Cooperating with others • Observing critically • Taking responsibility for learning
• Talk about safety and warning signs • Talk about weather emergencies and emergency plans • Listen to a conversation about reporting an unsafe situation • Listen to a news story about different jobs • Discuss dangers in the home and workplace **Grammar listening:** • Listen for sentences with the same meaning **Pronunciation:** • "ough" words	**L1:** 0.1.2, 0.1.5, 3.4.1, 3.4.2, 4.3.1, 4.8.1, 7.4.5 **L2:** 0.1.2, 0.1.5, 0.2.1, 2.3.3, 3.4.2, 7.4.2, 7.4.7 **L3:** 0.1.2, 0.1.5, 7.4.7 **L4:** 0.1.2, 0.1.5, 4.3.4, 6.7.4, 7.4.7**L5:** 0.1.2, 0.1.5, 3.4.2, 7.4.4 **RE:** 0.1.2, 0.1.5, 0.2.1, 3.4.2, 4.8.1, 7.3.1, 7.3.2	**L1:** 36.03, 44.01, 49.10, 49.16 **L2:** 44.01, 49.02, 49.16, 49.17 **L3:** 44.01, 49.01, 49.02, 49.09, 49.13, 49.16, 49.17 **L4:** 36.03, 44.01, 49.02, 49.09, 49.16, 49.17 **L5:** 38.01, 44.01, 49.02, 49.09, 49.16, 49.17 **RE:** 39.01, 44.01, 49.01, 49.13, 49.16, 49.17	Most SCANS are incorporated into this unit, with and emphasis on: • Acquiring and evaluating information • Organizing and marinating information • Problem solving	Most SCANS are incorporated into this unit, with and emphasis on: • Acquiring and evaluating information • Organizing and marinating information • Problem solving
• Talk about useful skills for different situations • Listen to conversations to determine workplace hierarchy • Listen to an automated phone menu • Discuss the importance of good interpersonal skills **Grammar listening:** • Listen to and match main clauses with adjective clauses **Pronunciation:** • Saying *yes* and *no* in informal situations	**L1:** 0.1.2, 0.1.5, 0.2.1, 4.1.7, 4.4.1, 4.6.1, 4.8.1, 7.4.5 **L2:** 0.1.2, 0.1.5, 0.2.1, 4.6.2 **L3:** 4.6.5, 7.4.7 **L4:** 0.1.2, 0.1.5, 4.2.1, 6.0.3, 6.0.4, 6.0.5, 6.1.2 **L5:** 0.1.2, 0.1.5, 4.4.1, 4.8.7, 7.4.4, 7.5.6 **RE:** 0.1.2, 0.1.5, 0.2.1, 7.2.6, 7.3.1, 7.3.2, 7.3.4	**L1:** 35.02, 36.04, 39.01, 49.10 **L2:** 39.01, 49.02, 49.13, 49.16 **L3:** 35.03, 49.02, 49.16 **L4:** 36.05, 36.06, 40.01, 49.01, 49.02, 49.09 **L5:** 38.01, 49.02, 49.04, 49.09, 49.16 **RE:** 39.01, 49.02, 49.13, 49.16	Most SCANS are incorporated into this unit, with an emphasis on: • Creative thinking • Interpreting and communicating information • Reasoning	Most EFFs are incorporated into this unit, with an emphasis on: • Conveying ideas in writing • Reading with understanding • Solving problems and making decisions

Unit	Life Skills & Civics Competencies	Vocabulary	Grammar	Critical Thinking & Math Concepts	Reading & Writing
Unit 7 **Buy Now, Pay Later** page 88	• Identify banking services • Identify various monthly expenses • Talk about financial needs and goals • Negotiate and compromise • Ask and answer questions about monthly expenses in order to plan a budget • Read an interest-rate chart	• Personal finance and banking • Budgeting terms **In other words:** • Making suggestions **Idiom note:** • *It's a deal.*	• Present unreal conditional • Questions with present unreal conditionals • Present unreal conditionals with *be*	• Analyze a budget • Speculate about ways that money affects people's lives • Interpret interest-rate chart • Reflect on feelings about money **Real-life math:** • Calculate monthly expenses **Problem solving:** • Find ways to help friend with money problems	• Read and write an essay about money • Read an article on financial planning **Writer's note:** • Avoiding *I* in a formal essay
Unit 8 **Satisfaction Guaranteed** page 102	• Identify various types of shopping • Describe purchase problems • Write an email to complain about purchase problems • Call and place an order over the phone • Identify organizations that protect consumers	• Shopping terms • Purchase problem terms • Consumer protection terms **In other words:** • Apologizing **Idiom note:** • *sold out*	• Adjectives ending in *-ed* and *-ing* • Adverbs of degree • *So...that, such...that,* and *such a/an...that* • The suffix *-ful*	• Reflect on favorite ways to shop • Speculate about possible problems with items purchased • Reflect on a life experience • Interpret a store's catalog • Interpret information about consumer rights **Real-life math:** • Calculate the cost of catalog order **Problem solving:** • Find solutions to problems with a purchase	• Read and write an email about problems with an order • Read an article about consumer rights **Writer's note:** • Using words like *first, second,* and *finally*
Unit 9 **Take Care** page 116	• Talk about personal health • Identify healthy changes in lifestyle • Give different forms of advice • Ask and answer questions about health issues • Confirm advice • Understand health insurance plans	• Health • Medical conditions • Health insurance **In other words:** • Confirming advice **Idiom notes:** • *cut back on* • *cut out*	• Advice with *should, had better,* and *ought to* • Practice *should, had better, have to* and *must* • Verbs with gerunds and infinitives • Verbs for talking about health and sickness	• Reflect on how heredity and lifestyle can affect health • Speculate on changes people make to improve their health • Analyze immunization poster • Interpret information about health insurance **Real-life math:** • Analyze an immunization record **Problem solving:** • Find ways to help a person make healthy lifestyle changes	• Read and write about healthy lifestyle changes • Read an article about health insurance **Writer's note:** • Letter writing

Listening & Speaking	CASAS Life Skills Competencies	Standardized Student Syllabi/ LCPs	SCANS Competencies	EFF Content Standards
• Talk about banking services and managing money • Discuss budgeting • Talk about ways to save money • Listen to a conversation about ways to save money **Grammar listening:** • Listen to a negotiation conversation **Pronunciation:** • Pauses with commas	**L1:** 0.1.2, 0.1.5, 1.4.6, 1.5.1, 1.5.2, 4.8.1, 7.4.5 **L2:** 0.1.2, 0.1.5, 7.2.2, 7.2.4, 7.2.5 **L3:** 0.1.2, 0.1.5, 0.2.1, 7.2.2, 7.2.5, 7.2.6 **L4:** 0.1.2, 0.1.5, 1.5.1, 6.0.3, 6.0.4, 6.1.1, 6.1.2, 7.4.7 **L5:** 0.1.2, 0.1.5, 0.2.1, 1.1.5, 7.4.4 **RE:** 0.1.2, 0.1.5, 0.2.1, 1.5.1, 7.3.1, 7.3.2, 7.3.4, 7.4.7	**L1:** 49.02, 49.10 **L2:** 49.02, 49.03, 49.13, 49.16 **L3:** 39.01, 49.01, 49.02, 49.09, 49.13, 49.16 **L4:** 49.02, 49.09, 49.16, 49.17 **L5:** 39.01, 49.02, 49.06, 49.09, 49.16 **RE:** 39.01, 49.01, 49.02, 49.16, 49.17	Most SCANS are incorporated into this unit, with an emphasis on: • Acquiring and evaluating information • Interpreting and communicating information • Writing	Most EFFs are incorporated into this unit, with an emphasis on: • Conveying ideas in writing • Cooperating with others • Solving problems and making decisions
• Talk about different types of shopping • Discuss problems experienced when purchasing merchandise • Listen to conversations about a catalog • Listen to a conversation about a problem with a purchase • Discuss consumer rights **Grammar listening:** • Listen for information using participial adjectives **Pronunciation:** • Linked consonants and vowels	**L1:** 0.1.2, 0.1.5, 0.2.1, 1.3.1, 7.2.3, 7.4.5 **L2:** 0.1.2, 0.1.5, 0.2.1, 1.3.3, 1.6.3, 7.4.4 **L3:** 0.1.2, 0.1.5, 7.4.7 **L4:** 0.1.2, 0.1.5, 1.3.3, 1.3.4, 6.0.3, 6.0.4, 6.2.1, 6.2.3, 6.2.5, 7.2.5 **L5:** 0.1.2, 0.1.5, 0.2.1, 1.6.2, 1.6.3, 7.4.2, 7.4.4 **RE:** 0.1.2, 0.1.5, 0.2.1, 4.8.1, 7.2.6, 7.3.1, 7.3.2, 7.3.4	**L1:** 39.01, 45.01, 49.02, 49.10 **L2:** 38.01, 39.01, 45.06, 49.01, 49.02, 49.13, 49.16 **L3:** 49.09, 49.16, 49.17, 50.04, 50.05 **L4:** 49.02, 49.09, 49.16, 51.05 **L5:** 38.01, 39.01, 49.02, 49.04, 49.09, 49.16 **RE:** 39.01, 49.01, 49.02, 49.09, 49.13, 49.16	Most SCANS are incorporated into this unit, with an emphasis on: • Arithmetic/Mathematics • Creative thinking • Seeing things in the mind's eye	Most EFFs are incorporated into this unit, with an emphasis on: • Conveying ideas in writing • Reflecting and evaluating • Solving problems and making decisions
• Talk about ways to stay healthy • Listen to people's health goals and doctors' advice • Listen to a conversation at a doctor's office • Talk about health insurance issues **Grammar listening:** • Listen to speakers give advice and strong advice **Pronunciation:** • "s" and "ch" sounds	**L1:** 0.1.2, 0.1.5, 3.5.9, 4.8.1 **L2:** 0.1.2, 0.1.5, 0.2.1, 3.5.9 **L3:** 0.1.2, 0.1.5, 0.2.1, 3.5.9, 7.4.7 **L4:** 0.1.2, 0.1.5, 0.2.1, 3.1.3, 3.5.9, 6.0.3, 6.0.4, 6.1.1, 7.5.6 **L5:** 0.1.2, 0.1.5, 2.5.6, 3.2.3, 3.5.9, 7.4.4 **RE:** 0.1.2, 0.1.5, 3.5.9, 4.8.1, 7.2.6, 7.3.1, 7.3.4	**L1:** 41.06, 49.02, 49.10 **L2:** 39.01, 41.06, 49.01, 49.13, 49.16 **L3:** 39.01, 41.06, 49.01, 49.02, 49.09, 49.17 **L4:** 39.01, 41.03, 41.06, 49.02, 49.09, 49.16, 49.17 **L5:** 38.01, 49.02, 49.06, 49.09, 49.16, 50.02 **RE:** 41.06 49.01, 49.02, 49.03, 49.16, 49.17	Most SCANS are incorporated into this unit, with and emphasis on: • Acquiring and evaluating information • Advocating and influencing • Applying technology to the task • Advocating and influencing	Most EFFs are incorporated into this unit, with an emphasis on: • Conveying ideas in writing • Reading with understanding • Solving problems and making decisions

Unit	Life Skills & Civics Competencies	Vocabulary	Grammar	Critical Thinking & Math Concepts	Reading & Writing
Unit 10 **Get Involved!** **page 130**	• Identify community services • Express concern about a community issue • Call a community official for information about an issue or event • Identify ways to get involved in a community • Address community problems • Recognize environmental issues in a community	• Community involvement • Community services • Recycling and dumping terms **In other words:** • Showing understanding **Idiom note:** • *put in (my) two cents*	• Indirect information questions • Indirect questions with *if* and *whether* • Statements with *wh-* and *if/whether* phrases • The suffix *-ment*	• Analyze a community services directory • Speculate on ways to get involved in a community • Analyze an editorial cartoon • Interpret a newspaper editorial on recycling, dumping and related issues **Real-life math:** • Analyze a pie chart **Problem solving:** • Find ways to help with community problems	• Read and write about a community issue • Read a notice of public hearings • Read a newspaper article on community involvement **Writer's note:** • Special purposes of paragraphs in a letter
Unit 11 **Find It on the Net** **page 144**	• Identify Internet and website information • Recognize changes in use of technology • Ask for and clarify instructions about Internet use • Ask and answer questions about partner's life • Offer and respond to help • Identify renters' rights	• The Internet • Website terms **In other words:** • Offering help **Idiom notes:** • *when it comes to* • *it's about time*	• Tag questions and short answers with *be* • Tag questions and short answers with *do* • Question words for clarification	• Analyze a website menu • Compare and contrast technological changes in the past ten years • Speculate about ways to find new homes • Interpret a web article on renters' rights • Speculate about ways the Internet can help renters and home buyers **Real-life math:** • Calculate daily number of hits on a website **Problem solving:** • Learn to work with family members	• Read about changes in the use of technology • Write about using technology • Read an article about renters' rights **Writer's note:** • Using time expressions
Unit 12 **How did I do?** **page 158**	• Identify leadership qualities • Identify personal goals and plans • Ask and answer questions about talents and future plans • Respond to positive and negative feedback • Participate in a performance review • Make polite suggestions and requests	• Achievement terms • Leadership qualities **In other words:** • Responding to feedback **Idiom note:** • *deal with*	• Gerunds after prepositions • Gerunds after *be* + adjective + preposition • Polite requests and suggestions with gerunds • Compound adjectives	• Reflect on personal leadership qualities • Interpret evaluations • Sequence events from an article • Compare and contrast life in the present to life in the past **Real-life math:** • Survey the class, calculate percentages for each answer, and make a pie chart **Problem solving:** • Find ways to help a community	• Read an application essay • Write an application statement • Read an article about a personal achievement **Writer's note:** • Using topic sentences

Listening scripts
pages 172–182

Grammar charts
pages 183–192

Vocabulary list
pages 193–195

Index
pages 196–198

Listening & Speaking	CASAS Life Skills Competencies	Standardized Student Syllabi/ LCPs	SCANS Competencies	EFF Content Standards
• Discuss community services and involvement • Talk about ways to improve a community • Talk about community meetings and pubic hearings • Listen to directions to city hall • Discuss community problems **Grammar listening:** • Listen for sentences with the same meaning **Pronunciation:** • Pauses in long sentences	**L1:** 0.1.2, 0.1.5, 0.2.1, 5.6.1, 7.4.5 **L2:** 0.1.2, 0.1.5, 0.2.1, 0.2.3, 5.6.1, 5.6.2 **L3:** 5.6.2, 7.5.6 **L4:** 0.1.2, 0.1.5, 1.1.3, 5.6.1, 6.0.3, 6.0.4, 6.1.2, 6.7.4, 7.4.7, 7.5.6 **L5:** 0.1.2, 0.1.5, 2.5.6, 5.6.1, 5.7.1, 7.4.4 **RE:** 0.1.2, 0.1.5, 4.8.1, 5.6.1, 5.7.1, 7.2.6, 7.3.1, 7.3.2, 7.3.4	**L1:** 39.01, 49.02, 49.09, 49.10 **L2:** 39.01, 49.01, 49.03, 49.13, 49.16 **L3:** 49.01, 49.02, 49.09, 49.17 **L4:** 49.01, 49.09, 49.16, 49.17, 51.01 **L5:** 38.01, 47.03, 49.02, 49.06, 49.16 **RE:** 47.03, 49.01, 49.02, 49.13, 49.16, 49.17	Most SCANS are incorporated into this unit, with an emphasis on: • Arithmetic/Mathematics • Creative thinking • Seeing things in the mind's eye	Most EFFs are incorporated into this unit, with an emphasis on: • Cooperate with others • Learning through research • Taking responsibility for learning
• Listen to and talk about ways to use computers and the Internet • Talk about ways to find new homes • Listen to an interview about designing a website • Discuss ways landlords and tenants can get along **Grammar listening:** • Listen to questions and complete with the correct tag **Pronunciation:** • Falling and rising intonation of tags	**L1:** 0.1.2, 0.1.5, 0.2.1, 4.8.1, 7.4.4 **L2:** 0.1.2, 0.1.5, 0.2.1, 1.4.1, 4.5.5, 4.5.6, 7.4.4, 7.4.7 **L3:** 0.1.2, 0.1.5, 0.1.6, 0.2.1, 7.4.7, 7.5.6 **L4:** 0.1.2, 0.1.5, 0.1.6, 6.0.3, 6.0.4, 6.1.2, 7.5.6 **L5:** 0.1.2, 0.1.5, 1.4.1, 1.4.2, 1.4.3, 1.4.5, 2.5.6, 7.4.4, 7.4.7 **RE:** 0.1.2, 0.1.5, 0.1.6, 0.2.1, 4.8.1, 7.2.6, 7.3.1, 7.3.2, 7.3.4, 7.4.7	**L1:** 38.01, 39.01, 49.02, 49.10 **L2:** 38.01, 39.01, 49.13, 49.16, 49.17 **L3:** 39.01, 49.01, 49.09, 49.13, 49.17 **L4:** 49.02, 49.09, 51.05 **L5:** 38.01, 45.01, 45.07, 49.06 **RE:** 39.01, 49.02, 49.13, 49.17	Most SCANS are incorporated into this unit, with an emphasis on: • Creative thinking • Interpreting and communicating information • Listening	Most EFFs are incorporated into this unit, with an emphasis on: • Conveying ideas in writing • Listening actively • Reflecting and evaluating
• Talk about life achievements • Discuss leadership qualities • Listen to conversations between employees and their supervisors • Talk about ways employers can give positive and negative feedback **Grammar listening:** • Listen for sentences with the same meaning **Pronunciation:** • Word grouping in long sentences	**L1:** 0.1.2, 0.1.5, 0.2.1, 4.8.1, 7.4.5 **L2:** 0.1.2, 0.1.5, 0.2.1, 7.1.1 **L3:** 0.1.2, 0.1.5, 0.2.1, 0.2.4, 7.4.7 **L4:** 0.1.2, 0.1.5, 4.4.4, 6.0.3, 6.0.4, 6.2.3, 6.4.2, 6.4.3, 6.7.4, 7.5.6 **L5:** 0.1.2, 0.1.5, 2.5.6, 7.2.2, 7.4.4 **RE:** 0.1.2, 0.1.5, 0.2.1, 4.8.1, 7.1.1, 7.2.6, 7.3.1, 7.3.2, 7.3.4, 7.5.6	**L1:** 39.01, 49.02, 49.10 **L2:** 39.01, 49.13, 49.16 **L3:** 39.01, 49.03, 49.09, 49.13, 49.17, 50.06 **L4:** 49.02, 49.09, 49.16, 51.05 **L5:** 38.01, 49.06 **RE:** 39.01, 49.02, 49.13, 49.16	Most SCANS are incorporated into this unit, with and emphasis on: • Knowing how to learn • Participating as a member of a team • Seeing in the mind's eye	Most EFFs are incorporated into this unit, with an emphasis on: • Observing critically • Reading with understanding • Using math to solve problems and communicate

A Word or Two About Reading Introductions to Textbooks

Teaching professionals rarely read a book's introduction. Instead, we flip through the book's pages, using the pictures, topics, and exercises to determine whether the book matches our learners' needs and our teaching style. We scan the reading passages, conversations, writing tasks, and grammar charts to judge the authenticity and accuracy of the text. At a glance, we assess how easy it would be to manage the pair work, group activities, evaluations, and application tasks.

This Introduction, however, also offers valuable information for the teacher. Because you've read this far, I encourage you to read a little further to learn how *Step Forward's* key concepts, components, and multilevel applications will help you help your learners.

Step Forward's Key Concepts

Step Forward is...

- the instructional backbone for single-level and multilevel classrooms.
- a standards-based, performance-based, and topic-based series for low-beginning through high-intermediate learners.
- a source for ready-made, four-skill lesson plans that address the skills our learners need in their workplace, civic, personal, and academic lives.
- a collection of learner-centered, communicative English-language practice activities.

The classroom is a remarkable place. *Step Forward* respects the depth of experience and knowledge that learners bring to the learning process. At the same time, *Step Forward* recognizes that learners' varied proficiencies, goals, interests, and educational backgrounds create instructional challenges for teachers.

To ensure that our learners leave each class having made progress toward their language and life goals, *Step Forward* works from these key concepts:

- **The wide spectrum of learners' needs makes using materials that support multilevel instruction essential.** *Step Forward* works with single-level and multilevel classes.
- **Learners' prior knowledge is a valuable teaching tool.** Prior knowledge questions appear in every *Step Forward* lesson.

- **Learning objectives are the cornerstone of instruction.** Each *Step Forward* lesson focuses on an objective that derives from identified learner needs, correlates to state and federal standards, and connects to a meaningful communication task. Progress toward the objective is evaluated at the end of the lesson.
- **Vocabulary, grammar and pronunciation skills play an essential role in language learning. They provide learners with the tools needed to achieve life skill, civics, workplace, and academic competencies.** *Step Forward* includes strong vocabulary and grammar strands and features pronunciation and math lesson extensions in each unit.
- **Effective instruction requires a variety of instructional techniques and strategies to engage learners.** Techniques such as Early Production Questioning, Focused Listening, Total Physical Response (TPR), Cooperative Learning, and Problem Solving are embedded in the *Step Forward* series, along with grouping and classroom management strategies.

The *Step Forward* Program Components

The *Step Forward* program has four levels:

- Book 1: low-beginning
- Book 2: high-beginning
- Book 3: low-intermediate
- Book 4: intermediate to high-intermediate

Each level of *Step Forward* correlates to *The Oxford Picture Dictionary*. For pre-literacy learners, *The Basic Oxford Picture Dictionary Literacy Program* provides a flexible, needs-based approach to literacy instruction. Once learners develop strong literacy skills, they will be able to transition seamlessly into *Step Forward Student Book 1*.

Each *Step Forward* level includes the following components:

Step Forward Student Book

A collection of clear, engaging, four-skill lessons based on meaningful learning objectives.

Step Forward Audio Program

The recorded vocabulary, focused listening, conversations, pronunciation, and reading materials from the *Step Forward Student Book*.

Step Forward Step-By-Step Lesson Plans with Multilevel Grammar Exercises CD-ROM

An instructional planning resource with interleaved *Step Forward Student Book* pages, detailed lesson plans featuring multilevel teaching strategies and teaching tips, and a CD-ROM of printable multilevel grammar practice for the structures presented in the *Step Forward Student Book*.

Step Forward Workbook

Practice exercises for independent work in the classroom or as homework.

Step Forward Multilevel Activity Book

More than 100 photocopiable communicative practice activities and 72 picture cards; lesson materials that work equally well in single-level or multilevel settings.

Step Forward Test Generator CD-ROM with ExamView® Assessment Suite

Hundreds of multiple choice and life-skill oriented test items for each *Step Forward Student Book*.

Multilevel Applications of *Step Forward*

All the *Step Forward* program components support multilevel instruction.

Step Forward is so named because it helps learners "step forward" toward their language and life goals, no matter where they start. Our learners often start from very different places and language abilities within the same class.

Regardless of level, all learners need materials that bolster comprehension while providing an appropriate amount of challenge. This makes multilevel materials an instructional necessity in most classrooms.

Each *Step Forward* lesson provides the following multilevel elements:

- **a general topic or competency area** that works across levels. This supports the concept that members of the class community need to feel connected, despite their differing abilities.
- **clear, colorful visuals and realia** that provide pre-level and on-level support during introduction, presentation and practice exercises, as well as prompts for higher-level questions and exercises.

In addition, *Step Forward* correlates to *The Oxford Picture Dictionary* so that teachers can use the visuals and vocabulary from *The Oxford Picture Dictionary* to support and expand upon each lesson.

- **learner-centered practice exercises** that can be used with same-level or mixed-level pairs or small groups. *Step Forward* exercises are broken down to their simplest steps. Once the exercise has been modeled, learners can usually conduct the exercises themselves.
- **pre-level, on-level, and higher-level objectives for each lesson and the multilevel strategies** necessary to carry out the lesson. These objectives are featured in the *Step-By-Step Lesson Plans*.
- **Grammar Boost pages in the Step Forward Workbook that provide excellent "wait time" activities** for learners who complete an exercise early, thus solving a real issue in the multilevel class.
- **a variety of pair, whole class, and small group activities** in the *Step Forward Multilevel Activity Book*. These activities are perfect for same-level and mixed-level grouping.
- **customizable grammar and evaluation exercises** in the *Step Forward Test Generator CD-ROM with ExamView® Assessment Suite*. These exercises make it possible to create evaluations specific to each level in the class.

Professional Development

As instructors, we need to reflect on second language acquisition in order to build a repertoire of effective instructional strategies. The *Step Forward Professional Development Program* provides research-based teaching strategies, tasks, and activities for single- and multilevel classes.

About Writing an ESL Series

It's collaborative! *Step Forward* is the product of dialogs with hundreds of teachers and learners. The dynamic quality of language instruction makes it important to keep this dialog alive. As you use this book in your classes, I invite you to contact me or any member of the *Step Forward* authorial team with your questions or comments.

Jayme Adelson-Goldstein

Jayme Adelson-Goldstein, Series Director
Stepforwardteam.us@oup.com

GUIDE TO THE *STEP FORWARD* SERIES

Step Forward: **All you need to ensure your learners' success. All the *Step Forward Student Books* follow this format.**

LESSON 1: VOCABULARY teaches key words and phrases relevant to the unit topic, and provides conversation practice using the target vocabulary.

New vocabulary is introduced through vibrant art and high-interest listening texts.

Standards-based objectives are identified at the beginning of every lesson.

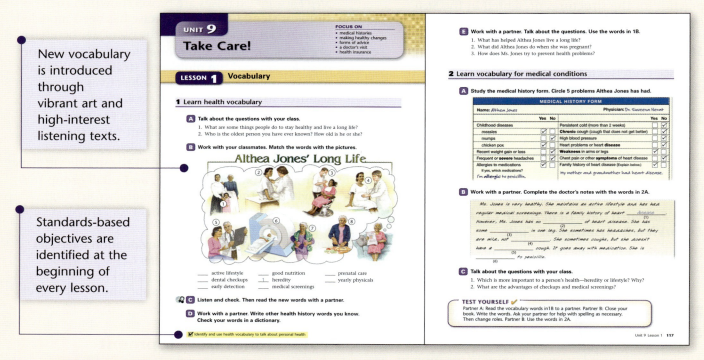

LESSON 2: REAL-LIFE WRITING expands on vocabulary learned in Lesson 1 and furthers learners' understanding through reading and writing about a life skills topic.

Learners write about their personal experiences using the vocabulary.

Life skills readings help learners practice the vocabulary in natural contexts.

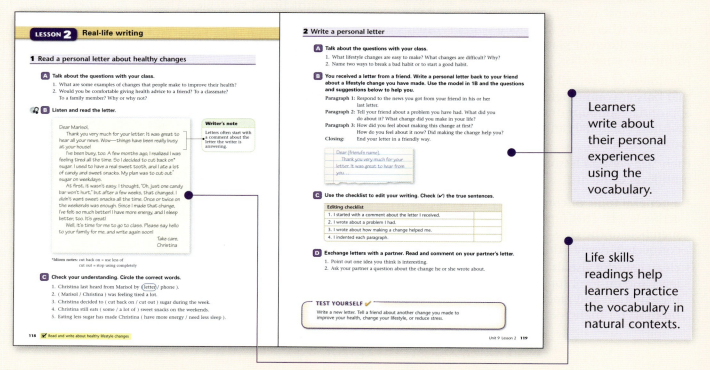

LESSON 3: GRAMMAR provides clear, simple presentation of the target structure followed by thorough, meaningful practice of it.

Clear grammar charts make learning grammar easy.

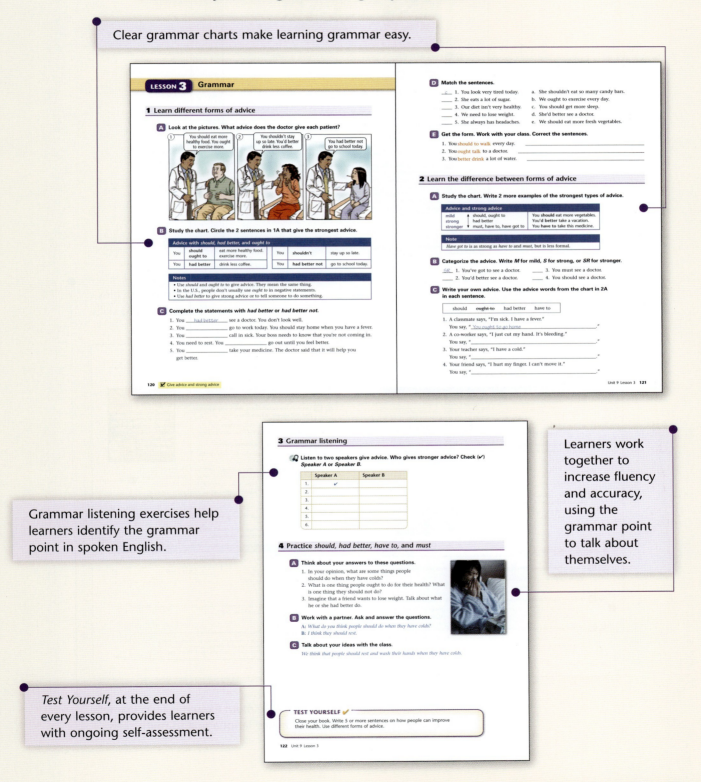

Grammar listening exercises help learners identify the grammar point in spoken English.

Learners work together to increase fluency and accuracy, using the grammar point to talk about themselves.

Test Yourself, at the end of every lesson, provides learners with ongoing self-assessment.

LESSON 4: EVERYDAY CONVERSATION provides learners with fluent, authentic conversations to increase familiarity with natural English.

Model dialogs feature authentic examples of everyday conversation.

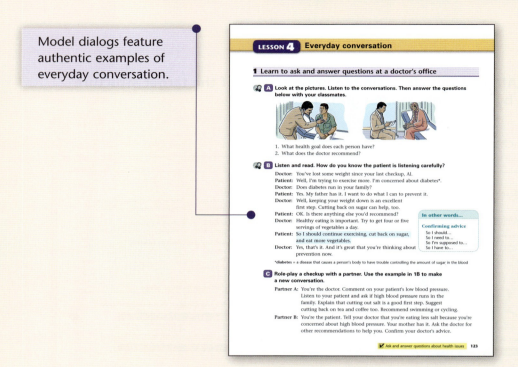

Pronunciation activities focus on common areas of difficulty.

Listening activities build listening skills.

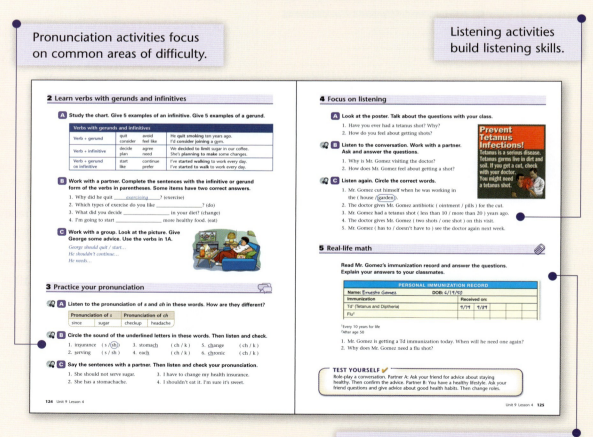

Real-life math exercises help learners practice language and math skills.

LESSON 5: REAL-LIFE READING develops essential reading skills and offers both life skill and pre-academic reading materials.

High-interest readings recycle vocabulary and grammar.

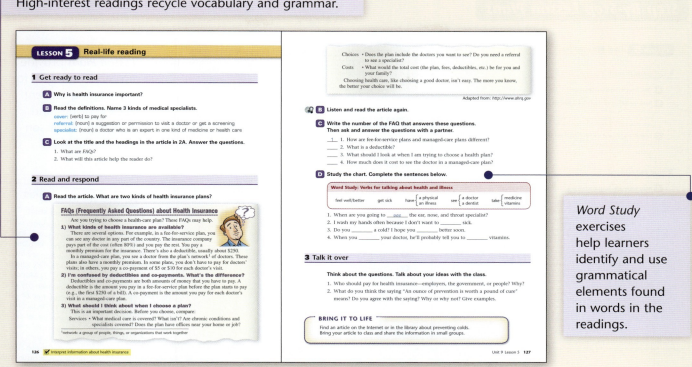

Word Study exercises help learners identify and use grammatical elements found in words in the readings.

REVIEW AND EXPAND includes additional grammar practice and communicative group tasks to ensure your learners' progress.

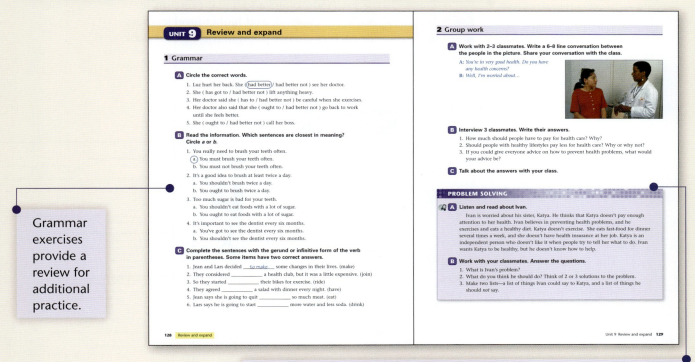

Grammar exercises provide a review for additional practice.

Problem solving tasks encourage learners to use critical thinking skills and meaningful discussion to find solutions to common problems.

Step Forward offers many different components.

Step-By-Step Lesson Plans

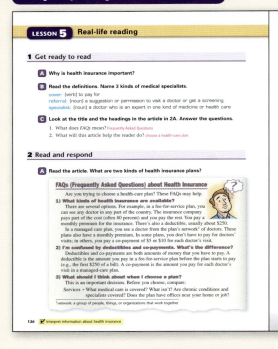

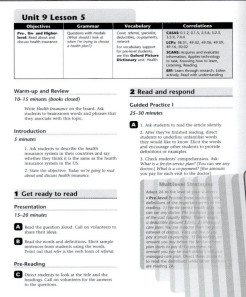

The *Step-By-Step Lesson Plans* provide tips and strategies for conducting *Student Book* activities and applying the lesson to the multilevel classroom.

Multilevel Strategies

Adapt 2A to the level of your students.
- **Pre-level** Provide these students with definitions of the important terms in the reading. 1) *Fee-for-service health plan:* You can see any doctor. The insurance pays part of the cost (usually 80%). There's usually a deductible (around $250). 2) *Managed-care plan:* You see a doctor from the plan's network of doctors. Visits are free or you pay a small co-payment. 3) *Deductible:* an amount you pay before the fee-for-service plan starts to pay 4) *Co-payment:* an amount you pay for each doctor's visit in a managed-care plan. Direct these students to read the definitions while other students are reading 2A.

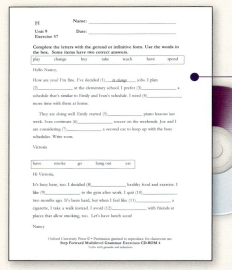

The *Multilevel Grammar Exercises CD-ROM*, a free CD-ROM included with the *Step-By-Step Lesson Plans*, offers additional exercises for pre-level, on-level, and higher-level learners for each grammar point in the *Student Book*.

Workbook

The *Workbook* offers additional exercises ideal for independent practice, homework, or review.

Multilevel Activity Book

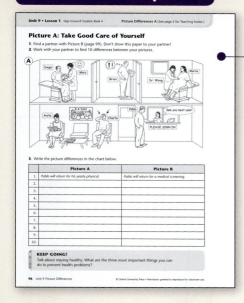

The *Multilevel Activity Book* features over 80 reproducible activities to complement the multilevel classroom through a variety of pair, small group, and whole-class activities.

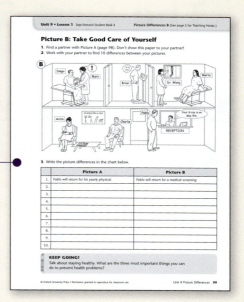

Audio Program

Audio CDs and Cassettes feature the listening exercises from the *Student Book* as well as conversations, pronunciation, and readings.

Test Generator

The *Test Generator CD-ROM with ExamView® Assessment Suite* offers hundreds of test items for each *Student Book*. Teachers can print out ready-made tests or create their own tests.

Professional Development

Professional Development Task 8

Imagine you want your learners to practice listening carefully during a group task. One behavior you could demonstrate would be leaning forward. Make a list of at least three other behaviors or expressions that careful listeners use.

The *Professional Development Program* offers instructors research-based teaching strategies and activities for single- and multilevel classes, plus Professional Development Tasks like this one.

The First Step

1 Get to know your classmates

  Listen and repeat.

A: Excuse me. Is anyone sitting here?
B: No. Someone was sitting here, but she left. Have a seat!
A: Thanks. I'm Estela, by the way.
B: Hi Estela. I'm Ara.
A: Ara? Is that a Persian name?
B: No, it's Armenian. I came here four years ago.
A: I've been here for two years. I'm from El Salvador.
B: Do you know anything about this class?
A: Not really. But I'm sure we'll learn a lot!

B Practice the conversation with 3 classmates. Use your own information.

2 Review verb tenses

A Study the sentences and the time lines. Then complete the charts with the verb tenses from the box.

| Future | Present perfect | Simple past |
| Past continuous | Present continuous | ~~Simple present~~ |

1. _Simple present_

I study everyday.

3. _Simple past_

I studied yesterday.

5. _Present perfect_

I've studied for four years.

2. _Present continuous_

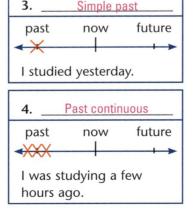

I'm studying English now.

4. _Past continuous_

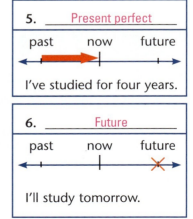

I was studying a few hours ago.

6. _Future_

I'll study tomorrow.

☑ Greet others; use various verb tenses; identify word families

The First Step

Objectives	Grammar	Vocabulary	Correlations
On-, Pre-, and Higher-level: Greet others, use various verb tenses, and identify word families	Parts of speech (noun, adjective, verb, adverb)	Country names and adjectives For vocabulary support, see these **Oxford Picture Dictionary** topics: World Map, Describing Things, Personal Information	**CASAS:** 0.1.2, 0.1.4, .0.1.5, 0.2.1, 7.4.5 **LCPs:** 39.01, 49.09, 49.10, 50.02 **SCANS:** Listening, Socialability, Speaking **EFF:** Listen actively, Speak so others can understand

Warm-up

10–15 minutes (books closed)

Tell the students a little bit about yourself. Then ask them questions in different tenses. *Where do you work? Are you taking any other classes? Where did you last study English? What were you doing at this time last year? How long have you attended this school? What will you do when you finish this class?* As you ask questions, learn the students' names and write a sentence on the board. *Olga works in a restaurant. Chan is taking a computer class.*

Introduction

5 minutes

1. Say: *Now we know something about a few people. It's time for more of us to get to know each other.*

2. State the objective: *Today we're going to get to know each other, review verb tenses, and talk about word families.*

1 Get to know your classmates

Presentation I

15–20 minutes

A 1. Direct students to look at the picture. Ask: *Where are these people? What are they doing?*

2. Read the instructions aloud. Direct students to read the conversation silently and listen for the answer to this question: *Where is Ara from?* Call on a volunteer for the answer. Point out Armenia on a world map.

3. Play the audio. Ask students to listen and repeat the conversation.

Guided Communicative Practice

15–20 minutes

B 1. Model the conversation with a volunteer using your own information.

2. Direct students to practice the conversation with three different partners. Tell them to remember the first names of their classmates. Participate in the exercise and provide feedback.

C 1. Ask students to write sentences about the classmates they met. Encourage them to ask each other for help with spelling names and nationalities.

2. Call on volunteers to read a sentence aloud and point out the student about whom it was written.

2 Review verb tenses

Guided Communicative Practice II

20–25 minutes

A 1. Introduce the new topic: *Now we're going to review verb tenses.*

2. Direct students to study the timeline. Use the sentences on the board from the warm-up to check comprehension. Elicit the verb and the tense of each sentence.

3. Direct students to work individually to write the correct tense for the sentences under the chart. Call on volunteers for the answers.

B 1. Direct students to look at the picture. Ask: *Why do you think they are working together?*

2. Read and have students repeat the questions. Ask them to work with a partner to identify the tense and then ask and answer the questions. Monitor and provide feedback.

3 Word Families

Presentation II

15–20 minutes

A 1. Introduce the new topic: *Now we're going to learn about word families.* Write *Noun, Adjective, Verb,* and *Adverb* on the board. Elicit an example of each, and write the words in the correct columns.

2. Direct students' attention to the chart. Point out that the example words are all related and are called a word family.

3. Ask students to work individually to complete the sentences below the chart. Go over the answers as a class.

4. Refer students to the words on the board, and elicit the complete family for each word. Point out that not all words have a "family member" in every part of speech.

Guided Practice

15–20 minutes

 B 1. Ask students to look up the word *help* in their dictionaries.

2. Direct them to work individually to complete the sentences in the chart. Go over the answers as a class.

> **TIP** Make a transparency of the page from the dictionary that lists *help,* and look at the parts of speech as a class. Point out other useful features in the dictionary, particularly example sentences. Encourage students to use an all-English learner's dictionary.

Communicative Practice

20–25 minutes

 C 1. Read the instructions aloud. Assign a time limit (ten minutes). Ask students to work with their partners to find a word family in the dictionary.

2. Tell students to complete the *Word* and *Part of Speech* columns in their charts and write an example sentence for each word. Ask them not to use the example sentence from the dictionary.

D Call on volunteers to write two of their sentences from 3C on the board. Ask the class to identify the parts of speech. Then have the volunteers write their charts on the board, so the class can check their answers.

> ## Multilevel Strategies
>
> Adapt 2C to the level of your students. Explain that you will be watching them so that you can determine their levels and target your instruction to their individual needs.
>
> • **Pre-level** Provide these students with skeleton sentences for *care. The teacher _____ about her students. Please drive _____. You have to be _____ when you walk down the stairs. When you are sick, you need medical _____.* Write these sentences on the board. Tell students that if 2C is difficult, they can use the sentences on the board.
>
> • **Higher-level** Tell these students to find an additional word family and write sentences for it.
>
> Monitor student practice and make a note of which students will need extra help or extra challenges.

Evaluation

10–15 minutes

Dictate several sentences using word families and different tenses. *Maria drives to school every day. That driver is talking on the phone. He has always worked very slowly. We came home the slow way. Will you please slow down?* Ask students to label the verb tenses and to identify the parts of speech for the words related to *drive* and *slow.* Collect and correct the dictations.

To compress this lesson: Omit the evaluation.

To extend this lesson: Brainstorm word families. Call on volunteers to say two related words—for example, *beautiful-beauty, quick-quickly, work-work.* Write the words on the board. Have students work with a partner to write sentences for the words. Tell them to use all of the tenses from 2A. Call on volunteers to share their sentences with the class.

B Work with a partner. Read the questions and identify the tenses. Then ask and answer the questions.

1. What are you thinking about right now? 1. present continuous
2. What do you do on weekends? 2. simple present
3. How long have you studied English? 3. present perfect
4. What did you do last Saturday? 4. simple past
5. Where will you speak English this week? 5. future

3 Word families

A Look at the chart. Then complete the sentences.

Word	Part of speech
study	verb
student	noun

Word	Part of speech
studious	adjective (adj.)
studiously	adverb (adv.)

1. Sara is a part-time _____student_____.
2. She _____studies_____ hard every day.
3. She does research every night. She's really _____studious_____.
4. She's working _____studiously_____ because she has a biology exam tomorrow.

B Look in a dictionary to find the word family for the word *help*. Then complete the chart.

Word	Part of speech	Example
help	noun	This dictionary is a big ___help___. I like it a lot.
help	verb	I think this class will really ___help___ me.
helpful	adj.	Our teacher is friendly and very ___helpful___.
helpfully	adv.	Ara ___helpfully___ gave me his pencil.

C Work with a partner. Look in the dictionary for another word family. Then complete the chart.

Word	Part of speech	Example

D Talk about your word family with the class.

FOCUS ON
- personalities and learning styles
- describing yourself
- action and non-action verbs
- expressing opinions about education
- test anxiety

It Takes All Kinds!

| LESSON **1** | **Vocabulary** |

1 Learn personality and talent vocabulary

A Talk about the questions with your class.

1. Which are you best at—math, languages, or sports?
2. Do you like to draw? Why or why not?

B Work with your classmates. Match the words with the pictures.

| __3__ adventurous | __7__ athletic | __6__ musical | __4__ social |
| __5__ artistic | __2__ mathematical | __8__ quiet | __1__ verbal |

C Listen and check. Then read the new words with a partner.

D Work with a partner. Write other personality and talent words you know. Check your words in a dictionary.

✔ Identify personality traits, talents, and learning styles

Unit 1 Lesson 1

Objectives	Grammar	Vocabulary	Correlations
On-level: Describe and talk about personality types and learning styles **Pre-level:** Identify personality types and describe learning styles **Higher-level:** Explain personality types and learning styles	Adjectives (*She is adventurous.*)	Personality types and learning styles For vocabulary support for pre-level students, see this **Oxford Picture Dictionary** topic: Studying	**CASAS:** 0.1.2, 0.1.5, 0.2.1, 4.8.1, 7.4.5, 7.4.9 **LCPs:** 39.01, 49.02, 49.10, 49.16 **SCANS:** Participates as member of a team, Reading, Seeing things in the mind's eye **EFF:** Cooperate with others, Listen actively, Observe critically, Read with understanding, Speak so others can understand, Reflect and evaluate

Warm-up and Review

10–15 minutes (books closed)

Tell students what you like to do in your free time—for example, cook, read, play basketball. Elicit things that they like to do, and write them on the board.

Introduction

5 minutes

1. Ask students which of the activities on the board a musical (or artistic or athletic) person might like to do. Tell them things we like to do in our free time are a reflection of our personalities and also of our learning styles.

2. State the objective: *Today we're going to learn about personality types and learning styles.*

1 Learn personality vocabulary

Presentation I

20–25 minutes

A Write *Math, Languages, Sports*, and *Drawing* on the board. Ask for a show of hands to find out how many students enjoy or think they are good at each one. Elicit words from the warm-up that are related to these words.

B 1. Direct students to look at the pictures. Ask: *Do these people enjoy the same activities?*

2. Group students and assign roles: leader, fact checker, recorder, and reporter. Explain that students work with their groups to match the words and pictures.

3. Check comprehension of the roles. *Who looks up the words in a dictionary?* [fact checker] *Who writes the numbers in the book?* [recorder] *Who tells the class your answers?* [reporter] *Who helps everyone and manages the group?* [leader]

4. Set a time limit (three minutes). As students work together, copy the wordlist onto the board.

5. Call "time." Have reporters take turns giving their answers. Write each group's answer on the board next to the word.

C 1. To prepare students for listening, say: *One of these people is going to describe her classmates.* Ask students to listen and check their answers.

2. Have students check the wordlist on the board and then write the correct numbers in their books.

3. Pair students. Set a time limit (three minutes). Monitor pair practice to identify pronunciation issues.

4. Call "time" and work with the pronunciation of any troublesome words or phrases

D 1. Ask students to work with their partners from 1C to brainstorm a list of related words.

2. Elicit words from the class. Write them on the board. Ask students to copy them into their vocabulary notes for the unit.

Guided Practice

5–10 minutes

 E 1. Model the conversation with a volunteer.

2. Set a time limit (three minutes). Direct students to practice with a partner.

3. Ask volunteers to act out one of their conversations for the class.

2 Learn vocabulary for learning styles

Presentation II

15–20 minutes

 A 1. Direct students to look at the title of the article. Introduce the new topic: *Now we're going to read about learning styles.* Ask students to look quickly at the article and identify how many learning styles it talks about. Say and have students repeat the three words.

2. Ask students to read the article silently.

3. Check comprehension. Ask: *Who learns best by hearing new information?* [Tony] *Who remembers best by writing or taking notes?* [Ria]

Guided Practice

10–15 minutes

 B 1. Have students work with a partner to match the names with the actions.

2. Go over the answers as a class.

 Before students answer the questions in 2C, demonstrate note taking. Write your own answer to question 1 on the board in long form. *I think that I am a visual learner because I always have to see the words in writing before I can remember them.* Ask: *Is this what I mean by* take notes? *Which words did I really need to write?* Erase all of the words except *visual* and *words in writing.*

Communicative Practice and Application

10–15 minutes

 C 1. Give students a minute to make notes of their answers to the questions. Call on individuals to share their ideas with the class.

2. Ask students to reflect on how their learning styles should affect your teaching. *Which class activities will be most beneficial to visual, auditory, and kinesthetic learners?*

Evaluation

10–15 minutes (books closed)

TEST YOURSELF

1. Direct students to work individually to write a list of words from the lesson. Assign a time limit (three minutes). Call "time" and direct students to work with a partner to combine their lists and put the words in alphabetical order.

2. Circulate and monitor students' progress.

3. Ask a volunteer to write his or her pair's list on the board. Ask other students to add words to the list.

Multilevel Strategies

Target the *Test Yourself* to the level of your students.

• **Higher-level** After these students have worked with a partner to alphabetize their lists, ask them to write three to five sentences explaining words from the list.

To compress this lesson: Conduct 1B as a whole-class activity.

To extend this lesson: Use personality adjectives.
1. Ask students to interview a partner about what activities he or she enjoys.
2. Have them introduce their partners to the class and tell about his or her personality and favorite activities.

And/Or have students complete **Workbook 4 page 2** and **Multilevel Activity Book 4 pages 18–19**.

E Work with a partner. Practice the conversation. Use the words in 1B.

A: What kind of person are you?

B: I'm pretty athletic. How about you?

A: Well, I'm not very athletic, but I'm artistic.

2 Learn vocabulary for learning styles

A Read the article. Who are you more like—Ria, Tony, or Trang?

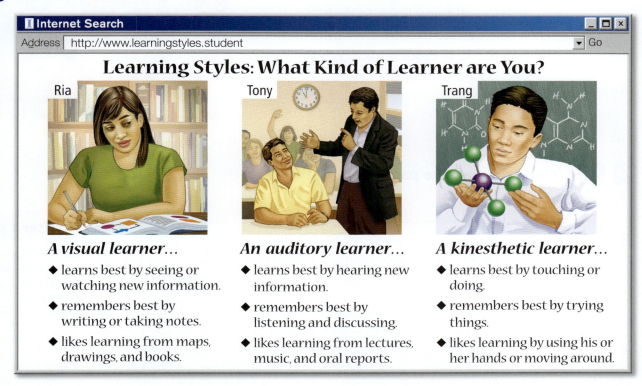

Internet Search

Address | http://www.learningstyles.student | Go

Learning Styles: What Kind of Learner are You?

Ria

A visual learner…

- ◆ learns best by seeing or watching new information.
- ◆ remembers best by writing or taking notes.
- ◆ likes learning from maps, drawings, and books.

Tony

An auditory learner…

- ◆ learns best by hearing new information.
- ◆ remembers best by listening and discussing.
- ◆ likes learning from lectures, music, and oral reports.

Trang

A kinesthetic learner…

- ◆ learns best by touching or doing.
- ◆ remembers best by trying things.
- ◆ likes learning by using his or her hands or moving around.

B Work with a partner. Match the names with the actions.

When there is a problem with the computer,

___c___ 1. Ria   a. asks someone to tell him how to fix it.

___a___ 2. Tony   b. tries to fix the problem.

___b___ 3. Trang   c. reads the instruction book.

C Talk about the questions with your class.

1. Which words in this lesson describe you? Which describe your friends and classmates?
2. How many visual, auditory, and kinesthetic learners are there in your class?

TEST YOURSELF ✓

Close your book. Work with a partner. Make a list of as many new words from the lesson as you can. Alphabetize your list. Then check your spelling in a dictionary.

1 Read about learning styles

A **Look at the pictures. Talk about the questions with your class.**

1. Name something you have recently learned to do. How did you learn to do it?
2. How do you like to learn new information? From a teacher? From books? Why?

B **Listen and read the paragraph.**

My Learning Style

by Carlos Morales

I think I'm an auditory learner. When I have to learn something new, I like to hear about it first. For example, ← at work I remember things if my boss tells me about them, but I often forget information if I read it in a memo. At home, I don't spend much time reading newspapers or magazines. I prefer to listen to the news on TV or on the radio. When I'm cooking or doing housework, I like to listen to interviews on radio talk shows. I learn a lot from them! In class, I understand best when I hear new information from the teacher. I don't learn very well from sources like books or websites. I'm really social and I like studying and learning with other people.

Writer's note

You can introduce an example with *For example* and a comma (,).

C **Check your understanding. Mark the sentences T (true), F (false), or NI (no information).**

_F_ 1. The writer likes to learn new information by reading.

_T_ 2. He'd rather listen to TV and radio news than read the newspaper.

_F_ 3. When he's cleaning or cooking, he watches TV.

_NI_ 4. When he studies at home, he turns the radio on.

_T_ 5. In the classroom, he learns by listening to his teacher.

☑ Write a paragraph to describe one's learning style

Unit 1 Lesson 2

Objectives	Grammar	Vocabulary	Correlations
On- and Higher-level: Analyze, write, and edit a paragraph about learning styles **Pre-level:** Read and write about learning styles	Simple-present tense (*I remember things if my boss tells me about them.*)	Learning-style vocabulary For vocabulary support for pre-level students, see this **Oxford Picture Dictionary** topic: Studying	**CASAS:** 0.1.2, 0.1.5, 0.2.1, 0.2.3, 7.4.7, 7.4.9 **LCPs:** 39.01, 49.02, 49.13, 49.16, 49.17 **SCANS:** Knowing how to learn, Listening, Participates as member of a team, Reading, Speaking **EFF:** Convey ideas in writing, Listen actively, Read with understanding, Reflect and evaluate

Warm-up and Review

10–15 minutes (books closed)

Make signs that say *Auditory, Kinesthetic,* and *Visual*. Place them in different parts of the room, and ask students to stand near the learning style they most identify with. Tell them to talk with their group members about why they identify with that learning style.

Introduction

5 minutes

1. Call on representatives from each group to share some information from their discussion.

2. State the objective: *Today we're going to write a paragraph about our learning styles.*

1 Read about learning styles

Presentation

20–25 minutes

A Write *Auditory, Visual,* and *Kinesthetic* on the board (or use the three signs from the warm-up). Elicit answers to questions 1 and 2. Ask students which learning style each of their answers exemplifies, and write them in the correct column. Point out that although one learning style may be dominant, most people use all of them at different times. Leave the lists on the board for students to refer to for their 2B writing assignment.

B 1. Tell students they are going to read and listen to a man describing his learning style.

2. Direct students to read the paragraph silently. Check comprehension. Ask: *What three places does he talk about?* [work, home, and school] *What's his example of auditory learning at work?* [He doesn't remember memos, but he remembers if his boss tells him.]

3. Play the audio. Have students read along silently.

4. Draw students' attention to the *Writer's note*. Ask them to find *For example* in the paragraph. Point out that it begins a new sentence.

Guided Practice I

10 minutes

C Have students work independently to mark the statements T (true), F (false), and NI (no information). Write the answers on the board.

Multilevel Strategies

Seat pre-level students together for 1C.

• **Pre-level** While other students are working on 1C, ask these students *Yes/No* and *Or* questions about the reading. *Is he a visual learner or an auditory learner? Does he prefer to read information or to hear it? Does he read very much?* Give students time to copy the answers to 1C from the board.

2 Write about your learning style

Guided Practice II

20–25 minutes

 A 1. Read the questions. Elicit students' answers.

2. Use student responses to add new examples to the lists on the board from 1A.

B 1. Direct students to look back at the paragraph in 1B. Focus their attention on the structure of the paragraph. Ask them to look through the paragraph quickly and find the introductory phrases that the writer uses to show he is switching to a new topic. *[At work, At home, In class]*

2. Read the questions aloud, and elicit various ways to answer them.

3. Check comprehension of the exercise. Ask: *Are you writing a list of answers to the questions, or are you writing a paragraph?* [a paragraph] *What's the difference?* [A paragraph is about one topic; the first sentence is indented; sentences are continuous.] *Do you need a title?* [yes]

4. Have students work individually to write their paragraphs.

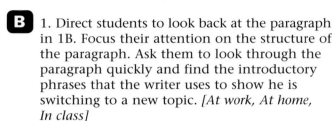

Multilevel Strategies

While the other students are completing 2B, work with the pre-level students.

• **Pre-level** Read each question aloud. Elicit various answers and ask students to write their own answers before you move onto the next question.

C 1. Lead students through the process of using the *Editing checklist*. Read each sentence aloud, and ask students to check their papers before moving onto the next item.

2. Allow students a few minutes to edit their writing as necessary.

Communicative Practice

10 minutes

 D 1. Read the instructions aloud. Emphasize to students that they are responding to their partners' work, not correcting it.

2. Use the paragraph in 1B to model the exercise. *I think the part about listening to talk shows is interesting. I'd like to ask the writer if her boss gets angry when she forgets the information in memos.*

3. Direct students to exchange papers with a partner and follow the instructions.

4. Call on volunteers to share some interesting things they read in their partners' paragraphs.

Application and Evaluation

20 minutes

TEST YOURSELF

1. Review the instructions aloud. Assign a time limit (15 minutes), and have students work independently. Give students notice when they have five minutes left.

2. Before collecting students' work, remind them to use the *Editing checklist*. Collect and correct students' writing.

Multilevel Strategies

Adapt the *Test Yourself* to the level of your students.

• **Pre-level** Provide these students with three questions to answer in writing about their partners. *What kind of learner is your partner? How does he or she learn new information? Does he or she prefer studying with other people or alone?*

To compress this lesson: Assign the *Test Yourself* for homework.

To extend this lesson: Have students apply learning styles to language learning.
1. Draw a large chart on the board with two rows and three columns. Label the rows *Grammar* and *Vocabulary*. Label the columns *Kinesthetic, Auditory,* and *Visual.*
2. As a class, brainstorm study strategies for each combination, and write them in the chart. For example: For grammar, an auditory learner might discuss the grammar with a friend; a visual learner might underline examples in a reading; a kinesthetic learner might act out sentences or do matching activities with index cards.

And/Or have students complete **Workbook 4 page 3** and **Multilevel Activity Book 4 page 20**.

2 Write about your learning style

A **Talk about the questions with your class.**

1. How are you similar to the writer in 1B?
2. How are you different from the writer in 1B?

B **Write a paragraph about your learning style. Use the model in 1B and the questions below to help you.**

- What kind of learner do you think you are?
- How do you remember new information?
- What do you do at home to learn new information?
- How do you learn best in class?
- Which do you prefer—studying and learning alone or with other people?

My Learning Style

by (your name)

I think I'm a visual learner.

I learn best by seeing new

information…

C **Use the checklist to edit your writing. Check (✔) the true sentences.**

Editing checklist	
1. I described my learning and studying styles.	
2. I included one or more examples.	
3. I introduced one example with *For example* and a comma (,).	
4. Every sentence starts with a capital letter and ends with a period.	

D **Exchange paragraphs with a partner. Read and comment on your partner's work.**

1. Point out one example that you think is interesting.
2. Ask your partner a question about his or her learning style.

TEST YOURSELF ✔

Write a new paragraph. Describe your partner's or another person's learning style.

1 Learn action verbs in the present

A **Read the story. Name 3 creative things Antonia does.**

Antonia is the most creative person in our class. She (works) in an office during the day, but on the weekends she (paints) pictures and (writes) poems. She (doesn't watch) TV.

Right now Antonia isn't painting pictures and she isn't writing poems. She's making a blouse. She (makes) all of her own clothes. She paints pictures, writes poems, and makes all of her own clothes.

B **Study the charts. Circle the 5 simple present action verbs and underline the 3 present continuous action verbs in the story above.**

ACTION VERBS IN THE SIMPLE PRESENT AND THE PRESENT CONTINUOUS

Simple present	Present continuous
Antonia often **makes** her own clothes.	She **is making** a blouse.
She **doesn't watch** TV.	She **isn't watching** TV now.
They sometimes **write** poems.	They **are writing** poems now.
They **don't paint** pictures very often.	They **aren't painting** pictures now.

Note
Most verbs describe actions. These verbs are called action verbs.

C **Complete the sentences with the simple present or the present continuous form of the verbs in parentheses.**

1. Pedro Santana _____<u>works</u>_____ at a university in the math department. (work)

2. In his free time, he _____<u>writes</u>_____ math books for school children. (write)

3. Today is Saturday, and Pedro _____<u>isn't working</u>_____ at the university now. (not work)

4. Right now, he and his family _____<u>are painting</u>_____ their house. (paint)

5. The Santanas _____<u>don't watch</u>_____ much TV on weekends. (not watch)

6. His children _____<u>aren't doing</u>_____ their homework now. (not do)

7. Now they _____<u>are helping</u>_____ Pedro paint. (help)

8. Pedro always _____<u>tells</u>_____ his friends, "It's important for families to do things together." (tell)

Unit 1 Lesson 3

Objectives	Grammar	Vocabulary	Correlations
On- and Higher-level: Use and listen for action and non-action verbs to express feelings and opinions **Pre-level:** Recognize action and non-action verbs in statements about feelings and opinions	Simple present and present continuous with action and non-action verbs (*She's making a sweater. She makes all of her own clothes.*)	Personality, free-time activities For vocabulary support for pre-level students, see these **Oxford Picture Dictionary** topics: Studying, Hobbies and Games	**CASAS:** 0.1.2, 0.2.1, 7.4.7 **LCPs:** 49.16, 49.17, 50.02 **SCANS:** Listening, Reading, Speaking, Writing **EFF:** Convey ideas in writing, Listen actively, Observe critically, Read with understanding, Reflect and evaluate, Speak so others can understand

Warm-up and Review

10–15 minutes (books closed)

Review the concepts of visual, auditory, and kinesthetic learners by asking students to describe what each type of learner likes to do. As they provide examples, write the verb phrases on the board: *take notes, read books, draw pictures, fix things.*

Introduction

5–10 minutes

1. Point out that most (or all) of the words on the board are actions, or things that we physically do. Provide an example. *I'm a visual learner. I like to read. Liking is not an action, but reading is an action.*

2. State the objective: *Today we're going to use action and non-action verbs to talk about learning styles in the present tense.*

1 Learn action verbs

Presentation I

20–25 minutes

A 1. Direct students to look at the picture. Ask: *Do you like her dress?*

2. Read the instructions aloud. Ask students to read the paragraph silently to find the three creative things Antonia does. Call on individuals for the answers.

B 1. Read and have students repeat the sentences in the chart. Elicit the difference in meaning between simple present and present continuous. [Simple present refers to habitual activities; present continuous refers to activities happening now.]

2. Direct students to underline the present-continuous action verbs in the paragraph in 1A. Go over the answers as a class.

3. Ask: *Why are those two sentences present continuous while all of the others are simple present?* [The others talk about what Antonia usually does. The two present-continuous sentences describe what she is doing now.]

4. Assess students' understanding of the charts. Elicit negative and affirmative sentences in simple present and present continuous using the verbs on the board from the warm-up. *I sometimes fix cars on the weekends. I'm not fixing a car right now.*

Guided Practice I

15–20 minutes

C Ask students to work individually to complete the sentences. Ask volunteers to write the answers on the board.

Multilevel Strategies

For 1C, seat same-level students together.

• **Pre-level** While other students are completing 1C, ask pre-level students to copy the sentences from the chart in 1B. Tell them to use a different verb from the one in the chart. Give them time to copy the answers to 1C after they are written on the board.

2 Learn non-action verbs in the simple present

Presentation II

20–25 minutes

 A 1. Introduce the new topic. Say: *Now we're going to talk about non-action verbs. These verbs describe things like feelings. They don't describe things that we do.*

2. Read the instructions aloud. Direct students to read the sentences in the chart and find the answer to the question. Read and have students repeat the list of other non-action verbs. Read the notes.

3. Elicit a sample sentence for each verb.

 Students may question why *think* is on the list of non-action verbs. Point out that when *think* means *believe* it is a non-action verb. *Think* also can refer to the action of thinking, in which case it can be used in the continuous. *I am thinking about my mother.* *See* and *have* also have "action" meanings. *I'm seeing the doctor today. She's having a party.* In addition, non-action verbs are sometimes used in the continuous in informal spoken English. *I'm loving my new job. Wait! I'm remembering something!* Using the verb in a non-standard form makes it sound more active and emphatic.

Guided Practice I

10–15 minutes

B 1. Have students work with a partner to complete the conversation.

2. Call on two volunteers to read the conversation aloud.

3. Ask students to read the conversation with their partners.

> ### Multilevel Strategies
>
> After 1B, provide more practice with non-action verbs.
>
> • **Pre-level** While other students are writing a conversation, review simple-present tense with this group. Write *think, need,* and *hear* on the board. Ask students to write a negative and an affirmative third-person simple-present sentence with each verb. Use *own* as an example: *He owns that business. She doesn't own a car.* Have volunteers read their completed sentences aloud.
>
> • **On- and Higher-level** While you are working with pre-level students, ask these students to write an original conversation using four of the verbs from the chart and two action verbs. Have volunteers read their conversations aloud. Ask other students to identify the non-action verbs.

C Ask students to work individually to complete the sentences. Call on a volunteer to read the completed sentences aloud.

 After 2C, use non-action verbs to practice expressing opinions in the third-person simple present. Put students in mixed-level groups. Tell each group to write three statements of opinion in the third person using non-action verbs. *Seaweed tastes delicious. Our teacher doesn't like grammar.* To increase the variety of statements, assign three verbs to each group. Have group members read the statements. If other students disagree, tell them to respond. *No, it doesn't! Yes, she does!*

2 Learn non-action verbs in the simple present

A Study the charts. Is *be* an action verb or a non-action verb?   a non-action verb

NON-ACTION VERBS IN THE SIMPLE PRESENT

Non-action verbs
Ari **likes** books about science and travel.
He **knows** a lot about the outdoors.
Ari **thinks** everyone should spend time outdoors.
He **sees** a lot of different things on his travels.
Ari **has** a website with pictures from his trips.
He **is** a good photographer.

More non-action verbs		
believe	need	smell
dislike	own	sound
forget	possess	taste
hate	remember	understand
hear	seem	want
love		

Notes
• We use non-action (stative) verbs to describe feelings, knowledge, beliefs, and the senses.
• These verbs are usually **not** used in the present continuous:
He knows a lot.
* He is knowing a lot. (INCORRECT)

B Work with a partner. Complete the conversation. Use the words in the box.

think   ~~remember~~   seem   have   know   don't understand

A: Do you _____remember_____ the page number for
(1)
our homework assignment?

B: Yes, it's page 23.

A: Thanks. Hey, these questions _____seem_____ really easy.
(2)

B: Great! By the way, does this book _____have_____ an answer key?
(3)

A: I don't _____know_____. OK, let's get started.
(4)

B: Uh-oh. I _____don't understand_____ question one. Do you?
(5)

A: No. I don't. I _____think_____ this assignment is going to take all day!
(6)

C Circle the correct words.

1. I really (**love** / am loving) to study history.
2. I (**study** / am studying) history every Saturday.
3. I also (**like** / am liking) to read.
4. Right now I (read / **am reading**) an interesting book about U.S. history.
5. I (**know** / am knowing) a lot about history.
6. I (**think** / am thinking) everyone should learn about the past.

3 Grammar listening

Listen to the speakers. Are they using action verbs or non-action verbs? Check (✔) Action or Non-action.

	Action	Non-action
1.		✔
2.	✔	
3.		✔
4.	✔	
5.	✔	
6.		✔

4 Practice action and non-action verbs

A **Think about your answers to these questions.**

1. How do you remember new words?
   Name two different ways.
2. Do you think that English is an easy language?
   Why or why not?
3. How do you feel when you speak English?
4. What do you like about English?
   What do you dislike?
5. What are three things that you often do
   in your English class?
6. Which of these things are you doing today?
7. What are you doing right now that you always do in class?

B **Work with a partner. Ask and answer the questions in 4A.**

A: *How do you remember new words?*
B: *Well, sometimes I repeat the new word. Other times, I use it in a sentence.*

C **Talk about your partner with the class.**

Nancy sometimes repeats a new word. Sometimes she uses it in a sentence.

TEST YOURSELF ✔

Close your book. Write 5 sentences about yourself and 5 about your classmates. Use a simple present or present continuous verb in each sentence. Use at least 3 non-action verbs.

---

3 Grammar listening

Guided Practice II

10–15 minutes

1. Say a couple of sentences about one of your students. *Carlos goes to the park every weekend. He plays soccer and eats a picnic lunch.* Ask the students whether you used action or non-action verbs to talk about Carlos. Say: *Now we're going to listen to sentences about different people. Decide whether the verbs are action or non-action.*

2. Play the audio. Direct students to read along silently without writing.

3. Replay the audio. Ask students to check the correct column.

4. Go over the answers as a class.

> ### Multilevel Strategies
>
> Replay the *Grammar listening* to allow pre-level students to catch up while you challenge on- and higher-level students.
>
> • **Pre-level** Have these students listen again to complete the chart.
>
> • **On- and Higher-level** Have these students write the verbs they hear.

4 Practice action and non-action verbs

Communicative Practice and Application

20–25 minutes

A 1. Read the questions aloud.

2. Ask students to think about and note their answers.

B 1. Put students in pairs. Read and have students repeat the questions.

2. Direct students to ask their partners the questions. Tell them to make notes of each other's answers. Model the exercise by asking a volunteer the first question. Have the class tell you how to write the answer in note form.

3. Check comprehension of the exercise. Ask: *Do you need to write your partner's answers in complete sentences?* [no]

C 1. Call on individuals to share what they learned about their partners.

2. Discuss the students' ideas as a class. Ask students how they are similar to and different from their partners.

Evaluation

10–15 minutes (books closed)

TEST YOURSELF

Ask students to write the sentences independently. Collect and correct their writing.

> ### Multilevel Strategies
>
> Target the *Test Yourself* to the level of your students.
>
> • **Pre-level** Allow these students to write five sentences about themselves only.
>
> • **Higher-level** Have these students write a paragraph in response to this prompt: *What are some similarities and differences in the way you and your partner feel about learning English?*

To compress this lesson: Conduct 1C as a whole-class activity.

To extend this lesson: After the *Grammar listening*, have volunteers make statements with action and non-action verbs. Have the class identify the verbs as action or non-action.

And/Or have students complete **Workbook 4 pages 4–5**, **Multilevel Activity Book 4 pages 21–22**, and the corresponding **Unit 1 Exercises** on the **Multilevel Grammar Exercises CD-ROM 4.**

Unit 1 Lesson 4

Objectives	Grammar	Vocabulary	Correlations
On-, Pre-, and Higher-level: Express agreement and disagreement about educational topics, and listen for opinions	Present-tense questions (*What does visual mean?*)	*Agree, disagree, opinion, appropriate* For vocabulary support for pre-level students, see this **Oxford Picture Dictionary** unit and topic: Areas of Study, Studying	**CASAS:** 0.1.2, 0.2.1, 1.1.3, 1.1.8, 6.0.3, 6.0.4, 6.1.4, 6.7.2 **LCPs:** 39.01, 49.02, 49.03, 49.09 **SCANS:** Arithmetic/Mathematics, Listening, Seeing things in the mind's eye **EFF:** Listen actively, Observe critically, Read with understanding, Use math to solve

Warm-up and Review

10–15 minutes (books closed)

Write *How do you learn English?* on the board, and elicit students' ideas about effective learning methods. Write their ideas on the board.

Introduction

5 minutes

1. Say: *You may think one of these is a good learning method, but your partner might not agree. We all have different opinions. It's important to know how to agree and disagree.*

2. State the objective: *Today we're going to learn how to express opinions about education.*

1 Learn to express opinions about education

Presentation I

15–20 minutes

A 1. Direct students to look at the picture. Ask: *Which class would you rather go to?*

2. Play the audio. Give students a minute to note their answers to the questions. Call on volunteers to share their opinions.

Guided Practice

20–25 minutes

B 1. Read the instructions aloud. Play the audio. Ask students to read along silently and listen for the answer to the question. Elicit the answer.

2. Ask students to read the conversation with a partner. Circulate and monitor pronunciation. Model and have students repeat difficult words or phrases.

3. Say and have students repeat the expressions in the *In other words* box. Elicit the placement of the expressions in the conversation. Ask volunteers to read the conversation using expressions from the box.

Communicative Practice and Application

15–20 minutes

C 1. Ask students to read the instructions silently. Check their comprehension of the exercise. Ask: *What are the two roles? What is the situation?* Elicit examples of what each partner might say.

2. Set a time limit (five minutes). Ask students to act out the role-play in both roles. Encourage students to incorporate their own ideas. Ask one to three volunteer pairs to act out their conversations for the class. Tell students who are listening to decide whether Partner A or Partner B was more persuasive.

Multilevel Strategies

For 1C, adapt the role-play to the level of your students.

• **Pre-level** Provide the first two lines for these students. *A: I think you should call the teacher Mr. or Ms. B: I'm not sure I agree.* _____.

1 Learn to express opinions about education

 A Look at the picture. Listen to the conversations. Then answer the questions below with your classmates.

1. Do the man and woman agree on how many students should be in a class? What is the man's opinion? What is the woman's opinion?
2. Do they agree that teaching is hard work? What is the man's opinion? What is the woman's opinion?

 B Listen and read. What do the people disagree about?   the best way to learn English

A: I think watching TV is the best way to learn English.
B: I'm not sure I agree. I think it's better to talk and listen to people.
A: Really? Why do you think so?
B: Because when you talk to people, there's real communication.
A: You have a point, but I still think watching TV is best.

In other words...

Disagreeing politely
I'm not sure I agree.
You have a point, but…
Maybe you're right, but…
That's true, but…

C Role-play a conversation about opinions with a partner. Use the example in 1B to make a new conversation.

Partner A: State your opinion. You think that the best way to talk to a teacher is to use *Mr.* or *Ms.* and the teacher's last name. Listen to your partner's opinion. Explain that you think that using a teacher's first name doesn't sound polite.

Partner B: Disagree politely with your partner. Say that you prefer to call teachers by their first names. Explain that you think this is OK when both students and teachers are adults.

☑ Express agreement and disagreement about educational topics   **11**

2 Review *Yes/No,* information, and *or* questions

A Study the charts. Then match the questions with the answers.

Yes/No questions and short answers

A: **Do** you agree?	A: **Does** watching TV help you learn?
B: Yes, I **do**.	B: No, it **doesn't**.

Information questions

A: **Why** do you think so?	A: **Who** agrees with you?
B: Because I heard it on the radio.	B: Everyone agrees with me!

Or questions

A: Does he like to learn from books **or** TV?	A: Do they agree **or** disagree?
B: He likes to learn from books.	B: They agree.

_c_ 1. When do you study?

_a_ 2. Do you need a quiet place to study?

_e_ 3. Do you like or dislike the Internet?

_d_ 4. What does *visual* mean?

_b_ 5. How much does this book cost?

a. Yes, I do.

b. $12.99.

c. After my children are asleep.

d. It means using your eyes.

e. I like it, but I don't use it often.

B Work with a partner. Ask and answer the questions.

1. What is one thing you remember about school in the past?
2. Do you think learning English is easy? Why or why not?

3 Practice your pronunciation

A Listen to the pronunciation of the *t* sounds in these sentences.

The pronunciation of *t*

	The *tt* in *better* is pronounced /d/.
It's better to talk and listen.	The *t* in *talk* is pronounced /t/.
There's real communication.	The *t* in *listen* is not pronounced.
	The *t* in *communication* is pronounced /sh/.

B Work with a partner. How do you think the *t* is pronounced in these words? Write *d, t, sh,* or *NP* (not pronounced).

_t_ 1. study

_t_ 2. teacher

_t_ 3. after

_sh_ 4. education

_d_ 5. little

_NP_ 6. mortgage

C Listen and check. Then read the words with a partner.

2 Review *Yes/No,* information, and *Or* questions

Presentation II
10–15 minutes

 A 1. Introduce the new topic. Say: *Now we're going to review* Yes/No *and* Or *questions, so we can talk about our opinions.*

2. Read the instructions aloud. Give students time to study the charts silently. Ask: *What are the first words in* Or *questions?*

3. Have students work with a partner to match the questions and answers. Call on volunteers to read the questions and answers aloud. Write the number-letter match on the board.

4. Ask partners to take turns reading the questions and answers aloud.

 After 2A, provide more practice with question formation. Have students work in pairs to create short opinion polls about a topic of interest to them. Tell each pair to write at least one *Yes/No,* one information, and one *Or* question. Monitor and provide feedback on the questions. Make a note of common errors, and go over them with the class. Direct the pairs to walk around the classroom asking their questions. Call on volunteers to share any interesting information they learned about their classmates.

Guided Practice and Application
30–35 minutes

B 1. Model the questions and answers with a volunteer.

2. Set a time limit (five minutes). Direct students to ask several partners the questions.

3. Call on individuals to share how their answers were similar to or different from their partners'.

 After 1B, practice agreeing and disagreeing. Write *Education in the U.S.* on the board. Draw a happy face and a sad face underneath it. Ask students what they think or what they have heard about the positive and negative aspects of the educational system in the U.S. Write their ideas on the board. Direct them to work with a partner to practice expressing their opinions and agreeing and disagreeing politely. Monitor and provide feedback.

For a follow-up writing assignment, have students write a "letter to the editor" expressing their opinions on education in the U.S. Allow less-advanced writers to describe a typical school day in their native country.

3 Practice your pronunciation

Pronunciation Extension
10–15 minutes

A 1. Write *letter, education, whistle,* and *take* on the board. Say the words and ask students to repeat them. Underline the letter *t* in each word. Ask: *Does* t *represent the same sound in each word?* Say: *Now we're going to focus on four different ways to pronounce* t.

2. Play the audio. Direct students to listen for the pronunciation of *t.*

3. Ask students to repeat the sentences in the chart.

B Have students work with a partner and write *t, d, sh,* or *NP.*

C 1. Play the audio. Ask students to listen and check their answers. Go over the answers as a class.

2. Have students take turns reading the words with a partner.

4 Focus on Listening

Listening Extension

20–25 minutes

A Read the questions aloud, and elicit answers from volunteers. Write the students' ideas or key vocabulary on the board.

B 1. Read the list of issues aloud. Ask students to predict some things that the speakers might say about each issue.

2. Play the audio. Tell students to check the issues the people talk about on the radio show.

C 1. Direct students to look at the chart before listening.

2. Check comprehension of the exercise. Ask: *Do you check if you agree or disagree, or if the speakers agree or disagree?* [the speakers]

3. Replay the audio and have students work individually to complete the chart. Go over the answers as a class.

> ### Multilevel Strategies
>
> For 4C, replay the interview to challenge on- and higher-level students while allowing pre-level students to catch up.
>
> • **Pre-level** Have these students listen again to complete their charts.
>
> • **On- and Higher-level** Write *Dr. Kwang* and *Mr. Holt* on the board. Ask students to take notes on the arguments they hear from each person. As you go over the answers for 4C, elicit the speakers' opinions about each issue.

5 Real-life math

Math Extension

5–10 minutes

1. Direct students to look at the graph. Ask: *Which year had the highest number of students per class?*

2. Read the explanation of *average*. Have students work individually to read and answer the question.

3. Ask a volunteer to write the problem and the solution on the board.

Evaluation

10–15 minutes

TEST YOURSELF

1. Model the role-play with a volunteer. Then switch roles.

2. Pair students. Check comprehension of the exercise by eliciting examples of what each partner might say.

3. Set a time limit (five minutes), and have the partners act out the role-play in both roles.

4. Circulate and monitor. Encourage pantomime and improvisation.

5. Provide feedback.

> ### Multilevel Strategies
>
> Target the *Test Yourself* to the level of your students.
>
> • **Pre-level** Ask students to use this skeleton conversation: *A: I think the school should offer classes on the weekend because _____. B: I don't agree. Students don't like weekend classes because _____. A: That's true, but I still think they should offer weekend classes.*
>
> • **Higher-level** Ask these students to create an original argument about a change at the school.

To compress this lesson: Do the *Real-life math* as a whole-class activity.

To extend this lesson: After 4C, elicit the students' opinions about the statements in the chart. Have a class discussion. Encourage students to disagree politely.

And/Or have students complete **Workbook 4 page 6** and **Multilevel Activity Book 4 page 23**.

4 Focus on listening

A Look at the picture. Talk about the questions with your class.

1. Where are the people?
2. What are they doing?

B Listen to the conversation. Check (✔) the issues the people talk about.

✔ 1. teachers' salaries   ____ 3. cafeteria food   ✔ 5. safety

✔ 2. class size   ____ 4. libraries   ✔ 6. need for books

C Listen again. Do the speakers agree or disagree on the best solutions to the problems? Check (✔) *Agree* or *Disagree*.

	Solutions	Agree	Disagree
1.	Pay teachers more.	✔	
2.	Build new schools.		✔
3.	Raise taxes.		✔
4.	Put in security cameras.		✔
5.	Buy new books and computers.	✔	

5 Real-life math

A Look at the graph and answer the question.

What was the average* number of students per class at Hills Adult School for the four-year period from 2003 to 2006? _____ 22 _____

*average = total number of students for 4 years, divided by 4

B Explain your answer to your classmates.

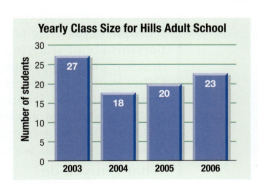

Yearly Class Size for Hills Adult School

TEST YOURSELF ✔

Role-play a conversation about weekend classes. Partner A: You think schools should have some weekend classes. Explain why. Partner B: Disagree politely. You think most students don't like weekend classes. Explain why. Then change roles.

1 Get ready to read

A **How do you feel about taking tests?**

B **Read the definitions. Which word can you use to describe your work?** manageable

college entrance exam: (noun) a test students take to get into a college or university
concentrate: (verb) to give all your attention to something
manageable: (adj.) not too big or difficult to control

C **Look at the title, the picture, and the section headings in the article in 2A. What do you think the article is about?**

2 Read and respond

A **Read the article. What is test anxiety?** Test anxiety occurs when people feel extremely nervous about studying for or taking a test.

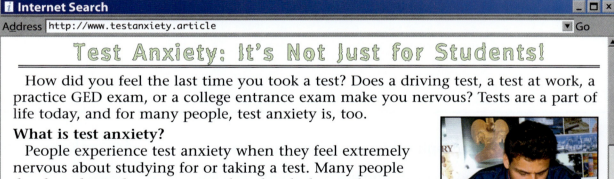

Internet Search _ □ x
Address http://www.testanxiety.article   ▼ Go

Test Anxiety: It's Not Just for Students!

How did you feel the last time you took a test? Does a driving test, a test at work, a practice GED exam, or a college entrance exam make you nervous? Tests are a part of life today, and for many people, test anxiety is, too.

What is test anxiety?
People experience test anxiety when they feel extremely nervous about studying for or taking a test. Many people develop physical symptoms such as headaches and nausea. Other symptoms of test anxiety are emotional, such as crying easily and feeling annoyed or frustrated. The major problem with test anxiety, though, is its effect on our ability to think clearly. Anxiety can make it difficult to concentrate or remember what we've learned.

What can you do?
Experts recommend using these strategies[1] to control test anxiety:
• Prepare for tests. Decide on a study schedule and follow it.
• Take good care of yourself. Get enough sleep, eat well, exercise, and give yourself some relaxation time.
• Get to the exam a little early—about 15 minutes.

[1]strategies: plans you use to achieve something

Unit 1 Lesson 5

Objectives	Grammar	Vocabulary	Correlations
On- , Pre-, and Higher-level: Read about and discuss test anxiety	Simple-past and simple-present tense (*I took the driving test. I think children take too many tests.*)	*Challenge, college-entrance exam, faint, manageable* For vocabulary support for pre-level students, see this **Oxford Picture Dictionary** topic: Feelings	**CASAS:** 0.1.2, 0.1.5, 0.2.1, 2.5.6, 7.4.4, 7.4.7, 7.4.9 **LCPs:** 39.01, 49.06, 49.16, 49.17 **SCANS:** Acquires and evaluates information, Uses computers to process information **EFF:** Listen actively, Read with understanding, Speak so others can understand, Take responsibility for learning

Warm-up and Review

10–15 minutes (books closed)

Draw a happy face and sad face on the board as column heads. Elicit words that describe feelings, and ask students which column they belong in. Write the words. If students run out of ideas, describe situations to elicit more "feeling" words. *How do you feel at the doctor's office? On a roller coaster? When you can't understand what someone is saying?*

Introduction

5 minutes

1. Add the word *anxiety* to the board. Tell students that it means extreme nervousness. If most of the words on the board are adjectives, point out that *anxious* is the adjective form of *anxiety.*

2. State the objective: *Today we're going to read and write about test anxiety.*

1 Get ready to read

Presentation

15–20 minutes

A Read the question aloud. Circle any words on the board that students use to describe their feelings about taking tests.

B Read the words and definitions. Elicit sample sentences from students using the words.

Pre-Reading

C 1. Direct students to look at the title, the picture, and the section headings. Call on a volunteer to say what the article is about.

2. Ask students to guess what strategies the article will recommend for dealing with test anxiety.

2 Read and respond

Guided Practice I

25–30 minutes

A 1. Ask students to read the article silently.

2. Direct students to underline unfamiliar words they would like to know. Elicit the words and encourage other students to provide definitions or examples.

3. Check comprehension. Ask: *What are some symptoms of anxiety?* [headaches, nausea, crying easily, feeling annoyed and frustrated, difficulty concentrating]

Multilevel Strategies

Adapt 2A to the level of your students.

• **Pre-level** Provide these students with a summary of the ideas in the reading. *1. Many people experience test anxiety. Test anxiety can cause headaches, nausea, and emotional symptoms. Test anxiety makes it difficult to concentrate. 2. You can control test anxiety. Prepare for the test. Take care of your health. Come to the test early. When you feel nervous, take deep breaths.*

Direct these students to read the summary while other students are reading 2A.

Guided Practice II

15–20 minutes

B 1. Play the audio. Have students read along silently.

2. Elicit and discuss any additional questions about the reading.

C Have students work individually to circle the correct answers. Go over the answers as a class. Write them on the board.

Multilevel Strategies

For 2C, work with pre-level students.

• **Pre-level** Ask these students questions about the summary while other students are completing 2C. *What are some symptoms of test anxiety? How can you control test anxiety?* Give students time to copy the answers to 2C from the board.

3 Talk it over

Communicative Practice

15–20 minutes

1. Read the questions aloud. Set a time limit (three minutes). Have students work independently to think about the questions and write their answers in note form.

2. Call on individuals to share their ideas and experiences.

Application

5–10 minutes

BRING IT TO LIFE

Read the instructions aloud. Provide students with URLs where they can find free learning-style tests.

TIP

Before students do the *Bring It to Life* assignment, type *learning-style test* into a search engine on the Internet to find a number of free learning-style test sites. Test formats vary from multiple choice, a *one-to-four* ranking system, and *never/seldom/often* choices. Print and make a transparency of the first page from several different tests. Go over them in class to familiarize your students with different ways of answering tests and to demonstrate the importance of following directions.

To compress this lesson: Conduct 2C as a whole-class activity.

To extend this lesson: Set up a debate about question 2 in *Talk it over*.
1. After students have discussed the question, elicit arguments and write them on the board under *Pros* and *Cons*.
2. Choose eight students (two groups of four) to be the debaters. Tell one side they are going to argue in favor of frequent testing in schools and the other that they are going to argue against it. Tell them to choose a role: 1, 2, 3, or 4. Number 1s will present the team's argument. Number 2s will respond to what the first team said. Number 3s will conclude. Number 4s will take notes and help teammates. Give students five minutes to talk with their teammates, choose their roles, and prepare their best arguments.
3. While the teams are preparing, explain to the rest of the class that they will be judges. Tell them they need to judge on how clear and convincing the arguments are, not on whether they agree or not.
4. Toss a coin to decide which team will go first. Have the Number 1s speak, then the Number 2s and Number 3s. Ask the class to choose a winning team. Applaud everyone for the effort.

And/Or have students complete **Workbook 4 page 7** and **Multilevel Activity Book 4 pages 24–25**.

- If you feel very nervous during the exam, take a few deep breaths. Calm down by saying to yourself, "I studied and I'm going to do fine on this test."

Tests are a fact of modern life, and most of us feel some anxiety when we have to take them. The next time you have to take a test, follow the experts' suggestions to bring your anxiety to a manageable level. You'll see: they help!

Adapted from: *www.hsc.edu and www.sdc.uwo.ca*

B Listen and read the article again.

C Circle the correct answer or answers.

1. Someone with test anxiety might feel ____.
   a. annoyed
   b. energetic
   c. nauseous

2. The most serious problem with test anxiety is its effect on our ____.
   a. emotions
   b. health
   c. ability to concentrate

3. If the test begins at 2:00, you should arrive at ____.
   a. 1:00
   b. 1:45
   c. 2:00

4. The experts advise people with test anxiety to ____.
   a. talk to other people taking the test
   b. take deep breaths
   c. calm down

5. Experts say test-taking strategies can help you ____.
   a. manage anxiety
   b. sleep at night
   c. study

3 Talk it over

Think about the questions. Talk about your ideas with the class.

1. Name a test you have taken in the U.S. How did you feel before you took it? After you took it?
2. Some people think that children have to take too many tests in school. Do you agree? Why or why not?

BRING IT TO LIFE

Use the library or the Internet to find a learning-styles test. Take the test and check your results. Bring your test to class. Do you agree with the results? Why or why not? Talk about your ideas with your classmates.

1 Grammar

A Circle the non-action verbs and underline the action verbs.

1. Lucy <u>goes out</u> with her friends every weekend, and she (loves) social events.
2. She (has) 100 phone numbers in her cell phone, and she <u>calls</u> her friends every week.
3. Her brothers, Steve and Ben, (seem) less social because they <u>spend</u> a lot of time at home.
4. Ben <u>reads</u> about the stars and planets because he (likes) astronomy.
5. Steve <u>doesn't talk</u> much, but he (remembers) everything he <u>reads</u>.

B Complete the conversations. Circle the correct words.

A: Juan ((thinks) / is thinking) that Hills Adult School is a good school.
(1)
B: I ((agree) / am agreeing) with him. They ((have) / are having) good teachers.
(2)   (3)
A: I've heard that they (start / (are starting)) some new classes now.
(4)
B: That's right. I (go / (am going)) there right now. (Are you wanting / (Do you want)) to
(5)   (6)
come with me?

C Match the parts of the questions. Then ask your partner the questions.

<u>b</u> 1. When do we   a. include?
<u>e</u> 2. Do you like morning classes   b. get our books?
<u>d</u> 3. Does the school sell books   c. a lot of homework?
<u>f</u> 4. Do you know   d. or give them to students?
<u>a</u> 5. What does the price of the class   e. or evening classes?
<u>c</u> 6. Does the teacher give   f. everyone's name yet?

D Read the answers. Complete the questions with the simple present.

1. A: Why _____<u>does Mitch hate</u>_____ tests?
   B: Mitch hates tests because he often doesn't do well on them.
2. A: How <u>does he feel</u>_____ before an exam?
   B: He feels nauseous before an exam.
3. A: What time <u>does he get up</u>_____ when he has an exam?
   B: He gets up at 5 a.m. when he has an exam.
4. A: What <u>do experts say</u>_____ about test anxiety?
   B: Experts say we can control test anxiety.

Unit 1 Review and expand

Objectives	Grammar	Vocabulary	Correlations
On-, Pre-, and Higher-level: Expand upon and review unit grammar and life skills	Action and non-action verbs (*I'm going to school. I agree with him.*) Present-tense questions (*Does the class start at 9:00?*)	*Social, astronomy* For vocabulary support for pre-level students, see this **Oxford Picture Dictionary** topic: Studying	**CASAS:** 0.1.2, 0.1.5, 0.2.1, 4.8.1, 7.3.1, 7.3.2, 7.3.4, 7.4.9 **LCPs:** 39.01, 49.01, 49.13, 49.16, 49.17, 50.02 **SCANS:** Creative thinking, Interprets and communicates information **EFF:** Convey ideas in writing, Listen actively, Read with understanding, Solve problems

Warm-up and Review

10–15 minutes (books closed)

1. Review the *Bring It to Life* assignment from Lesson 5.

2. Have students who brought learning-style tests in read some of the questions aloud. Ask other students how they would answer the questions.

3. Discuss the questions in the *Bring It to Life* assignment on page 15. Elicit any interesting vocabulary that students found on the tests.

Introduction and Presentation

5 minutes

1. Ask a volunteer for his or her opinion: *Mia, what do think of this test?* Write a sentence about the student using *think* or *agree. Mia thinks the test is interesting. Mia doesn't agree with the test results.*

2. State the objective: *Today we're going to review the grammar we have studied in this unit in order to talk about different ways of learning.*

1 Grammar

Guided Practice

40–45 minutes

A Read the instructions aloud and go over the first sentence. Direct students to work individually to read the rest of the sentences and find the action and non-action verbs. Go over the answers as a class.

B Have students work individually to circle the correct answers. Ask volunteers to read the completed sentences aloud.

C Have students work individually to match the parts of the questions. Call on volunteers to read the completed questions aloud. Have students ask and answer the questions with a partner.

D Have students work with their partners to complete the questions. Direct them to ask and answer the questions aloud. Ask volunteers to write the completed questions on the board.

Multilevel Strategies

For 1D, seat same-level students together.

• **Pre-level** Work through 1D with these students, eliciting and discussing the correct form for each question before moving on to the next one.

• **On- and Higher-level** While you are working with pre-level students, ask these students to complete the exercise and then write two more questions and answers, one with an action verb and one with a non-action verb. Have volunteers read their new questions and answers to the class.

2 Group work

Communicative Practice

20–35 minutes

 1. Direct students, in groups of three to four, to focus on the picture. Ask: *Where are these people? Do you think they are friends?*

2. Assign roles: leader, recorder, and reporters. Explain that students work with their groups to write a conversation between the people in the picture.

3. Check comprehension of the roles. Ask: *Who writes the conversation?* [recorder] *Who will read the conversation to the class?* [reporters] *Who helps everyone and manages the group?* [leader] *Who creates the conversation]?* [everyone]

4. Set a time limit (five minutes) to complete the exercise. Circulate and answer any questions.

5. Have reporters from each group read the group's conversation to the class.

Multilevel Strategies

For 2A, use mixed-level groups.
- **Pre-level** Assign these students the role of reporter.
- **On-level** Assign these students the role of recorder.
- **Higher-level** Assign these students the role of leader.

 1. Have students walk around the room to conduct these interviews. To get students moving, tell them to interview three new people not in their groups for 2A.

2. Set a time limit (five minutes) to complete the exercise.

3. Tell students to make a note of their classmates' answers but not to worry about writing complete sentences.

Multilevel Strategies

Adapt the mixer in 2B to the level of your students.
- **Pre-level** Allow these students to ask and answer the questions without writing.
- **Higher-level** Have students ask two additional questions and write all answers.

 Call on individuals to report what they learned about their classmates. Encourage students to make generalizations. *Two out of four students are visual learners.*

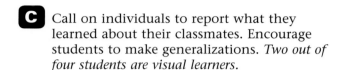

PROBLEM SOLVING

15–25 minutes

 1. Ask: *Can you study when other people in your house are watching TV or listening to music?* Tell students they will read a story about a woman who is having trouble studying. Direct students to read Rita's story silently.

2. Ask: *Are Rita's roommates students?* [No, they aren't.] *What do they like to do in the evening?* [They like to talk and play music.]

3. Play the audio and have students read along silently.

B **1.** Elicit answers to question 1. Have volunteers write answers to question 2 on the board until all of the class ideas have been put up.

2. Discuss the pros and cons of each solution.

3. Pair students. Have them write a short letter giving advice to Rita.

Evaluation

30–35 minutes

To test students' understanding of the unit grammar and life skills, have them take the Unit 1 Test on the *Step Forward Test Generator CD-ROM* with *ExamView® Assessment Suite.*

Learning Log

To help students record and discuss their progress, use the *Learning Log* on page T-200.

To extend this review: Have students complete **Workbook 4 page 8, Multilevel Activity Book 4 page 26**, and the **Unit 1 Exercises** on the **Multilevel Grammar Exercises CD-ROM 4.**

2 Group work

A Work with 2–3 classmates. Write a 6–8 line conversation between the people in the picture. Share your conversation with the class.

A: *What's your opinion of this program?*
B: *Well,…*

B Interview 3 classmates. Write their answers.

1. What are three words from this unit that describe you?
2. What is one word from this unit that doesn't describe you?
3. Do you think you are mostly a visual, an auditory, or a kinesthetic learner?
4. What is the best way for you to study? Why?
5. In your opinion, what's the best way to control test anxiety?

Fernando
1. artistic, social, visual

C Talk about the answers with your class.

PROBLEM SOLVING

A Listen and read about Rita.

Rita lives with two roommates. They're all good friends. Rita works part-time and goes to school. Her roommates aren't students; they work. Rita's classes are challenging, and she often has a lot of homework. She studies best when the apartment is quiet. But when her roommates come home from work, they don't want to be quiet. They want to enjoy the evening. When they talk and play music, Rita can't concentrate. She doesn't know what to do.

B Work with your classmates. Answer the questions.

1. What is Rita's problem?   Rita studies best when her apartment is quiet, but her roommates like to talk and play music.
2. What could she do? Think of 2 or 3 solutions to her problem.
3. Write a short letter to Rita. Tell her what you think she should do.

Keeping Current

FOCUS ON
- getting the news
- writing a news story
- past passives
- talking about the news
- reading a news report

LESSON **1** Vocabulary

1 Learn newspaper vocabulary

A Talk about the questions with your class.

1. How do you get the news?
2. What kind of news is the most important to you?

B Work with your classmates. Match the words with the pictures.

  3   classified ads   **5**   entertainment section   **4**   lifestyle section

  2   editorial page   **1**   front page   **6**   sports section

C Listen and check. Then read the new words with a partner.

D Work with a partner. Write other newspaper words you know.
Check your words in a dictionary.

✔ Identify and use news vocabulary to talk about news habits

Unit 2 Lesson 1

Objectives	Grammar	Vocabulary	Correlations
On-level: Describe news-reading habits, and talk about the news **Pre-level:** Identify ways to get the news and use news vocabulary **Higher-level:** Talk and write about the news, and explain about reading the news	Simple-present tense (*I usually read the headlines.*)	Newspaper sections and news words For vocabulary support for pre-level students, see these **Oxford Picture Dictionary** topics: Emergencies and Natural Disasters, U.S. History, Government and Military Service, Civil Rights and Responsibilities	**CASAS:** 0.1.2, 0.1.5, 0.2.1, 4.8.1, 7.4.4 **LCPs:** 38.01, 39.01, 49.02, 49.09 **SCANS:** Interprets and communicates information, Listening, Participates as member of a team, Seeing things in the mind's eye **EFF:** Speak so others can understand, Use information and communication technology

Warm-up and Review

10–15 minutes (books closed)

Pass out different sections of a newspaper. Give students a couple of minutes to look through them. Ask students to look at the headings (not to read the articles). Then elicit what they found in their sections.

Introduction

5 minutes

1. Tell students which sections of the newspaper you usually read and why you like them.

2. State the objective: *Today we're going to learn vocabulary for talking about newspapers and the news.*

1 Learn newspaper vocabulary

Presentation I

20–25 minutes

A 1. Write *news* on the board, and elicit students' answers to question 1. List their ideas. Ask students how often they check the various news sources.

2. Discuss question 2. To clarify *kind of news,* ask: *Are you most interested in the local news? Sports news?*

B 1. Direct students to look at the newspaper section in 1B. Ask: *What's the biggest story in this newspaper today?* ["World Leaders Meet"]

2. Group students and assign roles: leader, fact checker, recorder, and reporter. Explain that students work with their groups to match the words and pictures.

3. Check comprehension of the roles. Ask: *Who looks up the words in a dictionary?* [fact checker] *Who writes the numbers in the book?* [recorder] *Who tells the class your answers?* [reporter] *Who helps everyone and manages the group?* [leader]

4. Set a time limit (three minutes). As students work together, copy the wordlist onto the board.

5. Call "time." Have reporters take turns giving their groups' answers. Write each group's answer on the board next to the word.

C 1. To prepare students for listening, say: *Now we're going to hear people talk about which parts of the newspaper they like to read.* Ask students to listen and check their answers.

2. Have students check the wordlist on the board and then write the correct numbers in their books.

3. Pair students. Set a time limit (two minutes). Call "time" and work with the pronunciation of any troublesome words or phrases.

D 1. Ask students to work with a partner to brainstorm a list.

2. Elicit words from the class. Write them on the board. Ask students to copy them into their vocabulary notes for the unit.

E 1. Model the conversation with a volunteer. Model it again using other information from 1B.

2. Set a time limit (three minutes). Direct students to practice the conversation with several partners.

3. Ask volunteers to repeat one of their conversations for the class.

2 Learn more news vocabulary

Presentation II

15–20 minutes

 A 1. Introduce the new topic. *Now we're going to talk about another place to get the news.* Direct students to look at the website. Ask: *What kind of website is this?*

2. Ask students to read the web site. Elicit and answer questions about unfamiliar vocabulary.

Guided Practice

10–15 minutes

 B 1. Have students work individually to match the words and definitions.

2. Call on volunteers to read the matching words and definitions aloud.

3. Ask questions about the vocabulary. *What are current events? Where can you learn the freeway conditions? What are the headlines on this web page?*

Communicative Practice and Application

 C 1. Give students a minute to make notes of their answers to the questions. Call on individuals to share their ideas with the class.

2. Ask for a show of hands to find out how many students read the news every day.

> **TIP**
> If you have access to the Internet in class, expose students to the major English news sites. Pair the students and provide each pair with a URL of an online news site. Have the pairs look at the site and find the top story. The top story might be the one at the top of the page, it might have the biggest headline, or it might be labeled "top story." Ask students to copy the headline and share their findings. Take a survey of how many sites had the same top story. If you don't have access to the Internet in class, print out the home page of several news websites to do this activity.

Evaluation

10–15 minutes (books closed)

TEST YOURSELF

1. Pair students. Direct Partner B to close the book and listen to Partner A dictate five words from 1B. Ask students to switch roles when they finish. Then have Partner B dictate five words from 2B.

2. Direct both partners to open their books and check their spelling when they finish.

3. Circulate and monitor student work.

> **Multilevel Strategies**
> Target the *Test Yourself* to the level of your students.
> • **Higher-level** Direct these students to write a sentence defining each of the words their partner dictates.

To compress this lesson: Conduct 1B as a whole-class activity.

To extend this lesson: Have students practice categorizing the news.
1. Pair students and provide them with several sections of a newspaper. (You can use the same newspapers from the warm-up.) Tell each pair to copy or cut out two or three headlines from the paper.
2. Have the pairs exchange headlines. Then ask each pair to read the new headline aloud and to guess which section it came from. Alternatively, write the section titles on the board, and have pairs tape their headlines in the correct place. Go over the answers as a class. Discuss new vocabulary.

And/Or have students complete **Workbook 4 page 9** and **Multilevel Activity Book 4 pages 28–29**.

E Work with a partner. Practice the conversation. Use the words in 1B.

A: Do you read the editorial page every day?

B: Not every day. But I always check the sports section. What about you?

A: I usually just read the front page.

2 Learn more news vocabulary

A Look at the website. What kind of website is this?   a news website

B Work with a partner. Match the news vocabulary with the definitions.

1. _e_ top story
2. _a_ traffic report
3. _c_ current events
4. _b_ weather forecast
5. _d_ headlines

a. information about highway conditions
b. information on the state, local and national weather
c. news stories and events that have happened recently
d. the titles of important news stories
e. the most important or most recent news event

C Talk about the questions with your class.

1. Which section of the newspaper is most interesting or important to you?
2. Do you read a newspaper or visit a news website every day? Why or why not?
3. What kind of news do you never read?

TEST YOURSELF ✔

Work with a partner. Partner A: Read the vocabulary words in 1B to your partner. Partner B: Close your book. Write the words. Ask your partner for help with spelling as necessary. Then change roles. Partner B: Use the words in 2B.

1 Read a news story

A Look at the picture. Talk about the questions with your class.

1. What happened on this street?
2. How do you think the neighbors feel?

B Listen and read the news story.

Police Called in Lakeland

Tues. November 8 A group of teenagers painted graffiti on an empty building in Lakeland last night. Angry neighbors saw them and called the police. The police responded to the call, and the teens were taken to the Lakeland Police Station.

Neighbors disagree about the graffiti. Some people don't like it. They say that it is changing the way the neighborhood looks. However, the building's owner, Mr. Anwar Suk, doesn't mind the graffiti. He says that it is neighborhood art. Next week, the chief of police will hold a community meeting to talk about the neighborhood disagreement.

> **Writer's note**
>
> A news story answers the questions *who, what, when, where,* and *why.*

C Check your understanding. Work with a partner. Ask and answer the questions.

1. What happened? Where did it happen? When did it happen? Teens painted graffiti on an empty building last night.
2. Why were the teenagers taken to the police station? Neighbors called the police.
3. What is the neighborhood disagreement? The community disagrees on whether the graffiti is bad for the neighborhood or just artistic.
4. What is going to happen next? The police will have a community meeting.

  Summarize a news story or current event

Unit 2 Lesson 2

Objectives	Grammar	Vocabulary	Correlations
On- and Higher-level: Analyze, write, and edit a news story **Pre-level:** Read and write a news story	Simple-past tense (*They called the police.*)	*Graffiti, responded, disagreement* For vocabulary support for pre-level students, see this **Oxford Picture Dictionary** topic: Crime	**CASAS:** 0.1.2, 0.1.5, 7.2.1, 7.4.4 **LCPs:** 49.02, 49.03, 49.13, 49.16 **SCANS:** Interprets and communicates information, Listening, Reading, Seeing things in the mind's eye, Writing **EFF:** Convey ideas in writing, Listen actively, Read with understanding, Reflect and evaluate

Warm-up and Review

10–15 minutes (books closed)

Bring in a picture or show a short video clip from a recent big news story. If you don't have a picture, write a "headline" on the board for the event. *New President Elected. Hundreds Injured in Earthquake.* Ask questions (who, what, why, where, when) about the news story. As students answer, write the past-tense forms of the verbs they use on the board. Remind them that when they tell about an event, many of the verbs they use will be in the simple-past tense.

Introduction

5 minutes

1. Say: *If you answer the questions who, what, why, where, and when, you've probably covered the important information about any story.*

2. State the objective: *Today we're going to read and write news stories that answer these five questions.*

1 Read a news story

Presentation

20–25 minutes

A 1. Direct students to look at the picture. Ask: *Is this a nice neighborhood?*

2. Elicit answers to questions 1 and 2.

B 1. Tell students they are going to read and listen to a story about graffiti. Play the audio. Have students read along silently.

2. Elicit students' questions about vocabulary.

3. Draw students' attention to the *Writer's note.* Ask them if all of these questions are addressed in the story.

Guided Practice I

10 minutes

C Have students work in pairs to ask and answer the questions. Call on individuals to share their answers with the class.

Multilevel Strategies

For 1C, challenge on- and higher-level students while working with pre-level students.

• **Pre-level** While other students are working on 1C, ask these students questions about the reading. *What did the teenagers paint on the building? Who called the police? How does the building owner feel about the graffiti? How do other neighbors feel? Why are they having a meeting?*

• **On- and Higher-level** Write these questions on the board for these students to discuss after they finish 1C: *Who do you agree with—the neighbors or Mr. Suk? Why? Should the neighbors have any rights over Mr. Suk's building? Why or why not?* After allowing students to discuss the questions, ask volunteers to share their ideas with the class.

2 Write a news story

Guided Practice II

20–25 minutes

A 1. Read question 1 aloud. Elicit students' answers and write them on the board.

2. Choose one of the events on the board, and ask volunteers *who, what, where, when,* and *why* questions in order to elicit the story.

B 1. Direct students to look back at the article in 1B. Focus students' attention on the change from past tense in the first paragraph to present tense in the second paragraph. Elicit the reason for the change.

2. Read the questions for paragraph 1 aloud. Ask: *What tense will this paragraph be in?* [past] *Should you write the questions in your story?* [no]

3. Read the questions for paragraph 2 aloud. Point out that the story will end with speculation about the future.

4. Draw students' attention to the placement of the title and the paragraph indentions. Remind them to follow those conventions when they write. Have students work individually to write their stories.

> ### Multilevel Strategies
>
> Adapt 2B to the level of your students.
>
> • **Pre-level** Work with this group to write a story together. Elicit the answers to the questions, and compose the story sentence by sentence.
>
> • **Higher-level** After these students finish, ask them to underline all of the verbs in their stories and discuss their verb-tense choices with a partner.

 1. Lead students through the process of using the *Editing checklist*. Read each sentence aloud, and ask students to check their papers before moving onto the next item.

2. Allow students a few minutes to edit their writing as necessary.

Communicative Practice

10 minutes

D 1. Read the instructions aloud. Emphasize to students that they are responding to their partners' work, not correcting it.

2. Use the article in 1B to model the exercise. *I think the part about the owner of the building is interesting. I'd like to ask the writer about what the graffiti looks like.*

3. Direct students to exchange papers with a partner and follow the instructions.

4. Call on volunteers to share some interesting things they read in their partners' articles.

Application and Evaluation

20 minutes

TEST YOURSELF

1. Read the instructions aloud. Ask students to share their ideas with the class. *What has happened at school recently? In your workplace? In your neighborhood?* Assign a time limit (15 minutes), and have students work independently. Give students notice when they have five minutes left.

2. Before collecting students' work, remind them to use the *Editing checklist*. Collect and correct students' writing.

To compress this lesson: Assign the *Test Yourself* for homework.

To extend this lesson: Have students practice talking about past events.
1. Play a short video (two to three minutes) of a news event with the sound off. Use footage from television or the Internet, or choose a scene from a movie—for example, a scene of robbers breaking into a bank or a depiction of a natural disaster.
2. Have students tell their partners about what they saw, including the answers to the *who, what, where, when,* and *why* questions. Tell them to invent the answers if necessary. Circulate and monitor.
3. Wrap up by eliciting and writing vocabulary that was necessary for telling the story.

And/Or have students complete **Workbook 4 page 10** and **Multilevel Activity Book 4 page 30**.

2 Write a news story

A Talk about the questions with your class.

1. Name three or four recent local, national, or international events.
2. Choose one event. What happened?

B Write a news story about a recent event in your community, in the nation, or in the world. Use the model in 1B and the questions below to help you.

Paragraph 1: What happened?
When and where did it happen?
Who was involved?
Why did it happen?

Paragraph 2: How did people react to the event?
What do you think is going to happen next?

> Robbery in Lakeland
> Two men robbed a bank in Lakeland
> yesterday...

C Use the checklist to edit your writing. Check (✔) the true sentences.

Editing checklist	
1. My news story tells about an event that happened recently.	
2. It answers the questions *who, what, when, where,* and *why.*	
3. My story has two paragraphs.	
4. The first line of each paragraph is indented.	

D Exchange stories with a partner. Read and comment on your partner's work.

1. Point out one part of the story that you think is interesting.
2. Ask your partner a question about the current event in his or her news story.

TEST YOURSELF ✔

Write a new news story about another interesting event at your workplace, in your neighborhood, or at your school.

1 Learn the past passive

A **Read the article. What caused the accident on Highway 437?** fog

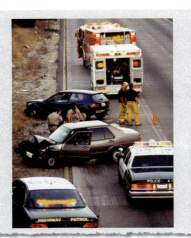

Highway 437 Closed by Multi-Car Accident

by Min Pham

Highway 437 was closed by the police for six hours last night after heavy fog caused a multi-car accident. Paramedics arrived in two ambulances. Several people were taken to the hospital. The highway was closed while the damaged cars were removed from the road. The highway was reopened just before midnight.

B **Study the chart. Underline the 4 past passive sentences in the article above.**

The past passive		
⌐ **Subject** ¬	⌐ *was/were* + **past participle** ¬	
An accident	**was caused**	by the fog last night.
Min	**wasn't taken**	to the hospital by the paramedics.
Several people	**were taken**	to the hospital after the accident.
The cars	**weren't removed**	for two hours because of the fog.

Notes

• We usually use the active voice to say what people or things do.
  The paramedics took the injured people to the hospital.
• We use the passive voice when we don't know who performed the action, when it isn't important who performed the action, or when it's clear who performed the action.
  The injured people were taken to the hospital. (It's clear that they were taken by the paramedics.)

C **Complete the sentences with the past passive. Use the verbs in parentheses.**

1. The accident ___was caused___ by the heavy fog. (cause)

2. The road ___was closed___ by the police. (close)

3. The article ___was written___ after the accident. (write)

4. The pictures ___were taken___ by a local news photographer. (take)

✔ Use the past passive to discuss and write about current events

Unit 2 Lesson 3

Objectives	Grammar	Vocabulary	Correlations
On- and Higher-level: Use past passive to discuss current events, and listen for information in news stories **Pre-level:** Identify the past passive in news stories	Simple past passive (*Drivers were surprised by the fog.*)	*Injured, damaged, removed* For vocabulary support for pre-level students, see these **Oxford Picture Dictionary** topics: Emergencies and Natural Disasters, Weather	**CASAS:** 0.1.2, 0.1.5, 7.2.1, 7.4.4 **LCPs:** 49.01, 49.02, 49.03, 49.09, 49.16, 50.02 **SCANS:** Knowing how to learn, Listening, Seeing things in the mind's eye **EFF:** Convey ideas in writing, Listen actively, Read with understanding, Speak so others can understand, Reflect and evaluate

Warm-up and Review

10–15 minutes (books closed)

Review past participles. Have students line up at the board in two teams. Direct one team member at a time to approach the board. Call out a verb in base form. The first person to correctly write the participle wins a point for the team. Allow team members to call out the answers to help their teammates at the board. Leave the participles on the board.

Introduction

5–10 minutes

1. Use the participles on the board to write several past-passive sentences that sound like news stories. *An election was held last night. Houses were damaged by the wind.*

2. State the objective: *Today we're going to learn how to use the past passive to describe news events.*

1 Learn the past passive

Presentation I

20–25 minutes

 1. Direct students to look at the photo in the news article. Ask: *What happened?*

2. Read the instructions aloud. Ask students to read the news story silently to find the answer to the question. Call on a volunteer for the answer.

B 1. Read the chart through sentence by sentence. Then read it again and have students repeat after you. Read the *Notes* aloud.

2. Direct students to underline the examples of the past passive in 1A.

3. Go over the answers as a class. As you elicit each answer, ask about the cause of each action. *Who closed the highway?* [the police] *Where were several people taken?* [to the hospital]

4. Assess students' understanding of the charts. Ask: *Which is more important: who closed the highway or that the highway was closed?*

Guided Practice I

15–20 minutes

C Ask students to work individually to complete the sentences. Go over the answers as a class. Ask volunteers to write the answers on the board.

Multilevel Strategies

After 1C, seat same-level students together.

- **Pre-level** Work with this group. Say several sentences and have these students identify whether they are active or passive.

- **On- and Higher-level** Have these students use the participles from the warm-up to write passive sentences. Tell them to include the *by* + noun phrase if they think it's important. Ask volunteers to put their answers on the board.

Guided Practice II

D 1. Read the first sentence and the corrected version aloud. Elicit the form of the past passive. [*be* + past participle]

2. Direct students to work individually to rewrite the sentences. Ask volunteers to write their corrected versions on the board.

Multilevel Strategies

For 1E, provide an extra challenge for the higher-level students while you work with the pre-level students.

• **Pre-level** Take these students through the step-by-step process of transforming each sentence to passive. *What is the verb? What is the participle of (close)? In this sentence, what (was closed)?*

• **On- and Higher-level** While you are working with the pre-level students, have these students ask a partner these questions: *Have you ever seen an accident? What happened?* Tell students to use past-passive sentences to describe some of the things they saw. Ask volunteers to share their stories with the class.

E Have students work individually to rewrite the sentences in the passive. Ask volunteers to write the answers on the board.

TIP For more practice with passive sentences, have students write passive riddles.

1. Put the following sentence on the board as a model: *It was invented by Thomas Edison.* Ask students to guess what *It* was. [the light bulb]

2. Group students and provide each group with a large sheet of paper. Have the groups write three to four passive sentences with "mystery" subjects. Write possible sentence beginnings on the board: *It was written... It was built... They were destroyed... It was conquered... It was performed... It was sung....*

3. Post the papers and have the rest of the class guess the missing subjects.

2 Learn past-passive questions

Presentation II

20–25 minutes

A 1. Introduce the new topic. *Now we're going to ask questions with the past passive.*

2. Read the instructions aloud. Call on a volunteer for the answer to the question. Read and have students repeat the questions in the chart.

Guided Practice I

10–15 minutes

B Direct students to work independently to complete the conversation. Have them read the conversation with a partner when they finish. Ask a volunteer pair to read the conversation aloud for the class.

TIP For more practice with past-passive questions after 2B, post some of the news story pictures or headlines you have used during this unit. As a class, brainstorm questions about each story. Write the questions on the board.

As an alternative practice, write news categories on the board: *Local, National, World, Health, Technology, Education, Traffic Report, Weather Forecast.* Pair students and assign each pair one of the categories. Then have students write a passive "headline" under their pair's category on the board. Tell them to write about a real event if possible. Correct the "headlines" together. As a class, brainstorm past-passive questions about the headlines.

D Get the form. Work with your class. Correct the sentences.

1. The Teller School was close on Thursday because of a fire.

   The Teller School was closed on Thursday because of a fire.

2. The fire caused by lightning.

   The fire was caused by lightning.

3. Parents was told to pick up their children.

   Parents were told to pick up their children.

4. The school was reopen on Friday.

   The school was reopened on Friday

E Rewrite the sentences in the past passive. Use *by* + noun to say who performed the action.

1. After the accident, the police closed Highway 437.

   After the accident, Highway 437 was closed by the police.

2. The paramedics took the injured people to the hospital.

   The injured people were taken to the hospital by the paramedics.

3. The tow trucks removed the cars from the highway.

   The cars were removed from the highway by the tow trucks.

4. The police reopened the highway an hour later.

   The highway was reopened an hour later by the police.

2 Learn past passive questions

A Study the charts. Which words come first in *Yes/No* questions?   Was/Were

PAST PASSIVE QUESTIONS

Yes/No questions
A: **Was** the highway **reopened**? B: Yes, it was.
A: **Were** people **taken** to the hospital? B: Yes, they were.

Information questions
A: When **was** the highway **reopened**? B: It was reopened an hour after the accident.
A: Where **were** the injured people **taken**? B: They were taken to City Hospital.

B Complete the conversation with the past passive of the verbs in parentheses.

A: There was a big accident on the highway this morning.

B: Really? What caused the accident?

A: It ___was caused___ by two deer. (cause) They ran across the road.
   (1)

B: ___Was___ anyone ___hit___? (hit)
   (2)   (2)

A: No. Thankfully no one ___was hit___. (hit)
   (3)

B: What about the deer? ___Were___ they ___hurt___? (hurt)
   (4)   (4)

A: One deer ___was hit___ (hit). It ___wasn't hurt___. (not hurt)
   (5)   (6)

3 Grammar listening

🎧 **Listen to each statement. Check (✔) the sentence that has a similar meaning.**

1. ____ a. Our car hit a tree.
   ✔ b. A tree hit our car.
2. ✔ a. The neighbors gave the information to the reporter.
   ____ b. The reporter gave the information to the neighbors.
3. ____ a. The teenagers' parents called the police.
   ✔ b. The police called the teenagers' parents.
4. ____ a. A fire caused an electrical problem.
   ✔ b. An electrical problem caused the fire.

4 Practice the past passive

A **Think of 3 news stories you have heard in the last few months. Answer as many of the questions as you can.**

1. What was built? Where? Why? When?
2. Who was rescued?
3. What was closed?
4. What was damaged?
5. Who was robbed? What was stolen?

B **Work with a partner. Talk about the news stories that you thought of. Use the past passive.**

A: *A few weeks ago a woman was rescued in the mountains.*
B: *Really? Who rescued her?*
A: *I think she was rescued by the park service.*

C **Talk about the news stories with the class.**

A woman was rescued in the mountains.

TEST YOURSELF ✔

Close your book. Write 5 sentences about your classmates' news stories. Use the past passive.

3 Grammar listening

Guided Practice II

10–15 minutes

1. Say: *Now we're going to listen to some statements about past events.*

2. Play the audio. Direct students to read along silently and point to the statement that has a similar meaning to the one they hear. Review the answer to number 1. Ask a volunteer what he or she heard.

3. Replay the audio. Stop after every statement, and ask students to check the correct sentence.

4. Ask volunteers to read the correct answers aloud.

> ### Multilevel Strategies
>
> For the *Grammar listening,* replay each statement to allow pre-level students to catch up while you challenge higher-level students.
>
> • **Pre- and On-level** Have these students listen again to choose the correct sentences.
>
> • **Higher-level** Direct these students to write the sentences they hear. When you have played all the sentences, ask volunteers to write them on the board. Compare the sentences on the board with their answers to the *Grammar listening.*

4 Practice the past passive

Communicative Practice and Application

20–25 minutes

A 1. Direct students to look at the photos. Ask about each picture. *What happened? Has that happened in the news recently?*

2. Give students time to think about or write answers to the questions. Call on individuals and ask them to share their ideas with the class. Write the ideas on the board.

B Model the conversation with a volunteer. Then model it again using other information from the board. Direct students to practice the conversation with several partners.

C Call on volunteers to share the news stories they found the most interesting.

Evaluation

10–15 minutes

TEST YOURSELF

Ask students to write the sentences independently. Collect and correct their writing.

> ### Multilevel Strategies
>
> Target the *Test Yourself* to the level of your students.
>
> • **Pre-level** Ask these students to copy the following sentences and then reorder them in the correct sequence. *A waitress was carried out of the building by the firefighters. The neighbors called 911. A fire started in the kitchen of Sam's restaurant last night. The flames were seen by neighbors.* Ask students to identify whether the sentences are active or passive.
>
> • **Higher-level** Have students write a short paragraph in response to this prompt: *Describe a recent news event. Use at least three sentences in the past passive. Write three questions about your story for a partner to answer.* Have students who finish early read their paragraphs to a partner and ask the partner the three questions.

To compress this lesson: Have students practice 4B with only one partner.

To extend this lesson: Distribute newspapers to pairs or small groups of students. Ask them to look for headlines that they can convert into past-passive sentences. Have volunteers share their sentences with the class.

And/Or have students complete **Workbook 4 pages 11–12, Multilevel Activity Book 4 pages 31–32,** and the corresponding **Unit 2 Exercises** on the **Multilevel Grammar Exercises CD-ROM 4.**

Unit 2 Lesson 4

Objectives	Grammar	Vocabulary	Correlations
On-, Pre-, and Higher-level: Give opinions about current events and listen for information in a news story	Reflexive pronouns (*Did you see it yourself?*)	*Protesters, prohibited, make sense, limit* For vocabulary support for pre-level students, see these **Oxford Picture Dictionary** topics: Emergencies and Natural Disasters, U.S. History	**CASAS:** 0.1.2, 0.1.5, 0.2.1, 6.0.3, 6.0.4, 6.1.2, 7.4.4 **LCPs:** 39.01, 49.02, 49.09, 49.16, 49.17 **SCANS:** Acquires and evaluates information, Arithmetic/Mathematics, Seeing things in the mind's eye **EFF:** Listen actively, Read with understanding, Use math to solve problems and communicate

Warm-up

10–15 minutes (books closed)

Talk about protests. Ask: *What is a protest? What do people do during a protest? Have you seen any protests? What were the people protesting?*

 This topic may recall frightening memories for some students. Keep the discussion general, and don't call on students to share their personal experiences unless they volunteer.

Introduction

5 minutes

1. Tell students that protests are common in the U.S., but they usually concern local issues and are nonviolent. Protests are an accepted way for groups of people to express their disagreement.

2. State the objective: *Today we're going to learn how to express agreement and disagreement about current events.*

1 Learn to talk about a current event

Presentation I

20–30 minutes

 1. Direct students to look at the picture. Ask: *Does this protest look peaceful?*

2. Play the audio. Give students a minute to answer the questions. Go over the answers as a class.

Guided Practice

20–25 minutes

B 1. Play the audio. Read the instructions aloud. Ask students to read along silently and find the answer to the question. Elicit the answer.

2. Ask students to read the conversation with a partner. Circulate and monitor pronunciation. Model and have students repeat difficult words or phrases.

3. Say and have students repeat the expressions in the *In other words* box. Elicit the placement of the expressions in the conversation. Ask volunteers to act out the conversation using expressions from the box.

Communicative Practice and Application

15–20 minutes

C 1. Ask students to read the instructions silently. Elicit examples of what each partner might say.

2. Set a time limit (five minutes). Ask students to act out the role-play in both roles. Ask volunteer pairs to act out their conversations for the class. Tell students who are listening to note how Partner B expresses agreement.

Multilevel Strategies

For 1C, adapt the role-play to the level of your students.

• **Pre-level** Provide these students with the beginning of the conversation: *A: Did you hear about the protest yesterday? B: No. What was it about? A: The school board wanted to _____.*

1 Learn to talk about a current event

 A Look at the picture. Listen to the conversation. Then answer the questions below with your classmates.

1. What did the city want to do?
2. Why did the protesters disagree with the city?

 B **Listen and read. What did the protesters want?** They wanted to save a hundred-year-old tree.

A: Did you hear about the protest yesterday?

B: No. What was it about?

A: The city wanted to cut down a hundred-year-old tree in the park, and protesters tied themselves to the tree.

B: A hundred trees?

A: No, not a hundred trees, a *hundred-year-old* tree. The protesters were very upset.

B: I can understand that. We have to protect the environment. So was the tree cut down?

A: No. To make a long story short,* the protesters won. The tree was saved.

*Idiom note: to make a long story short = to tell the most important fact

In other words...

Expressing agreement
I can understand that.
That makes sense to me.
I'd agree with that.

C **Role-play a conversation about a current event with a partner. Use the example in 1B to make a new conversation.**

Partner A: Tell your friend about a story on the news: there was a protest at the high school because the school board wanted to prohibit cell phones in school. The students were upset and protested at lunch. The students won. Cell phones weren't prohibited.

Partner B: At first, you don't understand your friend. You think the school wanted to sell phones to students. You understand the students. Cell phones are important in an emergency. Ask if cell phones were prohibited.

☑ Discuss, clarify, and give opinions about a current event 25

2 Learn reflexive pronouns

A Study the charts. How do reflexive pronouns end? *They end in -self.*

Subject pronouns	Reflexive pronouns	Notes
I	myself	• Reflexive pronouns end with *-self* or *-selves*.
you	yourself	• They are used when the subject and object of the sentence refer to the same people or things.
he	himself	I hurt **myself**.
she	herself	• Use *by* + reflexive pronoun to say that someone or something is alone or does something without help.
it	itself	
we	ourselves	She went **by herself**. = She went alone.
you	yourselves	
they	themselves	

B Work with a partner. Complete the sentences with reflexive pronouns.

1. Did you see the protest ___yourself___, or did you hear about it on the news?
2. We were watching the news, and we saw ___ourselves___ on TV!
3. Did you and Paul go by ___yourselves___, or did Tim go with you?
4. He was surprised to see a picture of ___himself___ in the newspaper.

C Work with a partner. Ask and answer the question.

What are some things you like to do by yourself?

3 Practice your pronunciation

A Listen to the conversation. Notice how the speakers use stress to clarify their meaning.

A: The city wanted to cut down a hundred-year-old tree.
B: A hundred trees?
A: No, not a hundred trees, *a hundred-year-old* tree.

B Work with a partner. Underline the words you think are stressed.

1. A: The tree wasn't cut down.
   B: It was cut down?
   A: No, it wasn't cut down.

2. A: The protesters were very upset.
   B: The police were upset?
   A: No, the protesters.

C Listen and check. Then practice the conversations in 3A and 3B with a partner.

2 Learn reflexive pronouns

Presentation II
10–15 minutes

 A 1. Draw your face on the board. Say: *I'm drawing myself.* Ask a male and a female volunteer to do the same. Say: *She's drawing herself. He's drawing himself.* Thank the students and say: *Thank you for drawing yourselves.* Have them sit down. Say: *They drew themselves.* Introduce the new topic: *Now we're going to learn about reflexive pronouns.*

2. Write on the board: *They drew themselves on the board.* Ask: *What is the verb?* [drew] *What is the subject of the verb?* [they] *What is the object?* [themselves] *Are the subject and object talking about different people or the same people?* [same]

3. Read the information in the chart aloud. Have students repeat the reflexive pronouns. Elicit the answer to the question in the instructions.

Guided Practice
20–25 minutes

> **TIP**
> In 2B, point out that the expression in number 3 (*by* + reflexive pronoun) means "alone" or "without help." Have students practice the expression with several pronouns. *My daughter cooked dinner by _____. My father lives by _____.*

B Have students work individually to complete the sentences with reflexive pronouns. Go over the answers as a class.

> ### Multilevel Strategies
> Allow pre-level students extra time to finish 2B while challenging on- and higher-level students.
>
> • **On- and Higher-level** Have these students write two or three original sentences with reflexive pronouns while the pre-level students are finishing the exercise. Have volunteers put their sentences on the board.

Communicative Practice and Application
15–20 minutes

 C 1. Read the question aloud, and elicit possible answers.

2. Set a time limit (five minutes). Ask students to take turns asking and answering the question with several partners.

3 Practice your pronunciation

Pronunciation Extension
10–20 minutes

 A 1. Write this exchange on the board: *A: There was a protest last night. B: Last week? A: No, last night.* Ask a volunteer to read part B, and model the conversation for the class. Ask students which word you stressed in the last sentence. [night] Say: *Now we're going to focus on using stress to clarify meaning.*

2. Play the audio. Direct students to listen for the stressed words.

3. Ask what would happen if you didn't stress the words. [The listener might misunderstand again.]

B After students finish reading, have them work with a partner to underline the words they think will be stressed.

C 1. Play the audio and have students check their work. Go over the answers as a class.

2. Have partners practice the conversations in 3A and 3B. Circulate and monitor pronunciation.

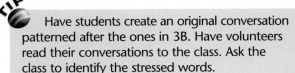

> **TIP**
> Have students create an original conversation patterned after the ones in 3B. Have volunteers read their conversations to the class. Ask the class to identify the stressed words.

4 Focus on Listening

Listening Extension

20–25 minutes

A Read the questions aloud, and elicit answers from volunteers. Encourage students to respond to each other's ideas. After one student speaks, ask other students for their opinions. *Do you agree or disagree with what he/she said? Why?*

B 1. Read the questions aloud. Ask students to predict what kind of news story they will hear.

2. Play the audio. Elicit the answers to the questions.

C 1. Direct students to read the questions before listening.

2. Replay the audio. Have students work individually to circle the correct words. Go over the answers as a class.

> ### Multilevel Strategies
>
> Replay the news story to challenge on- and higher-level students while allowing pre-level students to catch up.
>
> • **Pre-level** Have these students listen again and circle the words.
>
> • **On- and Higher-level** Ask these students to listen for and write the past-passive verbs in the news report. [*were told, were opened, were asked*] The higher-level students may also notice the present passive [*is expected*] and the present continuous passive [*are being brought*].
>
> After you go over the answers to 4C, elicit the passive verbs and discuss their context.

5 Real-life math

Math Extension

10–15 minutes

A Direct students to read the story silently and write the answer to the question.

B 1. Elicit how to construct the problem. [number who left home minus number who returned on Thursday minus number who returned on Friday]

2. Call on a volunteer to write the problem and solution on the board.

Evaluation

10–15 minutes

TEST YOURSELF

1. Model the role-play with a volunteer. Then switch roles

2. Pair students. Check comprehension of the exercise by asking what each partner might say. Elicit some statements or questions Partner B might use.

3. Set a time limit (five minutes), and have the partners act out the role-play in both roles.

4. Circulate and monitor. Encourage pantomime and improvisation.

5. Provide feedback.

> ### Multilevel Strategies
>
> Target the *Test Yourself* to the level of your students.
>
> • **Pre-level** Ask these students to use this skeleton conversation: *A: There was a protest yesterday. B: What was it about? A: The protesters want/don't want _____ B: I agree with them because _____.*
>
> • **Higher-level** Ask these students to try the role-play with two different issues.

To compress this lesson: Conduct 3C as a whole-class activity.

To extend this lesson: Have students write a story or a conversation with reflexive pronouns.
1. Group students and tell each group to write a story or a conversation that includes at least four reflexive pronouns. Tell them the story can be silly, but it should make sense.
2. Have a reporter (or reporters) read the group's work aloud for the class. Ask classmates to identify the reflexive pronouns and determine if they were used correctly.

And/Or have students complete **Workbook 4 page 13** and **Multilevel Activity Book 4 page 33**.

4 Focus on listening

A **Talk about the questions with your class.**

1. How often do you listen to news on the radio?
2. When is reporting the news a dangerous job? Give examples.

B **Listen to the news story. Answer the questions.**

1. Where is the news reporter?   the Florida Gulf Coast
2. What weather condition is causing problems?   a hurricane

C **Listen again. Circle the correct words.**

1. People think that the hurricane will arrive (today /(Wednesday)).
2. Timothy is the name of the (reporter /(hurricane)).
3. People have to leave their homes ((today)/ tomorrow).
4. People will be able to stay in ((schools)/ hotels) during the hurricane.
5. Local officials asked news reporters to (stay /(leave)).
6. Ron Avery is a reporter for ((Channel 4)/ Channel 5) News.

5 Real-life math

A **Read the story and answer the question.**

Before the hurricane hit, 100,000 Floridians left their homes. Luckily, when the hurricane hit, very few homes were damaged. On Thursday, 75,000 people returned to their homes; another 24,500 were allowed to return on Friday. However, some homes are still without electricity or water. Local officials expect the rest of the people to return home tomorrow.

On the day the story was written, how many people were still out of their homes?

_____500_____

B **Explain your answer to your classmates.**

TEST YOURSELF ✔

Role-play a conversation about a community protest. Partner A: Tell your partner that there was a protest yesterday. Explain why the protesters were upset.
Partner B: You don't know about the protest. You agree with the protesters. Explain why. Then change roles.

1 Get ready to read

A Which news source do you prefer: radio, TV, newspapers, magazines, or the Internet? Why?

B Read the definitions. Which word is the opposite of *rise*?   drop

drop: (verb) to fall
figure: (noun) a number
poll: (noun) a set of questions used to get an idea of people's opinions

C Look at the title and the graph in the magazine article in 2A. What do you think the article is about? Circle *a* or *b*.

a. the percent of people who enjoy talking about the news
b. people and their news habits

2 Read and respond

A Read the article. What has changed over the last 10 years?   how people get the news

Americans and the News

Where do you get the news? Do you like local, network, or cable TV news? Do you read the newspaper or magazines? Do you get your news online, or do you listen to the news on the radio? How much time do you spend every day getting the news? These are just some of the questions Americans answered in a poll on news habits. The results may surprise you.

People's news habits changed between 1994 and 2004. One change that isn't a surprise is the rise in online news. In 2004, 29 percent of people in the U.S. reported that they regularly[1] got the news online. In 1994, that figure was under 2 percent. Over the same 10 years, the percent of people who regularly got the news from the newspaper dropped from 58 percent

[1] regularly: often; frequently; almost every day

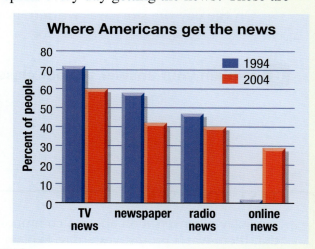

Where Americans get the news

Percent of people

| 1994 |
| 2004 |

TV news   newspaper   radio news   online news

   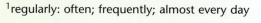 Use previewing skills to predict the content of a magazine article

Unit 2 Lesson 5

Objectives	Grammar	Vocabulary	Correlations
On-, Pre-, Higher-level: Read about and discuss where people get the news	*I think* + noun clause (*I think [that] there is too much bad news on TV.*)	*drop, figure, poll, regularly* For vocabulary support for pre-level students, see these **Oxford Picture Dictionary** topics: Describing Things, Feelings, Entertainment	**CASAS:** 0.1.2, 0.1.5, 0.2.1, 7.4.4 **LCPs:** 39.01, 49.02, 49.16, 49.17 **SCANS:** Applies technology to task, Creative thinking, Interprets and communicates information, Listening, Writing **EFF:** Take responsibility for learning, Read with understanding, Speak so others can understand

Warm-up and Review

10–15 minutes (books closed)

Write *News Sources* on the board. Elicit the names of local newspapers and popular TV news shows and news websites. Write them on the board.

Introduction

5 minutes

1. Ask students for a show of hands about each name on the board. *Do you watch/read _____?*

2. State the objective: *Today we're going to read about and discuss where people usually get their news.*

1 Get ready to read

Presentation

15–20 minutes

A Read the questions. Ask volunteers to tell where they get the news and why they choose that source.

B Read the words and definitions. Elicit sample sentences from students if they are familiar with the words. If not, provide these sentences: *I don't think the bookkeeper's figures are correct. They took a poll to find out who people were voting for. The number of people who watch TV news has dropped.*

Pre-Reading

C 1. Direct students to look at the title and the graph. Ask them to circle *a* or *b* without reading the article. Go over the answer as a class.

2. Have students make some predictions about what they will read. *Who do you think reads more newspapers—older or younger people? Where do you think most people get their news?*

2 Read and respond

Guided Practice I

25–30 minutes

A 1. Read the instructions aloud. Ask students to think about the question as they read the article silently.

2. After students finish reading, elicit answers to the question. Ask: *Did the percentage of people who get their news from TV go up or down?* [down]

3. Direct students to underline unfamiliar words they would like to know. Elicit the words and encourage other students to provide definitions or examples.

Multilevel Strategies

Adapt 2A to the level of your students.

• **Pre-level** Direct these students to study the graph while other students are reading 2A.

Guided Practice II

15–20 minutes

 B 1. Play the audio. Have students read along silently.

2. Elicit and discuss any additional questions about the reading.

Multilevel Strategies

Seat same-level students together for 2C.

- **Pre-level** Have these students use the information from the graph to answer the questions.
- **On- and Higher-level** Have these students complete 2C individually and then discuss these questions in pairs or small groups: *What are the advantages and disadvantages of the different news sources? Do you think the changes reflected in the chart are positive or negative?* Call on volunteers to share their ideas with the class.

C Ask students to work independently to write answers to the questions. Go over the answers as a class.

TIP Make a class graph like the one in 2A. Ask questions using the information from the graph: *Do you watch or listen to the news? Do you watch non-news TV?* Write the numbers on the board. Draw a vertical and horizontal axis on the board. Discuss the poll numbers as percentages. *How many students equal 10% of our class?* Have volunteers complete the graph on the board using the poll numbers. Discuss the differences and similarities between your class graph and the 2004 numbers in the book.

3 Talk it over

Communicative Practice

15–20 minutes

1. Read the questions. Set a time limit (three minutes). Have students work independently to think about the questions and write their answers in note form.

2. Call on individuals to share their ideas about each question. Ask other students to respond to the ideas they hear. For question 3, make a list of pros and cons for telling children about current events.

Application

5–10 minutes

BRING IT TO LIFE

Read the instructions aloud. Ask students to plan where they will get their article. Write the names of local papers, news magazines, and reputable Internet news addresses on the board. For students who will not be able to read a regular news article, provide adapted news articles from an ESL newspaper. (If you don't have a subscription to an ESL newspaper, such articles can be found online.)

To compress this lesson: Conduct 2C as a whole-class activity.

To extend this lesson: Play "spot the errors" with news stories.
1. Put students in mixed-level groups. Direct each group to write a familiar news story that includes three wrong facts.
2. Have a reporter from each group read the news story aloud to the class. Have the class identify and correct the wrong information. *The hurricane didn't hit Wyoming. It hit Florida.*

And/Or have students complete **Workbook 4 page 14** and **Multilevel Activity Book 4 pages 34–35**.

to 42 percent. The percent of people who regularly got the news from the radio dropped from 47 percent to 40 percent.

Age makes a difference. Only 23 percent of people under 30 said that they have read a newspaper recently.

People also reported the amount of time they spent getting the news compared with the time they spent on other activities. The results showed that people spent more time getting the news than they spent watching non-news TV, reading, making personal phone calls, exercising, or shopping.

Technology may change, but one thing stays the same: people want to know what's going on.

Adapted from: *http://people-press.org*

B **Listen and read the article again.**

C **Work with a partner. Ask and answer the questions.**

1. What was the poll about? news habits
2. Which news source became more popular from 1994 to 2004? online news
3. Which news sources became less popular? TV, newspaper, and radio news
4. Which news sources are most popular now?
5. Which news sources will be popular in the future?

3 Talk it over

Think about the questions. Talk about your ideas with the class.

1. Some people think that there is too much bad news on TV.
   Do you agree? Why?
2. Do you think that news reporters sometimes create news?
   If so, give an example.
3. Should parents and teachers talk to children about current events
   even if the news might upset them? Why or why not?

BRING IT TO LIFE

Read a local, national, or international news story in a newspaper or magazine, or on the Internet. Bring the article to class and talk about how the article answers the questions *who, what, where, when,* and *why.*

1 Grammar

A Rewrite the sentences in the past passive. Use *by* + noun when it is important to mention the person or thing performing the action.

1. A fire damaged two apartments in our building.

   Two apartments in our building were damaged by a fire.

2. Someone in the building pulled the fire alarm.

   The fire alarm was pulled by someone in the building.

3. Two neighbors put the fire out.

   The fire was put out by two neighbors.

4. Electrical problems caused two fires on our block last year.

   Two fires on our block last year were caused by electrical problems.

5. The owners replaced the electrical system in the building.

   The electrical system in the building was replaced by the owners.

B Read the answers. Complete the questions.

1. **A:** When _was the article about the protest written_?

   B: The article about the protest was written on Monday.

2. **A:** What _were the protesters called in the article_?

   B: The protesters were called "neighborhood leaders" in the article.

3. **A:** Where _were these pictures taken_?

   B: These pictures were taken at a club.

4. **A:** Why _was the club closed_?

   B: The club was closed because neighbors protested.

C Complete the conversations. Use reflexive pronouns.

1. **A:** Did the teenagers clean the building ___themselves___?

   B: Yes, they did. They bought the paint ___themselves___, too.

2. **A:** Why are you looking at ___yourself___ in the mirror?

   B: Because I gave ___myself___ a haircut. How do I look?

   A: Ummm…, fine.

3. **A:** You and I should treat ___ourselves___ to some ice cream.

   B: You go ahead. I'm on a diet.

   A: You're too hard on ___yourself___. You look great!

Unit 2 Review and expand

Objectives	Grammar	Vocabulary	Correlations
On-, Pre-, and Higher-level: Expand upon and review unit grammar and life skills	Past passive (*The fire was put out quickly.*) Reflexive pronouns (*He was talking to himself.*)	Current events, local events, natural disasters, protests For vocabulary support for pre-level students, see these **Oxford Picture Dictionary** topics: Describing Things, Emergencies and Natural Disasters	**CASAS:** 0.1.2, 0.1.5, 0.2.1, 4.8.1, 7.2.4, 7.3.1, 7.3.2, 7.3.4 **LCPs:** 39.01, 49.02, 49.16 **SCANS:** Acquires and evaluates information, Creative thinking, Listening, Participates as member of a team **EFF:** Cooperate with others, Read with understanding, Solve problems and make decisions

Warm-up and Review

10–15 minutes (books closed)

1. Review the *Bring It to Life* assignment from Lesson 5.

2. Have students who did the exercise discuss what they read about. Have students who didn't do the exercise ask *who, what, where, why,* and *when* questions about the news stories.

Introduction and Presentation

5 minutes

1. Write one or two active-voice sentences on the board. *My mother cleaned the house yesterday. Someone threw trash onto the street again today.*

2. Ask volunteers to identify the verbs. Call on a volunteer to convert the sentences to passive voice. Discuss the *by* phrase, which is not always necessary in the second sentence.

3. State the objective: *Today we're going to review using the past passive and reflexive pronouns to talk about the news.*

1 Grammar

Guided Practice

40–45 minutes

A 1. Direct students to read the sample answer in number 1. Ask: *Is the* by *phrase necessary? Are we missing any important information if we just say,* Two apartments in our building were damaged? [yes] Tell students to include the *by* phrase only if it contains important information.

2. Have students work individually to complete the sentences. Ask volunteers to write the answers on the board.

B Have students work individually to complete the questions. Have volunteers write the questions on the board.

Multilevel Strategies

For 1A and 1B, seat same-level students together.

• **Pre-level** Work with these students as a group. Help them work out each answer. Give everyone time to copy it into their books before you move onto the next question.

• **On- and Higher-level** While you are working with pre-level students, direct these students to finish the exercises individually. When they finish, challenge them to write four to five passive sentences with verbs that have irregular participles. Let them choose from an irregular verb list, or provide them with these additional verbs to use: *throw, eat, put, sing, ring, bite, take, bring, teach, catch, draw.* Ask volunteers to write their sentences on the board.

C Have students work individually to complete the sentences. Ask volunteers to read the resulting conversations aloud.

2 Group work

Communicative Practice

20–35 minutes

 A 1. Direct students, in groups of three to four, to focus on the picture. Ask: *What are they talking about? What do you think she is saying?*

2. Assign roles: leader, recorder, and reporters. Explain that students work with their groups to write a conversation.

3. Check comprehension of the roles. Ask: *Who writes the conversation?* [recorder] *Who will read the conversation to the class?* [reporters] *Who helps everyone and manages the group?* [leader] *Who creates the conversation?* [everyone]

4. Set a time limit (five minutes) to complete the exercise. Circulate and answer any questions.

5. Have reporters from each group read the group's conversation to the class.

B 1. Have students walk around the room to conduct these interviews. To get students moving, tell them to interview three new people not in their groups for 2A.

2. Set a time limit (five minutes) to complete the exercise.

3. Tell students to make a note of their classmates' answers but not to worry about writing complete sentences.

Multilevel Strategies

For 2A and 2B, use same-level groups.

• **Pre-level** For 2A, ask students to write a short conversation of two or three exchanges. For 2B, allow pre-level students to ask and answer the questions without writing.

• **Higher-level** For 2A, ask students to write a longer conversation of five or six sentences per speaker. For 2B, have these students expand question 3 to include the most important national, world, and local events.

C Call on individuals to report what they learned about their classmates. Encourage students to make generalizations: *Most people think _____ was one of the most important news stories this year.*

15–25 minutes

 A 1. Ask: *Did you pay more or less attention to the news before you came to the U.S.? Why?* Tell students they will read a story about a man who is having difficulty keeping up with the news. Direct students to read Anton's story silently.

2. Ask: *What did Anton do before he came to the U.S.? What has changed?*

3. Play the audio and have students read along silently.

B 1. Elicit answers to question 1. Have volunteers write answers to question 2 on the board until all of the class ideas have been put up.

2. Discuss the pros and cons of each solution.

3. Pair students. Ask them to write a short letter giving advice to Anton.

Evaluation

30–35 minutes

To test students' understanding of the unit grammar and life skills, have them take the Unit 2 Test on the *Step Forward Test Generator CD-ROM* with *ExamView® Assessment Suite.*

Learning Log

To help students record and discuss their progress, use the *Learning Log* on page T–200.

To extend this review: Have students complete **Workbook 4 page 15** and **Multilevel Activity Book 4 page 36,** and the **Unit 2 Exercises** on the **Multilevel Grammar Exercises CD-ROM 4**.

2 Group work

A Work with 2–3 classmates. Write a 6–8 line conversation between the people in the picture. Share your conversation with the class.

A: *Did you hear about...?*
B: *No, I didn't. What...?*

B Interview 3 classmates. Write their answers.

1. Where do you get the news? What do you like about your news source?
2. Do you think people have a responsibility to know about current events? Why or why not?
3. In your opinion, what have been the 3 most important events in the news this year?

C Talk about the answers with your class.

PROBLEM SOLVING

A Listen and read about Anton.

Before Anton came to the United States, he always read the newspaper, watched the news on TV, and followed the international news on the Internet. He loved to talk to his friends about current events.

However, since Anton came to the U.S., getting the news hasn't been so easy. He thinks it is very hard to understand TV and radio news in English. At work, his co-workers talk about current events at lunch. Anton would like to be able to talk about his opinions, too.

B Work with your classmates. Answer the questions.

1. What is Anton's problem?   He wants to talk about current events with his co-workers, but it's hard for him to understand the news in English.
2. What should Anton do? Think of 2 or 3 solutions to his problem.
3. Write a short letter to Anton. Tell him what you think he should do.

UNIT **3**

FOCUS ON
- travel problems and solutions
- using the telephone
- reported speech
- planning a trip
- cell-phone communication

Going Places

LESSON 1 **Vocabulary**

1 Learn vocabulary for travel emergencies

A **Talk about the questions with your class.**

1. How do you like to travel—by car, by bus, or by train? Why?
2. What are some things you always take with you when you travel? Why?

B **Work with your classmates. Match the words with the pictures.**

_3_	call the auto club	_1_	have a breakdown	_8_	send a tow truck
_6_	change a tire	_5_	have a flat tire	_2_	turn on the hazard lights
_9_	get directions	_4_	raise the hood	_7_	use a safety triangle

C **Listen and check. Then read the new words with a partner.**

D **Work with a partner. Write other travel emergency words you know. Check your words in a dictionary.**

Identify and use travel emergency vocabulary to state problems and solutions

Unit 3 Lesson 1

Objectives	Grammar	Vocabulary	Correlations
On-level: Describe travel emergencies and give advice for travel problems **Pre-level:** Identify travel emergencies and give advice for travel problems **Higher-level:** Talk and write about travel emergencies, and give advice for travel problems	Present tense (*He's locked out of the car.*) Past tense (*I had a breakdown on the highway.*)	Travel emergencies and travel problems For vocabulary support for pre-level students, see this **Oxford Picture Dictionary** unit: Transportation	**CASAS:** 0.1.2, 0.1.5, 0.2.1, 2.5.1, 4.8.1, 7.2.5, 7.4.5, 7.4.7 **LCPs:** 39.01, 44.01, 49.02, 49.03, 49.10, 49.17 **SCANS:** Interprets and communicates information, Participates as member of a team, Seeing things in the mind's eye **EFF:** Cooperate with others, Speak so others can understand

Warm-up and Review

10–15 minutes (books closed)

Show a picture of a car, or draw a car on the board. Elicit the names of car parts (inside and out), and write them on the board.

Introduction

5 minutes

1. Point to different car parts listed on the board, and ask students what can go wrong with them.

2. State the objective: *Today we're going to learn words for travel emergencies and problems.*

1 Learn vocabulary for travel emergencies

Presentation I

20–25 minutes

A Write *travel* on the board, and elicit students' answers to the questions. Write their ideas for question 2 on a large sheet of paper. Keep this list for the extension at the end of the lesson.

B 1. Direct students to look at the pictures. Ask: *Has either of these things ever happened to you?*

2. Group students and assign roles: leader, fact checker, recorder, and reporter. Explain that students work with their groups to match the words and pictures.

3. Check comprehension of the roles. Ask: *Who looks up the words in a dictionary?* [fact checker] *Who writes the numbers in the book?* [recorder] *Who tells the class your answers?* [reporter] *Who helps everyone and manages the group?* [leader]

4. Set a time limit (three minutes). As students work together, copy the wordlist onto the board.

5. Call "time." Have reporters take turns giving their answers. Write each group's answer on the board next to the word.

C 1. To prepare students for listening, say: *Now we're going to listen to these people talk about their car problems.* Ask students to listen and check their answers.

2. Have students check the wordlist on the board and then write the correct numbers in their books.

3. Pair students. Set a time limit (three minutes). Monitor pair practice to identify pronunciation issues.

4. Call "time" and work with the pronunciation of any troublesome words or phrases.

5. Replay the audio and challenge students to listen for additional information about each of the car problems. Call on volunteers to share what they heard.

D 1. Ask students to work with their partners from 1C to brainstorm a list of related words.

2. Elicit words from the class. Write them on the board. Ask students to copy them into their vocabulary notes for the unit.

Guided Practice

5–10 minutes

 E 1. Set a time limit (three minutes). Direct students to ask and answer the questions with a partner.

2. Call on volunteers to share their answers with the class.

2 Learn vocabulary for travel problems

Presentation II

15–20 minutes

 A 1. Direct students to look at the pictures. Introduce the new topic: *Now we're going to talk about other problems you can have while you're traveling.*

2. Say and have students repeat the captions.

3. Ask students to work individually to match the pictures to the sentences. Go over the answers as a class.

4. Check comprehension. Say: *There are too many cars, so I'm _____.* [stuck in traffic] *I don't know where I am. I'm _____.* [lost]

Guided Practice

10–15 minutes

 B 1. Model the conversation with a volunteer. Model it again using different words from 2A.

2. Set a time limit (three minutes). Direct students to practice with a partner.

3. Call on volunteers to act out one of their conversations for the class.

Communicative Practice and Application

10–15 minutes

> Before students answer the questions in 2C, demonstrate note taking. Write your own answer to question 1 on the board in long form. *Once I was driving home from work, and I had a breakdown.* Ask: *Is this what I mean by* take notes? *Which words did I really need to write?* Erase all of the words except *breakdown*. Explain that taking notes allows the class to move forward with the discussion.

 C 1. Give students a minute to make notes of their answers to the questions. Call on individuals to share their ideas with the class.

2. Write *Travel Emergencies* and *Solutions* on the board. Write the students' ideas under each one.

Evaluation

10–15 minutes (books closed)

TEST YOURSELF

1. Make a two-column chart on the board with the headings *Travel Emergencies/Problems* and *Solutions*. Have students close their books and give you an example for each column. Have students copy the chart into their notebooks.

2. Give students five to ten minutes to test themselves by writing the words they recall from the lesson.

3. Call "time" and have students check their spelling in a dictionary. Circulate and monitor students' progress.

4. Direct students to share their work with a partner and add additional words to their charts.

> ### Multilevel Strategies
> Target the *Test Yourself* to the level of your students.
>
> • **Higher-level** Have these students complete the chart and then write sentences with *if* and *should*.

To compress this lesson: Conduct 1B as a whole-class activity.

To extend this lesson: Take out the list of items from 1A, question 2. Ask students if they want to add anything to the list after finishing the lesson. Write their ideas. Have groups work together to rank the list from the most important to the least important. Call on a reporter from each group to justify the group's "top three."

And/Or have students complete **Workbook 4 page 16** and **Multilevel Activity Book 4 pages 38–39**.

E **Work with a partner. Ask and answer the questions. Use the words in 1B.**

1. How do you know there is a travel emergency with the bus? With the cars?
2. What happened to the people in the pictures? What are they doing?

2 Learn vocabulary for travel problems

A **Look at the pictures. Match the pictures with the statements.**

a

b

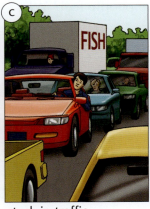
c

d

out of gas   lost   stuck in traffic   locked out of the car

  __d__ 1. She should call the auto club. She needs a locksmith.

  __a__ 2. He should walk to a gas station.

  __b__ 3. She should ask for directions.

  __c__ 4. He's going to be late. He should call his boss.

B **Work with a partner. Practice the conversation. Use the words in 2A.**

A: I can't believe this!

B: What's the problem?

A: I'm locked out of my car. What should I do?

B: You should call the auto club.

C **Talk about the questions with your class.**

1. What problems have you had while traveling by car or bus? What did you do?
2. What should you do if you have a car problem while you are driving?

TEST YOURSELF ✔

Close your book. Categorize the new words in two lists: *Travel Emergencies and Problems* and *Solutions*. Check your spelling in a dictionary. Compare your lists with a partner.

1 Read about using the phone

A **Look at the pictures. Talk about the questions with your class.**

1. Who do you think each person is calling?
2. How do the people feel? Why?

Please press one for road assistance...

Please leave a message at the tone...

B **Listen and read the story.**

> How I Made Friends with the Phone
>
> by Ahmed Bell
>
> When I first came to this country, it was very difficult for me to use the phone. I could understand people in person, but listening to people on the phone was a different story. I remember the first time I called about a job. The secretary said, "Can you hold?" and I said, "Hold what?" I didn't know that "hold" can mean "wait".
>
> My worst phone problem was automated messages with choices or menus. When I called the bank, for example, I couldn't understand the computer voice, and I couldn't get the information I needed. Sometimes, I called offices at night when the offices were closed. I could listen to their automated messages for English practice.
>
> Now, using the phone is much easier for me. I enjoy making phone calls, and I like it when people call me.

Writer's note

To repeat a speaker's words, add a comma (,) and quotation marks (" ").

C **Check your understanding. Circle the correct words.**

1. When the writer first came to the U.S., using the phone was (impossible / (very hard)).
2. He ((could) / couldn't) understand most people when he spoke to them in person.
3. He didn't understand a secretary when she asked him to (call again / (wait)).
4. He learned how to understand automated messages by ((listening) / leaving messages).

☑ Describe and report on experiences using the phone

Unit 3 Lesson 2

Objectives	Grammar	Vocabulary	Correlations
On- and Higher-level: Analyze, write, and edit a story about using the phone **Pre-level:** Read a story and write about using the phone	Past tense (*I didn't understand the secretary.*)	*Automated, and so on, quotation marks* For vocabulary support for pre-level students, see this **Oxford Picture Dictionary** topic: The Telephone	**CASAS:** 0.1.2, 0.1.5, 0.2.1, 7.4.7, 7.5.6 **LCPs:** 39.01, 49.01, 49.02, 49.03, 49.16, 49.17 **SCANS:** Creative thinking, Interprets and communicates information, Seeing things in the mind's eye **EFF:** Convey ideas in writing, Listen actively, Read with understanding, Reflect and evaluate

Warm-up and Review

10–15 minutes (books closed)

Ask students to name places they call where they encounter automated message systems (banks, utility companies, credit-card companies, stores, schools, movie theaters, etc.). Write the places on the board. Discuss their experiences with these automated messages.

Introduction

5 minutes

1. Elicit and write typical phone expressions one might hear when calling the places on the board. *This is _____. Please hold. You have the wrong number. Can I take a message? Press the pound key.*

2. State the objective: *Today we're going to read and write about using the phone.*

1 Read about using the phone

Presentation

20–25 minutes

A 1. Direct students to look at the pictures. Ask questions 1 and 2.

2. Write students' answers to question 1 on the board.

B 1. Say: *Now we're going to read a story by Ahmed Bell. Ahmed is writing about the difficulty he had understanding phone conversations when he first came to the U.S.*

2. Direct students to read the story silently. Ask: *What did the secretary say that confused him?* [Can you hold?] *How did he practice understanding automated messages?* [He called the offices late at night.]

3. Play the audio. Have students read along silently.

4. Draw students' attention to the *Writer's note.* Point out that quotation marks are only used when you repeat a speaker's exact words.

Guided Practice I

10 minutes

C Have students work independently to circle the answers. Ask volunteers to write the answers on the board.

Multilevel Strategies

Seat pre-level students together for 1C.

• **Pre-level** While other students are working on 1C, ask these students questions about the reading. *What did the secretary say? What does* hold *mean on the phone? What happened when he called the bank? Can he understand phone messages now?* Give students time to copy the answers to 1C from the board.

2 Write about using the phone

Guided Practice II

20–25 minutes

A 1. Read the questions. Elicit students' answers.

2. Write some of the students' ideas on the board, so they can refer to them during the writing assignment.

B 1. Direct students to look back at the story in 1B. Focus students' attention on the structure of the story. Elicit the topic of the first and second paragraphs. Point out the introductory sentence and the concluding sentence.

2. Read the questions for paragraph 1 aloud, and elicit some examples that students might include in their paragraphs. Do the same with the paragraph 2 and 3 questions. Point out the placement of the title and indentations in the example.

3. Check comprehension of the exercise. Ask: *How many paragraphs do you need to write?* [three] *What do you do with the first sentence of each paragraph?* [indent]

4. Have students work individually to write their stories.

Multilevel Strategies

Adapt 2B to the level of your students.

• **Pre-level** Direct these students to write one paragraph, using the questions for paragraph 1 as a guide. Provide them with a topic sentence: *When I first came to the U.S., it was difficult to understand phone conversations.*

• **Higher-level** Tell these students to include at least two examples of direct speech with commas and quotation marks.

C 1. Lead students through the process of using the *Editing checklist*. Read each sentence aloud, and ask students to check their papers before moving on to the next item.

2. Allow students a few minutes to edit their writing as necessary.

Communicative Practice

10 minutes

D 1. Read the instructions aloud. Emphasize to students that they are responding to their partners' work, not correcting it.

2. Use the story in 1B to model the exercise. *I think the part about practicing by calling at night is interesting. I'd like to ask the writer if he still has any problems on the phone and what they are.*

3. Direct students to exchange papers with a partner and follow the instructions.

4. Call on volunteers to share interesting things they read in their partners' stories.

Application and Evaluation

15 minutes

TEST YOURSELF

1. Review the instructions aloud. Have the class brainstorm some ideas and write them on the board. Assign a time limit (ten minutes), and have students work independently. Give students notice when they have five minutes left.

2. Before collecting students' work, remind them to use the *Editing checklist*. Collect and correct students' writing.

Multilevel Strategies

Adapt the *Test Yourself* to the level of your students.

• **Pre-level** Ask these students to write a paragraph in response to these questions: *Think of a time when you couldn't understand someone. Who were you talking to? What did you say? How did you feel?*

To compress this lesson: Assign the *Test Yourself* for homework.

To extend this lesson: Role-play a communication difficulty. Put students in mixed-level groups. Tell each group to write a telephone conversation in which one person doesn't understand the other. Have reporters from each group read the conversations aloud. Encourage pantomime and humor.

And/Or have students complete **Workbook 4 page 17** and **Multilevel Activity Book 4 page 40**.

2 Write about using the phone

A **Talk about the questions with your class.**

1. How is speaking in English on the phone different from communicating in person?
2. Do you get nervous when you have to use the phone? Why or why not?

B **Write about your phone experience. Use the model in 1B and the questions below to help you.**

Paragraph 1: When you first came to the U.S., was it difficult to understand English on the phone? Give an example of something you didn't understand.

Paragraph 2: What was your worst phone experience? What happened? How did you get better at using the phone?

Paragraph 3: How do you feel about using the phone now?

> My Worst Phone Experience
>
> When I first came to the U.S., it was difficult for me
> to use the phone. I couldn't understand...

C **Use the checklist to edit your writing. Check (✔) the true sentences.**

Editing checklist	
1. I wrote about the past and the present.	
2. I wrote about one of my experiences using the phone.	
3. I used the simple past to write about the past.	
4. I used a comma and quotation marks to repeat a speaker's words.	

D **Exchange stories with a partner. Read and comment on your partner's work.**

1. Point out one sentence that you think is interesting.
2. Ask your partner a question about his or her phone experience.

TEST YOURSELF ✔

Write a new story about another communication problem you had in English—on the phone or talking to someone in person.

1 Learn reported speech

A Look at the pictures. Where is Monty? Where are his friends?

Monty

Monty's friends

B Study the charts. Circle the example of reported speech in 1A.

REPORTED SPEECH WITH STATEMENTS

Quoted speech
Monty said, "**I'm stuck** in traffic."
Lia said, "**I'm waiting** for a tow truck."
They said, "**We don't have** a map."

Reported speech	
He said	(that) **he was** stuck in traffic.
She said	(that) **she was waiting** for a tow truck.
They said	(that) **they didn't have** a map.

Notes
• Use reported speech to tell what someone said or wrote.
• For quoted speech in the simple present, the reported speech is in the simple past.
• For quoted speech in the present continuous, the reported speech is in the past continuous.

C Fred invited his friends to dinner, but some of them called because they had problems getting to his home. What did they say? Complete the sentences with reported speech.

1. Luis said, "I'm lost."

   Luis said that __he was lost__.

2. Dora said, "The bus is stuck in traffic."

   Dora said __the bus was stuck in traffic__.

3. Alice and Kim said, "We don't know the address."

   Alice and Kim said __they didn't know the address__.

4. Sarah said, "I'm looking for a parking space."

   Sarah said that __she was looking for a parking space__.

☑ Use reported speech to relay messages and information

Unit 3 Lesson 3

Objectives	Grammar	Vocabulary	Correlations
On- and Higher-level: Use reported speech to write messages, and listen for reported speech in statements about travel problems **Pre-level:** Identify reported speech in statements about travel problems	Reported speech (*He said that he was lost.*)	*Pull off, pull over, hood, radiator, hazard lights, street sign.* For vocabulary support for pre-level students, see this **Oxford Picture Dictionary** topics: Basic Transportation, Public Transportation	**CASAS:** 0.1.2, 0.1.5, 0.2.1 **LCPs:** 39.01, 49.09, 49.13, 50.07 **SCANS:** Knowing how to learn, Listening, Seeing things in the mind's eye, Speaking **EFF:** Convey ideas in writing, Listen actively, Observe critically, Speak so others can understand, Reflect and evaluate

Warm-up and Review

10–15 minutes (books closed)

Ask students to tell you about a time they had car trouble or a time they had a problem while traveling. Write their quotes on the board. *Tara said, "I got a flat tire." Kendra said, "I missed my flight."* Leave these sentences on the board.

Introduction

5–10 minutes

1. Circle the commas and the quotation marks in the sentences on the board. Say: *I use these because I'm writing the exact words that the speakers used. Sometimes I want to report what you said, but I don't want to use the exact words.*

2. State the objective: *Today we're going to use reported speech to talk about travel problems.*

1 Learn reported speech

Presentation I

20–25 minutes

A Direct students to look at the pictures. Read the questions aloud, and elicit students' answers.

B 1. Read the first quoted speech and reported speech sentences in the chart aloud. Elicit the differences. Do the same for the rest of the sentences. Read the *Notes* aloud.

2. Direct students to circle the example of reported speech in 1A. Go over the answer as a class.

3. Indicating the first quoted-speech sentence in the chart, ask: *Are these the exact words Monty used?* [yes]

4. Read the reported-speech sentences aloud, and have students repeat after you.

5. Assess students' understanding of the charts. Elicit the process of changing the direct-speech sentences you wrote on the board during the warm-up to reported speech. *Do I need the comma after said?* [no] *Do I need the quotation marks?* [no] *What do I change I to?* [he or she]

Guided Practice I

15–20 minutes

C Ask students to work individually to complete the sentences. Ask volunteers to write the answers on the board.

Multilevel Strategies

For 1C, seat same-level students together.

• **Pre-level** While other students are completing 1C, work with these students. Ask them to identify the pronouns and verbs that need to be changed, and go over the changes together.

• **On- and Higher-level** After these students finish 1C, ask them to write a quoted-speech sentence and change it into a reported-speech sentence. Ask volunteers to write their sentence pairs on the board.

Guided Practice II

5–10 minutes

 D 1. Direct students to look at number 1. Ask them to identify the verb form in the sentence and in its corrected version. Use a timeline to demonstrate that *said* and *was on Elk Road* happened at the same time (in the past). Say: *We don't know where he is now.*

2. Go through each of the remaining sentences. Elicit the verb form, and direct students to rewrite the sentences with the correct form. Call on volunteers for the answers.

 After 1D, play a reported-speech "circle" game. Tell each student to write a short present-tense statement about cars or travel. Have students stand in a circle around the room. Have each student say his or her sentence aloud. (If you have a large class, allow students to work with a partner to write the sentence.) Tell students they need to try to remember who said what. Allow them to take notes.

After everyone has spoken, call on individuals to report what one of their classmates said. *June said she had an old car.* Remind them that with reported speech, it isn't necessary to use the exact words as long as the idea is the same. Help students with verb tense and pronoun usage.

2 Learn reported speech with *told* + noun or pronoun

Presentation II

20–25 minutes

 A 1. Introduce the new topic. *Now we're going to learn reported speech with* told.

2. Rewrite the sentences on the board from the warm-up using *told.* *Kendra told us that she missed her flight. Tara told the class that she got a flat tire.*

3. Ask the students to identify the difference between the sentence with *said* and the sentence with *told.* [use of a pronoun or noun after *told* but not *said*]

4. Read the questions above the chart aloud. Ask students to read the chart to find the answer. Read the reported-speech sentences aloud, and elicit the answer to the question.

5. Read the *Notes* aloud. Point out that object pronouns are not used after *say.*

Guided Practice I

10–15 minutes

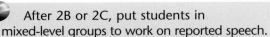 **B** Ask students to work individually to complete the sentences. Call on volunteers to read the completed sentences aloud. Write the answers on the board.

 After 2B or 2C, put students in mixed-level groups to work on reported speech.

1. Tell each group to write a conversation with four short present-tense statements. Tell them not to include any questions. Ask the groups to choose one person as the "narrator." The narrator will tell about the conversation using reported speech.

2. Write a conversation on the board as an example. *John: We have a flat tire. Mary: That's OK. There's a spare in the trunk. I can change the tire. John: You're the best wife in the world, dear.* Ask two volunteers to read the parts of Mary and John. Then "report" their conversation to the class: *John said they had a flat tire. Mary told John there was a spare in the trunk…*

3. Assign a time limit (five minutes) for writing the conversation. Have two reporters from each group act out the conversation. Have the narrator tell about the conversation using reported speech. Encourage the narrator to use both *told* and *said.*

C Ask students to work individually to complete the reported speech sentences. Have a volunteer write the completed sentences on the board.

Multilevel Strategies

For 2C, seat same-level students together.

• **Pre-level** Work with this group. Elicit the object pronouns and verb forms before students write each sentence.

• **On- and Higher-level** Ask these students to write three to five additional reported-speech sentences using *told.* Ask volunteers to put their sentences on the board.

D Get the form. Work with your class. Correct the sentences.

Ali called this morning.

1. He said that he **is** on Elk Road.   He said that he was on Elk Road.
2. He **says** he was calling from a gas station.   He said he was calling from a gas station.
3. He said that he **has** a flat tire.   He said that he had a flat tire.
4. He said he **is** going to be late.   He said he was going to be late.

2 Learn reported speech with *told* + noun or pronoun

A Study the charts. Is Lee a man or a woman? How do you know?

a woman   The 3rd example says Bob told her.

REPORTED SPEECH WITH *TOLD* + NOUN OR PRONOUN

Quoted speech		Reported speech	
		Bob said	
Bob said, "Lee, **I have** a flat tire."		Bob told **Lee**	(that) **he had** a flat tire.
		Bob told **her**	
They said, "**We're waiting** for the bus."		They said	(that) **they were waiting** for the bus.
		They told **me**	

Notes
• Use *said* to report a person's words.
• Use *told* to report a person's words and to report on who the person is speaking to.
• Use a noun (*Lee*, etc.) or an object pronoun (*her, me*, etc.) after *told*.

B Complete the sentences with *said* or *told*.

1. Bob ___said___ he was changing his tire.
2. Yan ___told___ Lisa that she didn't belong to an auto club.
3. The teacher ___told___ us that there was a car in the parking lot with its lights on.
4. My friends ___said___ they wanted to buy a new car.

C Look at the quoted speech. Complete the reported speech. Use object pronouns.

1. Mr. Ruiz stopped Liz in the hall. He said, "I need the key to the closet."

   Mr. Ruiz told ___her that he needed the key to the closet___.

2. Tia phoned John. She said, "I'm calling about the homework."

   Tia told ___him (that) she was calling about the homework___.

3. Ken emailed his parents. He said, "I'm taking driving lessons."

   Ken told ___them (that) he was taking driving lessons___.

4. Tasha called my sister and me. She said, "I'm locked out of my apartment."

   Tasha told ___us (that) she was locked out of her apartment___.

3 Grammar listening

Listen to the conversations. Write the missing words.

1. David said that _____ *he was* _____ lost.
2. Patricia said that ___ *she had* _____ a flat tire.
3. Gina said that ___ *she was waiting* _____ for a tow truck.
4. Sam and Joe said that ___ *they were stuck* _____ in traffic.
5. They said that ___ *they were taking* _____ the bus.
6. Cindy said that ___ *she didn't have* _____ a cell phone.
7. Hank said that ___ *he wasn't going* _____ to class.
   He also said that ___ *his car was* _____ out of gas.
8. Maria said that ___ *she needed* _____ a map.

4 Practice reported speech

A **Work with your classmates. Ask your classmates these questions. Take notes on their answers.**

1. Do you have a car?
2. What's your favorite form of transportation?
3. Do you like to travel?
4. Are you planning to take a trip soon?

B **Work with a partner. Tell your partner what your classmates said.**

A: *Max said that he had a used car.*
B: *June told me that she didn't have a car.*

TEST YOURSELF ✔

Close your book. Write 5 sentences about things your partner told you in 4B.
Use reported speech with *told* or *said*.

3 Grammar listening

Guided Practice II

10–15 minutes

1. Say: *Now we're going to listen to some reported-speech sentences about travel problems.*

2. Play the audio. Direct students to read along silently without writing.

3. Replay the audio. Ask students to complete the sentences. If necessary, replay each sentence before moving on to the next one.

4. Ask volunteers to write the sentences on the board.

Multilevel Strategies

Adapt the *Grammar listening* to the level of your students.

• **Pre-level** Direct these students to use a separate sheet of paper to write the words they can. Allow them to copy the completed answers into their books after volunteers put them on the board.

4 Practice reported speech

Communicative Practice and Application

20–25 minutes

A 1. Direct students to look at the photo. Ask about what is happening in the picture.

2. Read and have students repeat the questions.

3. Direct students to walk around the room asking two or three different people the questions. To get students moving, tell them they must speak to people who sit at a different table or in another part of the room. Tell them to make notes of each other's answers.

4. Model the exercise by asking a volunteer the first question. Have the class tell you how to write the answer in note form.

5. Check comprehension of the exercise. Ask: *Do you ask the questions of the person sitting next to you?* [no] *Do you ask only one person the questions?* [no]

B Tell students to work with a partner to report what their classmates said. Model the exercise by calling on several volunteers. Monitor and provide feedback on students' use of reported speech.

Evaluation

10–15 minutes (books closed)

TEST YOURSELF

Ask students to write the sentences independently. Collect and correct their writing.

Multilevel Strategies

Target the *Test Yourself* to the level of your students.

• **Pre-level** Provide skeleton sentences for these students to complete. *1. _____ (name) said that he/she had a car. 2. _____ (name) said that his/her favorite form of transportation was _____ (name). 3. _____ (name) said that he/she was/wasn't planning to take a trip soon.*

To compress this lesson: Conduct 1C as a whole-class discussion.

To extend this lesson: Have students paraphrase a conversation. Play a short conversation from a movie, television show, or commercial. Ask students to report on the conversation to a partner.

And/Or have students complete **Workbook 4 pages 18–19, Multilevel Activity Book 4 pages 41–42,** and the corresponding **Unit 4 Exercises** on the **Multilevel Grammar Exercises CD-ROM 4.**

Unit 3 Lesson 4

Objectives	Grammar	Vocabulary	Correlations
On-, Pre-, and Higher-level: Make travel plans and listen to phone messages	Conditionals for giving advice (*If I were you, I'd check the website.*)	*Inquire, confirm, check-in, check-out, charges* For vocabulary support for pre-level students, see this **Oxford Picture Dictionary** topics: Basic Transportation, Public Transportation	**CASAS:** 0.1.2, 0.1.5, 0.2.1, 2.2.1, 6.0.3, 6.0.4, 6.2.1, 6.2.3, 6.2.5 **LCPs:** 39.01, 40.02, 43.02, 43.04, 49.02, 49.09, 51.03 **SCANS:** Acquires and evaluates information, Arithmetic/Mathematics, Knowing how to learn **EFF:** Listen actively, Use math to solve problems and communicate

Warm-up and Review

10–15 minutes (books closed)

Show pictures of famous places in the U.S., and ask students to identify them. Find out who has visited the different places and whether anyone has plans to visit them in the future.

Introduction

5 minutes

1. Ask about each place that your students have been to or want to go to. *How would you get there? Where would you stay?*

2. State the objective: *Today we're going to learn to make travel plans.*

1 Learn to make travel plans

Presentation I

15–20 minutes

A 1. Direct students to look at the ads. Ask questions. *Did you ever call for motel reservations? Did you ever look at a hotel website?*

2. Play the audio. Give students a minute to answer the questions. Go over the answers as a class.

Guided Practice

20–25 minutes

B 1. Play the audio. Ask students to read along silently and listen for the answer to the question. Elicit the answer.

2. Ask students to read the conversation with a partner. Circulate and monitor pronunciation. Model and have students repeat difficult words or phrases.

3. Say and have students repeat the expressions in the *In other words* box. Elicit the placement of the expressions in the conversation. Ask volunteers to read the conversation using expressions from the box.

Communicative Practice and Application

15–20 minutes

C 1. Ask students to read the instructions silently. Check their comprehension of the exercise. Ask: *What are the two roles? What is the situation?* Elicit examples of what each partner might say.

2. Set a time limit (five minutes). Ask students to act out the role-play in both roles. Ask one to three volunteer pairs to act out their conversations for the class. Tell students who are listening to write Partner B's advice.

Multilevel Strategies

For 1C, adapt the role-play to the level of your students.

• **Pre-level** Provide the beginning of the conversation for these students. *A: I'm going to San Francisco. A friend told me to use a map website. What do you think? B: I think it's a good idea _____.*

1 Learn to make travel plans

 **A** **Look at the ads. Listen to the conversations. Then answer the questions below with your classmates.**

1. What website does Artie recommend?
2. Where does Rhonda think her friend should stay?

B **Listen and read. Who knows more about planning a trip—A or B?** B

A: I'm planning a trip to Florida. I've never been there before.

B: Great. Do you have a hotel reservation?

A: No, I don't. My sister told me to use the Internet.

B: That's a good idea. If I were you, I'd try *hotels.int*.

A: Is it hard to use?

B: It's easy, and I'll bet* you can get a good price. Why don't you try it?

A: OK, I will. Thanks for the advice.

*****Idiom note:** I'll bet (OR I bet) = I'm sure

> **In other words...**
>
> **Making suggestions**
> If I were you, I'd...
> Why don't you...?
> You could...
> How about trying...?

C **Role-play a conversation about planning a trip with a partner. Use the example in 1B to make a new conversation.**

Partner A: You are planning to drive to San Francisco for the first time. You need directions. A friend told you to use a map website. Ask if it's hard to use.

Partner B: You agree that a map website is a good idea. Recommend *drivethere.map*. Explain that it's easy, and you can get maps and travel tips.

2 Learn reported speech with instructions

A Study the charts. Do you use *said* or *told* with *me* for reported instructions? told

REPORTED SPEECH WITH INSTRUCTIONS

Quoted Speech	Reported Speech
Laila said, "Use a map website."	Laila **told me to use** a map website.
Mati said, "Don't take Highway 75."	Mati **told me not to take** Highway 75.
Tomas said, "Please drive."	Tomas **said to drive**.

Note
Use an infinitive (*to* + verb OR *not to* + verb) to report an instruction.

B Work with a partner. Look at the pictures. Report Pedro and Lois' instructions.

1. _Pedro told Lois to call him every day._   3. _Pedro told Lois not to drive at night._
2. _Lois told Pedro not to worry._   4. _Lois told Pedro to relax_

3 Practice your pronunciation

A Listen to the pronunciation of the letter *s* in these sentences.

Pronounced *s*	Pronounced *z*
Try thi<u>s</u> web<u>s</u>ite.	It i<u>s</u> easy to u<u>s</u>e.

B Work with a partner. How do you think the letter s is pronounced in these words? Circle s or z.

1. use   s (z)   3. sister   (s) z   5. cats   (s) z
2. hotels   s (z)   4. please   s (z)   6. does   s (z)

C Listen and check. Then read the words with a partner.

TIP

If you have access to the Internet in class, have students plan a trip online. You can do this anytime after 1C. Have students work with a partner. For a short version of the activity, have students choose a place in your state to visit, and show them how to find driving directions online. Have each pair tell another pair about where they are going and how to get there.

For a more involved version of this activity, have students choose a place anywhere in the world to visit. Direct them to find information about the place using a search engine, and show them how to make plane and hotel reservations online. Have each pair present their vacation plans and cost to the class.

Multilevel Strategies

For 2B, seat same-level students together.

• **Pre-level** Work with these students to complete the exercise as a group. Read each quote and elicit the necessary information for writing it in reported speech. *Who said "Don't worry"? Whom did she say it to? Should we use* said *or* told *in this case?* After you have worked through each sentence, have the group copy it into their books.

• **On- and Higher-level** While you are working with the pre-level students, tell these students to write three to five more things that Lois and Pedro might tell each other to do.

2 Learn reported speech with instructions

Presentation II and Guided Practice

10–15 minutes

A 1. Introduce the new topic. *Now we're going to learn reported speech for giving instructions.*

2. Read the instructions aloud. Direct students to study the chart. Call on a volunteer to answer the question.

3. Check comprehension of the chart. Write several "quotes" on the board. *"Take sunscreen." "Wear comfortable shoes." "Don't forget to take pictures!"* Elicit and write the reported speech. *My mother told me to wear comfortable shoes.*

Guided Communicative Practice

15–20 minutes

B 1. Direct students to look at the pictures. Ask: *Who is going away? How does Pedro feel?*

2. Have students work individually to write the sentences in reported speech. Ask volunteers to write the sentences on the board.

3. Ask students to use reported instructions to tell a partner about some good advice they have received about traveling or driving. Call on volunteers to share the advice with the class.

3 Practice your pronunciation

Pronunciation Extension

10–15 minutes

A 1. Write *He always tries to get his tickets on sale.* on the board. Say the sentence and ask students to repeat it. Underline each *s* and pronounce just those words so that students can hear the difference in the pronunciation of *s*. Say: *Now we're going to focus on two pronunciations of the letter* s.

2. Play the audio. Direct students to listen for the *s* sounds.

3. Replay the audio and have students repeat the sentences.

B Have students work with a partner to predict how the words will be pronounced.

C Play the audio. Direct students to listen and check their work. Go over the answers as a class. Have students repeat the words.

4 Focus on Listening

Listening Extension

20–25 minutes

A Read the questions aloud, and elicit answers from volunteers. Encourage students to respond to each other's ideas. After one student speaks, ask other students for their opinions. *Do you feel the same way? Why or why not?*

B 1. Say: *We are going to listen to a motel automated message system. What do you think you can do on it?*

2. Play the audio. Ask students to listen for and check two things you can do on the system. Elicit the answers.

C 1. Direct students to read the sentences before listening.

2. Replay the audio and have students work individually to write the correct number or symbol. Go over the answers as a class.

> ### Multilevel Strategies
>
> For 4C, write the numbers *1, 2, 3, 4,* and # on the board, and replay the automated phone message. Stop after each sentence.
>
> • **Pre-level** Write the key words on the board to help these students find the correct answer.
>
> • **On- and Higher-level** Elicit the key words from these students, and write them on the board. *1. make reservations, 2. locate nearest motel, 3. reserve rooms for a wedding, 4. employment information, # (pound key) hear the message again.*

5 Real-life math

Math Extension

5–10 minutes

1. Say: *Billy has made reservations at a motel. This is the email he received to confirm those reservations.* Direct students to read the email silently and work individually to answer the questions.

2. Call on volunteers to answer questions 1 and 2. Write the multiplication problem on the board.

3. Call on another volunteer to solve the problem.

Evaluation

10–15 minutes

TEST YOURSELF

1. Model the role-play with a volunteer. Then switch roles.

2. Pair students. Check comprehension of the exercise by eliciting things that each partner might say.

3. Set a time limit (five minutes), and have the partners act out the role-play in both roles.

4. Circulate and monitor. Encourage pantomime and improvisation.

5. Provide feedback.

> ### Multilevel Strategies
>
> Target the *Test Yourself* to the level of your students.
>
> • **Pre-level** Ask these students to use this skeleton conversation: *A: I want to go somewhere this weekend. Where should I go? B: How about _____. A: How do I get there? B: _____. A: Where _____.*
>
> • **Higher-level** Direct these students to talk about several places.

To compress this lesson: Conduct *Real-life math* as a whole-class activity.

To extend this lesson: Write postcards.

1. Pass out pictures of nice places cut from a magazine or printed from the Internet. Have each student attach a picture to a piece of paper and write a "postcard" on it. Tell them to say how they got to the place and where they are staying, as well as how they are enjoying their trip.

2. Have small groups share their postcards and discuss their imaginary vacations. Tell the groups to decide which one had the most exciting vacation and which had the most relaxing one.

And/Or have students complete **Workbook 4 page 20** and **Multilevel Activity Book 4 page 43.**

4 Focus on listening

A **Talk about the questions with your class.**

1. Where do you hear: *Press 1 for…, Press 2 for…,* etc.?
2. Are automated messages easy or difficult for you to follow or understand? Why?

B **Listen to the automated message. Check (✔) 2 things you can't do on this message system.**

- [ ] Make a reservation.
- [✔] Get room service.
- [✔] Order a wedding cake.
- [ ] Get information about jobs.
- [ ] Find a nearby hotel.
- [ ] Hear the message again.

C **Listen again. Write the numbers or the symbols the people should press.**

1. Omar wants to have a company meeting at a Motel 22.   3
2. Elena wants to find a Motel 22 near her home.   2
3. Billy wants a reservation at the Motel 22 in Dallas, Texas.   1
4. Juanita needs to hear the choices again.   #
5. Kevin is looking for a job at a Motel 22.   4

5 Real-life math

A **Read the confirmation email for a hotel reservation and answer the questions.**

1. How many nights is Billy planning to stay at the Motel 22?   2

2. How much is Billy's room per night (room rate plus taxes and charges)? $87.55

3. What will be the total cost of his stay at Motel 22? $175.10

B **Explain your answers to your classmates.**

Email - Message (Plain Text)

File   Edit   View   Insert   Format   Tools   Actions   Help

Reply   Reply to All   Forward   Print   Save   Delete

From: reservations@motel22
To: blewis@fince.ma
Subject: Your reservation
Date: 9/1

Dear Billy Lewis:
We are pleased to confirm your reservation at Motel 22. Please check the summary below. We look forward to seeing you!

Location: Motel 22, 1800 Clark Ave., Dallas, TX
Check-in (arrive): Wed, 10/14 [3 p.m.]
Check-out (leave): Friday, 10/16 [12 p.m.]
Room Rate: $79.00 per night;
Taxes and Charges: $8.55 per night
To modify or cancel this reservation, please call us at 1-800-555-2222.

TEST YOURSELF ✔

Role-play a conversation about making travel arrangements. Partner A: You want to take a trip for the weekend, but you're not sure where you want to go, how you should travel, or where to stay. Partner B: You always use the Internet to plan your trips. Give your friend advice. Then change roles.

1 Get ready to read

A Do you use a cell phone? How have cell phones changed the way people communicate?

B Read the definitions. Which word means *become bigger*? increase

get in touch with: [verb] to contact, talk or write to
increase: [verb] to get larger; grow
mobility: [noun] the ability to move around, or travel, easily
wireless: [adj.] without wires

C Scan the first paragraph of the magazine article in 2A. Then mark the sentences T (true) or F (false).

  T   1. More than 50 percent of people in the U.S. carry cell phones.

  F   2. From 1994 to 2004, the number of cell phones in the U.S. increased from 24 million to 80 million.

2 Read and respond

A Read the article. Why do people have cell phones?

They want to be more accessible, have greater mobility, and feel safer. They don't want to hear other people's conversations in public places or have a cell phone call interrupt a face-to-face conversation.

Our Love–Hate Relationship with Cell Phones

Cell phones are a fact of modern life. More than 50 percent of people in the U.S. carry them. From 1994 to 2004, the number of cell phones in the U.S. increased from 24 million to 180 million.

Why do people have cell phones? When researchers asked this question, most people said that they wanted to be more accessible,[1] that they wanted to have greater mobility, or that a cell phone made them feel safe. Cell phones allow us to spend more time talking to family and friends. We use them on the go—when we are waiting in line or walking the dog. And they do make us feel safer. We know that we can get in touch with each other in case of an emergency.

[1] accessible: easy to talk to; easy to reach

☑ Interpret a magazine article on cell phones; scan an article for numbers

Unit 3 Lesson 5

Objectives	Grammar	Vocabulary	Correlations
On-, Pre-, and Higher-level: Read about and discuss cell phones	Adjectives with *-less* (*useless, worthless*)	*Get in touch with, increase, mobility, wireless, accessible* For vocabulary support for pre-level students, see this **Oxford Picture Dictionary** topic: The Telephone	**CASAS:** 0.1.2, 0.1.5, 0.2.1, 2.1.4, 7.4.4, 7.4.7 **LCPs:** 39.01, 49.02, 49.04, 49.09, 49.16, 49.17 **SCANS:** Creative thinking, Listening, Reading, Speaking **EFF:** Learn through research, Read with understanding, Take responsibility for learning, Uses information and communicates technology

Warm-up and Review

10–15 minutes (books closed)

Write *cell phone* on the board. Ask the class to brainstorm all of the words they associate with cell phones. Write them on the board.

Introduction

5 minutes

1. Categorize the words on the board: *cell-phone features, opinions about cell phones, cell-phone manners.*

2. State the objective: *Today we're going to read about and discuss cell phones.*

1 Get ready to read

Presentation

15–20 minutes

A Read the questions aloud, and elicit students' answers.

B Read the words and definitions. Elicit sample sentences from students using the words. Point out that *mobility* is a noun and that the adjective form is *mobile*, as in *mobile phone* and *mobile home*. Provide a sample sentence. *Mobility is important in many jobs.*

Pre-Reading

C 1. Direct students to read the sentences and then scan the first paragraph to find out if they are true or false. Direct students to put down their pencils, or otherwise signal you, when they have found the answers.

2. Read the title. Ask students to predict what the article will say about what we love and hate about cell phones.

2 Read and respond

Guided Practice I

25–30 minutes

A 1. Ask students to read the article silently.

2. After students finish reading, direct them to underline unfamiliar words they would like to know. Elicit the words and encourage other students to provide definitions or examples.

3. Check comprehension. Ask: *Why do people want cell phones? What are some of the problems with cell phones?*

Multilevel Strategies

Adapt 2A to the level of your students.

• **Pre-level** Provide these students with a summary of the ideas in the reading. *From 1994 to 2004, the number of cell phones in the U.S. increased from 24 million to 180 million. We like cell phones because people can call us anytime, they give us mobility, and they make us feel safe. People often use cell phones when they are waiting in line or driving. But cell phones also cause problems. Most people don't want to listen to other people's conversations in public places, and cell phone calls interrupt face-to-face conversations.*

Direct these students to read the summary while other students are reading 2A.

Guided Practice II

15–20 minutes

B 1. Play the audio. Have students read along silently.

2. Elicit and discuss any additional questions about the reading.

C Have students ask and answer the questions with a partner. Call on volunteers to share their answers.

Multilevel Strategies

Adapt 2C to the level of your students.

• **Pre-level** Tell these students to use their summaries to answer the questions. After you have gone over the answers with the class, write them on the board, and give these students time to copy them.

D 1. Read the information in the chart aloud. Elicit and discuss any questions the students have about *-less*. Say the words and have students repeat them.

2. Direct students to work individually to complete each sentence. Write the answers on the board.

Multilevel Strategies

After 2D, seat pre-level students together.

• **Pre- and On-level** Direct these students to write a sentence with each of the words in the chart.

• **Higher-level** Ask these students to look up *helpless, hopeless, meaningless,* and *priceless* in their dictionaries. Have them write a sentence for each word.

3 Talk it over

Communicative Practice

15–20 minutes

1. Read the questions aloud. Set a time limit (three minutes). Have students work independently to think about the questions and write their answers in note form.

2. Call on volunteers to share their ideas. Ask for a show of hands to find out how many students feel they cannot imagine life without a cell phone.

Application

5–10 minutes

BRING IT TO LIFE

Read the instructions aloud. Ask students what they know about cell-phone plans to help them anticipate vocabulary they will find in the ads. Write the vocabulary on the board: *mobile-to-mobile calling, roaming, family plan, accessories, voice mail, carrier, brand, ringtones, and speakerphone.*

To compress this lesson: Conduct 2D as a whole-class activity.

To extend this lesson: Learn text-messaging abbreviations.
1. Tell students that when people send text messages, they like to abbreviate to save time. These abbreviations can be confusing if you aren't familiar with them. Write several text messages on the board. *C U @ 4, Thx 4 ur msg, Whr R U?, CU L8TR.*
2. Ask students to work with a partner to write the messages out in standard English. Go over the answers as a class. [See you at 4:00. Thanks for your message. Where are you? See you later.] Share other common abbreviations with students: *LOL (laughing out loud), BRB (be right back), IMO (in my opinion).*

And/Or have students complete **Workbook 4 page 21** and **Multilevel Activity Book 4 pages 44–45.**

Cell phones have changed our lives and our ideas of politeness and privacy. Most of us don't enjoy listening to other people's phone conversations in public places, but we don't always have a choice. Cell-phone calls interrupt our conversations and can disturb the people around us. When we get a call in the middle of a face-to-face conversation, we have to make a decision about who to talk to, and that decision can hurt people's feelings.

Cell phones can cause problems, but they have real advantages when they're used for the right reasons. Whether you love cell phones or hate them, we can probably all agree that wireless communication is here to stay.

Source: *www.CTIA-The Wireless Association®*

B **Listen and read the article again.**

C **Work with a partner. Answer the questions with information from the article.**

1. What are two situations in which people often use cell phones? *waiting in line and walking dogs*
2. What are two situations in which it is not polite to use cell phones? *in public places and in the middle of face-to-face conversations*

D **Study the chart. Complete the sentences with the correct words.**

Word Study: The suffix -*less*			
Add –*less* to the end of some nouns to form adjectives.			
Word	**Meaning**	**Word**	**Meaning**
wireless	without a wire	harmless	not harmful or dangerous
useless	without a use; not useful	speechless	unable to speak

1. A cell phone is __useless__ if you forget to charge the battery.

2. ____Wireless____ communication, such as cell phones, is common today.

3. When he called, I couldn't think of what to say. I was ____speechless____ with surprise.

4. My co-worker thinks cell phones are dangerous, but experts say they're ____harmless____.

3 Talk it over

Think about the question. Talk about your ideas with the class.

Many people say that they cannot imagine life without a cell phone.
Do you feel the same way? Why or why not?

BRING IT TO LIFE

Use the newspaper, the Internet, or store flyers to find information on cell-phone calling plans. Bring your information to class. Compare services with your classmates. Which plans have the best services?

1 Grammar

A Complete the sentences. Use reported speech.

1. Patty said, "I need directions to the bus station."

   Patty said that __she needed directions to the bus station__.

2. She also said, "I want to use a map website."

   She also told me that __she wanted to use a map website__.

3. Her co-workers said, "We don't know the zip code for the bus station."

   Her co-workers told her that __they didn't know the zip code for the bus station__.

B Read the reported speech. What did the speakers say? Write the quoted speech.

1. Abram said that he didn't understand his cell-phone bill.

   Abram said, "__I don't understand my cell-phone bill.__"

2. Eddy's mother said Eddy was staying home today.

   Eddy's mother said, "__Eddy is staying home today.__"

3. Sandra and her roommate said they had a new phone number.

   Sandra and her roommate said, "__We have a new phone number.__"

C Complete the sentences with *him, her, us,* or *them.*
Use the words in parentheses.

1. We told __them__ to meet us here. (Aldo and Mary)
2. They told __her__ that they were locked out of their car. (Mrs. Ikito)
3. Ms. Ikito told __us__ that they were waiting for the auto club. (my family and me)
4. I told __him__ that Aldo and Mary needed an extra set of keys. (Mr. Ikito)
5. We told __them__ where Aldo and Mary were waiting. (Mr. and Mrs. Ikito)

D Change the instructions to reported speech.

1. "Please call a tow truck," Ms. Holton said to her husband.

   Ms. Holton told him to call a tow truck.

2. "Stop at the intersection," Ali said to the taxi driver.

   Ali told the taxi driver to stop at the intersection.

3. "Turn on the hazard lights," Gina said to Mrs. Perlas.

   Gina told Mrs. Perlas to turn on the hazard lights.

4. "Don't forget the map," my brother said to his friends.

   My brother told his friends not to forget the map.

Unit 3 Review and expand

Objectives	Grammar	Vocabulary	Correlations
On-, Pre-, and Higher-level: Expand upon and review unit grammar and life skills	Reported speech (*She said that she needed directions.*)	Transportation vocabulary For vocabulary support for pre-level students, see this **Oxford Picture Dictionary** topics: Basic Transportation, Public Transportation	**CASAS:** 0.1.2, 0.1.5, 0.2.1, 4.8.1, 7.3.1, 7.3.2, 7.3.4 **LCPs:** 39.01, 49.01, 49.02, 49.16 **SCANS:** Creative thinking, Problem solving, Seeing things in the mind's eye, Speaking **EFF:** Convey ideas in writing, Listen actively, Read with understanding, Solve problems and make decisions

Warm-up and Review

10–15 minutes (books closed)

1. Review the *Bring It to Life* assignment from Lesson 5.

2. Write a comparison chart on the board: *Contract, Minutes, Monthly Charge.* Have students who did the exercise share the information they found. Write it in the chart on the board. Ask other students to determine the best deal based on the information they see on the board. Discuss other factors that might affect plan choice: *special international rates, type and price of phone included with the plan, charge for extra lines.*

Introduction and Presentation

5 minutes

1. Using reported speech, write several sentences about what was said during the warm-up. *I asked you to take out the ads you found. (Marco) said that GG&T had the best phone plan. (Luisa) said she wanted a lot of night and weekend minutes on her plan.*

2. State the objective: *Today we're going to review reported speech in order to talk about transportation.*

1 Grammar

Guided Practice

40–45 minutes

A 1. Read the first sentence, and elicit changes that were required to write the quoted speech as reported speech. Indicating the reported speech sentences on the board, ask students what the direct quote was. Elicit the differences.

2. Direct students to work individually to complete the exercises. Ask volunteers to write the answers on the board.

B 1. Read the first sentence. Draw students' attention to the changes in punctuation as well as in pronoun and verb use.

2. Direct students to work individually to complete the exercise. Ask volunteers to write the answers on the board.

C Have students work individually to complete the sentences. Ask volunteers to read the completed sentences aloud. Write the answers on the board.

D Have students work with a partner to change the instructions and requests to reported speech. Ask volunteers to write the sentences on the board.

Multilevel Strategies

For 1D, pair pre-level students with on- and higher-level students.

• **Pre-level** Ask these students to read the quoted-speech sentence to their partners. Allow them to copy the reported-speech sentences.

• **On- and Higher-level** Ask these students to write the reported-speech sentence and read it to their partners.

2 Group work

Communicative Practice

20–35 minutes

 1. Direct students, in groups of three to four, to focus on the picture. Say: *Lin called Sue. Why do you think she called?*

2. Assign roles: leader, recorder, and reporters. Explain that students work with their groups to write the conversation.

3. Check comprehension of the roles. Ask: *Who writes the conversation?* [recorder] *Who will read the conversation to the class?* [reporters] *Who helps everyone and manages the group?* [leader] *Who creates the conversation?* [everyone]

4. Set a time limit (five minutes) to complete the exercise. Circulate and answer any questions.

5. Have reporters from each group read the group's conversation to the class.

> ### Multilevel Strategies
>
> For 2A, use mixed-level groups.
> - **Pre-level** Assign these students the role of reporter.
> - **On-level** Assign these students the role of recorder.
> - **Higher-level** Assign these students the role of leader.

 1. Have students walk around the room to conduct these interviews. To get students moving, tell them to interview three new people not in their groups for 2A.

2. Set a time limit (five minutes) to complete the exercise. Tell students to make a note of their classmates' answers but not to worry about writing complete sentences.

> ### Multilevel Strategies
>
> Adapt the mixer in 2B to the level of your students.
> - **Pre-level** Allow these students to ask and answer the questions without writing.
> - **Higher-level** Have these students ask two additional questions and write all answers.

 Call on individuals to report what they learned about their classmates. Write the "best advice" ideas on the board.

PROBLEM SOLVING

15–25 minutes

 1. Ask: *Would you drive your car on a long trip?* Tell students they will read a story about a man who is deciding whether or not to drive to another city. Direct students to read Kofi's story silently.

2. Ask: *How much is the airfare?* [$400 roundtrip] *How old is the car?* [more than 10 years old] *How much are new tires?* [$500] *How much does Kofi have in the bank?*[$800]

3. Play the audio and have students read along silently.

 1. Elicit answers to question 1. Have volunteers write answers to question 2 on the board until all of the class ideas have been put up.

2. Have the class vote on Kofi's best course of action.

3. Pair students. Have them write a short letter giving advice to Kofi.

Evaluation

30–35 minutes

To test students' understanding of the unit grammar and life skills, have them take the Unit 3 Test on the *Step Forward Test Generator CD-ROM* with *ExamView® Assessment Suite*.

> ### Learning Log
>
> To help students record and discuss their progress, use the *Learning Log* on page T–200.

To extend this review: Have students complete **Workbook 4 page 22, Multilevel Activity Book 4 page 46,** and the **Unit 3 Exercises** on the **Multilevel Grammar Exercises CD-ROM 4.**

2 Group work

A Work with 2–3 classmates. Write a 6–8 line conversation between the people in the picture. Eve is asking about Lin. Sue is reporting what Lin told her. Share your conversation with the class.

Eve: *Is Lin OK? What did she say?*
Sue: *She…*

B Interview 3 classmates. Write their answers.

1. When you travel, do you like to go somewhere new or somewhere you've visited before? Why?
2. What is the best travel advice you have ever heard? Why?
3. What are 3 things every traveler should know before leaving home?

C Talk about the answers with your class.

PROBLEM SOLVING

A Listen and read about Kofi.

Kofi needs to make a trip to another city for a job interview. The airfare would be about $400 roundtrip. He wants to drive because he thinks it will be cheaper. Kofi is worried about his car, though. It broke down last week, and he had to pay a mechanic $200 to fix it. It's running all right now, but the car is more than 10 years old. He wants to be sure he won't have another breakdown on his trip. His car also needs new tires. New tires would cost about $500. Kofi has $800 in the bank.

B Work with your classmates. Answer the questions.

1. What is Kofi's problem? Kofi needs to make a trip for a job interview, but he's worried about his car. He can fly for $400 or buy new tires for $500.
2. What could he do? Think of 2 or 3 solutions to his problem.
3. Write a short letter to Kofi. Tell him what you think he should do.

UNIT **4**

FOCUS ON
• career planning resources
• writing a cover letter
• the past perfect
• job interviews
• making a career plan

Get the Job

LESSON **1** **Vocabulary**

1 Learn career-planning vocabulary

A **Talk about the questions with your class.**

1. Think about your future. What kind of work would you like to do?
2. What are some ways you can get more information about this kind of work?

B **Work with your classmates. Match the words with the picture.**

___1___	apply for financial aid	___6___	take an interest inventory
___4___	look at job listings	___3___	take a training class
___2___	see a career counselor	___5___	use the resource center

C **Listen and check. Then read the new words with a partner.**

D **Work with a partner. Write other career planning words you know. Check your words in a dictionary.**

✔ Identify and use career-planning vocabulary to discuss job-training opportunities

Unit 4 Lesson 1

Objectives	Grammar	Vocabulary	Correlations
On-level: Describe and talk about career planning and job training opportunities **Pre-level:** Identify and describe career planning and job training opportunities **Higher-level:** Talk and write about career planning and job training	*Should* and *would* (*She should go to the career planning center. I'd like to be a medical assistant.*)	Career planning and job training vocabulary For vocabulary support for pre-level students, see this **Oxford Picture Dictionary** unit: Work	**CASAS:** 0.1.2, 0.1.5, 0.2.1, 4.1.4, 4.4.2, 4.4.5, 4.8.1, 7.4.5 **LCPs:** 37.01, 39.01, 35.03, 49.10 **SCANS:** Decision making, Listening, Participates as member of a team, Seeing things in the mind's eye **EFF:** Observe critically, Plan, Reflect and evaluate, Speak so others can understand

Warm-up and Review

10–15 minutes (books closed)

Write *Good Jobs* on the board. Ask students to name what they would consider to be good jobs. Write them on the board.

Introduction

5 minutes

1. Ask for a show of hands. *How many people would like to have one of these jobs on the board? How many people know how to plan for getting the job they want?*

2. State the objective: *Today we're going to learn career planning and job training vocabulary.*

1 Learn career planning vocabulary

Presentation I

20–25 minutes

A Write *career planning* on the board, and elicit students' answers to questions 1 and 2. Write their ideas for question 2 on the board.

B 1. Direct students to look at the picture. Ask: *What is this place? What are the people doing?*

2. Group students and assign roles: leader, fact checker, recorder, and reporter. Explain that students work with their groups to match the words and pictures.

3. Check comprehension of the roles. Ask: *Who looks up the words in a dictionary?* [fact checker] *Who writes the numbers in the book?* [recorder] *Who tells the class your answers?* [reporter] *Who helps everyone and manages the group?* [leader]

4. Set a time limit (three minutes). As students work together, copy the wordlist onto the board.

5. Call "time." Have reporters take turns giving their answers. Write each group's answer on the board next to the word.

C 1. To prepare students for listening, say: *We're going to listen to a description of the things you can do at a career center.* Ask students to listen and check their answers.

2. Have students check the wordlist on the board and then write the correct numbers in their books.

3. Pair students. Set a time limit (three minutes). Monitor pair practice to identify pronunciation issues.

4. Call "time" and work with the pronunciation of any troublesome words or phrases.

5. Replay the audio and challenge students to listen for additional information about each of the career center's services. Call on volunteers to share what they heard.

D 1. Ask students to work with their partners from 1C to brainstorm a list of related words.

2. Elicit words from the class. Write them on the board. Ask students to copy them into their vocabulary notes for the unit.

Guided Practice

5–10 minutes

 1. Model the conversation with a volunteer. Model it again using other information from 1B.

2. Set a time limit (three minutes). Direct students to practice with a partner.

3. Ask volunteers to act out one of their conversations for the class.

2 Learn more career planning vocabulary

Presentation II

15–20 minutes

 1. Direct students to look at the flyer. Introduce the new topic: *Now we're going to read about some job training opportunities.*

2. Read the instructions aloud. Ask students to look at the boldfaced headings to answer the question. Call on volunteers for the answers. Say and have students repeat the phrases.

Guided Practice

10–15 minutes

B Ask students to work with a partner to complete the sentences. Ask volunteers to read the completed sentences aloud. Write the answers on the board.

> ### Multilevel Strategies
>
> For 2B, used mixed-level pairs.
>
> • **Pre-level** Ask these students to read the incomplete sentences aloud to their partners and write the completion.
>
> • **On- and Higher-level** Ask these students to supply the missing words.

Communicative Practice and Application

10–15 minutes

C Give students a minute to make notes of their answers to the questions. Call on individuals to share their ideas with the class.

 If you have access to the Internet in class, show students some of the resources available on a job training website. You can find links to job training in your area through your state government website.

Evaluation

10–15 minutes (books closed)

TEST YOURSELF

1. Direct students to work individually to write a list of words from the lesson. Assign a time limit (three minutes). Call "time" and direct students to work with a partner to combine their lists and put the words in alphabetical order.

2. Circulate and monitor students' progress.

3. Ask a volunteer pair to write its list on the board. Ask other students to add words to the list.

> ### Multilevel Strategies
>
> Target the *Test Yourself* to the level of your students.
>
> • **Higher-level** After these students have worked with a partner to alphabetize their lists, ask them to write three to five sentences defining words from the list.

To compress this lesson: Conduct 1B as a whole-class activity.

To extend this lesson: Look at want ads.
1. Put students in groups. Pass out want ads cut from the newspaper or printed off the Internet. Tell the groups to look for the five ads they think are the most interesting.
2. Ask a reporter from each group to present the group's ads to the class. Tell them to share any training or experience requirements that are mentioned in the ads.

And/Or have students complete **Workbook 4 page 23** and **Multilevel Activity Book 4 pages 48–49**.

E Work with a partner. Practice the conversation. Use the words in 1B.

A: Good morning. Can I help you?

B: Yes, please. Is this where I sign up to use the resource center?

A: Yes, it is. Have a seat, and someone will be right with you.

2 Learn more career-planning vocabulary

A Look at the flyer. What kinds of training opportunities are available?

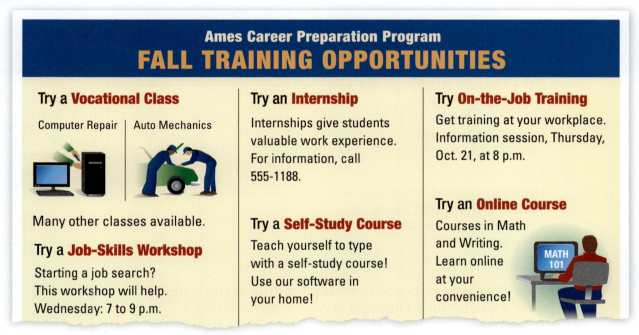

Ames Career Preparation Program
FALL TRAINING OPPORTUNITIES

Try a Vocational Class

Computer Repair | Auto Mechanics

Many other classes available.

Try a Job-Skills Workshop

Starting a job search?
This workshop will help.
Wednesday: 7 to 9 p.m.

Try an Internship

Internships give students valuable work experience. For information, call 555-1188.

Try a Self-Study Course

Teach yourself to type with a self-study course! Use our software in your home!

Try On-the-Job Training

Get training at your workplace. Information session, Thursday, Oct. 21, at 8 p.m.

Try an Online Course

Courses in Math and Writing. Learn online at your convenience!

MATH 101

B Work with a partner. Complete the sentences. Use the words in 2A.

1. Loc wants a promotion. He should ask his boss about ____on-the-job training____.
2. Brenda likes using the Internet. She should try an ____online course____.
3. Joe needs work experience. He should ask about an ____internship____.
4. Mai has always wanted to be a mechanic. She could take a ____vocational class____.
5. Tonio is starting to look for work. He should go to a ____job-skills workshop____.
6. Mira stays at home with her children. She could try a ____self-study course____.

C Talk about the questions with your class.

1. What would you like to do at a career center? Why?
2. Think of a job or career you would like to have. How could you prepare for it?

TEST YOURSELF ✔

Close your book. Work with a partner. Make a list of as many new words from the lesson as you can. Alphabetize your list. Then check your spelling in a dictionary.

1 Read a cover letter

A Look at the cover letter. Talk about the questions with your class.

1. What is a cover letter?
2. Who do people send a cover letter to?

B Listen and read the cover letter.

Mr. Luis Sanchez
2394 Geneva Avenue, #443
Bayside, FL 34748
(836) 555-3992
lsanchez@cobe.net
July 26, 2007

Ms. Lee Porter
Director, Human Resources
Vanit's Department Store, Inc.
1000 Oleander Drive
Bayside, FL 34748

Dear Ms. Porter:

This letter is in response to your job listing at the Ames Career Center for a customer service representative. I am enclosing my resume.

I have two years' experience as a cashier, and I've completed a training class in customer skills. My computer skills are excellent, and I am fluent in English and Spanish. I am reliable, organized, and hardworking.

I would like very much to meet with you. I have listed my contact information above. Thank you for considering me for this position.

Sincerely yours,
Luis Sanchez
Luis Sanchez

Writer's note

In a business letter, include your contact information and the job title and address of the person you are writing to.

C Check your understanding. Mark the sentences T (true), F (false), or NI (no information).

_T_ 1. Luis is applying for a job at Vanit's.

_F_ 2. Luis is writing to Ms. Porter because he met her at a job skills workshop.

_F_ 3. Luis doesn't know how to use a cash register.

_T_ 4. In his cover letter, Luis says why he is a good person for the job.

_NI_ 5. Luis has applied for several jobs.

✔ Write a cover letter to a potential employer

Unit 4 Lesson 2

Objectives	Grammar	Vocabulary	Correlations
On- and Higher-level: Analyze, write, and edit a cover letter **Pre-level:** Read a cover letter, and write about job experience	Contrast simple present, present perfect, and present continuous (*I am reliable. I have completed training. I'm enclosing my resume.*)	*Cover letter, contact information, enclose, fluent,* resume adjectives For vocabulary support for pre-level students, see these **Oxford Picture Dictionary** topics: Job Skills, Job Search	**CASAS:** 0.1.2, 0.1.5, 0.2.3, 4.1.2, 7.4.7 **LCPs:** 49.02, 49.13, 49.16, 49.17 **SCANS:** Knowing how to learn, Listening, Reading, Speaking, Writing **EFF:** Convey ideas in writing, Listen actively, Read with understanding, Reflect and evaluate, Speak so others can understand

Warm-up and Review

10–15 minutes (books closed)

Write *Positive Adjectives* on the board. Have the students brainstorm adjectives that they might use to describe themselves in a cover letter: *reliable, dependable, organized, hardworking, enthusiastic, motivated.* Call on volunteers to give you an example of how they demonstrate such behaviors.

Introduction

5 minutes

1. Say: *When you apply for a new job you need to sell yourself or make yourself look good to employers. One opportunity you have for this is in the cover letter.*

2. State the objective: *Today we'll learn how to write a cover letter.*

1 Read a cover letter

Presentation

20–25 minutes

A Read the questions aloud, and elicit the answers. Ask students if they have ever written a cover letter. Explain that while a resume provides important background information for the employer, a cover letter allows you to explain why you are the right person for the job.

B 1. Say: *Now we're going to read a cover letter.* Ask students to look at the letter and tell you who wrote it and to whom it's addressed.

2. Direct students to read the letter silently. Check comprehension. Ask: *What job is Luis applying for?* [customer-service representative] *What are his qualifications?* [cashier experience, job training, computer skills, bilingual]

3. Play the audio. Have students read along silently.

4. Draw students' attention to the *Writer's note.* Elicit Luis's contact information and the job title of the person he is writing to.

Guided Practice I

10 minutes

C Have students work independently to mark the statements T (true), F (false), or NI (no information). Write the answers on the board. Ask students to correct the false statements.

Multilevel Strategies

For 1C, seat pre-level students together.

• **Pre-level** While other students are working on 1C, ask these students questions about the reading. *Did Luis enclose his resume with the letter? Does he have sales experience? How are his computer skills?* Give students time to copy the answers to 1C from the board.

2 Write a cover letter

Guided Practice II
20–25 minutes

A 1. Direct students to look at the classified ads.

2. Give students time to read and think about the questions. Elicit their answers. Write other jobs they would like to apply for on the board.

B 1. Direct students to look back at the cover letter in 1B. Focus students' attention on the verb tenses in the letter. Ask them to look through the letter quickly and underline the one present-continuous and two present-perfect verbs. Elicit the reason for those tense choices and discuss any questions.

2. Read through the questions. Point out how Luis answered these questions in his letter.

3. Check comprehension of the exercise. Ask: *How many paragraphs do you need to write?* [three] *What information goes at the beginning of the letter?* [contact information, title and address of person you are writing to]

4. Have students work individually to write their letters.

Multilevel Strategies

Adapt 2B to the level of your students.

• **Pre-level** Tell these students to refer to the model in 1B for formatting their contact information and the addressee's information. Provide a skeleton letter to help them write the body.

This letter is in response to your job listing for a _____. I am enclosing my resume.
I have _____ experience as a _____.
I have training in _____. I am _____.
I would like to meet with you. Thank you for considering me for this position.
Sincerely yours,

_____

C 1. Lead students through the process of using the *Editing checklist.* Read the sentences aloud, and answer any questions. Then ask students to check their papers.

2. Allow students a few minutes to edit their writing as necessary.

Communicative Practice
10 minutes

D 1. Read the instructions aloud. Emphasize to students that they are responding to their partners' work, not correcting it.

2. Use the letter in 1B to model the exercise. *I think the sentence about his experience and training will help him get an interview. I'd like to ask the writer about what he learned in the customer-skills training.*

3. Direct students to exchange papers with a partner and follow the instructions.

4. Call on volunteers to share interesting things they read in their partners' letters.

Application and Evaluation
20 minutes

TEST YOURSELF

1. Review the instructions aloud. Assign a time limit (15 minutes), and have students work independently. Give students notice when they have five minutes left.

2. Before collecting students' work, remind them to use the *Editing checklist.* Collect and correct students' writing.

Multilevel Strategies

Adapt the *Test Yourself* to the level of your students.

• **Pre-level** Write questions for these students to answer. *What job would you like to have? What experience and/or training do you have that prepares you for the job? What skills do you have?*

To compress this lesson: Assign the *Test Yourself* for homework.

To extend this lesson: Have students practice "selling" themselves. Direct them to tell three partners about what makes them a good employee or a good student.

And/Or have students complete **Workbook 4 page 24** and **Multilevel Activity Book 4 page 50**.

2 Write a cover letter

A Look at the classified ad. Talk about the questions with your class.

1. Would you like to apply for one of these jobs? If so, which one? If not, why not?
2. Think of a company in your area that you would like to work for. What job would you like to apply for?

> **Help Wanted**
>
> Bayside Health. **Nursing Aide**. No exp. req.; good English a must. **Front Desk Clerk**. Exp. with the public req. **Computer Technician**. PT, exp. preferred. Send resume to Ms. Larai Ondo, Human Resources Director, 11475 Elm St., Bayside, FL 34747, or ondo@bayh.fl. No calls, please.

B Write a cover letter to Bayside Health or another company. Use the model in 1B and the questions below to help you.

To start: What is your contact information?
Who are you writing to? What is the person's title and address?
Paragraph 1: What job are you applying for? What are you sending?
Paragraph 2: What are your qualifications (your education and experience)?
Paragraph 3: What would you like to do? How can the employer contact you?
To end: Sign your letter.

> (your contact information)
> (person's name, title, and address)
> Dear...
> This letter...

C Use the checklist to edit your writing. Check (✔) the true sentences.

Editing checklist	
1. I included my contact information and the title and address of the person I am writing to.	
2. My letter explains why I am writing.	
3. I described my experience, skills, and personal characteristics.	
4. I signed my letter.	

D Exchange letters with a partner. Read and comment on your partner's work.

1. Point out one sentence that you think will help your partner get an interview.
2. Ask your partner a question about his or her qualifications.

TEST YOURSELF ✔

Write a new cover letter for another job from 2A.

1 Learn the past perfect

A Read the story about Luis. What did he do before and after his interview?

Before his interview, he read some information about the company and planned some questions to ask. After his interview, he wrote Ms. Porter a thank-you note.

On Thursday, Luis Sanchez got a phone call from Ms. Porter at Vanit's Department store. She <u>had read</u> Luis' resume, and she wanted to interview him at 3:00 that afternoon.

When Luis arrived for the interview, he <u>had already read</u> some information about the company, and he <u>had planned</u> some questions to ask. He <u>hadn't completed</u> an application. He did that while he was waiting.

When the interview was over, Luis felt that he'd <u>done</u> well. Later, he wrote Ms. Porter a thank-you note.

B Study the chart and the time line. Underline the 5 past perfect verbs in 1A.

THE PAST PERFECT

Affirmative and negative statements		
Subject	*had/had not* + past participle	
He	**had planned**	some questions before he arrived.
He	**hadn't completed**	an application before he arrived.

The Past Perfect

past   now

✕   ✕

Ms. Porter read   Ms. Porter called Luis.
Luis' resume.

Note

Use the past perfect to show that an event happened before another event in the past. The past perfect shows the earlier event.
     Ms. Porter **had read** Luis' resume before she called him.
     (First Ms. Porter read Luis' resume. Then she called him.)

C Complete the sentences with the past perfect form of the verbs in parentheses.

1. Ms. Porter called Luis after she <u>   had read   </u> his resume. (read)

2. On Tuesday, Luis was worried because Ms. Porter <u> hadn't called </u> him. (not call)

3. Luis <u> hadn't looked </u> at Vanit's website when Ms. Porter called him. (not look)

4. Luis <u> had prepared </u> some questions before he went to the interview. (prepare)

5. A career counselor <u> had given </u> Luis some advice before the interview. (give)

Unit 4 Lesson 3

Objectives	Grammar	Vocabulary	Correlations
On- and Higher-level: Use the past perfect to write about applying for jobs, and listen for information about life experience **Pre-level:** Identify the past perfect in sentences about applying for jobs and life experience, and use past participles	Past perfect (*He felt that he had done well.*)	Job search vocabulary For vocabulary support for pre-level students, see this **Oxford Picture Dictionary** topic: Job Search	**CASAS:** 0.1.2, 0.1.5, 0.2.1, 7.4.7 **LCPs:** 39.01, 49.01, 49.02, 49.16, 49.17, 50.02 **SCANS:** Interprets and communicates information, Listening, Reading, Speaking **EFF:** Convey ideas in writing, Cooperate with others, Listen actively, Read with understanding, Reflect and evaluate

Warm-up and Review

10–15 minutes (books closed)

Write these sentences on the board out of order: *She was called in for an interview. She wrote a cover letter. She got the job. She sent it to the company with her resume. Maria saw a job ad in the newspaper. She dressed carefully for the interview.* Ask volunteers to rewrite the sentences in the correct order. Leave the sentences on the board.

Introduction

5–10 minutes

1. Elicit the tense of the story on the board. Say: *We tell stories in the simple past when we are telling them in sequence. First Maria saw the ad; then she wrote the letter; then she sent it to the company. But sometimes we want to put two ideas together, so we use the verb tense to show the sequence of events.* Write on the board *Maria wrote a cover letter for a job she had seen in the paper.* Underline *had seen.* Say: *This tells us that she saw the ad before she wrote the letter. This tense is called the past perfect.*

2. State the objective: *Today we're going to use the past perfect to talk about applying for jobs.*

1 Learn the past perfect

Presentation I

20–25 minutes

A 1. Direct students to look at the picture. Ask: *What's he doing? How does he feel?*

2. Read the question. Ask students to read the story silently to find the answer. Call on volunteers for the answers.

B 1. Read the sentences in the chart. Elicit the form of the verb: *had* + past participle.

2. Direct students to underline the past-perfect verbs in the story in 1A. Go over the answers as a class.

3. Read the *Note* aloud. Discuss the meaning of each past-perfect verb in the story. Say: *Ms. Porter had read Luis's resume before what?* [before she called him about an interview] *Luis had found information about the company before what?* [before he arrived at the interview]

4. Read the chart through sentence by sentence. Then read it again, and have students repeat after you.

5. Assess students' understanding of the charts. Use the sentences from the warm-up to elicit more past-perfect verbs. *They called (Maria) in for an interview because she had _____. She felt good at the interview because she had _____.*

Guided Practice I

15–20 minutes

C Ask students to work individually to complete the sentences. Ask volunteers to write the answers on the board.

Guided Practice II

5–10 minutes

 Read each sentence aloud. Direct students to underline the past-perfect and the simple-past verb in each sentence. Ask students to choose *a* or *b*. Ask for a show of hands to see how many chose each option.

Multilevel Strategies

After 1D, provide more practice with the past perfect.

• **Pre-level** Provide these students with a series of sentences containing a simple-past and a past-perfect verb. Ask them to underline the verbs and label them as *1* or *2* to indicate which action happened first. 1. *By the time she got home, the manager had called her twice. 2. He applied for a job he had learned about at the career center. 3. She felt qualified for the job because she had worked at a restaurant. 4. He was ready for the questions because he had prepared. 5. She hadn't slept much the night before she went to the interview.* Go over the answers together.

• **On- and Higher-level** Provide these students with pictures of people or have them look through magazines. Tell them to write sentences about what was happening at the time of the picture and what they imagine had happened before. *She was sad because she hadn't done well on the interview. He looked tired because he had stayed up late the night before.*

2 Learn past perfect questions

Presentation II

20–25 minutes

 1. Introduce the new topic. *Now we're going to ask and answer questions in the past perfect.*

2. Read and have students repeat the questions and answers. Point out the simple-past verbs in the chart. Emphasize that the past perfect is used to talk about something that happened before another event in the past (the event in the simple past).

Multilevel Strategies

Use mixed-level pairs for 2B.

• **Pre-level** Ask these students to read the complete question or answer (the one without the blank) aloud to their partners.

• **On- and Higher-level** Ask these students to read the incomplete question or answer and to supply the completion.

Guided Practice I

10–15 minutes

 Ask students to work with a partner to complete the sentences. Have them read their questions and answers aloud with their partners. Call on volunteer pairs to read the questions and answers aloud. Write the answers on the board.

 After 2B, have students practice short answers in different tenses. Ask questions and call on different students to answer. *Do you have a job? Did you work last year? Have you ever gone on a job interview? Would you like to find a job? Had you ever studied past perfect before we began this lesson?*

D **Get the meaning. Work with your class. What happened first? Circle *a* or *b*.**

1. When I started the training class, I had already tried a self-study course.
   a. I started a training class.
   b. I tried a self-study course.

2. Unfortunately, we arrived after the counselor had left.
   a. The counselor left.
   b. We arrived.

3. After I sat down, I realized that I had forgotten to sign in.
   a. I sat down.
   b. I forgot to sign in.

2 Learn past perfect questions

A **Study the charts. What verb is used in the short answers?** had

PAST PERFECT QUESTIONS

Yes/No questions	Information questions
A: **Had** you **sent** a resume before you called? B: Yes, I **had**. OR No, I **hadn't**.	A: How many jobs **had** you **applied** for before you got this job? B: I had applied for two jobs before I got this job.
A: **Had** all the applicants **sent** resumes? B: Yes, they **had**. OR No, they **hadn't**.	A: Which classes **had** they **taken** before they started their internships? B: They had taken computer classes before they started their internships.

B **Look at the answers. Then complete the questions with the past perfect.**

1. A: What _had you looked at_ before you applied for the job?

   B: Before I applied for the job, I had looked at the company's website.

2. A: _Had Pietro finished_ the training class before he applied for the job?

   B: Yes, he had. Pietro finished the training class two weeks ago.

3. A: How many people _had they interviewed_ before you?

   B: I don't know how many people they had interviewed before me.

4. A: Why _had she gone_ to Vanit's before she applied

   for the job there?

   B: She had gone to Vanit's to shop before she applied for the job there.

5. A: _Had you worked_ in an office before you applied

   for the internship?

   B: No, I hadn't. I had worked in a restaurant, but not in an office.

3 Grammar listening

🎧 **Listen to Mopati talk about his life. Circle the correct words.**

1. Before Mopati came to the U.S., he had always lived in a (small town /(big city)).
2. Now he lives in a ((small town)/ big city).
3. Before Mopati came to the U.S., he had studied ((French)/ English).
4. Now he studies (French /(Spanish)).
5. Before Mopati came to the U.S., he had always wanted to be a (teacher /(businessman)).
6. Now he wants to be a ((teacher)/ businessman).

4 Practice the past perfect

A **Think about your answers to these questions.**

1. What are two things you'd never seen before you came to the U.S.?
2. What is one thing you'd never done before you came to the U.S.?
3. What's one word you'd never heard before you started this class?

B **Work with a partner. Ask and answer the questions.**

A: *What are two things you'd never done before you came to the U.S.?*
B: *I'd never…*

C **Talk about your ideas with the class.**

Before Franco came to the U.S., he had never…

TEST YOURSELF ✔

Close your book. Write 4 sentences about your partner's answers. Use the past perfect.

3 Grammar listening

Guided Practice II

10–15 minutes

1. Ask: *Had you studied English before you came to the U.S.?* Say: *Now we're going to listen to a man named Mopati talk about things he had done in his country before he came to the U.S.*

2. Play the audio. Direct students to read along silently without writing.

3. Replay the audio. Ask students to circle the correct words.

4. Go over the answers as a class.

4 Practice the past perfect

Communicative Practice and Application

20–25 minutes

A 1. Direct students to look at the photos. Ask: *What is he/she doing? What place is that? Have you ever been there?*

2. Direct students to read the questions silently and note their answers.

B 1. Put students in pairs. Read and have students repeat the questions in 4A.

2. Direct students to ask their partners the questions. Tell them to make notes of each other's answers. Model the exercise by asking a volunteer the first question. Have the class tell you how to write the answer in note form.

3. Check comprehension of the exercise. Ask: *Do both partners need to answer the questions?* [yes] *Do you need to write your partner's answers in complete sentences?* [no]

C Discuss the students' ideas as a class. Elicit several completions for this sentence: *Most students had never _____ before they came to the U.S.*

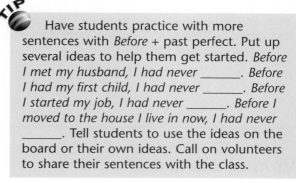

Have students practice with more sentences with *Before* + past perfect. Put up several ideas to help them get started. *Before I met my husband, I had never _____. Before I had my first child, I had never _____. Before I started my job, I had never _____. Before I moved to the house I live in now, I had never _____.* Tell students to use the ideas on the board or their own ideas. Call on volunteers to share their sentences with the class.

Evaluation

10–15 minutes (books closed)

TEST YOURSELF

Ask students to write the sentences independently. Collect and correct their writing.

Multilevel Strategies

Target the *Test Yourself* to the level of your students.

• **Pre-level** Provide skeleton sentences for these students to complete. *Before I came to the U.S., I had never seen _____. Before I started this class, I had never heard the word _____. Before I came to the U.S., I had never _____.*

• **Higher-level** Ask these students to write four sentences about their partners and four sentences about themselves.

To compress this lesson: Conduct 1C as a whole-class discussion.

To extend this lesson: Provide more practice with the past perfect.
1. Write the following questions on the board: *1. Why was he nervous at the interview? 2. Why did he get fired? 3. Why did she celebrate after the interview? 4. Why didn't he pass the class? 5. Why couldn't she answer the questions?*
2. Direct students to work with a partner to write answers to the questions using the past perfect and *because. He was nervous at the interview because he had arrived late.*

And/Or have students complete **Workbook 4 pages 25–26, Multilevel Activity Book 4 pages 51–52,** and the corresponding **Unit 4 Exercises** on the **Multilevel Grammar Exercises CD-ROM 4.**

Unit 4 Lesson 4

Objectives	Grammar	Vocabulary	Correlations
On-, Pre-, and Higher-level: Interview for a job, and listen for employment history	Simple past, past perfect, and present perfect (*He got the job. He hadn't worked before. He has learned a lot.*)	*applicant, file clerk, responsibilities* For vocabulary support for pre-level students, see these **Oxford Picture Dictionary** topics: Jobs and Occupations, Job Skills, Job Search	**CASAS:** 0.1.2, 0.1.5, 0.2.1, 4.1.5, 6.0.3, 6.0.4, 6.1.1, 6.6.6, 7.4.7, 7.5.6 **LCPs:** 39.01, 49.02, 49.09, 49.16, 49.17, 51.05 **SCANS:** Arithmetic/Mathematics, Seeing things in the mind's eye **EFF:** Listen actively, Read with understanding, Use math to solve problems and communicate

Warm-up and Review

10–15 minutes (books closed)

Write *Job Interview* on the board. Ask students what advice they would give to someone going on a job interview. Write their ideas on the board in categories: *Dress, Behavior, Preparation.*

Introduction

5 minutes

1. Say: *All of these things are important, but of course the most difficult part is what you actually say to the interviewer. What questions will he or she ask, and how will you answer?*

2. State the objective: *Today we'll learn how to respond to job-interview questions.*

1 Learn to respond to interview questions

Presentation I

15–20 minutes

 1. Direct students to look at the pictures. Ask students to predict which woman will have a better job interview.

2. Play the audio. Give students a minute to read and think about the questions. Go over the answers as a class.

Guided Practice

20–25 minutes

 1. Read the instructions aloud. Play the audio. Ask students to read along silently and listen for the answer to the question. Elicit the answer.

2. Ask students to read the conversation with a partner. Circulate and monitor pronunciation. Model and have students repeat difficult words or phrases.

3. Say and have students repeat the expressions in the *In other words* box. Elicit the placement of the expressions in the conversation. Ask volunteers to read the conversation using expressions from the box.

Communicative Practice and Application

15–20 minutes

 1. Ask students to read the instructions silently. Check comprehension of the exercise by eliciting examples of what the applicant and interviewer might say.

2. Set a time limit (five minutes). Ask students to act out the role-play in both roles. Ask volunteer pairs to act out their conversations for the class. Tell students who are listening to note which expressions the applicants use to check understanding.

Multilevel Strategies

For 1C, adapt the role-play to the level of your students.

• **Pre-level** Provide these students with the beginning of the conversation. *Interviewer: Have you had much experience? Applicant: I've worked as an office assistant for six months. Before that _____.*

1 Learn to respond to interview questions

A Look at the pictures. Listen to the conversations. Then answer the questions below with your classmates.

Ms. Jones

Ms. Adams

1. Whose interview is longer—Ms. Jones' or Ms. Adams'? Why?
2. In your opinion, which applicant does the interviewer think is better? Why?

B Listen and read. Do you think Luis will get the job?

Ms. Porter: Tell me about yourself, Mr. Sanchez. Have you had much experience?

Luis: Do you mean with customers?

Ms. Porter: Yes, and other work experience, too.

Luis: Well, I've been a cashier in a convenience store for two years. Before that, I worked as a stock clerk.

Ms. Porter: How about training?

Luis: Well, I took a self-study course in customer skills last month. Before that, I'd already learned a lot about customer service on the job.

Ms. Porter: Very good. You have just the skills we need.

> **In other words...**
>
> **Checking understanding**
> Do you mean...?
> You mean...?
> Is that...?

C Role-play an interview with a partner. Use the example in 1B to make a new conversation.

Partner A: You're the interviewer. Ask about the applicant's experience and training. Give the applicant positive feedback.

Partner B: You are interviewing for a job as an office manager. Listen to the interviewer's first question and check your understanding. Talk about your work experience. You've been an office assistant for six months; before that you were a file clerk for a construction company. You took a computer-skills class this year and an online course in office management last year.

☑ Answer questions appropriately at a job interview; clarify meaning

2 Compare the simple past, the past perfect, and the present perfect

A Study the chart. Mark the statements below T (true) or F (false).

Simple past	Sam **got** his first job in a hospital in 1998. He **took** English classes from 1999 to 2002.
Past perfect	Sam **had** already **taken** a training class when he got the job, but he **hadn't worked** in a hospital before.
Present perfect	Sam **has worked** at the hospital since 1998. He **has learned** a lot of English at his job.

  _F_ 1. Sam hasn't learned to speak English yet.

  _T_ 2. Sam had already gotten his job before he started English classes.

  _F_ 3. Sam got the job and then took a training class.

  _T_ 4. Sam is still a hospital worker.

B Work with a partner. Circle the correct words.

I deliver letters and packages by bicycle. (**I've had** / I had) this job for three months, and I
(1)
like it a lot. (**I'd worked** / I've worked) as a delivery driver before (I've gotten / **I got**)
(2)   (3)
this job, but (**I didn't like** / I haven't liked) driving all day. On my bicycle,
(4)
(**I've learned** / I learned) a lot more about the city. I also get a lot more exercise—
(5)
(**I've lost** / I lost) ten pounds already!
(6)

C Work with a partner. Ask and answer the questions.

1. Are you working now? If so, how long have you worked at your present job?
2. Had you worked before you got this job? If so, what did you like about that job?

3 Practice your pronunciation

A Listen. Notice how speaker B uses rising intonation to check understanding.

1. A: Tell me about your experience.   2. A: What were your responsibilities?
   B: Do you mean in construction? ↗   B: You mean at my last job? ↗

B Practice the conversations with a partner. Use rising intonation to check
understanding. Then listen and check.

1. A: Tell me about your last job.   3. A: Have you had any training?
   B: My last job in an office?   B: Computer training?

2. A: What experience have you had?   4. A: Do you have any questions?
   B: Experience in the U.S.?   B: Questions about the job?

2 Compare the simple past, the past perfect, and the present perfect

Presentation II

10–15 minutes

 1. Introduce the new topic. *Now we're going to contrast the simple past, the past perfect, and the present perfect. We'll use all of these tenses to talk about work.*

2. Read the sentences in the chart aloud. Direct students to work individually to mark the sentences T (true) or F (false). Go over the answers as a class.

Guided Practice

15–20 minutes

 Direct students to work with a partner to circle the correct words. Call on volunteers to read the completed sentences aloud.

Multilevel Strategies

Seat same-level students together for 2B.

• **Pre-level** Work with these students as a group. Read each sentence aloud using the correct tense. Direct students to circle the words they hear. Ask questions about the meaning of the sentence. For the first sentence, say: *I've had this job for three months. Am I still working at the job?*

• **On- and Higher-level** Direct these students to complete the paragraph with their partners. Put an additional exercise on the board for them to complete while you are working with the pre-level students. *I (be) _____ in this English class for _____. Before I (begin) _____ this class, I (study) _____ in _____.* Challenge students to add sentences to create a paragraph about their experience with studying English. Ask two volunteers to read their paragraphs to the class.

Communicative Practice and Application

10–15 minutes

 1. Model the questions and answers with a volunteer.

2. Set a time limit (five minutes). Have students ask the questions of several partners.

3 Practice your pronunciation

Pronunciation Extension

10–15 minutes

 1. Write *A: Tell me about your first English class. B: My first English class* on the board. Direct a volunteer to say sentence A. Reply, saying sentence B with falling intonation, as if you were reading a book title. Have a different volunteer say sentence A. Respond with rising intonation, to indicate a check of understanding. Ask students which version was a question. Write the question mark at the end of the sentence and repeat the rising intonation. Say: *Now we're going to focus on using rising intonation to check understanding.*

2. Play the audio. Direct students to listen for the rising intonation.

3. Replay the audio and ask students to repeat sentence B.

 1. Direct students to practice the conversations with a partner. Monitor and provide feedback on rising intonation.

2. Replay the audio and ask students to listen for the rising intonation.

 Have students practice producing their own comprehension checks. Write questions on the board. *1. Where did you work before you came here? 2. Where did you study before? 3. What will you do when you finish school? 4. Have you studied English for very long? 5. Do you study every day?* Tell students to take turns asking these questions with a partner and responding with a check for understanding.

4 Focus on Listening

Listening Extension

20–25 minutes

A Read the questions aloud, and elicit answers from volunteers. Encourage students to respond to each other's ideas. After one student speaks, ask other students if their ideas about resumes are similar to or different from their classmates'.

B 1. Direct students to look at Hanna's resume. Ask: *What information does she need to include on this resume?*

2. Play the audio and direct students to answer the questions. Call on volunteers for the answers.

C 1. Direct students to read the sentences before listening.

2. Replay the audio and have students work individually to circle the correct words. Go over the answers as a class. Write them on the board.

> ### Multilevel Strategies
>
> Adapt 1C to the level of your students.
>
> • **Pre-level** While other students are completing 1C, write questions on the board for these students to answer. *Does Hanna's friend help her with her resume? Should Hanna include her ESL class? When did she finish her ESL class? Where did she graduate from high school?* Call on volunteers for the answers. Allow these students to copy the answers to 1C from the board.

5 Real-life math

Math Extension

5–10 minutes

1. Direct students to look at the resume and work individually to answer the questions.

2. Call on a volunteer to explain how he or she worked out the problems.

Evaluation

10–15 minutes

TEST YOURSELF

1. Model the role-play with a volunteer. Then switch roles.

2. Pair students. Check comprehension of the exercise by eliciting things the interviewer and the applicant might say.

3. Set a time limit (five minutes), and have the partners act out the role-play in both roles.

4. Circulate and monitor. Encourage pantomime and improvisation.

5. Provide feedback.

> ### Multilevel Strategies
>
> Target the *Test Yourself* to the level of your students.
>
> • **Pre-level** Ask these students to use this skeleton conversation: *Employer: Have you had much experience? Applicant: Yes. I've worked _____. E: How about training? A: Yes, I _____. E: Very good!*

To compress this lesson: Conduct *Real-life math* as a whole-class activity.

To extend this lesson: Have students write an "imaginary" resume.
1. Put students in mixed-level groups. Tell them to imagine that you are going to hire an aide for your beginning ESL class. They need to write a resume for someone who would make a good candidate for the job.
2. Write *Employment History*, *Education*, and *Other* on the board. Tell them to include three jobs under *Employment History*, two pieces of information under *Education*, and at least one sentence under *Other* explaining why their candidate would be good for the job.
3. Have each group write its candidate's resume on a large sheet of paper. Post the papers in the front of the room, and have the class vote on who should get the job.

And/Or have students complete **Workbook 4 page 27** and **Multilevel Activity Book 4 page 53**.

4 Focus on listening

A **Talk about the questions with your class.**

1. What is a resume for? What information is usually on a resume?

2. Have you ever written a resume? If so, when did you write it?

B **Listen to the conversation. Answer the questions.**

1. Is Hanna taking a training course now? Yes, she is.

2. Has Hanna typed her resume yet? No, she hasn't.

C **Listen again. Circle the correct words.**

1. Hanna (has /(hasn't)) finished her training class yet.

2. For the training class, Liz tells Hanna to write the month she started the class to (now /(present)).

3. For her English class, Hanna should write the name of the school, the place, the name of the (teacher /(class)), and the year she studied there.

4. Hanna finished high school in ((her country)/ the U.S.)

HANNA LEE
4482 THIRD STREET
AUSTIN TX 78701
(512) 555-1435
EDUCATION

5 Real-life math

A **Read part of Hanna's resume and answer the questions.**

1. How long had Hanna been a cashier before she became a home health-care aide?

   1 year and 7 months

2. How long did she work as a file clerk?

   3 years and 8 months

B **Explain your answers to your classmates.**

Employment history	
6/1/05 – present	Home health-care aide, Sunnyside Associates, Austin
11/1/03 – 5/31/05	Cashier, Tannelo Department Stores, Austin
9/1/99 – 4/28/03	File Clerk, Central Market Supplies, Austin

TEST YOURSELF ✔

Role-play a job interview. Decide on the job together. Partner A: You're the applicant. Answer the interviewer's questions. Partner B: You're the employer. Ask questions to find out your partner's qualifications for the job. Then change roles.

1 Get ready to read

A What do you think is the best way to find a good job?

B Read the definitions. Which word is something a student wants to receive?   scholarship

field: (noun) profession; area or subject of study or work
scholarship: (noun) money from the government or other group to help pay for school
variety: (noun) a number of different kinds of things

C Look at the title and the headings in the article in 2A. What do you think the article is about?

2 Read and respond

A Read the article. What are the three steps to finding a career?

Make a career plan.
Improve your skills.
Find the right job.

Career Planning: $teps to $uccess

Are you tired of the same old job, day after day? Are you ready for a career? Here are the steps to take.

1. Make a career plan.
➡ Make a list of your skills. Include your work skills (using a cash register, repairing cars), your life skills (using a computer, taking care of children, speaking different languages), and your "people skills" (working with others, communicating ideas).
➡ Make a list of interesting jobs or careers. If you can, take an interest inventory or a skills inventory to help you decide which career seems right for you. Find out which fields are expected to grow over the next ten years.

2. Improve your skills.
➡ After you've identified a career,[1] find out what education or training you need.

[1] identify a career: find or choose a career

Some careers, especially in medical or technical fields, require special training. A career counselor or a career website can help you find opportunities for training.
➡ Training can be expensive. Financial aid can help you pay. Financial aid options include scholarships, loans, and work-study programs.

3. Find the right job.
➡ Use a variety of job-search resources. Look for possible employers in the newspaper, on the Internet, or at a career center. Networking, or just talking to people, can also help.
➡ Be organized in your job search. Make notes every time you contact a company. Write down the names and job titles of people you talk to.
➡ Be patient. Finding the right job can take time, but it's worth it. Good luck!

Source: *www.acinet.org*

Unit 4 Lesson 5

Objectives	Grammar	Vocabulary	Correlations
On-, Pre-, and Higher-level: Read about and discuss career planning	Verbs and nouns (*He employs three people. He is an employer.*)	*Field, scholarship, variety* For vocabulary support for pre-level students, see these **Oxford Picture Dictionary** topics: Schools and Subjects, Jobs and Occupations, Job Skills, Job Search	**CASAS:** 0.1.2, 0.1.5, 2.5.6, 4.1.9, 7.4.4, 7.4.7 **LCPs:** 35.04, 38.01, 49.04, 49.09, 49.16, 49.17 **SCANS:** Interprets and communicates information, Knowing how to learn, Listening, Speaking **EFF:** Learn through research, Read with understanding, Take responsibility for learning

Warm-up and Review

10–15 minutes (books closed)

Write *Skills* on the board, and elicit examples. List the students' ideas on the board. Encourage them to think of interpersonal skills as well as work skills.

Introduction

5 minutes

1. Say: *Everybody has skills, whether they have had job experience or not. Some skills come from job training or education, but some you learn in your life outside of work. Knowing what skills you have is the first step in planning a career.*

2. State the objective: *Today we're going to read and write about career planning.*

1 Get ready to read

Presentation

15–20 minutes

A Read the question aloud. Elicit students' ideas.

B Read the words and definitions. Elicit sample sentences from students using the words. Write the sentences on the board.

Pre-Reading

C 1. Direct students to look at the title and the headings. Elicit answers to the question.

2. Ask students to look over the article quickly and identify the three steps.

2 Read and respond

Guided Practice I

25–30 minutes

A 1. Ask students to read the article silently.

2. After students finish reading, direct them to underline unfamiliar words they would like to know. Elicit the words and encourage other students to provide definitions or examples.

3. Check comprehension. Ask: *What are the three kinds of skills?* [work, life, people] *How can you improve your skills?* [education, training] *What are some places to look for a job?* [newspaper, Internet, career center]

Multilevel Strategies

Adapt 2A to the level of your students.

• **Pre-level** Provide these students with a summary of the reading. *Here are steps to planning for a career: 1. Make a career plan. List your skills. List interesting jobs. 2. Improve your skills. Get training for the job you want. Look for financial aid to help you pay for training. 3. Find the right job. Look for work in the newspaper, on the Internet and at career centers. Talk to people about the job you want.*

Direct these students to read the summary while other students are reading 2A.

Guided Practice II

15–20 minutes

B 1. Play the audio. Have students read along silently.

2. Elicit and discuss any additional questions about the reading.

C Direct students to work individually to circle the correct words. Ask volunteers to read the completed sentences aloud. Write the answers on the board.

Multilevel Strategies

For 2C, work with pre-level students.

• **Pre-level** Ask these students questions about their summary while other students are completing 2C. What's the first step? How can you improve your skills? How can you pay for training? Where can you look for work? Give students time to copy the answers to 2C from the board.

D 1. Read the information in the chart aloud. Elicit and discuss any questions the students have about the *–er* and *–ee* suffix. Say the words and have students repeat them.

2. Direct students to work individually to write the correct words to complete each sentence. Write the answers on the board.

Multilevel Strategies

For 2D, seat pre-level students together.

• **Pre-level** Direct these students to copy the words from the chart into their notebooks with a definition. Allow them to look in their dictionaries if necessary.

3 Talk it over

Communicative Practice

15–20 minutes

1. Read the questions aloud. Set a time limit (three minutes). Have students work independently to think about the questions and write their answers in note form.

2. Call on individuals to share their answers with the class. Ask students to share what they think was the most important piece of advice they heard today. Write those ideas on the board.

Application

5–10 minutes

BRING IT TO LIFE

Talk to students about career-interest inventories and skills surveys. Explain that interest inventories will ask about what kinds of activities you like to do and skill surveys will ask about what you know how to do.

To compress this lesson: Conduct 2D as a whole-class activity.

To extend this lesson: Teach action verbs.
1. Tell students that career counselors often recommend that people use action verbs in their resumes and cover letters. Write these words on the board: *design, develop, create, build, maintain, prepare, supply, transport.*
2. As a class, brainstorm sentences using these verbs that might appear in a cover letter or resume. Encourage students to use their own experience.

And/Or have students complete **Workbook 4 page 28** and the **Multilevel Activity Book 4 pages 54–55**.

B Listen and read the article again.

C Scan the article. Circle the correct words.

1. Start a career plan by making a list of ((your skills and interests) / job resources).
2. The article says that taking care of children is a ((life skill) / people skill).
3. Choose a field that will probably (pay well / (grow)) over the next ten years.
4. Work-study programs are one example of (skills / (financial aid)).
5. When you network, you (take an interest inventory / (talk to people)).
6. The article says it's important to find (a job quickly / (the right job)).

D Study the chart. Complete the sentences with the correct words.

> **Word Study: Suffixes -er and -ee**
>
> Add *-er* to the end of some verbs to show the person who performs an action.
> Add *-ee* to the end of some verbs to show the person who receives the result of the action.
> An **employer** employs an **employee**.
>
> | Verb | Nouns | |
> | --- | --- | --- |
> | employ | employer | employee |
> | train | trainer | trainee |
> | pay | payer | payee |

1. Ms. Adams has been an ___employee___ here for several years. Her _____employer_____ thinks that she is an excellent worker.
2. Mr. Jonson is a computer _____trainer_____. He has 15 _____trainees_____ in his class right now.
3. The person who receives a check is the _____payee_____. The person who writes it is the _____payer_____.

3 Talk it over

Think about the questions. Talk about your ideas with the class.

1. What work skills do you have? What other skills do you have?
2. Think about people you know. How did they get their jobs?

> **BRING IT TO LIFE**
> Find a skills inventory or career-interest inventory at the library, at a career center, or on the Internet. Complete the inventory. What careers does it tell you to look at? Do you agree? Talk about your ideas with your classmates.

1 Grammar

A Read the situations. Write new sentences with the past perfect and *before*.

1. In May 2005, Yuri had three interviews at Calto, Inc. In July, the company offered him a job.

   Yuri had had three interviews at Calto, Inc. before the company offered him a job.

2. At 4 p.m., the interviewer called with good news. At 5 p.m., Leila got home.

   The interviewer had called with good news before Leila got home.

3. On Tuesday, Rico took a skills inventory. On Wednesday, the career counselor met with him.

   Rico had taken a skills inventory before the career counselor met with him.

4. In the morning, Yolanda went to the company's website. In the afternoon, she wrote her cover letter.

   Yolanda had gone to the company's website before she wrote her cover letter.

B Read the applicant's answers. Write the career counselor's questions. Use the past perfect.

1. **A:** _How long had you worked in the factory before you left for the U.S.?_

   B: I had worked in the factory for two years before I left for the U.S.

2. **A:** _Had you gone to a career center before you called me?_

   B: Yes, I had. I had gone to a career center before I called you.

3. **A:** _Had you taken a skills inventory before you came here?_

   B: No, I hadn't taken a skills inventory before I came here.

4. **A:** _How many times had you been here before you made this appointment?_

   B: I'd been here five times before I made this appointment.

C Complete the sentences. Use the past perfect or the present perfect of the verbs in parentheses.

1. Mahmoud _____had_____ already _____accepted_____ another job when Ms. Simms called him. (accept)

2. Alice _has learned_ a lot about working with people in her present job. (learn)

3. I _have taken_ two online courses since I got my GED. (take)

4. Donata _had worked_ as a translator before she came to this country. (work)

5. Irene _had_ never _thought_ about a career in sales before she got her present job as a salesperson. (think)

Unit 4 Review and expand

Objectives	Grammar	Vocabulary	Correlations
On-, Pre-, and Higher-level: Expand upon and review unit grammar and life skills	Past perfect (*He had already accepted another job when she called him.*)	Career-preparation vocabulary For vocabulary support for pre-level students, see this **Oxford Picture Dictionary** unit: Work	**CASAS:** 0.1.2, 0.1.5, 0.2.1, 4.8.1, 7.2.4, 7.3.1, 7.3.2, 7.3.4 **LCPs:** 35.03, 39.01, 49.01, 49.02, 49.13 **SCANS:** Acquires and evaluates information, Creative thinking, Listening, Reading, Speaking **EFF:** Convey ideas in writing, Cooperate with others, Solve problems and make decisions

Warm-up and Review

10–15 minutes (books closed)

1. Review the *Bring It to Life* assignment from Lesson 5.

2. Have students who did the exercise share their career inventory and results with the class. Ask them to read several of the questions aloud. Elicit responses from other students.

Introduction and Presentation

5 minutes

1. Write these sentences on the board: *Mei applied for three jobs. She finally got an interview.* Ask students: *What happened first?* Underline *applied* and connect the two sentences with *when.* Say: *How can I make it clear that Mei applied for the jobs first and then she got the interview?* [change *applied* to *had applied*.]

2. State the objective: *Today we're going to review the present perfect in order to talk about career preparation*

1 Grammar

Guided Practice

40–45 minutes

A 1. Read number 1 aloud. Elicit the changes from the simple past to the past perfect.

2. Read the second sentence aloud, and elicit a new version using the past perfect and *before.* Write it on the board.

3. Direct students to work individually to complete numbers 3 and 4. Ask volunteers to write the new sentences on the board.

B 1. Read the question and the answer in number 1 aloud. Point out the connection between *for two years* and *how long.*

2. Read the answer in number 2 aloud. Elicit the question and write it on the board.

3. Direct students to work individually to complete numbers 3 and 4. Ask volunteers to write the questions on the board.

C 1. Write two sentences about yourself on the board. *1. When I came to this school I _____ as a secretary. 2. I _____ at this school for ten years.* Say: *Look at sentence number 1. Is this sentence about the past or the present? How do you know? Did I work as a secretary at the same time I came to this school or before? Do I use the past perfect or the present perfect?* Write *had worked* in the blank. Say: *Look at sentence 2. Do I still work at this school? Should I use present perfect or past perfect?* Write *have worked* in the blank.

2. Have students work individually to complete the sentences. Ask volunteers to write the answers on the board.

2 Group work

Communicative Practice

20–35 minutes

 1. Direct students, in groups of three to four, to focus on the picture. Ask: *Who is the interviewer? Who is the interviewee?*

2. Assign roles: leader, recorder, and reporters. Explain that students work with their groups to write the conversation.

3. Check comprehension of the roles. *Who writes the conversation?* [recorder] *Who will read the conversation to the class?* [reporters] *Who helps everyone and manages the group?* [leader] *Who creates the conversation?* [everyone]

4. Set a time limit (five minutes) to complete the exercise. Circulate and answer any questions.

5. Have reporters from each group read the group's conversation to the class.

> ### Multilevel Strategies
>
> For 2A, use mixed-level groups.
> - **Pre-level** Assign these students the role of reporter.
> - **On-level** Assign these students the role of recorder.
> - **Higher-level** Assign these students the role of leader.

B 1. Have students walk around the room to conduct these interviews. To get students moving, tell them to interview three new people not in their groups for 2A. Set a time limit (five minutes) to complete the exercise.

2. Tell students to make a note of their classmates' answers but not to worry about writing complete sentences.

> ### Multilevel Strategies
>
> Adapt the mixer in 2B to the level of your students.
> - **Pre-level** Allow these students to ask and answer the questions without writing.
> - **Higher-level** Have these students ask two additional questions and write all answers.

C Call on individuals to report what they learned about their classmates. Encourage students to make generalizations. *Four out of four students had never made a list of their skills before we talked about career planning.*

PROBLEM SOLVING

15–25 minutes

 1. Ask: *Would you like to find a job? If you have a job, would you like a different job from the one you have now?* Tell students they will read a story about a woman who wants a new job. Direct students to read Jin's story silently.

2. Ask: *Where does she work? How long has she worked there? What are her skills? What kind of job would she like? Does she have skills and training for accounting?*

3. Play the audio and have students read along silently.

B 1. Elicit answers to question 1. Have volunteers write answers to question 2 on the board until all of the class ideas have been put up.

2. Put students into groups of three or four, and have them come to a consensus about the best solution for Jin's problem.

3. Pair students. Have them write a short letter giving advice to Jin. Call on volunteers to read their letters to the class.

Evaluation

30–35 minutes

To test students' understanding of the unit grammar and life skills, have them take the Unit 4 Test on the *Step Forward Test Generator CD-ROM* with *ExamView® Assessment Suite.*

> ### Learning Log
>
> To help students record and discuss their progress, use the *Learning Log* on page T–201.

To extend this review: Have students complete **Workbook 4 page 29, Multilevel Activity Book 4 page 56,** and the **Unit 4 Exercises** on the **Multilevel Grammar Exercises CD-ROM 4.**

2 Group work

A Work with 2–3 classmates. Write a 6–8 line conversation between the people in the picture. Share your conversation with the class.

A: *Tell me something about your experience.*
B: *Well,...*

B Interview 3 classmates. Write their answers.

1. Before you came to the U.S., what kind of career training had you had?
2. Before we talked about career planning in this class, had you ever made a list of your skills? Why or why not?
3. In your opinion, what is the most important thing people should do at a job interview?

C Talk about the answers with your class.

PROBLEM SOLVING

A Listen and read about Jin.

Jin works in her family's restaurant. She's worked there for three years, and she's very good at her job. She has learned to cook, wait on customers, use the cash register, and keep track of the restaurant's accounts. Jin likes helping her family, but she is thinking about her future. Before her family decided to come to the U.S., she had studied accounting at a technical school. Jin would like to work in the accounting field, but she doesn't know how to look for a job. She's never written a resume or gone on a job interview.

B Work with your classmates. Answer the questions.

1. What is Jin's problem? *Jin would like to work in the accounting field, but she doesn't know how to look for a job.*
2. What do you think Jin should do? Think of 2 or 3 solutions to her problem.
3. Write a short letter to Jin. Tell her what you think she should do.

Safe and Sound

FOCUS ON
- dangers, warnings, safety precautions
- preparing for an emergency
- modals of advice and warning
- giving warnings
- injuries on the job and at home

LESSON 1 Vocabulary

1 Learn vocabulary for safety hazards and warnings

A Talk about the questions with your class.

1. Where do you see safety or warning signs?
2. What safety or warning signs have you seen at or near your school?

B Work with your classmates. Match the words with the picture.

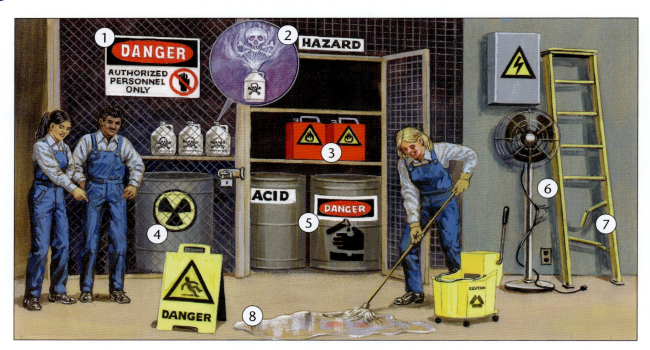

___7___	broken ladder	___6___	frayed cord	___1___	restricted area
___5___	corrosive chemicals	___2___	poisonous fumes	___8___	slippery floor
___3___	flammable liquids	___4___	radioactive materials		

C Listen and check. Then read the new words with a partner.

D Work with a partner. Write other words you know for safety hazards and warnings. Check your words in a dictionary.

☑ Identify and use safety hazard and warning vocabulary

Unit 5 Lesson 1

Objectives	Grammar	Vocabulary	Correlations
On-level: Describe and talk about safety hazards, warnings, and precautions **Pre-level:** Identify safety hazards, warnings, and precautions **Higher-level:** Talk and write about safety hazards, warnings, and precautions	Imperative (*Be alert.*)	Safety hazard, warning, and precaution vocabulary For vocabulary support for pre-level students, see this **Oxford Picture Dictionary** topic: Job Safety	**CASAS:** 0.1.2, 0.1.5, 3.4.1, 3.4.2, 4.3.1, 4.8.1, 7.4.5 **LCPs:** 36.03, 44.01, 49.10, 49.16 **SCANS:** Acquires and evaluates information, Participates as member of a team, Reading **EFF:** Listen actively, Observe critically, Reflect and evaluate, Speak so others can understand

Warm-up and Review

10–15 minutes (books closed)

Write *At Home* and *At Work* on the board. Ask students to name things that can cause accidents or injuries in each place. Write their ideas in the correct column.

Introduction

5 minutes

1. Say: *Anything that can cause an injury or an accident is a safety hazard.*

2. State the objective: *Today we're going to learn words for safety hazards and warnings, and we'll talk about safety procedures.*

1 Learn vocabulary for safety hazards and warnings

Presentation I

20–25 minutes

A Write *Safety* on the board, and elicit students' answers to questions 1 and 2. Point out any safety or warning signs that you have in your classroom—for example, warnings on the fire extinguisher.

B 1. Direct students to look at the picture. Ask: *Have you ever worked in a place like this?*

2. Group students and assign roles: leader, fact checker, recorder, and reporter. Explain that students work with their groups to match the words and pictures.

3. Check comprehension of the roles. Ask: *Who looks up the words in a dictionary?* [fact checker] *Who writes the numbers in the book?* [recorder] *Who tells the class your answers?* [reporter] *Who helps everyone and manages the group?* [leader]

4. Set a time limit (three minutes). As students work together, copy the wordlist onto the board.

5. Call "time." Have reporters take turns giving their answers. Write each group's answer on the board next to the word.

C 1. To prepare students for listening, say: *Now you're going to hear an employee talk about safety hazards.* Ask students to listen and check their answers.

2. Have students check the wordlist on the board and then write the correct numbers in their books.

3. Pair students. Set a time limit (three minutes). Monitor pair practice to identify pronunciation issues.

4. Call "time" and work with the pronunciation of any troublesome words or phrases.

5. Replay the audio and ask students to listen for additional information about each item.

D 1. Ask students to work with their partners from 1C to brainstorm a list of related words.

2. Elicit words from the class. Write them on the board. Ask students to copy them into their vocabulary notes for the unit.

Guided Practice

5–10 minutes

 1. Model the conversations with a volunteer. Model them again using other information from 1B.

2. Set a time limit (three minutes). Direct students to practice with a partner. Ask volunteers to act out one of their conversations for the class.

2 Learn vocabulary for safety precautions

Presentation II

15–20 minutes

 1. Direct students to look at the poster. Introduce the new topic: *Now we're going to talk about things you can do to prevent accidents, or safety procedures.*

2. Read the instructions aloud, and direct students to read the poster silently. Elicit their answers to the question. Elicit questions about vocabulary. Check comprehension. Ask: *Which safety rule am I following if I don't use the back parking lot at night?*

Guided Practice

10–15 minutes

 Have students work individually to match the safety rule with the example. Go over the answers as a class.

Communicative Practice and Application

10–15 minutes

 1. Give students a minute to make notes of their answers to the questions. Call on individuals to share their ideas with the class.

2. Make a two-column chart with the headings *Hazard* and *Prevention*. As students mention hazards, write them in the chart, and elicit the safety precautions associated with them.

> **TIP**
>
> After 2C, have your students look at real warning labels. You can find warning labels on cleaning products, toys, and electronic equipment; in appliance manuals; and on the Internet (type *warning label* into an image search engine). Write short warning-label sentences on the board, or make a transparency or photocopies of a longer label. Discuss the meaning of the sentences. Go over unknown vocabulary with students.

Evaluation

10–15 minutes (books closed)

TEST YOURSELF

1. Pair students. Direct Partner B to close the book and listen to Partner A dictate four phrases from 1B. Ask students to switch roles when they finish so Partner B can dictate the other four phrases.

2. Direct both partners to open their books and check their spelling when they finish.

3. Circulate and monitor student work.

> ### Multilevel Strategies
>
> Target the *Test Yourself* to the level of your students.
>
> • **Pre-level** Provide these students with a list to dictate from. *A: ladder, chemical, liquid, electrical cord, fumes; B: be alert, avoid, report, prevent, accident*
>
> • **Higher-level** Direct these students to write a sentence defining each of the phrases their partner dictates.

To compress this lesson: Conduct 1B as a whole-class activity.

To extend this lesson: Write safety advice. Put students in groups. Provide each group with a common item that could cause a safety problem. Cover any warning labels on the items. If you don't have actual items, give each group the name of an item that would contain a warning: *light bulb, small radio, box of matches, bottle of cleaning fluid, pair of roller skates, electrical cord.* Have the groups write safety advice for their items. Have a reporter from each group share the group's advice.

And/Or have students complete **Workbook 4 page 30** and **Multilevel Activity Book 4 pages 58–59**.

E Work with a partner. Practice the conversations. Use the words in 1B.

1. A: Be careful! That floor is slippery!

B: OK, thanks.

2. A: Watch out! Those fumes are poisonous.

B: Oh, OK. Thanks for the warning.

2 Learn vocabulary for safety precautions

A Look at the safety poster. Where do you think you might you see this poster?

Four Ways to Be Safe on Campus

Be Alert
Keep your eyes open. Watch for anything unusual in the area around you.

Avoid Isolated Areas
Walk in areas where there are people around you, especially at night.

Report Suspicious Activities Immediately
If you see something, tell someone about it.

Prevent Accidents
Follow all safety rules, and report dangerous situations.

B Match the safety advice with the examples.

_c_ 1. Be alert.

_d_ 2. Report suspicious activities.

_b_ 3. Avoid isolated areas.

_a_ 4. Prevent accidents.

a. You report broken equipment.

b. You walk along a busy street.

c. You notice the door to a building is unlocked.

d. Someone is entering a building through a window.

C Talk about the questions with your class.

1. Which of the safety hazards, warning signs, or situations from this lesson have you seen at home? At work? At school? Describe one situation or hazard.
2. How can people prevent accidents at home? At work? At school?
3. Which things in your home have warning or caution labels?

TEST YOURSELF ✔

Work with a partner. Partner A: Read the vocabulary words in 1B to your partner. Partner B: Close your book. Write the words. Ask your partner for help with spelling as necessary. Then change roles. Partner B: Use the words in 2B.

1 Read about emergency preparations

A **Talk about the questions with your class.**

1. What types of weather emergencies occur in your area?
2. Have you ever made an emergency plan?
   Why or why not?

Need help?

Weather emergencies

blizzard	hurricane
drought	tornado
flood	

B **Listen and read the emergency plan.**

Hurricane Emergency Plan by the Duval Family

I. Before

   A. Make emergency kit

      1. Supplies we have: canned food, can opener,
         blankets, radio

      2. Supplies to buy: batteries for radio, first-aid
         kit, bottled water, flashlight

   B. Get information

      1. Learn evacuation routes

      2. Identify emergency contact person

II. During

   A. Stay safe

      1. Stay indoors and away from windows

      2. Don't use candles or electrical equipment

   B. Be aware

      1. Watch for tornadoes

      2. Listen for warnings

III. After

   A. Check radio or TV for instructions

   B. Check house for damage

Writer's note

Use phrases or short sentences when you make an outline. You don't have to use articles (*a, an, the*) or ending punctuation.

C **Check your understanding. Mark the statements T (true), F (false), or NI (no information).**

  F   1. The Duval family already has a first-aid kit.

  T   2. The family needs to buy batteries.

  T   3. In the Duvals' area, tornadoes might occur during hurricanes.

  NI   4. The Duvals live in Florida.

Unit 5 Lesson 2

Objectives	Grammar	Vocabulary	Correlations
On- and Higher-level: Analyze, write, and edit an emergency plan **Pre-level:** Read and write about emergency preparedness	Imperative (*Stay indoors.*)	Emergencies and natural disasters For vocabulary support for pre-level students, see this **Oxford Picture Dictionary** topic: Emergencies and Natural Disasters	**CASAS:** 0.1.2, 0.1.5, 0.2.1, 2.3.3, 3.4.2, 7.4.2, 7.4.7 **LCPs:** 44.01, 49.02, 49.16, 49.17 **SCANS:** Acquires and evaluates information, Listening, Speaking, Writing **EFF:** Convey ideas in writing, Listen actively, Plan, Read with understanding, Speak so others can understand

Warm-up and Review

10–15 minutes (books closed)

Write *Earthquake, Fire, Flood, Tornado, Hurricane, Drought, Tsunami,* and *Blizzard* on the board. Elicit a description of each type of disaster. Ask students if they have ever experienced any of these emergencies or natural disasters.

TIP Some students enjoy talking about this topic, but others may be reminded of unpleasant experiences. Be sure to address questions to the class at large and only call on volunteers to answer.

Introduction

5 minutes

1. Say: *For every emergency we need to think of three things: how to prepare for (or prevent) it, what to do when it happens, and what to do afterwards.*

2. State the objective: *Today we're going to read and write an emergency plan.*

1 Read about emergency preparedness

Presentation

20–25 minutes

A 1. Read the words in the *Need help?* box, and have students repeat them.

2. Elicit answers to questions 1 and 2. Show students a map of the U.S., and ask which natural disasters usually happen in which areas.

B 1. Tell students they are going to read a family's plan for what to do before, during, and after a hurricane. Ask them to guess what they might read in the plan.

2. Direct students to read the plan silently. Check comprehension. Ask: *What supplies do they already have for their emergency kit? What information do they need?*

3. Play the audio. Have students read along silently.

4. Draw students' attention to the *Writer's note.* Elicit several words that would normally have an article.

Multilevel Strategies

Adapt 1B to the level of your students.

• **Pre-level** Write vocabulary and definitions on the board to help these students understand the reading. *Supplies: things that are necessary; Evacuation: leaving a dangerous place; Route: the way to go.*

Guided Practice I

10 minutes

C Have students work independently to mark the statements T (true), F (false), or NI (no information). Write the answers on the board.

TIP Take advantage of this lesson to go over your school's safety and fire-evacuation plan with your students.

2 Write an emergency plan

Guided Practice II

20–25 minutes

 1. Read the questions. Elicit students' answers.

2. List the emergencies on the board, and write students' preparation ideas under each one.

 1. Direct students to look back at the outline in 1B. Focus students' attention on the imperative sentences in the outline. Ask them to underline the first word in each sentence. Elicit the form of the verb [the base form], and point out how each sentence has the same structure.

2. Read the questions for each part of the outline aloud, and elicit possible answers.

3. Check comprehension of the exercise. Ask: *How many parts does your outline need?* [three] *What should each part cover?* [part 1—before, part 2—during, part 3—after] *Do you need to write long sentences?* [no]

4. Have students work individually to write their emergency plans.

> ### Multilevel Strategies
>
> Adapt 2B to the level of your students.
>
> • **Pre-level** Work with this group to create an outline together. Choose an emergency and brainstorm together for each part of the outline.

 1. Lead students through the process of using the *Editing checklist*. Read the sentences aloud, and answer any questions. Then ask students to check their papers.

2. Allow students a few minutes to edit their writing as necessary.

Communicative Practice

10 minutes

 1. Read the instructions aloud. Emphasize to students that they are responding to their partners' work, not correcting it.

2. Use the outline in 1B to model the exercise. *I think identifying an emergency-contact person is a good idea. I'd like to ask the writer what he or she is going to put in the first-aid kit.*

3. Direct students to exchange papers with a partner and follow the instructions.

4. Call on volunteers to share some interesting things they read in their partners' outlines.

 Use this lesson as an opportunity to invite a guest speaker to your classroom. Many public service agencies, such as the Red Cross or the fire department, have speakers who are trained to give presentations about emergency preparedness. Have your students prepare a list of questions to ask the speaker. Expand on the activity by having students write a thank-you note that mentions something important they learned.

Application and Evaluation

20 minutes

TEST YOURSELF

1. Review the instructions aloud. Assign a time limit (15 minutes), and have students work independently. Give students notice when they have five minutes left.

2. Before collecting students' work, remind them to use the *Editing checklist*. Collect and correct students' writing.

To compress this lesson: Assign the *Test Yourself* for homework.

To extend this lesson: After 2D, form groups of three. If possible, group students according to which emergency they wrote their plans for. Have each group present the three most important ideas to the class.

And/Or have students complete **Workbook 4 page 31** and **Multilevel Activity Book 4 page 60**.

2 Write an emergency plan

A Talk about the questions with your class.

1. What types of emergencies do people in your area prepare for?
2. What steps should people take to prepare for different kinds of emergencies?
3. Where can you get information about possible emergencies in your area?

B Outline a plan for an emergency in your area. Use the model in 1B and the questions below to help you.

Part 1: What should you do before the emergency?
What do you have? What should you buy?
What information should you get?
Part 2: How can you stay safe during the emergency?
What should you be aware of?
Part 3: What should you do after the emergency?

```
                          [Title]
        I.  Before...
             A.
             B.
        II. During...
             A.
             B.
        III. After...
             A.
             B.
```

C Use the checklist to edit your writing. Check (✔) the true sentences.

Editing checklist	
1. I gave my plan a title.	
2. I included plans for before, during, and after an emergency.	
3. I followed the format for an outline.	
4. I used phrases or short sentences.	

D Exchange plans with a partner. Read and comment on your partner's work.

1. Point out one good idea for emergency preparation.
2. Ask your partner a question about his or her plan.

TEST YOURSELF ✔

Write a new outline for a plan for another possible emergency at your workplace or school.

1 Learn about necessity and prohibition

A Read the article. What does the city official say that people have to do?

They have to prepare for an earthquake.

City Official Says Silton Bay Must Prepare for Major Earthquake

City Official Sam Andreas announced that Silton Bay is not prepared for a major earthquake. Andreas said, "People think that they <u>don't have to worry</u> about a major earthquake here, but they're wrong."

According to Andreas, people <u>have got to prepare</u>. They <u>have to buy</u> emergency food and medical supplies. People also <u>must make</u> an emergency plan. They <u>have to plan</u> where to go if their homes are damaged. After an earthquake, damaged homes will be tagged with red tags. People <u>must not enter</u> a home with a red tag.

PREPARE:
• FOOD
• MEDICAL SUPPLIES
• EMERGENCY PLAN

B Study the charts. Underline the 6 examples of *have to*, *have got to*, *must*, and *must not* in the article above.

HAVE TO, *HAVE GOT TO*, AND *MUST* FOR NECESSITY AND PROHIBITION

Necessity		
People	**have to** **have got to** **must**	prepare for emergencies.

Lack of necessity		
People in Florida	**don't have to**	prepare for earthquakes.

Prohibition		
After an earthquake, people	**must not**	enter a home with a red tag.

C Complete the sentences with *(don't) have to*, *have got to*, or *must not*.

1. You <u>must not</u> go out of the house during a hurricane.
2. I <u>don't have to</u> buy any canned food. I have some already.
3. She <u>doesn't have to</u> worry about floods. She lives in a safe area.
4. You <u>must not</u> use electrical equipment during a hurricane. It's extremely dangerous.
5. The tornado is coming! You <u>must not</u> go outside.
6. We <u>don't have to</u> watch the news on TV. We can listen to it on the radio instead.

✔ Use *have to*, *have got to*, and *must* to discuss necessity and prohibition

Unit 5 Lesson 3

Objectives	Grammar	Vocabulary	Correlations
On-, Pre-, and Higher-level: Use *have to, have got to,* and *must* to discuss necessity and prohibition, and listen for safety advice	Modals of necessity and prohibition (*You have to wear a hard hat.*)	Safety For vocabulary support for pre-level students, see these **Oxford Picture Dictionary** topics: Emergencies and Natural Disasters, Job Safety	**CASAS:** 0.1.2, 0.1.5, 7.4.7 **LCPs:** 44.01, 49.01, 49.02, 49.09, 49.13, 49.16, 49.17 **SCANS:** Interprets and communicates information, Knowing how to learn, Reading, Speaking, Writing **EFF:** Convey ideas in writing, Listen actively, Plan, Read with understanding, Reflect and evaluate

Warm-up and Review

10–15 minutes (books closed)

Write potentially dangerous situations on the board. *Swimming in the Ocean, Going Camping in the Mountains, Driving, Crossing the Street.* Ask volunteers to come to the board and write safety warnings under the appropriate situations. *Don't swim too far. Bring a flashlight. Don't speed. Look both ways.* Leave these sentences on the board.

Introduction

5–10 minutes

1. Say: *When we say* Don't swim too far! *we are giving a warning or strong advice. We can also say* You must not swim here *to express prohibition.*

2. State the objective: *Today we're going to talk about necessity and prohibition in order to give warnings or strong advice.*

1 Learn about necessity and prohibition

Presentation I

20–25 minutes

A 1. Direct students to look at the picture. Ask: *What is he talking about?*

2. Read the instructions aloud. Direct students to read the article to find the answer to the question. Elicit the answer.

B 1. Read the sentences in the chart.

2. Direct students to circle the examples of *have to, have got to,* and *must* in 1A. Go over the answers as a class.

3. Read the sentences in the chart again, and have students repeat after you.

4. Assess students' understanding of the charts. Ask them to change the imperative sentences on the board from the warm-up into sentences with *have to, have got to,* and *must.*

Guided Practice I

15–20 minutes

C Ask students to work individually to complete the sentences. Ask volunteers to write the answers on the board.

Multilevel Strategies

For 1C, use mixed-level pairs.

- **Pre-level** Direct these students to listen to their partners read the completed sentences aloud. Tell them to read the sentences back to their partners when they finish the exercise in order to check their answers.

- **On- and Higher-level** Have these students read the sentences to their partners, filling in the missing words as they go. Tell them to listen to their partners read the sentences back and check their work.

Guided Practice II

5–10 minutes

D Read each statement aloud. Refer students to the chart in 1B for the answer. Ask for a show of hands to see which choice students made for each item. Write the answers on the board.

> **TIP**
> Provide more practice with *have to, have got to,* and *must.* Write down a number of dangerous situations on pieces of paper. *The stove is on fire. You just heard a tornado warning. It looks like someone is drowning. Someone is choking. You run out of gas on the freeway. You see a car accident.* Make enough so that you can give every student one sentence. Tell students to walk around the room talking to different partners. Partner A reads the situation. Partner B tells about something you must, must not, and don't have to do in that situation. Then have students switch roles. When they finish, each student moves off to find a new partner.
>
> Once students are comfortable with *have to, have got to,* and *must,* contrast those modals with *should,* which expresses advice rather than necessity. Write another set of situations on the board. *I'm going downtown at night. I'm going roller-skating for the first time. I'm going to the desert. I'm going to the mountains. My baby just learned to walk. My house is going to be empty for a week. I'm going to have a barbecue. I'm going to the beach. I'm going to ride a motorcycle.* Direct students to tell you what you should do in each situation. Ask if there are also things you must and must not do.

2 Learn to express necessity in the past

Presentation II

20–25 minutes

A 1. Introduce the new topic. Say: *You have to do your homework.* Ask: *Is this sentence about the past, present, or future?* [present or future]

2. Read the instructions aloud. Direct students to read the chart silently to find the answer to the question. Elicit the answer.

3. Read and have students repeat the sentences in the chart.

Guided Practice I

10–15 minutes

B Have students work individually to circle the correct words to complete the sentences. Go over the answers as a class.

C Have students work individually to complete the sentences. Tell them to discuss their answers with a partner.

> **TIP**
> After 2C, provide more practice with *had to* and *didn't have to.* Write a list of questions on the board, and direct students to take turns asking a partner the questions and answering in complete sentences. *1. What did you have to do before you came to school today? 2. What did you have to do last weekend? 3. What did you have to do to enroll in this class? 4. What did you have to do to come to the U.S.? 5. What did you have to do last night?* After students have discussed what they had to do, direct them to go back and talk about things they didn't have to do in each situation and to explain why. *I didn't have to put gas in my car before I came to school today because I got gas yesterday.*

T-65

D Mark the statements N (necessary), NN (not necessary), or P (prohibited).

_P_ 1. That chemical has poisonous fumes. You must not use it in the house.

_N_ 2. We've got to prepare for emergencies.

_NN_ 3. You don't have to be afraid to walk at night when you walk with friends.

_N_ 4. We must fix the broken ladder before we use it.

_P_ 5. You must not stand by a window in a tornado.

2 Learn to express necessity in the past

A Study the chart. What words are used to express necessity in the past? had to

Necessity in the past	
Present	**Past**
This year, Rosa **has to** buy new supplies.	Last year, she **had to** buy a first-aid kit.
They**'ve got to** buy a new flashlight.	They **had to** buy a ladder last month.
Her husband **must** check the house for storm damage.	He **had to** repair the roof last November.
Their son **doesn't have to** go to school this week.	He **didn't have to** go to school last week.

Note
There are no past forms of *must* or *have got to* to express necessity. Use *had to* instead.

B Complete the sentences. Circle the correct words.

1. Rosa and her family (**had to** / have to) repair the roof last year.
2. Her husband (doesn't have to / **didn't have to**) replace the windows then.
3. Every year he (had to / **has to**) check the house for storm damage.
4. Now he (**has got to** / had to) replace the back door.
5. Their neighbor (**had to** / must) buy new furniture after the storm.
6. Now they (had to / **must**) make an emergency plan before the next big storm.

C Complete the sentences. Talk about your answers with a partner.

1. As a child when I was sick, I didn't have to _____.
2. One hundred years ago, when there was a hurricane, people probably
   had to _____.
3. Last week, I had to _____.
4. Last year, I had to _____.
5. Last year, I didn't have to _____.

3 Grammar listening

Listen to the emergencies. Choose the sentences with the same meaning. Circle _a_ or _b_.

1. (a.) We have to call 911.
   b. We don't have to call 911.
2. (a.) We have got to evacuate the area.
   b. We don't have to evacuate the area.
3. (a.) Children must go to the basement.
   b. Children must not go to the basement.
4. (a.) They have to leave the area.
   b. They don't have to leave the area.
5. a. Last year, they had to leave the area.
   (b.) Last year, they didn't have to leave the area.
6. (a.) Most people had to buy emergency supplies.
   b. Most people didn't have to buy emergency supplies.

4 Practice expressing necessity and prohibition

A **Think about the answers to these questions.**

1. What are three things people have to do to prepare for an emergency?
2. What are three things people must not do when they are driving a car?
3. What are three things you've got to do to learn English?

B **Work with a partner. Ask and answer the questions.**

A: *What are three things people have to do to prepare for an emergency?*
B: *They have to buy emergency supplies…*

C **Talk about your ideas with the class.**

People have to buy emergency supplies.

TEST YOURSELF ✔

Close your book. Write 5 sentences about what people *have to do, must do,* and *don't have to do* in the situations you discussed in 4C.

3 Grammar listening

Guided Practice II

10–15 minutes

1. Say: *Now we're going to listen to some emergency rules.*

2. Play the audio. Direct students to read along silently without writing.

3. Replay the audio. Ask students to choose the sentence with the same meaning.

4. Ask for a show of hands to find out how students answered. Settle disagreements by replaying segments as necessary.

Multilevel Strategies

Replay the *Grammar listening* to allow pre-level students to catch up while you challenge on- and higher-level students.

• **Pre-level** Have these students listen again to complete the exercise.

• **On- and Higher-level** Have these students close their books and write two of the sentences they hear.

4 Practice expressing necessity and prohibition

Communicative Practice and Application

20–25 minutes

A 1. Read the questions aloud.

2. Ask students to think about and note their answers.

B 1. Put students in pairs. Direct them to ask their partners the question. Tell them to make notes of each other's answers. Model the exercise by asking a volunteer. Have the class tell you how to write the answer in note form.

2. Check comprehension of the exercise. Ask: *Do both partners need to answer the question?* [yes] *Do you need to write your partner's answers?* [yes, in note form]

C 1. Call on volunteers to share their ideas with the class.

2. Write students' ideas on the board.

Evaluation

10–15 minutes (books closed)

TEST YOURSELF

Ask students to write the sentences independently. Collect and correct their writing.

Multilevel Strategies

Target the *Test Yourself* to the level of your students.

• **Pre-level** Allow these students to write three sentences. Provide these skeleton sentences for them to complete: *To stay safe, you have to _____. When you drive a car, you must _____. To learn English, you don't have to _____.*

To compress this lesson: Conduct 1C as a whole-class discussion.

To extend this lesson: After 4A, have students create a home-safety survey.
1. Put students in groups. Tell them to work together to create a survey with five *Yes/No* questions about home safety. *Do you have a fire extinguisher?* Tell each group member to copy the questions.
2. Have students ask their survey questions of students from other groups. Encourage them to move around and talk to different people, but tell them not to answer the same survey question twice.
3. Have the original groups reconvene and pool their results. Ask a reporter to share the group's results with the class. *Six out of ten people have a fire extinguisher at home.*

And/Or have students complete **Workbook 4 pages 32–33, Multilevel Activity Book 4 pages 61–62,** and the corresponding **Unit 5 Exercises** on the **Multilevel Grammar Exercises CD-ROM 4.**

Unit 5 Lesson 4

Objectives	Grammar	Vocabulary	Correlations
On-, Pre-, and Higher-level: Report unsafe conditions and listen for job information	Past of *should* (*You should have locked the door.*)	*Restricted, protective, retail* For vocabulary support for pre-level students, see this **Oxford Picture Dictionary** topic: Job Safety	**CASAS:** 0.1.2, 0.1.5, 4.3.4, 6.7.4, 7.4.7 **LCPs:** 36.03, 44.01, 49.02, 49.09, 49.16, 49.17 **SCANS:** Arithmetic/Mathematics, Knowing how to learn, Listening, Reading, Speaking **EFF:** Listen actively, Observe critically, Use math to solve problems and communicate, Reflect and evaluate

Warm-up and Review

10–15 minutes (books closed)

Write *Mistakes We Made* on a large sheet of paper. Write a list of safety-related mistakes that you have made in the past. *I left the oven on when I went to work. I didn't unplug the iron.* Ask students to tell you about mistakes they have made in the past, and write them on the board. Save this paper.

Introduction

5 minutes

1. Say: *If we make these mistakes at home, we have to take care of them. But if we see safety problems at work or on public property, we have to report them.*

2. State the objective: *Today we'll learn to report safety problems and listen for information about safety problems at work.*

1 Learn to report unsafe conditions

Presentation I

15–20 minutes

 1. Direct students to look at the picture. Elicit the safety problems.

2. Play the audio. Tell students to discuss the questions with a partner. Call on volunteers to share their answers.

Guided Practice

20–25 minutes

 1. Read the instructions aloud. Play the audio. Ask students to read along silently and listen for the answer to the question. Elicit the answer. Ask students to read the conversation with a partner. Circulate and monitor pronunciation. Model and have students repeat difficult words or phrases.

2. Say and have students repeat the expressions in the *In other words* box. Elicit the placement of the expressions in the conversation. Ask volunteers to read the conversation using expressions from the box. Read the *Idiom note.* Elicit other situations where students might hear this expression.

Communicative Practice and Application

15–20 minutes

 1. Ask students to read the instructions silently. Check comprehension of the exercise. Ask: *What are the two roles? What is the situation?* Elicit examples of what each partner might say.

2. Set a time limit (five minutes). Ask students to act out the role-play in both roles. Ask one to three volunteer pairs to act out their conversations for the class. Tell students who are listening to note which words Partner A uses for reporting the problem.

Multilevel Strategies

For 1C, adapt the role-play to the level of your students.

• **Pre-level** Provide the beginning of the conversation for these students. *A: Excuse me, I want to report a safety hazard. B: Yes, what is it? A: There's broken glass _____.*

1 Learn to report unsafe conditions

A Look at the picture. Listen to the conversations. Then ask and answer the questions below with your classmates.

1. What did the first employee report?
2. What did the second employee report?
3. What should people do in these situations?

There are a lot of boxes in front of the emergency exit. The back door won't close.

B Listen and read. What safety hazards does the employee report?

A: Excuse me. I want to report a safety hazard.

B: Yes? What is it?

A: There are a lot of boxes in front of the emergency exit. That's dangerous.

B: You're right. The delivery workers should have put the boxes in the storeroom. I'll take care of it.* Thanks.

A: There's something else, too.

B: Oh? What's that?

A: There seems to be a problem with the back exit. The door won't close.

B: Thanks for bringing it to my attention. I'll call maintenance.

Idiom note: take care of it = solve the problem

> **In other words...**
>
> **Reporting a problem**
>
> I want to report…
> There seem(s) to be…
> I noticed…

C Role-play a conversation about unsafe conditions with a partner. Use the example in 1B to make a new conversation.

Partner A: You're at the park. Tell a park employee about a safety hazard. There's broken glass near the playground. You also notice that the trash cans are full.

Partner B: You're a park employee. Listen to the visitor. You agree that someone should have cleaned up the glass. Tell the visitor you'll take care of the problems.

2 Learn *should have*

A Study the chart. **Where are the boxes?** in the hall

Should have	
Affirmative statements	**Negative statements**
You **should have put** the boxes in the storeroom. He **should have listened** to his manager.	You **should not have left** them in the hall. He **shouldn't have forgotten** the boxes.

Note
Use *should (not) have* + past participle to give an opinion about a situation in the past.

B Work with a partner. Write statements with *should have* or *shouldn't have*.

1. I didn't report the problem.

   You should have reported the problem.

2. We went into a restricted area.

   You shouldn't have gone into a restricted area.

3. They didn't wear protective gloves.

   They should have worn protective gloves.

4. She used a lamp with a frayed cord.

   She shouldn't have used a lamp with a frayed cord.

5. He climbed on the broken ladder.

   He shouldn't have climbed on the broken ladder.

3 Practice your pronunciation

A Listen to the pronunciation of *-ough* in these words. Then match each word with *-ough* with a word that has a similar sound.

   b   1. bought   a. stuff

   d   2. through   b. saw

   a   3. enough   c. go

   c   4. though   d. too

B Read the conversation with a partner. Then listen and check your pronunciation.

A: I bought a new lock for the restricted area.

B: Do you think one lock is enough?

A: Yes, if we put it through the handles of both doors.

B: Good. We still need a lock for the supply cabinet, though.

2 Learn the past of *should have*

Presentation II

10–15 minutes

 1. Introduce the new topic. *In the conversation in 1B, the employer says,* The workers should have put that stuff in the storeroom. *Did they put the stuff in the storeroom?*

2. Read the sentences in the chart and the *Note* aloud. Ask about the meaning of each sentence. *Did you put the boxes in the storeroom?* [no] *Did he listen to his manager?* [no] *We use* should have *to give advice about the past, but the advice is too late! We use* should have *to talk about things we wish we could change, but we can't.*

3. Take out the sentences from the warm-up, and demonstrate how to talk about them with *should have. I shouldn't have left the oven on. I should have unplugged the iron. She should have put the skateboard away.*

> ### Multilevel Strategies
>
> Adapt 2B to the level of your students.
>
> • **Pre-level** Provide these students with present-tense versions of the advice, and ask them to fill in an appropriate modal. *2. You _____ go into restricted areas. 3. You _____ wear protective gloves. 4. She _____ buy a new electrical cord. 5. He _____ climb on a broken ladder.*

Guided and Communicative Practice

15–20 minutes

 1. Have students work with a partner to write the sentences with *should have*. Ask volunteers to write their sentences on the board.

2. Direct students to tell their partners about something they didn't do in the past that they should have done and something they did in the past that they shouldn't have done.

> ### Multilevel Strategies
>
> After 2B, provide more practice with *should/should have* for all levels. Form mixed-level groups. Provide each group with one or two pictures, or provide a magazine, and ask students to look for a picture about which they can write a sentence with *should have*. (You can find good pictures for this on the Internet by typing words like *spilled, dropped, crashed, broke,* and *forgot* into an image search engine.)
>
> • **Pre-level** Have these students write a sentence about what should happen next.
>
> • **On- and Higher-level** Have these students write sentences about what should have (or should not have) happened.
>
> Have a reporter from each group share the group's pictures and sentences with the class.

3 Practice your pronunciation

Pronunciation Extension

10–15 minutes

 1. Write on the board: *He's still coughing even though he bought cough syrup.* Say the sentence and ask students to repeat it. Underline and pronounce the words with *ough*. Say: *Do these words sound the same or different? Now we're going to focus on different pronunciations of* ough.

2. Play the audio. Direct students to listen for the pronunciation of *ough*.

3. Have students match the words with the same sounds. Go over the answers as a class.

 1. Play the audio and have students read along silently.

2. Have partners read the conversation in both roles. Monitor and provide feedback on pronunciation of the *ough* words.

4 Focus on Listening

Listening Extension

20–25 minutes

A Direct students to look at the pictures. Ask them to check the job they think is the safest. Ask which job they think is most dangerous.

B Read and have students repeat the occupations. Tell students they are going to listen to a news interview about workplace safety. Play the audio and have them check the job that is not mentioned. Elicit the answer.

C 1. Direct students to read the sentences before listening.

2. Replay the audio and have students work individually to mark the sentences T (true) or F (false). Go over the answers as a class. Write the answers on the board.

> ### Multilevel Strategies
>
> Adapt 4C to the level of your students.
>
> • **Pre-level** Provide these students with *Yes/No* questions to answer. *Are jobs in education safe?* [yes] *Are there a lot of injuries for hospitality workers?* [yes] *Are telecommunication jobs dangerous?* [no] *Is the computer industry safe?* [yes] Call on volunteers for the answers.

2. Have students work individually to read and answer the question. Call on a volunteer for the answer.

Evaluation

10–15 minutes

TEST YOURSELF

1. Model the role-play with a volunteer. Then switch roles.

2. Pair students. Check comprehension of the exercise by eliciting examples of what the tenant and the superintendent might say.

3. Set a time limit (five minutes), and have the partners act out the role-play in both roles.

4. Circulate and monitor. Encourage pantomime and improvisation.

5. Provide feedback.

> ### Multilevel Strategies
>
> Target the *Test Yourself* to the level of your students.
>
> • **Pre-level** Provide the beginning of the conversation for these students: *Tenant: Excuse me, I want to report a safety hazard. Superintendent: Yes, what is it? T: _____.*

5 Real-life math

Math Extension

5–10 minutes

1. Direct students to look at the pie chart. Read the job categories, and elicit any questions about vocabulary. Elicit an example for each category.

To compress this lesson: Conduct *Real-life math* as a whole-class activity.

To extend this lesson: Report a safety hazard in writing.
1. Tell students to imagine that their apartment building has a safety hazard that the superintendent has not addressed. They need to write a letter to the landlord complaining about the problem.
2. Put students in multi-level groups. Have each group write a letter and read it to the class.

And/Or have students complete **Workbook 4 page 34** and **Multilevel Activity Book 4 page 63**.

4 Focus on listening

A Check (✔) the job you think is the safest. Talk about your answer with your class.

_____ teacher

_____ hotel worker

_____ computer technician

B Listen to the news story. Check (✔) the job that is NOT mentioned.

_____ librarian   _____ scientist   _____ telecommunications worker

✔ nurse   _____ teacher   _____ veterinarian

C Listen again. Mark the sentences T (true) or F (false).

_T_ 1. Teachers have a safer job than hotel workers.

_F_ 2. It's a little safer to work in computers than in telecommunications.

_T_ 3. Telecommunications workers have the safest jobs.

_T_ 4. In the computer industry, workers have to work very slowly.

_F_ 5. The injury/illness rate for scientists is 680 per 10,000.

5 Real-life math

A Read the chart about workplace safety. Then look at the groups of jobs below. Which group has the most illnesses and injuries? Group 2

Group 1: manufacturing jobs, construction jobs, transportation and warehouse jobs

Group 2: health-care and social-services jobs, retail jobs, hotel and vacation jobs

B Explain your answer to your classmates.

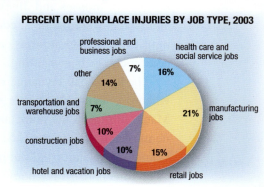

PERCENT OF WORKPLACE INJURIES BY JOB TYPE, 2003

professional and business jobs 7%
health care and social service jobs 16%
other 14%
transportation and warehouse jobs 7%
manufacturing jobs 21%
construction jobs 10%
hotel and vacation jobs 10%
retail jobs 15%

Source: *www.bls.gov*

TEST YOURSELF ✔

Role-play a conversation between a tenant and a superintendent about safety. Partner A: You noticed a dangerous situation in your apartment building. Tell the superintendent about the problem. Partner B: You are the superintendent. Listen and tell the tenant what you will do to solve the problem. Then change roles.

1 Get ready to read

A   **Name some jobs that are very dangerous. Which jobs are safe?**

B   **Read the definitions. Have you ever had a sprain or a strain?**

keep track of: (verb) to watch, keep a record of
sprain: (noun) an injury caused by suddenly twisting or turning a part of the body
strain: (noun) an injury caused by using a part of the body too much

C   **Scan the article. Check (✔) the most dangerous item in the home.**

_____ cleaning materials   _____ exercise equipment   ✔ basketballs

2 Read and respond

A   **Read the article. Which government agency keeps track of workplace injuries? Home injuries?** The Department of Labor keeps track of workplace injuries.
The U.S. Consumer Product Safety Commission keeps track of home injuries.

Accidents Can Happen Anywhere!

Accidents and injuries can happen at any time—at home or at work. Knowing which injuries are the most common can help employers, families, and individuals avoid and prevent them.

The U.S. Department of Labor keeps track of the amount of time people take off from work because of injuries and illnesses. In a recent survey, the Department of Labor found that sprains and strains were the most common reasons given for workers taking time off. Many of these injuries were back injuries caused by overexertion (too much hard physical work), accidents with equipment, or heavy lifting.

The home can be dangerous, too. Accidents happen when people are careless or when they don't use caution. Many injuries in the home are caused by everyday items. According to the U.S. Consumer Product Safety Commission, stairs and ramps are two of the most dangerous parts of the home. Bicycles, tools, and containers account for[1] many injuries that people go to emergency rooms for. However, a recent survey showed that the most dangerous item of all is the basketball!

[1]account for: to be responsible for

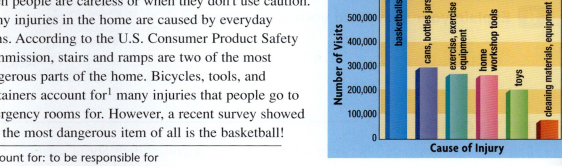

Number of Emergency Room Visits by Cause

☑ Read an article about safety statistics; scan for information

Unit 5 Lesson 5

Objectives	Grammar	Vocabulary	Correlations
On-, Pre-, and Higher-level: Read about and discuss accidents and injuries	Nouns and adjectives (*He is cautious. You need to use caution.*)	*Keep track of, sprain, strain, account for* For vocabulary support for pre-level students, see this **Oxford Picture Dictionary** topic: Symptoms and Injuries	**CASAS:** 0.1.2, 0.1.5, 3.4.2, 7.4.4 **LCPs:** 38.01, 44.01, 49.02, 49.09, 49.16, 49.17 **SCANS:** Decision making, Interprets and communicates information, Reading, Speaking **EFF:** Cooperate with others, Learn through research, Read with understanding, Take responsibility for learning

Warm-up and Review

10–15 minutes (books closed)

Review symptoms and injuries. Show pictures of injuries from *The Oxford Picture Dictionary* or another source. Ask volunteers to write the name of the injury or symptom on the board.

Introduction

5 minutes

1. Say: *Some of these injuries and symptoms occur because of an unsafe environment at work or at home.*

2. State the objective: *Today we're going to read and write about accidents at work and at home.*

1 Get ready to read

Presentation

15–20 minutes

A Read the question aloud, and elicit students' answers. Ask what kinds of accidents can happen at the different workplaces.

B Read the words and definitions. Elicit sample sentences from students using *keep track of*. Discuss students' experiences with sprains and strains.

Pre-Reading

C Read the instructions aloud, and tell students to scan the article as quickly as they can. Ask them to indicate when they have located the most dangerous item in the home by putting their pencils on their books or using another silent signal.

2 Read and respond

Guided Practice I

25–30 minutes

A 1. Read the instructions aloud. Ask students to read the article silently and think about the question.

2. After they're finished reading, direct students to underline unfamiliar words they would like to know. Elicit the words and encourage other students to provide definitions or examples.

3. Check comprehension. Ask: *Who keeps track of the amount of time people take off from work?* [the Department of Labor]

Multilevel Strategies

Adapt 2A to the level of your students.

• **Pre-level** Provide these students with a summary of the ideas in the reading. *Both the workplace and the home can be dangerous. Sprains and strains are the most common reasons people take time off from work. Many of these injuries are back injuries. In the home, accidents often happen through carelessness. Many accidents are caused by bicycles, tools, and containers, but basketballs caused the most injuries.*

Direct these students to read the summary while other students are reading 2A.

Guided Practice II

15–20 minutes

B 1. Play the audio. Have students read along silently.

2. Elicit and discuss any additional questions about the reading.

C Have students work individually to check the main idea. Go over the answers as a class.

> ### Multilevel Strategies
>
> Adapt 2C to the level of your students.
>
> • **Pre-level** Tell these students to refer to their summary to choose the main idea.

D 1. Read the words in the chart aloud. Elicit and discuss any questions the students have about the noun and adjective forms. Say the words and have students repeat them.

2. Provide sample sentences to remind students of the different uses of nouns and adjectives. *You need to use caution. He is a cautious person. She didn't notice the danger. Those chemicals are dangerous. The garbage is a health hazard. Smoking is hazardous to your health.*

3. Direct students to work individually to circle the correct word to complete each sentence. Write the answers on the board.

> ### Multilevel Strategies
>
> For 2D, seat pre-level students together.
>
> • **Pre-level** Direct these students to write two sentences using adjectives from the chart.
>
> • **On- and Higher-level** Ask these students to write two sentences using the noun and the adjective form of one of the words in the box.

3 Talk it over

Communicative Practice

15–20 minutes

1. Read the questions aloud. Set a time limit (three minutes). Have students work independently to think about the questions and write their answers in note form.

2. Call on volunteers to share their ideas with the class.

Application

5–10 minutes

BRING IT TO LIFE

Read the instructions aloud. Suggest that students type *household safety* or *home-health hazards* into an Internet search engine in order to find an article on this topic.

To compress this lesson: Conduct 2D as a whole-class activity.

To extend this lesson: After 2D, provide more practice with nouns and *-ous* adjectives.
1. Write more *-ous* adjectives on the board: *religious, courageous, humorous, marvelous, mountainous, poisonous.*
2. Elicit the noun form of each word. As a class, brainstorm a sentence for both forms of each word.

And/Or have students complete **Workbook 4 page 35** and the **Multilevel Activity Book 4 pages 64–65**.

Injuries and accidents cannot be avoided completely, but knowing where the dangers are can help. As always, when it comes to staying safe, prevention is the best strategy.

adapted from: *www.bls.gov and www.cpsc.gov*

B Listen and read the article again.

C Check (✔) the main idea of the article.

_____ 1. Most jobs are not dangerous, but some jobs can be very dangerous.

_____ 2. More injuries happen in the home than in the workplace.

✔ 3. Both the workplace and home can be dangerous.

D Study the chart. Then circle the correct words in the sentences below.

> **Word Study: Forming adjectives from nouns**
>
> Add -*ous* to the end of some nouns to form adjectives. There is sometimes a spelling change: cautio**n**—cautio**us**
>
> | Noun | Adjective |
> |---------|------------|
> | caution | cautious |
> | danger | dangerous |
> | hazard | hazardous |

1. Don't leave things on the stairs. It's a safety ((hazard) / hazardous).
2. Be (caution / (cautious)) around flammable liquids. They're a ((danger) / dangerous) at many workplaces.
3. That frayed cord is very (danger / (dangerous)). These chemicals look (hazard / (hazardous)), too.

3 Talk it over

Think about the questions. Talk about your ideas with the class.

1. Which do you think is more dangerous, the home or the workplace? Why?
2. What kinds of safety training should employers give their workers?

> **BRING IT TO LIFE**
> Use the newspaper, a magazine, or the Internet to find an article on safety at home. What problems or hazards does the article talk about? What safety procedures does the article suggest? Talk about your article with your classmates.

1 Grammar

A Complete the sentences with *must not* or *don't have to.*

1. To prevent falls, you ___must not___ walk on a wet floor.
2. You ___don't have to___ report that broken window. I already reported it.
3. People ___must not___ forget to report safety hazards.
4. You ___don't have to___ worry about emergencies if you're prepared.

B Read the information. Which sentences are closest in meaning? Circle *a* or *b*.

1. It's really important to use caution when you're going downstairs.
   (a.) You must be careful when you're going downstairs
   b. You must not be careful when you're going downstairs.

2. You don't have to buy an emergency kit. It's fine to make one yourself.
   a. You've got to buy an emergency kit.
   (b.) It isn't necessary to buy an emergency kit.

3. It could be dangerous to go out by yourself. Wait until someone can go with you.
   a. You don't have to go out by yourself.
   (b.) You must not go out by yourself.

4. We're required to put new batteries in the smoke alarms next month.
   a. We must put new batteries in the smoke alarms this month.
   (b.) We don't have to put new batteries in the smoke alarms this month.

C Randy's back hurts. Write sentences with *should have* or *shouldn't have.*

1. He moved boxes for two hours on Saturday.
   He shouldn't have moved boxes for two hours on Saturday.

2. He didn't ask for help.
   He should have asked for help.

3. He played basketball on Sunday.
   He shouldn't have played basketball on Sunday.

4. He lifted weights after he played basketball.
   He shouldn't have lifted weights after he played basketball.

5. He didn't rest his back.
   He should have rested his back.

Unit 5 Review and expand

Objectives	Grammar	Vocabulary	Correlations
On-, Pre-, and Higher-level: Expand upon and review unit grammar and life skills	Necessity and prohibition in the present and past (*You have to see a doctor. You shouldn't have lifted that box.*)	Safety For vocabulary support for pre-level students, see this **Oxford Picture Dictionary** topic: Job Safety	**CASAS:** 0.1.2, 0.1.5, 0.2.1, 3.4.2, 4.8.1, 7.3.1, 7.3.2 **LCPs:** 39.01, 44.01, 49.01, 49.13, 49.16, 49.17 **SCANS:** Creative thinking, Participates as member of a team, Problem solving, Speaking, Writing **EFF:** Convey ideas in writing, Listen actively, Solve problems and make decisions

Warm-up and Review

10–15 minutes (books closed)

1. Review the *Bring It to Life* assignment from Lesson 5.

2. Have students who did the exercise share one or two ideas from what they read. Invite other students to comment on or ask questions about the information.

Introduction and Presentation

5 minutes

1. Using information that the students discussed during the warm-up, write sentences with *have to* and *must*. *If you have small children, you must keep cleaning supplies in high cabinets. You have to have a smoke alarm in every room.*

2. State the objective: *Today we're going to review the grammar we've studied in this unit to talk about safety.*

1 Grammar

Guided Practice

40–45 minutes

A Have students work individually to complete the sentences. Ask volunteers to read the completed sentences to the class.

B Have students work with a partner to circle the correct answer. Call on volunteers for the answers.

C 1. Review the past of *should*. Write sentences on the board. *I tripped over my daughter's toy. Maya got shocked when she plugged in the frayed electrical cord. Roberto cut his foot when he walked outside barefoot.* Say: *These things already happened. How can we use* should *to talk about the past?* Elicit a sentence with *should have* or *shouldn't have* for each situation, and write it on the board.

2. Direct students to work with their partners to write the sentences. Ask volunteers to write their sentences on the board.

Multilevel Strategies

For 1C, seat pre-level students together.

• **Pre-level** While other students are completing 1C, assist these students. Read each sentence, elicit the advice, and have everyone write it down before you move on.

2 Group work

Communicative Practice

20–35 minutes

 A 1. Direct students, in groups of three to four, to focus on the picture. Ask: *Who are the people in this picture?*

2. Assign roles: leader, recorder, and reporters. Explain that students work with their groups to write the conversation.

3. Check comprehension of the roles. Ask: *Who writes the conversation?* [recorder] *Who will read the conversation to the class?* [reporters] *Who helps everyone and manages the group?* [leader] *Who creates the conversation?* [everyone]

4. Set a time limit (five minutes) to complete the exercise. Circulate and answer any questions.

5. Have reporters from each group read the group's conversation to the class.

Multilevel Strategies

For 2A, use mixed-level groups.

• **Pre-level** Assign these students the role of reporter.

• **On-level** Assign these students the role of recorder.

• **Higher-level** Assign these students the role of leader.

B 1. Have students walk around the room to conduct these interviews. To get students moving, tell them to interview three new people not in their groups for 2A.

2. Set a time limit (five minutes) to complete the exercise.

3. Tell students to make a note of their classmates' answers but not to worry about writing complete sentences.

Multilevel Strategies

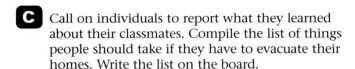

Adapt the mixer in 2B to the level of your students.

• **Pre-level** Allow these students to ask and answer the questions without writing.

• **Higher-level** Have students ask two additional questions and write all answers.

C Call on individuals to report what they learned about their classmates. Compile the list of things people should take if they have to evacuate their homes. Write the list on the board.

PROBLEM SOLVING

15–25 minutes

 A 1. Ask: *If you noticed a safety problem at work, would you be afraid to tell your boss?* Tell students they will read a story about a man who sees a safety problem at work. Direct students to read Mario's story silently.

2. Ask: *Are the employees trained in safety? Is the factory a dangerous place? What is the safety problem?* Play the audio and have students read along silently.

B 1. Elicit answers to question 1. Have volunteers write answers to question 2 on the board until all of the class ideas have been put up. Put students into groups of three or four. Have them vote on Mario's best course of action.

2. Pair students. Ask them to write a short letter giving advice to Mario. Call on volunteers to read their letters to the class.

Evaluation

30–35 minutes

To test students' understanding of the unit grammar and life skills, have them take the Unit 5 Test on the *Step Forward Test Generator CD-ROM* with *ExamView® Assessment Suite*.

Learning Log

To help students record and discuss their progress, use the *Learning Log* on page T–201.

To extend this review: Have students complete **Workbook 4 page 36**, **Multilevel Activity Book 4 page 66**, and the **Unit 5 Exercises** on the **Multilevel Grammar Exercises CD-ROM 4**.

2 Group work

A Work with 2–3 classmates. Write a 6–8 line conversation between the people in the picture. Share your conversation with the class.

A: *We need to make a family emergency plan.*
B: *OK. What do we have to do first?*

B Interview 3 classmates. Write their answers.

1. What is the most dangerous or unsafe situation you've ever seen? Did you report it? If you did, what happened?
2. Is it easy for you to report a dangerous or unsafe situation? Why or why not?
3. What are some things people should take with them if they have to evacuate their homes? What are some things they don't have to take?

C Talk about the answers with your class.

PROBLEM SOLVING

A Listen and read about Mario.

Mario works in a factory. He's worked there for a few months. The factory has a good safety-training program. Every employee is required to take a class and learn about keeping the workplace safe. Mario's co-workers follow the safety rules, but Mario has noticed one unsafe practice at his workplace. Some of the emergency exits are locked, even though a big sign on the door says, "This door must be unlocked at all times during work hours." Mario thinks that the emergency exits should be unlocked, but he doesn't know what to do.

B Work with your classmates. Answer the questions.

1. What is Mario's problem?   Mario thinks that the emergency exits should be unlocked.
2. Give Mario advice. Think of 3 or 4 solutions to his problem.
3. Write Mario a short letter. Tell him what you think he should do.

Getting Ahead

FOCUS ON
- interpersonal skills and personal qualities
- writing a recommendation
- adjective clauses
- asking for information
- building interpersonal skills

LESSON 1 **Vocabulary**

1 Learn vocabulary for interpersonal skills

A **Talk about the questions with your class.**

1. What skills do you think help people get better jobs?
2. Which of these skills are also useful at school, at home, and in the community?

B **Work with your classmates. Match the words with the pictures.**

__2__ ask for clarification	__5__ manage conflict	__4__ solve problems
__7__ give feedback	__6__ resolve disagreements	__3__ work on a team
__1__ make suggestions	__8__ respond to feedback	

C **Listen and check. Then read the new words with a partner.**

D **Work with a partner. Write other words that you know for interpersonal skills. Check your words in a dictionary.**

☑ Identify and use vocabulary for interpersonal skills and personal qualities

Unit 6 Lesson 1

Objectives	Grammar	Vocabulary	Correlations
On-level: Describe and talk about interpersonal skills and personal qualities **Pre-level:** Identify interpersonal skills and describe personal qualities **Higher-level:** Talk and write about interpersonal skills and personal qualities	Adjectives (*She is very reliable.*)	Interpersonal skills and personal qualities For vocabulary support for pre-level students, see this **Oxford Picture Dictionary** unit: Work	**CASAS:** 0.1.2, 0.1.5, 0.2.1, 4.1.7, 4.4.1, 4.6.1, 4.8.1, 7.4.5 **LCPs:** 35.02, 36.04, 39.01, 49.10 **SCANS:** Listening, Organizes and maintains information, Participates as member of a team **EFF:** Cooperate with others, Listen actively, Read with understanding, Speak so others can understand

Warm-up and Review

10–15 minutes (books closed)

Write several job locations on the board. *Restaurant, Factory, Hospital, School, Office.* Elicit the job titles of different people who work in each location, and write them in the correct category.

Introduction

5 minutes

1. Ask students which of the people at each job site work with each other. For example: Waiters interact with busboys, cooks, cashiers, and customers. Ask if any of the jobs don't require working with people.

2. State the objective: *Today we're going to talk about the interpersonal skills and qualities you need to succeed on the job.*

1 Learn vocabulary for interpersonal skills

Presentation I

20–25 minutes

A Write *skills* on the board, and elicit students' answers to the questions. Write their ideas on the board.

B 1. Direct students to look at the pictures. Ask *Where is she?* about each picture.

2. Group students and assign roles: leader, fact checker, recorder, and reporter. Explain that students work with their groups to match the words and pictures.

3. Check comprehension of the roles. Ask: *Who looks up the words in a dictionary?* [fact checker] *Who writes the numbers in the book?* [recorder] *Who tells the class your answers?* [reporter] *Who helps everyone and manages the group?* [leader]

4. Set a time limit (three minutes). As students work together, copy the wordlist onto the board.

5. Call "time." Have reporters take turns giving their answers. Write each group's answer on the board next to the word.

C 1. To prepare students for listening, say: *Now we're going to hear the woman in the picture talk about the importance of interpersonal skills.* Ask students to listen and check their answers.

2. Have students check the wordlist on the board and then write the correct numbers in their books.

3. Pair students. Set a time limit (three minutes). Monitor pair practice to identify pronunciation issues.

4. Call "time" and work with the pronunciation of any troublesome words or phrases.

5. Replay the audio and challenge students to listen for what the woman says about each skill. Elicit what they remember.

D 1. Ask students to work with their partners from 1C to brainstorm a list of related words.

2. Elicit words from the class. Write them on the board. Ask students to copy them into their vocabulary notes for the unit.

Guided Practice

5–10 minutes

 1. Model the conversation with a volunteer. Model it again using other information from 1B.

2. Set a time limit (three minutes). Direct students to practice with a partner.

3. Ask volunteers to act out one of their conversations for the class.

2 Learn vocabulary to describe personal qualities

Presentation II

15–20 minutes

 1. Direct students to look at the job evaluation. Introduce the new topic: *Now we're going to talk about personal qualities.*

2. Direct students to read the evaluation silently.

3. Read the personal-quality words aloud, and have students repeat them.

4. Check comprehension. Ask: *What do you call someone who never lies?* [honest] *What do you call someone who is always on time and completes all of his or her work?* [reliable]

Guided Practice

10–15 minutes

 Have students work individually to complete the sentences. Go over the answers as a class.

Communicative Practice and Application

10–15 minutes

 1. Give students a minute to make notes of their answers to the questions. Call on individuals to share their ideas with the class.

2. Write *In a Family* and *In a Class* on the board. Elicit the qualities students chose as most important, and write them in each category. Elicit examples of how a person demonstrates those qualities.

Evaluation

10–15 minutes (books closed)

TEST YOURSELF

1. Make a four-column chart on the board with the headings *I can…, I can't…, I am…,* and *I'm not….* Have students close their books and give you an example for each column.

2. Have students copy the chart into their notebooks.

3. Give students five to ten minutes to test themselves by writing words they recall from the lesson in each column.

4. Call "time" and have students check their spelling in a dictionary. Circulate and monitor students' progress.

5. Direct students to share their work with a partner and add additional words to their charts.

> ### Multilevel Strategies
> Target the *Test Yourself* to the level of your students.
> •**Higher-level** Have these students complete the chart and then write an example of how they demonstrate the skills and qualities in their *I can…* and *I am…* lists.

To compress this lesson: Conduct 1B as a whole-class activity.

To extend this lesson: Have students complete a self-evaluation.
1. Copy the chart in 2A on the board. Change the title to *Student Evaluation for* _____ and leave the *Rating* and *Comments* columns blank.
2. Direct students to copy the chart and complete it with ratings and comments about themselves as students. Allow but do not require them to share their self-evaluations with you.
And/Or have students complete **Workbook 4 page 37** and **Multilevel Activity Book 4 pages 68–69**.

E **Work with a partner. Practice the conversation. Use the words in 1B.**

A: Do you find it easy to respond to feedback?

B: Pretty easy. How about you?

A: It's not too easy, but I'm working on it.

2 Learn vocabulary to describe personal qualities

A **Read the evaluation. Describe Ayana's personal qualities.** She's reliable, responsible, honest, and tolerant.

Employee Evaluation for: _Ayana Abeb_

Section 1: Personal Qualities

EMPLOYEE IS...	RATING*	COMMENTS
reliable	4	is always on time; completes all work
responsible	4	works well without supervision
flexible	2	sometimes has difficulty making changes
honest	4	reports problems and follows company rules
independent	3	can work alone, but does best work on a team
tolerant	4	works well with everyone; listens to others' ideas

*4 = always 3 = usually 2 = sometimes 1 = rarely

B **Complete the sentences. Use the words in 2A.**

1. Ayana is _reliable_. I know she'll be here every day.

2. You can believe everything she says. She's very _____honest_____.

3. She doesn't like to make changes. She needs to be more _____flexible_____.

4. She's a good team player, but she is also _____independent_____.

5. She works hard when the supervisor isn't there. She's _____reliable_____.

6. She works well with everyone. She's _____tolerant_____.

C **Talk about the questions with your class.**

1. When you work on a team, which interpersonal skills and personal qualities are the most important? Why?

2. Which skills and qualities are most important in a family? In a class?

TEST YOURSELF ✔

Close your book. Make four lists about your interpersonal skills and personal qualities. _I can... I can't... I am... I'm not..._ Check your spelling in a dictionary. Compare your lists with a partner.

1 Read a recommendation

A Look at the *To, From,* and *RE* lines of the memo. Talk about the questions with your class.

1. Do Ms. Roberts and Mr. Scott work at the same company? How do you know?
2. What is the memo about?

B Listen and read the recommendation memo.

> **To:**   Annalise Roberts, Human Resources
> **From:** Martin Scott, Accounting
> **RE:**   Recommendation for Employee of the Month
>
> I would like to recommend Helen Lee for the Employee of the Month award.
>
> Ms. Lee has been working as a clerk in the accounting department since 2005. She is one of our most reliable and responsible employees. She does her work well and checks it carefully.
>
> Ms. Lee is a good team player. She makes helpful suggestions and often volunteers to stay late when we are especially busy. She gives 110% to make sure that the work gets done.
>
> I hope that you will consider Helen Lee for the Employee of the Month award.

Writer's note

A workplace memo includes *To, From,* and *RE* (subject) lines. Do not indent the paragraphs in a memo or business letter.

C Check your understanding. Complete the sentences with words from 1B.

1. Mr. Scott wrote a __memo__ to Ms. Roberts.
2. Mr. Scott is recommending Ms. Lee for the Employee of the Month ____award____.
3. Helen Lee is a _____clerk_____ in the accounting department.
4. Ms. Lee is good at working on a _____team_____.
5. Ms. Lee often makes good ____suggestions____.
6. When the office is busy, Ms. Lee often _____volunteers_____ to work late.

☑ Read and write a memo to recommend a co-worker

Unit 6 Lesson 2

Objectives	Grammar	Vocabulary	Correlations
On- and Higher-level: Analyze, write, and edit a recommendation letter **Pre-level:** Read a recommendation letter, and write about job performance	Present tense (*She does her work well and checks it carefully.*)	Interpersonal skills and personal qualities For vocabulary support for pre-level students, see this **Oxford Picture Dictionary** unit: Work	**CASAS:** 0.1.2, 0.1.5, 0.2.1, 4.6.2 **LCPs:** 39.01, 49.02, 49.13, 49.16 **SCANS:** Decision making, Interprets and communicates information, Knowing how to learn, Listening, Speaking **EFF:** Convey ideas in writing, Listen actively, Read with understanding, Speak so others can understand

Warm-up and Review

10–15 minutes (books closed)

Write *Employee of the Month* on the board. Find out if Employee-of-the-Month awards are offered at the students' jobs or if they have noticed the award in stores and other places they do business. Ask them what kinds of benefits the Employee of the Month gets. Benefits sometimes include a cash award, a certificate or plaque, the employee's photo in the newsletter or on the wall, a gift certificate, or a special parking place for the month.

Introduction

5 minutes

1. Ask students how they think the Employee of the Month is chosen. Explain that the process often involves letters of recommendation.

2. State the objective: *Today we're going to read and write a letter of recommendation.*

1 Read a recommendation

Presentation

20–25 minutes

A 1. Direct students to look at the *To:, From:,* and *Re:* lines of the memo. Explain that *Re:* means *Regarding,* which introduces the topic of the memo.

2. Elicit answers to questions 1 and 2.

B 1. Direct students to read the memo silently. Check comprehension. Ask: *What are Ms. Lee's good qualities?*

2. Play the audio. Have students read along silently.

3. Draw students' attention to the *Writer's note.* Ask students: *How do you know when there is a new paragraph if paragraphs aren't indented in a workplace memo?*

Guided Practice I

10 minutes

C Have students work independently to complete the sentences. Write the answers on the board.

Multilevel Strategies

Seat pre-level students together for 1C.

•**Pre-level** While other students are working on 1C, ask these students questions about the memo. *When did Ms. Lee start working in the office? Is she responsible? When does she volunteer to stay late?* Give students time to copy the answers to 1C from the board.

2 Write a recommendation

Guided Practice II

20–25 minutes

 A 1. Read the questions. Elicit students' answers.

2. Write students' ideas for question 2 on the board.

 B 1. Direct students to look back at the memo in 1B. Focus students' attention on the present-tense verbs. Ask them to look through the memo quickly and underline all of the present-tense verbs. Elicit the answers and discuss any questions.

2. Read through the questions, and elicit possible answers for each one.

3. Go over the words in the *Need help?* box.

4. Check comprehension of the exercise. Ask: *Are you going to write about a real person or someone you invented?* [a real person] *Does it have to be someone from this class?* [No, it can be someone from work.]

4. Have students work individually to write their recommendations.

> ### Multilevel Strategies
>
> Adapt 2B to the level of your students.
>
> •**Pre-level** Direct these students to write one-sentence answers to each of the questions in 2B

 C 1. Lead students through the process of using the *Editing checklist.* Read the sentences aloud, and answer any questions. Then ask students to check their papers.

2. Allow students a few minutes to edit their writing as necessary.

Communicative Practice

10 minutes

 D 1. Read the instructions aloud. Emphasize to students that they are responding to their partners' work, not correcting it.

2. Use the memo in 1B to model the exercise. *I think it's very important that she does her work well and checks it carefully. I'd like to ask the writer if Ms. Lee can work independently as well as on a team.*

3. Direct students to exchange papers with a partner and follow the instructions.

4. Call on volunteers to share some interesting things they read in their partners' memos.

Application and Evaluation

20 minutes

 Allow students to have some fun with this *Test Yourself* by writing a recommendation letter for a family member or a friend. Students can create new awards: Daughter of the Month, Friend of the Month, etc. Tell them to explain their nominees' personal qualities and what they do well.

TEST YOURSELF

1. Review the instructions aloud. Assign a time limit (15 minutes), and have students work independently. Give students notice when they have five minutes left.

2. Before collecting students' work, remind them to use the *Editing checklist.* Collect and correct students' writing.

To compress this lesson: Assign the *Test Yourself* for homework.

To extend this lesson: Have students talk about the qualities and skills of someone they admire.
1. Tell students to think of someone they admire: a famous person, a family member, or someone else they know. Write some "famous person" ideas on the board to help students who can't think of anyone.
2. Give students three minutes to take notes on the personal qualities and skills of the person.
3. Have each student tell a partner about the person they admire.

And/Or have students complete **Workbook 4 page 38** and **Multilevel Activity Book 4 page 70**.

2 Write a recommendation

A **Talk about the questions with your class.**

1. Imagine you are recommending someone for Employee or Student of the Month. Who would you recommend?
2. Which interpersonal skills and personal qualities does this person have? What does he or she do very well?

B **Write a memo to recommend the person you described in 2A. Use the model in 1B and the questions below to help you.**

To start: What information will you put in the *To, From,* and *RE* lines of your memo?

Paragraph 1: Who do you want to recommend for Employee or Student of the Month?

Paragraph 2: What are this person's special qualities?
What does he or she do very well?
What interpersonal skills does this person have?

To Close: How will you summarize your recommendation?
How will you end your memo?

> **Need help?**
>
> **Recommendations**
> does excellent work
> goes beyond the call of duty
> gives 110%
> goes the extra mile

To:
From:
RE:
I would like to recommend…

C **Use the checklist to edit your writing. Check (✔) the true sentences.**

Editing checklist	
1. I explained what the person does well.	
2. I described the person's personal qualities and interpersonal skills.	
3. My memo includes *To, From,* and *RE* lines.	
4. I grouped my ideas into paragraphs and did not indent them.	

D **Exchange memos with a partner. Read and comment on your partner's work.**

1. Point out the quality or skill you think is most important.
2. Ask a question about the person in your partner's memo.

TEST YOURSELF ✔

Write a new memo or note recommending someone for an award. Write about another person you know who works really hard.

1 Learn adjective clauses

A Read the conversation. What skill should Alicia work on?

She should make better eye contact with the customers who sit at her tables.

Manager: Here's your evaluation, Alicia. You're doing a great job!

Alicia: Thank you for saying so.

Manager: There's just one skill <u>that needs work</u>. Please try to make better eye contact with the customers <u>who sit at your tables</u>.

Alicia: OK, I will.

B Study the chart. Underline the 2 adjective clauses in the conversation above.

Adjective clauses after main clauses		
Main clause	**Adjective clause**	
There is one **skill**	which that	needs work.
Please greet the **customers**	who that	sit at your tables.

Notes

• Use adjective clauses to give more information about a noun in the main clause of a sentence:
    Alicia should greet the customers.
    A: Which customers should Alicia greet?
    B: Alicia should greet the customers **who sit at her tables.**
• Use *which* or *that* when the adjective describes a thing.
• Use *who* or *that* when the adjective clause describes a person.

C Combine the sentences with adjective clauses. Use *which* or *who*.

1. The manager made a suggestion. The suggestion helped Alicia.

   <u>The manager made a suggestion which helped Alicia.</u>

2. Alicia has many skills. The skills are important in her job.

   Alicia has many skills which are important in her job.

3. She always remembers the customers. The customers sit at her tables.

   She always remembers the customers who sit at her tables.

4. She is good at solving problems. Problems happen in the kitchen.

   She is good at solving problems which happen in the kitchen.

✔ Use adjective clauses to describe job applicants' experience and skills

Unit 6 Lesson 3

Objectives	Grammar	Vocabulary	Correlations
On- and Higher-level: Use adjective clauses to talk about job applicants' experience and skills, and listen for information about job applicants **Pre-level:** Identify adjective clauses in sentences about job applicants' experience and skills, and listen for information about job applicants	Adjective clauses (*Please greet customers who sit at your tables.*)	Interpersonal skills and job qualifications For vocabulary support for pre-level students, see this **Oxford Picture Dictionary** unit: Work	**CASAS:** 4.6.5, 7.4.7 **LCPs:** 35.03, 49.02, 49.16 **SCANS:** Acquires and evaluates information, Decision making, Interprets and communicates information, Speaking **EFF:** Cooperate with others, Listen actively, Read with understanding, Reflect and evaluate, Speak so others can understand

Warm-up and Review

10–15 minutes (books closed)

Scramble the words in these sentences, and write them on the board. *1A. Julie talks to the customers. 1B. The customers come to the front counter. 2A. Tom works with a team. 2B. The team designs catalogs. 3A. Jim spoke to the woman. 3B. The woman was interviewing new employees.* Give students time to unscramble the words. Ask volunteers to write them on the board correctly.

Introduction

5–10 minutes

1. Say: *When we write short sentences, we have to repeat words. Which words are repeated in sentences A and B? We can connect these sentences so that we don't have to repeat the words. For sentence 1, we can say,* Julie talks to the customers who come to the front counter. *The connecting clause is called an* adjective clause.

2. State the objective: *Today we're going to use adjective clauses to talk about job experience and skills.*

1 Learn adjective clauses

Presentation I

20–25 minutes

A 1. Direct students to look at the picture. Ask: *Who are these people?*

2. Read the instructions aloud. Ask students to read the conversation silently to find the answer to the question. Call on a volunteer for the answer.

B 1. Demonstrate how to read the grammar chart.

2. Direct students to underline the adjective clauses in the conversation in 1A. Go over the answers as a class.

3. Read the *Note* aloud. Ask students to identify the noun being described by the adjective clauses in the chart.

4. Read the chart through sentence by sentence. Then read it again, and have students repeat after you.

5. Assess students' understanding of the chart. Elicit ways to join the sentences on the board from the warm-up.

Guided Practice I

15–20 minutes

C Ask students to work individually to combine the sentences. Ask volunteers to write the answers on the board.

Multilevel Strategies

For 1C, seat same-level students together.

• **Pre-level** While other students are completing 1C, provide these students with the answers, and ask them to underline the adjective clause and circle the noun it describes.

T-78

Guided Practice II

5–10 minutes

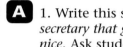 Have students work with a partner to correct the adjective clauses in the sentences. Go over the answers as a class.

2 Learn adjective clauses inside main clauses

Presentation II

20–25 minutes

A 1. Write this sentence on the board: *The secretary that gave me my application was very nice.* Ask students to identify the adjective clause and the noun it describes. Say: *Now we're going to learn about adjective clauses inside the main clause.*

2. Read the instructions aloud. Ask students to read the chart to find the answer to the question.

3. Read the sentences in the chart aloud. Ask students to read the main clauses independently and then read them with the adjective clauses.

Guided Practice I

10–15 minutes

> ### Multilevel Strategies
>
> Adapt 2B to the level of your students.
>
> **•Pre-level** Provide these students with the answers. Direct them to underline the adjective clause and circle the noun it describes.
>
> **•Higher-level** Direct students from this group who finish early to write an original sentence with an adjective clause inside the main clause. Have other students identify the clause and the noun it describes.

B Read number 1 aloud. Direct students to work individually to write the rest of the sentences. Ask volunteers to write the sentences on the board.

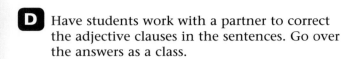

> For more practice with adjective clauses after 2B, write this paragraph on the board: *Marta wanted the manager position _____. She called the number _____ and made an appointment. The man _____ was very nice. He told her to get a letter of recommendation from a supervisor _____. He asked her to choose a time _____ for an interview.*
>
> Write these adjective clauses as a list: *1. that was announced in the company newsletter 2. that she spoke to 3. that was convenient for her 4. that she saw in the announcement 5. whom she had worked with.*
>
> Have students use the adjective clauses to complete the sentences of the paragraph. [1, 4, 2, 5, 3] To make the task more challenging, don't include the blanks in the paragraph, and have students find the appropriate spots for the clauses.

C Direct students to work individually to complete the sentences with their own ideas. Call on several volunteers to read their versions of each of the sentences.

> ### Multilevel Strategies
>
> Adapt 2C to the level of your students.
>
> **•Pre-level** Provide these students with adjective clauses, and have them choose which sentence to insert them into. *a. who go the extra mile b. that offers good benefits c. who can manage conflict and be a leader* [1b, 2a, 3c]

D **Get the form. Work with your class. Correct the sentences.**

1. Tyra's manager gave her feedback who helped her.

   Tyra's manager gave her feedback that (which) helped her.

2. He wants her to manage conflict with the people which work with her.

   He wants her to manage conflict with the people who (that) work with her.

3. Tyra is happy to have a new skill who will help her on her team.

   Tyra is happy to have a new skill that (which) will help her on her team.

2 Learn adjective clauses inside main clauses

A **Study the chart. Who made a suggestion?** The manager who (that) did Alicia's evaluation made a suggestion.

Adjective clauses inside main clauses			
		Main clause	
		Adjective clause	
The manager	who that	did Alicia's evaluation	made a suggestion.
The company	which that	gave him the job	closed last week.

B **Combine the sentences with adjective clauses. Two answers are possible.**

1. The manager was very happy. He had hired Alicia.

   The manager who had hired Alicia was very happy.

   The manager that had hired Alicia was very happy.

2. The suggestion was about making eye contact. It helped Alicia.

   The suggestion that (which) helped Alicia was about making eye contact.

   _____

3. The job opening was filled last week. It was advertised in the paper.

   The job opening that (which) was advertised in the newspaper was filled last week.

   _____

4. The woman quit after two days. She was hired last week.

   The woman who (that) was hired last week quit after two days.

   _____

C **Complete the sentences with adjective clauses. Use your own ideas.**

1. A company _____ is a good place to work.

2. People _____ are good employees.

3. A manager _____ is a good person to work for.

3 Grammar listening

A Listen to the conversations. Match the parts of the sentences.

_c_ 1. We're looking for people   a. who work well on a team.

_e_ 2. We need systems   b. that gets the job must be reliable.

_f_ 3. She got an evaluation   c. that can manage conflict.

_a_ 4. We're hiring people   d. who have the right experience.

_b_ 5. The person   e. that are reliable.

_d_ 6. We'll interview the applicants   f. which was very positive.

B Listen again and check your answers.

4 Practice adjective clauses

A A hotel has a full-time opening for a front-desk clerk. Look at the list of applicants for the job. How many have hotel experience? 3

Applicants for Desk Clerk Position:	
Applicant	Notes
1	speaks 5 languages but hasn't worked in a hotel
2	has a lot of experience in hotels in Europe
3	is a housekeeper here now. She's very reliable
4	is currently a desk clerk at a smaller hotel
5	is the hotel owner's nephew but has never had a job
6	has studied hotel management but hasn't worked in a hotel

B Work with a partner. You are managers at the hotel in 4A. Decide which applicant to hire. Give your opinion.

I think we should hire the person who…
The person that… would be better because…

C Tell the class which applicant you have decided to hire and why.

We want to hire the applicant who… because…

TEST YOURSELF ✔

Close your book. Write 5 sentences about your classmates' opinions in 4C.
Use adjective clauses to write about the job applicant's qualifications.

3 Grammar listening

Guided Practice II
10–15 minutes

A 1. Say: *Now we're going to listen to questions and answers with an employer.* Tell students to read the sentences before listening.

2. Play the audio. Direct students to match the parts of the sentences.

B 1. Replay the audio. Ask students to check or complete their work.

2. Call on volunteers to read the completed sentences aloud.

4 Practice adjective clauses

Communicative Practice and Application
20–25 minutes

A Read the instructions aloud. Direct students to look at the list of applicants to find the answer to the question. Elicit the numbers of the applicants with hotel experience.

B 1. Direct students to talk to a partner to decide whom to hire. Tell them to discuss the pros and cons of each applicant. Tell them to make notes on their decision-making process.

2. Check comprehension of the exercise. Ask: *Should you discuss every applicant or just the one that seems best?* [every applicant]

C 1. Call on pairs to share their decision and their reasons with the class.

2. Try to come to a class consensus on the top two or three candidates and on the least desirable candidate.

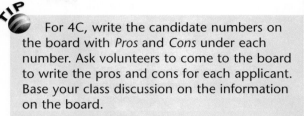

For 4C, write the candidate numbers on the board with *Pros* and *Cons* under each number. Ask volunteers to come to the board to write the pros and cons for each applicant. Base your class discussion on the information on the board.

Evaluation
10–15 minutes (books closed)

TEST YOURSELF

Ask students to write the sentences independently. Collect and correct their writing.

> **Multilevel Strategies**
>
> Target the *Test Yourself* to the level of your students.
>
> •**Pre-level** Provide skeleton sentences for these students to complete. *The woman who is a housekeeper here now is a good/bad candidate because _____. The person who is currently a desk clerk is a good/bad candidate because _____. The person who speaks five languages is a good/bad candidate because _____.*

To compress this lesson: Conduct 1C as a whole-class discussion. Assign 2C for homework.

To extend this lesson: Have students talk about their job preferences.
1. Put students in mixed-level groups. Write a series of skeleton sentences on the board: *1. I would like a job that _____. 2. I'd like to have a boss that _____. 3. I want to work in a place that _____. 4. I want to be the kind of employee that _____. 5. I'd like to have co-workers that _____.*
2. Have each person in the group complete sentence 1 orally. When they get back to the first person in the group, have a different student start with sentence 2. Model the activity with one of the groups. Monitor and provide feedback.

And/Or have students complete **Workbook 4 pages 39–40, Multilevel Activity Book 4 pages 71–72**, and the corresponding **Unit 6 Exercises** on the **Multilevel Grammar Exercises CD-ROM 4**.

Unit 6 Lesson 4

Objectives	Grammar	Vocabulary	Correlations
On-, Pre-, and Higher-level: Ask for information and listen for information in an automated phone message	Adjective clauses with *whose* (*She's the woman whose office is closest to the entrance.*)	*Payroll clerk, procedure, warehouse* For vocabulary support for pre-level students, see this **Oxford Picture Dictionary** unit: Work	**CASAS:** 0.1.2, 0.1.5, 4.2.1, 6.0.3, 6.0.4, 6.0.5, 6.1.2 **LCPs:** 36.05, 36.06, 40.01, 49.01, 49.02, 49.09 **SCANS:** Arithmetic/Mathematics, Creative thinking, Listening, Speaking **EFF:** Listen actively, Read with understanding, Reflect and evaluate, Use math to solve problems and communicate

Warm-up and Review

10–15 minutes (books closed)

Review question formation. Write *who, what, which, where, when, why, how,* and *whose* on the board. Call on volunteers to ask a question with one of the words. Challenge students not to use any verb that has already been used.

Introduction

5 minutes

1. Say: *These are the questions we use to ask for information. It is important to know how to ask for information. It is also important to know whom to ask for information.*

2. State the objective: *Today we're going to talk about getting information from the right people at work or school, and getting information from an automated phone message.*

1 Learn to ask for information

Presentation I

15–20 minutes

 1. Direct students to look at the organizational chart. Read the job titles aloud, and elicit the responsibilities of each person.

2. Play the audio. Give students a minute to answer the questions. Go over the answers as a class.

Guided Practice

20–25 minutes

 1. Read the instructions aloud. Play the audio. Ask students to read along silently and listen for the answer to the question. Elicit the answer.

2. Ask students to read the conversation with a partner. Circulate and monitor pronunciation. Model and have students repeat difficult words or phrases.

3. Say and have students repeat the expressions in the *In other words* box. Elicit the placement of the expressions in the conversation. Ask volunteers to read the conversation using expressions from the box.

Communicative Practice and Application

15–20 minutes

 1. Ask students to read the instructions silently. Check comprehension of the exercise. Ask: *What are the two roles? What is the situation?* Elicit examples of what each person might say.

2. Set a time limit (five minutes). Ask students to act out the role-play in both roles. Ask one to three volunteer pairs to act out their conversations for the class. Tell students who are listening to note how Partner A asks for information.

> ### Multilevel Strategies
>
> For 1C, adapt the role-play to the level of your students.
>
> •**Pre-level** Provide the beginning of the conversation for these students. *A: There's a problem with my class schedule. Whom should I see about it? B: You need to see _____.*

1 Learn to ask for information

 A **Look at the organizational chart. Listen to the conversations. Then answer the questions below with your classmates.**

MARTINEZ ELECTRONICS

George Martinez, General Manager

Marilyn Reese, Warehouse Manager

Gina Anderson, Human Resources Supervisor

Martin Gupta, Benefits Officer

Teresa Bell, Payroll Clerk   **Jun Kim,** Payroll Clerk

1. Who should Marta see about her schedule? the warehouse manager, Marilyn Reese
2. Who should Jamal talk to about the memo that he received? the benefits officer, Martin Gupta

B **Listen and read. Why shouldn't the employee talk to her manager first?**
The procedure is to go to Ms. Bell.

A: Hey! You look upset. What's wrong?

B: There's a problem with my paycheck.
   Who should I see about it?

A: Go see Ms. Bell.

B: Ms. Bell? Who's she?

A: You know. She's the woman whose office is next to
   the time clock.

B: Should I talk to my manager first?

A: Uh-uh. You should go directly to Ms. Bell.
   She's the person who takes care of payroll
   problems. That's the procedure here.

B: OK, thanks. I'll see you later.

> **In other words...**
>
> **Asking for information**
> Who should I see about...?
> Who do I talk to?
> What should I do?
> What do I do about...?

C **Role-play a conversation with a partner about asking for information. Use the example in 1B to make a new conversation.**

Partner A: You're a student and there's a problem with your class schedule. Ask your classmate who you should see about it. Ask if you should talk to your teacher first. Thank your classmate for helping you.

Partner B: You're a student. Your classmate asks you a question. Tell your classmate to see Mr. Ang, the coordinator. His office is downstairs. He takes care of schedule problems.

✔ Identify workplace hierarchy; problem-solve issues involving information   **81**

2 Learn adjective clauses with *whose*

A Study the chart. Who are Mr. and Mrs. Lopez? *They're the people whose children won awards.*

Adjective clauses with *whose*	
Main clause	**Adjective clause**
Ms. Bell is the **clerk**	**whose office** is next to the time clock.
Mr. and Mrs. Lopez are the **people**	**whose children** won awards.

Note
Adjective clauses with *whose* show who something belongs to.

B Work with a partner. Combine the sentences with *whose*. Then use the new sentence in a conversation.

1. Margaret is one of the cashiers. Her schedule is the same as Tom's.
   A: *Who is Margaret?*
   B: *She's the cashier whose schedule is the same as Tom's.*
2. Mr. Edwards is one of the teachers. His office is on the second floor.
3. Natasha and Jim are the employees. Their paychecks were lost.
4. Sophie is one of the managers. Her office is down the hall.

A: Who is Mr. Edwards?
B: He's the teacher whose office is on the second floor.
A: Who are Natasha and Jim?
B: They're the employees whose paychecks were lost.
A: Who's Sophie?
B: She's the manager whose office is down the hall.

C Work with a partner. Complete the sentences with adjective clauses.

1. Mr. Kelso is the teacher _whose class meets at three o'clock_____.
2. Terry is the manager _____.
3. Daria is the woman _____.
4. Mr. and Mrs. Silva are the people _____.

3 Practice your pronunciation

A Listen to the conversations. Notice how the speakers say *Yes* and *No*. Practice the conversations with a partner.

1. **A:** Do I talk to my manager first?
   B: Uh-uh. You go to Ms. Bell.
2. **A:** Does Mr. Sosa work here?
   B: Uh-huh. Do you need to talk to him?

Note: Do not use *Uh-uh* or *Uh-huh* in formal situations.

B Work with a partner. Ask and answer the questions. Use *Uh-huh* and *Uh-uh* to say *Yes* or *No*. Then add more information, as in 1A.

1. Do you work in an office?
2. Were you in class yesterday?
3. Have you ever gotten an award?
4. Do you like to work on a team?

2 Learn adjective clauses with *whose*

Presentation II

10–15 minutes

 1. Write: *That's the man that I met in the office. She's the woman who helped me fill out my application.* Elicit the adjective clauses and the nouns they describe. Underline the clauses and circle the nouns.

2. Introduce the new topic. *Now we're going to look at another kind of adjective clause.* Read the instructions aloud. Direct students to read the sentences in the chart to find the answer. Read the *Note* aloud.

Guided Practice

15–20 minutes

 1. Have students work with a partner to combine the sentences with *whose*. Model the conversation with a volunteer.

2. Call on volunteers to share their conversations with the class.

Communicative Practice and Application

15–20 minutes

 1. Have students work with a partner to complete the sentences using their own ideas.

2. Ask volunteers to write their sentences on the board.

Multilevel Strategies

After 2C, provide additional practice with adjective clauses. Use same-level pairs and target the practice to the level of your students.

•**Pre-level** Pair these students and provide them with definitions using adjective clauses. Tell one partner to read the definitions and the other to guess the answer. *A person who fixes pipes is a _____. The form that you fill out when you want a job is an _____. A person who types and files is a _____.*

•**On- and Higher-level** Direct these students to write their own definitions and have their partners guess the answers. Show some of the definitions you have written for pre-level students as an example.

After students have practiced with their partners, collect all of the definitions, and call out some of them for the class to answer.

3 Practice your pronunciation

Pronunciation Extension

10–15 minutes

 1. Ask several volunteers an obvious *Yes/No* question. *Are you a student? Are you a doctor?* Write their *Yes/No* answers on the board exactly as they say them. Say: *There are different ways to say yes and no depending on how formal the situation is.*

2. Play the audio. Direct students to listen for how the speakers say yes and no.

3. Have students practice the conversation with a partner.

B 1. Model the questions and answers with a volunteer.

2. Direct students to practice with a partner. Have one partner ask all of the questions and the other partner answer. Tell them to switch roles when they finish.

4 Focus on Listening

Listening Extension

20–25 minutes

A Read the questions aloud, and elicit answers from volunteers. After one student answers each question, ask other students for additional ideas.

B 1. Read the office names aloud, and elicit the function of each office.

2. Read the instructions and check comprehension of the exercise. Ask: *Are you going to write the extension number?* [no]

3. Play the audio. Have students number the departments in the order they hear them. Elicit the answers from the class.

C 1. Direct students to look at the chart before listening. Draw their attention to the sample answer.

2. Replay the audio and have students work individually to complete the chart. Go over the answers as a class.

Multilevel Strategies

Replay the message in 4C to challenge on- and higher-level students while allowing pre-level students to catch up.

•**Pre-level** Have these students listen again to complete the chart.

•**On- and Higher-level** Ask these students to note the reason for choosing Sales and Service or Customer Service. After you correct 4C, elicit the additional information.

5 Real-life math

Math Extension

5–10 minutes

1. Direct students to look at the pay stub. Review the meanings of each column head on the stub.

2. Ask students to work individually to figure out the answer to the question. Elicit the problem and the solution from a volunteer.

Evaluation

10–15 minutes

TEST YOURSELF

1. Model the role-play with a volunteer. Then switch roles.

2. Pair students. Check comprehension of the exercise by eliciting things that each neighbor might say.

3. Set a time limit (five minutes), and have the partners act out the role-play in both roles.

4. Circulate and monitor. Encourage pantomime and improvisation.

5. Provide feedback.

Multilevel Strategies

Target the *Test Yourself* to the level of your students.

•**Pre-level** Provide these students with the beginning of the conversation: *A: There's a problem with my _____. Should I call a repairperson? B: I think you should _____.*

To compress this lesson: Conduct *Real-life math* as a whole-class activity.

To extend this lesson: Go over an organizational chart for your school.
1. Show students an organizational chart for your school. Review the various job titles on the chart. Discuss which people students might need to speak to—for example, a teacher, a secretary, a counselor, the principal, a department head, the nurse.
2. Put students in groups, and ask them to discuss various reasons they might need to speak to each of the people. Go over their ideas as a class.

And/Or have students complete **Workbook 4 page 41** and **Multilevel Activity Book 4 page 73**.

4 Focus on listening

A **Talk about the questions with your class.**

1. What are some reasons employees call a company?
2. What are some reasons customers call a company?

B **Listen to the automated phone menu. Number the offices in the order you hear them.**

3	Business Services	6	Main Office
2	Customer Service	1	Sales and Service
5	Human Resources	4	Warehouse

C **Listen again. Complete the phone directory for Martinez Electronics.**

Office	Extension
Business Services	417
Customer Service	222
Human Resources	389
Main Office	555
Sales and Service	111
Warehouse	700

5 Real-life math

A **Read the problem and answer the question.**

Martinez Electronics		Name: Tom Tran			Check # 3133
Gross Pay	Social Security	Medicare	Federal Tax	State Tax	**Net Pay**
$421.40	$26.13	$6.11	$11.03	$13.80	**$355.36**

Tom called Ms. Bell in Payroll because he thinks there is an error on his paycheck. He thinks his net pay is incorrect. What should Tom's net pay be? _____$364.33_____

B **Explain your answer to your classmates.**

TEST YOURSELF ✔

Role-play a conversation between two neighbors. Partner A: Something in your apartment isn't working. Ask your partner who to call. You think you should call the repairperson. Partner B: Tell your neighbor that he or she needs to call the apartment manager first. Then change roles.

1 Get ready to read

A What do you think *people skills* are? Give some examples.

B Read the definitions. What are you enthusiastic about?

diverse: (adj.) including a lot of differences
enthusiastic: (adj.) excited, very positive
pay off: (verb) to produce a benefit

C Read the questions in 2C on page 85. Look for the answers as you read the article in 2A.

2 Read and respond

A Read the article. Did the students enjoy the training class?   Yes, they did.

Skills Training Pays Off for Local Residents

Last Thursday, the Pasco Adult Skills Program celebrated the end of its spring semester with a party for graduates of its 12-week *People Skills* training class. The graduates were enthusiastic about the program and its results.

"I learned about teamwork," said Daniela Victor, age 27. "Before I took this class, I thought that people who worked in groups could never get anything done. Now I know that when people work together, they get a lot more work done. I'm a more tolerant and more flexible person now.

"I really appreciated the emphasis[1] on language," said Musa Tahri, 45. "I needed to learn the right English to work in a group and manage conflict. Everything we did in class is paying off. The skills I learned are helping me at work, in my community, and even at home. I'm helping my kids learn to resolve disagreements and find solutions to problems by talking. Those skills are helping them in school, too!"

A third graduate, Diego Rosario, 66, was also enthusiastic. "I'm so glad I came here," said Rosario. "I've met men and women from all over the world, and I've learned a lot about working with diverse groups of people. I'm using the skills I learned to start a community parks group in my neighborhood."

Pasco Adult School's next *People Skills* training class is scheduled to begin in September. For more information, call (250) 555-1800.

[1]emphasis: a strong focus on something

☑ Use previewing strategies to better understand a reading passage

Unit 6 Lesson 5

Objectives	Grammar	Vocabulary	Correlations
On-, Pre-, and Higher-level: Read about and discuss skills training	Adjectives (*She's irresponsible.*)	Adjectives with *dis-, in-, ir-,* and *un-* prefixes For vocabulary support for pre-level students, see these **Oxford Picture Dictionary** topics: Job Skills, Job Search	**CASAS:** 0.1.2, 0.1.5, 4.4.1, 4.8.7, 7.4.4, 7.5.6 **LCPs:** 38.01, 49.02, 49.04, 49.09, 49.16 **SCANS:** Acquires and evaluates information, Listening, Reading, Selects technology, Speaking **EFF:** Cooperate with others, Learn through research, Read with understanding, Take responsibility for learning

Warm-up and Review

10–15 minutes (books closed)

Write *Shy, Outgoing, Honest, Reliable,* and *Funny* on the board. Elicit more examples of words that describe people's personalities. Write them on the board.

Introduction

5 minutes

1. Ask volunteers to come to the board and circle adjectives that describe positive employee traits. Ask if students think these attitudes or personality qualities are skills that can be learned.

2. State the objective: *Today we're going to read and discuss skills training.*

1 Get ready to read

Presentation

15–20 minutes

A Read the question aloud. Make any associations you can between students' answers and the adjectives on the board from the warm-up. *Outgoing people often have good people skills.*

B Read the words and definitions. Elicit sample sentences from students using the words.

Pre-Reading

C 1. Direct students to read the title of the article. Ask: *Does this mean they got money from the training?*

2. Read the questions on page 85 aloud. Ask students to look for the answers as they read the article.

2 Read and respond

Guided Practice I

25–30 minutes

A 1. Ask students to read the article silently.

2. After students are finished reading, direct students to underline unfamiliar words they would like to know. Elicit the words and encourage other students to provide definitions or examples.

3. Check students' comprehension. Ask: *How long was the training course?* [12 weeks] *How did the graduates feel about it?* [enthusiastic]

Multilevel Strategies

Adapt 2A to the level of your students.

•**Pre-level** Provide these students with a summary of the ideas in the reading. *Daniela, Musa, and Diego just graduated from a 12-week people-skills training class. Daniela learned about teamwork. Now she is more flexible and tolerant. Musa learned English skills that help him resolve conflicts at work, at home, and in the community. Diego learned about diverse groups of people. The class begins again in September.*

Direct these students to read the summary while other students are reading 2A.

Guided Practice II

15–20 minutes

B 1. Play the audio. Have students read along silently.

2. Elicit and discuss any additional questions about the reading. Discuss the meaning of the expression: *There's no* I *in* team.

C Tell students to ask and answer the questions with a partner. Call on volunteers for the answers.

Multilevel Strategies

Adapt 2C to the level of your students.

•**Pre-level** Write questions on the board for these students to ask and answer while other students are completing 2C. Tell them to refer to their summaries. *1. What class did the three students take? 2. What did Daniel learn? 3. Did Musa learn how to resolve conflicts at home? 4. What did Diego learn?* Call on volunteers for the answers.

D 1. Read the information in the chart aloud. Elicit and discuss any questions the students have about the prefixes. Say the words and have students repeat them.

2. Direct students to work individually to circle the correct word to complete each sentence. Write the answers on the board.

Multilevel Strategies

For 2D, seat pre-level students together.

•**Pre-level** While other students are completing 2D, direct these students to copy the words from the chart into their notebooks with a definition. Allow them to look in their dictionaries if necessary. Have them copy the answers to 2D from the board.

•**Higher-level** After they finish 2D, have these students look up an additional adjective with one of the prefixes. Ask them to write a sentence with the adjective on the board.

3 Talk it over

Communicative Practice

15–20 minutes

1. Read the questions aloud. Set a time limit (three minutes). Have students work independently to think about the questions and write their answers in note form.

2. Call on volunteers to share their ideas with the class.

Application

5–10 minutes

BRING IT TO LIFE

Read the instructions aloud. Students can easily find workplace cartoons on the Internet by typing *workplace cartoon* into a search engine. In addition, many well-known cartoonists have books that can be found at the library.

To compress this lesson: Assign 2D as homework.

To extend this lesson: After 2D, teach additional adjectives with *in-, un-, ir-,* and *dis-*.
1. Write the following words on the board: *incompetent, intolerant, unqualified, unprofessional, irrational, disorganized, dissatisfied.* Elicit the positive form of the adjective and discuss both meanings.
2. As a class, write a sample sentence for the positive form of each word.
3. Have students work in pairs or groups to write a sample sentence for the negative form of the word. Ask volunteers to write their sentences on the board.

And/Or have students complete **Workbook 4 page 42** and **Multilevel Activity Book 4 pages 74–75**.

B Listen and read the article again.

C Work with a partner. Ask and answer the questions.

1. What class did the three students take? *the 12-week People Skills training class*
2. What does Daniela Victor think now about people who work together? *She thinks that they get a lot more work done.*
3. What personal qualities did Daniela Victor develop in the class? *She's more tolerant and flexible.*
4. How is Musa Tahri using his new skills? *Musa is helping his children learn to resolve disagreements and find solutions to problems. Diego is starting a community parks group in his neighborhood.*

D Study the chart. Circle the correct words in the sentences below.

> **Word Study: The prefixes *dis-*, *in-*, and *un-***
>
> Add *dis-*, *in-*, *ir-*, and *un-* to the beginning of some adjectives to form negatives.
>
> | Adjective | Negative | Adjective | Negative |
> |---|---|---|---|
> | responsible | irresponsible | reliable | unreliable |
> | flexible | inflexible | honest | dishonest |

1. Some of my co-workers come late and are very (dependable /(unreliable)), but Laura is ((responsible)/ irresponsible) and always finishes her work on time.
2. Edward is (flexible /(inflexible)); he can't make changes. And sometimes he's (honest /(dishonest)) and breaks the company rules. The company shouldn't hire someone who's this (reliable /(irresponsible)).

3 Talk it over

Think about the questions. Talk about your ideas with the class.

1. Many people say that it's important to be able to work with diverse groups of people. Do you agree? Why or why not?
2. What are some things that help people in diverse groups work together?
3. How can you have good interpersonal skills in a language you don't know well?

BRING IT TO LIFE

Use the newspaper, a magazine, or the Internet to find an article or cartoon about interpersonal skills in the workplace. Bring it to class and talk about it with your classmates.

1 Grammar

A Circle the correct words.

1. The company (**that** / who) makes these boxes is in our town.
2. The people (which / **who**) work there say that it's a good company.
3. I know several people (who / **whose**) parents worked there.
4. The owner of the company is the person (**that** / which) hired me.
5. A lot of companies use the boxes (**which** / who) are made here.
6. The employees (who / **whose**) work is the best get awards every year.

B Match the parts of the sentences.

__c__ 1. The manager   a. whose benefits were increased was very happy.

__a__ 2. The employee   b. which require experience are harder to get.

__d__ 3. Employees   c. that prepared the report did a good job.

__b__ 4. Jobs   d. who are honest are very valuable.

C Combine the sentences. Use adjective clauses with *who, that,* or *which.*

1. I like working with people. People can resolve disagreements.

   I like working with people who can resolve disagreements.

2. Disagreements can cause big problems on the job. The disagreements aren't resolved.

   Disagreements which (that) aren't resolved can cause big problems on the job.

3. The manager gives a lot of feedback. She hired me.

   The manager who (that) hired me gives a lot of feedback.

4. The team won $100. The team solved the problem.

   The team which (that) solved the problem won $100.

D Combine the sentences. Use adjective clauses with *whose.*

1. Ms. Haines is the teacher. Her class always has the most students.

   Ms. Haines is the teacher whose class always has the most students.

2. Mr. Freeman is the art teacher. His students painted these pictures.

   The art teacher whose students painted these pictures is very proud.

3. Mr. Diaz was the counselor. His suggestions really helped me.

   Mr. Diaz was the counselor whose suggestions really helped me.

4. Mrs. Tanaka was the principal. Her office was very nice.

   Mrs. Tanaka was the principal whose office was very nice.

Unit 6 Review and expand

Objectives	Grammar	Vocabulary	Correlations
On-, Pre-, and Higher-level: Expand upon and review unit grammar and life skills	Adjective clauses (*I work at the company that makes those boxes.*)	Job skills For vocabulary support for pre-level students, see this **Oxford Picture Dictionary** unit: Work	**CASAS:** 0.1.2, 0.1.5, 0.2.1, 7.2.6, 7.3.1, 7.3.2, 7.3.4 **LCPs:** 39.01, 49.02, 49.13, 49.16 **SCANS:** Acquires and evaluates information, Interprets and communicates information, Problem solving **EFF:** Convey ideas in writing, Cooperate with others, Solve problems and make decisions

Warm-up and Review

10–15 minutes (books closed)

1. Review the *Bring It to Life* assignment from Lesson 5.

2. Have students who did the exercise share their cartoons with the class. Ask other students if they "get" the joke. Tell students which cartoon you think is the funniest.

Introduction and Presentation

5 minutes

1. Write sentences about the students' cartoons using adjective clauses. *The cartoon that Santiago brought in is very funny. The man who wrote the _____ cartoon is very famous. I like cartoons that _____.*

2. Ask students to identify the adjective clauses in your sentences and the nouns they describe.

3. State the objective: *Today we're going to review adjective clauses in order to talk about getting ahead.*

1 Grammar

Guided Practice

40–45 minutes

A Read the first sentence aloud. Direct students to work individually to circle the correct words. Go over the answers as a class.

B Tell students to read all of the sentence parts before matching them. Ask them to work individually. Call on volunteers to read the completed sentences aloud.

C Have students work with a partner to combine the sentences. Ask volunteers to write their sentences on the board.

D Have students work with their partners to combine the sentences. Ask volunteers to write their sentences on the board.

Multilevel Strategies

For 1C and 1D seat same-level students together.

•**Pre-level** Provide these students with the adjective clauses, and ask them to insert them in the right place in the sentence. *C: 2. that aren't resolved, 3. who hired me, 4. that solved the problem D: 1. whose class always has the most students, 2. whose students painted these pictures, 3. whose suggestions really helped me. 4. whose office was very nice.*

•**Higher-level** Have students from this group who finish the exercises early write two original sentences with an adjective clause (one with *whose*). Ask them to put their sentences on the board and have other students identify the adjective clauses.

2 Group work

Communicative Practice

20–35 minutes

 A 1. Direct students, in groups of three to four, to focus on the picture. Ask: *Who are these people? How do they feel? What do you think they are talking about?*

2. Assign roles: leader, recorder, and reporters. Explain that students work with their groups to write the conversation.

3. Check comprehension of the roles. Ask: *Who writes the conversation?* [recorder] *Who will read the conversation to the class?* [reporters] *Who helps everyone and manages the group?* [leader] *Who creates the conversation?* [everyone]

4. Set a time limit (five minutes) to complete the exercise. Circulate and answer any questions. Have reporters from each group read the group's conversation to the class.

> ### Multilevel Strategies
>
> For 2A, use mixed-level groups.
>
> •**Pre-level** Assign these students the role of recorder.
>
> •**On-level** Assign these students the role of reporter.
>
> •**Higher-level** Assign these students the role of leader.

B 1. Have students walk around the room to conduct these interviews. To get students moving, tell them to interview three new people not in their groups for 2A.

2. Set a time limit (five minutes) to complete the exercise. Tell students to make a note of their classmates' answers but not to worry about writing complete sentences.

> ### Multilevel Strategies
>
> Adapt the mixer in 2B to the level of your students.
>
> •**Pre-level** Allow these students to ask and answer the questions without writing.
>
> •**Higher-level** Have these students ask two additional questions and write all answers.

C Call on individuals to report what they learned about their classmates. Elicit their ideas about three things that every teacher should do. Tell them your opinion.

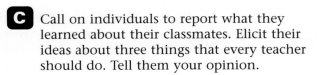
PROBLEM SOLVING

15–25 minutes

 A 1. Ask: *Did you ever work with a group that couldn't get along?* Tell students they will read a story about a woman who is trying to manage a difficult group. Direct students to read Lana's story silently.

2. Ask: *How many employees are on Lana's team?* [six] *What is happening with her group?* [They don't get along.]

3. Play the audio and have students read along silently.

B 1. Elicit answers to question 1. Have volunteers write answers to question 2 on the board until all of the class ideas have been put up.

2. Put students into groups of three or four, and have them discuss the pros and cons of each solution.

3. Pair students. Ask them to write a short letter giving advice to Lana. Call on volunteers to read their letters to the class.

Evaluation

30–35 minutes

To test students' understanding of the unit grammar and life skills, have them take the Unit 6 Test on the *Step Forward Test Generator CD-ROM* with *ExamView® Assessment Suite*.

> **Learning Log**
>
> To help students record and discuss their progress, use the *Learning Log* on page T-201.

To extend this review: Have students complete **Workbook 4 page 43, Multilevel Activity Book 4 page 76**, and the **Unit 6 Exercises** on the **Multilevel Grammar Exercises CD-ROM 4**.

2 Group work

A Work with 2–3 classmates. Write a 6–8 line conversation between the people in the picture. Share your conversation with the class.

A: *Let's take a look at your evaluation.*
B: *OK.*
A: *First, you're doing a good job at...*

B Interview 3 classmates. Write their answers.

1. Do you know someone who gets along with everyone? Who is it? How does he/she do it?
2. Which interpersonal skill would you like to develop? Why?
3. What are three things that every manager (or teacher or parent) should do? Why?

C Talk about your answers with your class.

PROBLEM SOLVING

A Listen and read about Lana.

Lana has just gotten a promotion at work. She is a team manager for a group of six employees. Lana really wants to be a success in her new job, but her group isn't really a team. Two of the people in her group don't like each other and argue a lot. There is one team member who talks all the time and another one who never says a word. The team members are from six different countries, and two of the countries they come from don't get along. Lana doesn't know what to do.

B Work with your classmates. Answer the questions.

1. What is Lana's problem? Lana is a team manager, but the employees in her group don't get along.
2. What should she do? Think of 2 or 3 solutions to her problem.
3. Write a short letter to Lana. Tell her what you think she should do.

Buy Now, Pay Later

FOCUS ON
- personal finance and budgeting
- essay writing
- present unreal conditionals
- negotiating and compromising
- financial planning

LESSON **1** Vocabulary

1 Learn vocabulary for personal finance and banking

A Talk about the questions with your class.

1. What are some services that banks and credit unions offer?
2. Are you good at managing money? What money skills do you have?

B Work with your classmates. Match the words with the picture.

1	assets	2	debts	3	insurance policy
5	auto loan	4	home loan	6	interest rate

C Listen and check. Then read the new words with a partner.

D Work with a partner. Write other personal finance and banking words you know. Check your words in a dictionary.

Identify and use financial and banking vocabulary to discuss budgeting

Unit 7 Lesson 1

Objectives	Grammar	Vocabulary	Correlations
On-level: Describe and talk about personal finance, banking, and budgeting **Pre-level:** Identify and describe personal finance, banking, and budgeting **Higher-level:** Talk and write about personal finance, banking, and budgeting	Past tense (*How much did we pay?*)	Personal finance, banking and budgeting For vocabulary support for pre-level students, see these **Oxford Picture Dictionary** topics: Money, The Bank	**CASAS:** 0.1.2, 0.1.5, 1.4.6, 1.5.1, 1.5.2, 4.8.1, 7.4.5 **LCPs:** 49.02, 49.10 **SCANS:** Listening, Participates as member of a team, Seeing things in the mind's eye, Speaking **EFF:** Cooperate with others, Listen actively, Observe critically, Plan, Speak so others can understand

Warm-up and Review

10–15 minutes (books closed)

Write *Where does the money go?* on the board. Ask students what things they spend most of their money on. Write their ideas on the board.

Introduction

5 minutes

1. Ask students to rank the items on the board from the ones that generally cost the most to the ones that cost the least.

2. State the objective: *Today we're going to learn words for personal finance, banking, and budgeting.*

1 Learn vocabulary for personal finance and banking

Presentation I

20–25 minutes

A Write *Banks and Credit Unions* and *Money Skills* on the board, and elicit students' answers to question 1 and 2. Note their ideas under the correct term.

B 1. Direct students to look at the pictures. Ask: *What are they looking at?*

2. Group students and assign roles: leader, fact checker, recorder, and reporter. Explain that students work with their groups to match the words and pictures.

3. Check comprehension of the roles. Ask: *Who looks up the words in a dictionary?* [fact checker] *Who writes the numbers in the book?* [recorder] *Who tells the class your answers?* [reporter] *Who helps everyone and manages the group?* [leader]

4. Set a time limit (three minutes). As students work together, copy the wordlist onto the board.

5. Call "time." Have reporters take turns giving their answers. Write each group's answer on the board next to the word.

C 1. To prepare students for listening, say: *We're going to listen to Roberto and Julia talk about their financial plans.* Ask students to listen and check their answers.

2. Have students check the wordlist on the board and then write the correct numbers in their books.

3. Pair students. Set a time limit (three minutes). Monitor pair practice to identify pronunciation issues.

4. Call "time" and work with the pronunciation of any troublesome words or phrases.

5. Replay the audio and challenge students to listen for more information about each item. Elicit what they heard.

D 1. Ask students to work with their partners from 1C to brainstorm a list of related words.

2. Elicit words from the class. Write them on the board. Ask students to copy them into their vocabulary notes for the unit.

Guided Practice

5–10 minutes

 E 1. Read the questions aloud, and elicit one answer for each question.

2. Set a time limit (three minutes). Direct students to ask and answer the questions with a partner.

3. Call on volunteers to share their answers with the class.

2 Learn budgeting vocabulary

Presentation II

15–20 minutes

 A 1. Direct students to look at the budget plan. Introduce the new topic: *Now we're going to learn budgeting vocabulary.*

2. Read the items in the chart aloud. Elicit definitions of *mortgage* and *premium*. Ask for examples of miscellaneous items.

3. Ask students to work individually to match the words with their definitions.

4. Read and have students repeat the words. Call on volunteers to read the matching definitions.

5. Check comprehension. Ask: *Is your rent payment a fixed expense or a variable expense?* [fixed] *What do you call the money you pay for insurance?* [a premium]

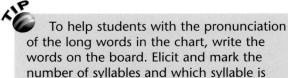

To help students with the pronunciation of the long words in the chart, write the words on the board. Elicit and mark the number of syllables and which syllable is stressed.

Guided Practice

10–15 minutes

 B 1. Model the conversation with a volunteer. Model it again using a different word from 2A.

2. Set a time limit (three minutes). Direct students to practice with a partner.

3. Call on volunteers to say one of their conversations for the class.

Communicative Practice and Application

10–15 minutes

 C 1. Give students a minute to make notes of their answers to the questions. Call on individuals to share their ideas with the class.

2. Write the students' advice on the board. Ask them if they follow their own advice.

Evaluation

10–15 minutes (books closed)

TEST YOURSELF

1. Direct students to work individually to write a list of words from the lesson. Assign a time limit (three minutes). Call "time" and direct students to work with a partner to combine their lists and put the words in alphabetical order.

2. Circulate and monitor students' progress. Ask a volunteer pair to write its list on the board. Ask other students to add words to the list.

> ### Multilevel Strategies
>
> Target the *Test Yourself* to the level of your students.
>
> •**Higher-level** After these students have worked with a partner to alphabetize their lists, ask them to write three to five sentences defining words from the list.

To compress this lesson: Conduct 1B as a whole-class activity.

To extend this lesson: Have students compare bank brochures. Put students in mixed-level groups. Give each group brochures from two different banks. (You can pick these up at the banks, or you can print them off the Internet. If you have access to computers in the class, you can do this together.) Direct each group to compare the two brochures by looking at types of accounts, fees, minimum balances, and interest rates. Ask a reporter from each group to share his/her group's findings.

And/Or have students complete **Workbook 4 page 44** and **Multilevel Activity Book 4 pages 78–79**.

E Work with a partner. Talk about the questions. Use the words in 1B.

1. What types of accounts and loans do banks offer?
2. What types of assets and debts do people often have?
3. What kinds of insurance do people often have?

2 Learn budgeting vocabulary

A Look at Julia and Roberto's budget. Match the words with their definitions.

Our budget: Sanchez-Ruiz family

Net Income		Julia's job	$1200 per month
		Roberto's job	$1200 per month
Expenses	Fixed Expenses	Rent	$900 per month
		Car insurance premium	$200 per month
	Variable Expenses	food	$400 per month
		utilities	$200 per month
		car (gas)	$300 per month
		miscellaneous (clothing, gifts, eating out, etc.)	$400 per month

Mortgage payment for house = $1,035 per month

_d_ 1. fixed expenses
_c_ 2. variable expenses
_a_ 3. income
_f_ 4. mortgage payment
_b_ 5. premium
_e_ 6. miscellaneous

a. money from a job or other sources
b. money you pay for insurance
c. things that cost a different amount each month
d. things that cost the same each month
e. things that don't fit in any other category
f. money you pay for a home loan

B Work with a partner. Practice the conversation. Use the words and amounts in 2A.

A: How much did we pay for utilities last month?

B: Look under variable expenses.

A: We paid $200! Wow! I didn't know it was that much.

C Talk about the questions with your class.

1. How does making a budget help a family?
2. Julia and Roberto want to save for a house. What advice can you give them?

TEST YOURSELF ✔

Close your book. Work with a partner. Make a list of as many new words from the lesson as you can. Alphabetize your list. Check your spelling in a dictionary.

1 Read an essay about money

A Talk about the questions with your class.

1. What are some ways that having or not having money affects people's lives?
2. In your opinion, do people pay too much attention to money? Explain your answer.

B Listen and read the essay about money.

> **Topic**
> Tell why you agree or disagree with this statement:
> "Money can't buy happiness." Limit your essay to 125 words.

Money Can't Buy Happiness

by Edwin Thomas

Money is important. People who have money have more comfortable lives than people who don't have money. They have more free time, more security, and more flexibility. Most people would probably say that they would like to have more money. However, many of these people would probably also agree that money can't buy happiness.

Happiness is a feeling. It can come from being with your family or your friends, from good news, from kind words, or from a happy event. Money can help make good things happen, but it can't buy time, friends, or love. Money can only buy things.

People can find happiness in everyday life and in other people. Sometimes money can help, but the statement is still true: "Money can't buy happiness."

> **Writer's note**
>
> Formal essays don't usually use the first-person pronoun *I* or statements like *I think…*or *In my opinion*.

C Check your understanding. Answer the questions.

1. According to Edwin, what 4 things can money buy?
    comfortable lives, free time, security, and flexibility

2. What does he think most people want? more money

3. According to Edwin, what things bring happiness? being with your family and friends, good news, kind words, a happy event

4. Does Edwin agree or disagree with the statement "Money can't buy happiness"?
    He agrees.

Unit 7 Lesson 2

Objectives	Grammar	Vocabulary	Correlations
On- and Higher-level: Analyze, write, and edit an essay about money **Pre-level:** Read an essay about money, and write a paragraph about money	*Can (Money can't buy happiness.)*	*Essay, security, flexibility* For vocabulary support for pre-level students, see this **Oxford Picture Dictionary** topic: The Bank	**CASAS:** 0.1.2, 0.1.5, 7.2.2, 7.2.4, 7.2.5 **LCPs:** 49.02, 49.03, 49.13, 49.16 **SCANS:** Creative thinking, Listening, Reading, Speaking, Writing **EFF:** Convey ideas in writing, Listen actively, Read with understanding, Reflect and evaluate, Speak so others can understand

Warm-up and Review

10–15 minutes (books closed)

Write on the board: *Money doesn't grow on trees. Time is money. Money is the root of all evil.* Elicit and discuss the meaning of each expression.

Introduction

5 minutes

1. Ask students if they know of sayings about money in their first language. Ask how they would translate the sayings into English.

2. State the objective: *Today we're going to read and write an essay about money.*

1 Read an essay about money

Presentation

20–25 minutes

A Elicit answers to questions 1 and 2. Write students' ideas for question 1 on the board.

B 1. Elicit the meaning of *essay*. Ask students when they might have to write an essay.

2. Direct students to read the essay silently. Check comprehension. Ask: *What does Edwin say money can buy?* [free time, security, flexibility] *What does he say it can't buy?* [time, friends, love]

3. Play the audio. Have students read along silently.

4. Draw students' attention to the *Writer's note.* Point out that we use these expressions in speaking because they "soften" our statement of opinion but that they are not necessary in writing.

Guided Practice I

10 minutes

C Have students work independently to answer the questions. Ask volunteers to write the answers on the board.

Multilevel Strategies

For 1C, challenge on- and higher-level students while working with pre-level students.

•**Higher-level** Write additional questions on the board for these students to answer after they finish 1C: *Look at the things Edwin says can bring happiness. What else can bring happiness? Did he leave out anything important that money can buy?* After volunteers have put up the answers to 1C, ask these students to share their ideas about the additional questions.

2 Write an essay about money

Guided Practice II

20–25 minutes

A Read the questions. Elicit students' answers. Write students' ideas about how people have changed the world with and without money on the board.

B 1. Read the prompt aloud. Tell students that 125 words is about half of a double-spaced typewritten (12-point font) page.

2. Direct students to look back at the essay in 1B. Focus students' attention on the first sentence of each paragraph. Point out that this sentence tells the reader what the rest of the paragraph will be about. Direct students to look at the last sentence of the first paragraph. Point out that this sentence signals a transition to the next paragraph.

3. Tell students that when they take a writing test, it's a good idea to quickly brainstorm some ideas before they begin writing. Use the questions for each paragraph to brainstorm ideas for the essay as a class.

4. Check comprehension of the exercise. Ask: *How many paragraphs do you need to write?* [three] Have students work individually to write their essays.

> ### Multilevel Strategies
>
> Adapt 2B to the level of your students.
>
> **•Pre-level** Direct these students to write two paragraphs answering the questions for paragraphs 1 and 2.

C 1. Lead students through the process of using the *Editing checklist*. Read the sentences aloud, and answer any questions. Then ask students to check their papers.

2. Allow students a few minutes to edit their writing as necessary.

Communicative Practice

10 minutes

D 1. Read the instructions aloud. Emphasize to students that they are responding to their partners' work, not correcting it.

2. Use the essay in 1B to model the exercise. *I think the part about how people with money have more free time, security, and flexibility is interesting. I'd like to ask the writer if he knows of any specific people whom he could use as examples of his ideas.*

3. Direct students to exchange papers with a partner and follow the instructions.

4. Call on volunteers to share some interesting things they read in their partners' essays.

Application and Evaluation

15 minutes

TEST YOURSELF

1. Review the instructions aloud. Remind students of the expressions that you discussed during the warm-up and introduction. Write the expressions on the board again. Assign a time limit (15 minutes), and have students work independently. Give students notice when they have five minutes left.

2. Before collecting students' work, remind them to use the *Editing checklist*. Collect and correct students' writing.

> ### Multilevel Strategies
>
> Adapt the *Test Yourself* to the level of your students.
>
> **•Pre-level** Direct these students to choose an expression and write one paragraph about it. Write questions to guide their writing. *What does the expression mean? Do you agree with it? Why or why not?*

To compress this lesson: Assign the *Test Yourself* for homework.

To extend this lesson: Talk about money and culture. Write these questions on the board: *In the U.S. and in your native country, is it polite to talk about how much things cost? Can you ask someone how much money they earn? When you go out to dinner with friends, who pays? If you divide the bill, how do you divide it? Do you think American attitudes toward money are different from attitudes toward money in your native country? If so, how are they different?* Put students in groups of three and ask them to discuss the questions. Ask a reporter from each group to share the group's ideas with the class.

And/Or have students complete **Workbook 4 page 45** and **Multilevel Activity Book 4 page 80**.

2 Write an essay about money

A **Talk about the questions with your class.**

1. Name three famous people who have a lot of money. What do you think their lives are like?
2. What have these three people done to change the world or to help others?
3. Name someone who has changed the world. Did the person use money to make changes?

B **Write an essay about money. Read the directions. Use the model in 1B and the questions below to help you.**

| **Topic** |
| Tell why you agree or disagree with this statement: "Money makes the world go around." Limit your essay to 125 words. |

Paragraph 1: How does money change the world? What would most people probably say that money can do?

Paragraph 2: What are some things in the world that money cannot change?

Paragraph 3: Is it true that money makes the world go around? If not, what "makes the world go around"?

> Money
> The statement that
> "money makes the world go
> around" is…

C **Use the checklist to edit your writing. Check (✔) the true sentences.**

Editing checklist	
1. I wrote about the topic in the directions.	
2. I gave my opinions without using *I*.	
3. I used commas between items in lists.	
4. My essay is not more than 125 words.	

D **Exchange essays with a partner. Read and comment on your partner's work.**

1. Point out one sentence you think is interesting.
2. Ask a question about one idea in your partner's essay.

TEST YOURSELF ✔

Think about a popular saying about money in your first language. Translate the saying and write a new essay that explains why you agree or disagree with the saying.

1 Learn present unreal conditional statements

A **Read the conversation. Can Molly go to college right now?** No, she can't. She doesn't have
Why or why not? enough money.

Isabel: If I go to the cafe for lunch, will you go with me?

Molly: Thanks, but I don't think so. I brought a sandwich from home. I'm really trying to save money.

Isabel: I know. If I didn't eat in the cafe every day, I'd save about $25 a week.

Molly: I'm saving for college—that's my dream. If I had enough money, I'd start today. But I don't, so I'm watching my expenses.

Isabel: Good for you, Molly! Go get your dream.

B **Study the chart. Underline the 2 examples of present unreal conditional statements in the conversation above.**

Present unreal conditional statements	
If **clause**	**Main clause**
If Molly **had** enough money,	she **could start** college now.
If she **had** enough money now,	she **wouldn't have to wait.**
If Isabel **didn't eat** in the cafe,	she **would save** money.

Notes
• Use unreal conditional statements to talk about unreal, untrue, or impossible situations: If Molly had enough money, she could start college now. (She doesn't have enough money. She can't start college now.) • In unreal conditionals, the *if* clause can also come after the main clause: Molly could start college now **if she had enough money.**

C **Complete the sentences to make present unreal conditional statements. Use the verbs in parentheses.**

1. It ____would be____ easier for Isabel to save money if she ____limited____ her spending. (be, limit)

2. If she ____took____ the bus, she ____would save____ a lot of money on parking. (take, save)

3. If she ____used____ Town Bank, she ____would get____ a higher interest rate. (use, get)

4. Isabel ____would save____ $100 a month if she ____brought____ her lunch. (save, bring)

Unit 7 Lesson 3

Objectives	Grammar	Vocabulary	Correlations
On- and Higher-level: Use the present unreal conditional to discuss financial needs and goals, and listen for unreal conditionals **Pre-level:** Recognize the present unreal conditional in discussions of financial needs and goals	Present unreal conditional (*If I had enough money, I could go to college now.*)	Finance and budgeting For vocabulary support for pre-level students, see this **Oxford Picture Dictionary** topic: Money	**CASAS:** 0.1.2, 0.1.5, 0.2.1, 7.2.2, 7.2.5, 7.2.6 **LCPs:** 39.01, 49.01, 49.02, 49.09, 49.13, 49.16 **SCANS:** Acquires and evaluates information, Listening, Reading, Speaking, Writing **EFF:** Convey ideas in writing, Listen actively, Read with understanding, Speak so others can understand

Warm-up and Review

10–15 minutes (books closed)

Write three things on the board that you want to do but can't do right now: *Visit China, remodel my kitchen, write a book.* Say: *I want to _____, but I can't because _____.* Ask students for examples of things they want to do but can't. Write them on the board.

Introduction

5–10 minutes

1. Write two sentences on the board about the things you want to do using the unreal conditional: *If I had money, I would visit China. If I had time, I would write a book.* Underline *had* in each sentence. Say: *I don't have time, and I don't have money. I use* if *with a past-tense verb to show that I am talking about something that isn't true at the moment or is impossible. This form is called the unreal conditional.*

2. State the objective: *Today we're going to use the present unreal conditional to discuss our financial needs and goals.*

1 Learn present unreal conditional statements

Presentation I

20–25 minutes

A 1. Direct students to look at the picture. Ask: *Where are they?*

2. Read the instructions aloud. Ask students to read the conversation silently to find the answer to the question. Call on a volunteer for the answer.

B 1. Demonstrate how to read the grammar chart.

2. Direct students to circle the two examples of the present unreal conditional in the conversation in 1A. Go over the answers as a class.

3. Ask about the tense of each conditional. *Molly says:* If I had enough money... *Does she mean now or in the past? Isabel says:* If I didn't eat in the café... *Does she mean now or in the past?*

4. Read the chart through sentence by sentence. Then read it again, and have students repeat after you.

5. Read and discuss the *Notes.*

6. Assess students' understanding of the charts. Elicit present unreal conditional sentences with the expressions on the board from the warm-up.

Guided Practice I

15–20 minutes

C Ask students to work individually to complete the sentences. Ask volunteers to write the answers on the board.

Guided Practice II

5–10 minutes

D Read each sentence aloud. Elicit the correct form of the verb. Ask students to write the corrected sentence.

> **TIP** After 1D, play a "chain" game. Have students stand in a circle. Write *If I had a million dollars, I would travel around the world.* on the board. Underline the second clause, and elicit a new sentence that uses that clause as the condition. *If I traveled around the world, I would stop in Spain. If I stopped in Spain, I would go to the beach.* Have students continue the chain until you've gone around the circle.

2 Learn present unreal conditional questions

Presentation II

20–25 minutes

A 1. Introduce the new topic. *Now we're going to ask questions with the unreal conditional.*

2. Read the questions and answers in the chart aloud. Read the *Note.*

3. Direct students to circle the correct words in the sentences under the chart. Go over the answers as a class.

Guided Practice I

10–15 minutes

B Have students work with a partner to complete the questions and answers. Tell them to take turns reading the completed questions and answers aloud.

D Get the form. Work with your class. Correct the sentences.

1. Sunny would spend less money if she shops at garage sales. ___Sunny would spend less money if she shopped at garage sales.___

2. If she did that, she will also meet her neighbors. ___If she did that, she would also meet her neighbors.___

3. She can start this weekend if she wanted to. ___She could start this weekend if she wanted to.___

2 Learn present unreal conditional questions

A Study the charts. Circle the correct words in the questions below.

Yes/No questions and short answers

A: **Would** Molly **go** to college **if** she **didn't have to work?**
B: Yes, she **would**.

A: **If** your son **wanted** a credit card, **would** you **give** him one?
B: No, I **wouldn't**.

Information questions

A: What **would** Molly **do** if she **had** enough money?
B: She **would go** to college.

A: **If** you **could live** anywhere, where **would** you **live?**
B: I **would live** in Hawaii.

Note

Don't use contracted forms (*she'd, he'd,* etc.) in affirmative short answers.

1. Who would you call if you (have / (had)) a money emergency?

2. Would he save a lot of money if he ((walked) / would walk) to work?

B Complete the questions and answers. Use the verbs in parentheses.

1. A: If you ____didn't need____ money, ___would___ you ___keep___ your second job? (not need, keep)

   B: Yes, I ___would___. I like that job.

2. A: If you ___had___ a car, ___would___ you ___drive___ to work? (have, drive)

   B: No, I _____wouldn't_____. Gas is too expensive.

3. A: How much money ___would___ she ___save___ if she _____didn't shop_____ at expensive stores? (save, not shop)

   B: She _____would save_____ fifty or sixty dollars a month. (save)

4. A: What ___would___ you ___do___ first if you ___wanted___ to buy a house? (do, want)

   B: I _____would get_____ some information on home loans. (get)

3 Grammar listening

Listen to the conversations. Check (✔) the true sentences.

1. _____ a. She has a credit card.
   _✔_ b. She has to carry cash.
2. _✔_ a. He uses a credit card.
   _____ b. He doesn't use a credit card.
3. _✔_ a. She has to study.
   _____ b. She rents a movie every night.
4. _✔_ a. He has to study.
   _____ b. He would like to rent a movie every night.

4 Practice present unreal conditionals

A **Think about your answers to these questions.**

1. If you had $100 to spend on your classroom or school, how would you spend the money? Why?
2. What would you do if you had $1,000 to spend on your classroom or school? Why?
3. If you could make one change in your school, what would you change?

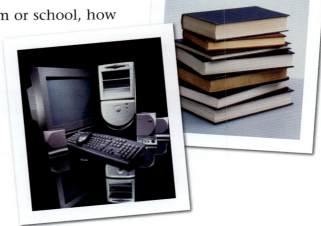

B **Work with a partner. Ask and answer the questions in 4A.**

A: *If you had $100 to spend on our classroom, how would you spend the money?*
B: *I would buy a dictionary for every student.*
A: *Why would you do that?*
B: *Well, I'd do it because...*

C **Talk about your ideas with the class. Which ideas do you like best?**

If we had $100 to spend on our classroom, we would...

TEST YOURSELF ✔

Close your book. Write 5 sentences about how you and your classmates would spend money on your classroom or school. Use present unreal conditionals.

---

3 Grammar listening

Guided Practice II

10–15 minutes

1. Say: *Now we're going to listen to people talk about their financial situations.*

2. Play the audio. Direct students to read along silently without writing.

3. Replay the audio. Ask students to check the true sentences.

4. Go over the answers as a class.

Multilevel Strategies

Replay the *Grammar listening* to allow pre-level students to catch up while you challenge on- and higher-level students.

•**Pre-level** Have these students listen again to check the true sentences.

•**On- and Higher-level** Have these students write one or two of the sentences they hear.

---

4 Practice present unreal conditionals

Communicative Practice and Application

20–25 minutes

A 1. Direct students to look at the pictures. Ask if you have the items in your classroom.

2. Read the questions aloud. Ask students to think about and note their answers.

B 1. Put students in pairs. Read and have students repeat the questions.

2. Direct students to ask their partners the questions. Tell them to make notes of each other's answers. Model the exercise by asking a volunteer the first question. Have the class tell you how to write the answer in note form.

3. Check comprehension of the exercise. Ask: *Do you need to write everything your partner says?* [no] Set a time limit for the exercise (four minutes), and observe and take note of issues that arise.

C Elicit the students' ideas, and write them on the board. Have the students vote for their favorite idea.

Evaluation

10–15 minutes (books closed)

TEST YOURSELF

Ask students to write the sentences independently. Collect and correct their writing.

Multilevel Strategies

Target the *Test Yourself* to the level of your students.

•**Pre-level** Provide skeleton sentences for these students to complete. *If I had one hundred dollars to spend on the classroom, I _____. If I had one thousand dollars to spend on the classroom, I _____. If I had five thousand dollars to spend on the classroom, I _____.*

•**Higher-level** Have these students include an explanation of why they would buy each item.

To compress this lesson: Conduct 1C as a whole-class discussion.

To extend this lesson: Encourage free conversation with conditionals.
1. Write *What would you do if _____?* on the board. Elicit several endings for the question.
2. Direct students to walk around the room asking and answering different versions of the question.

And/Or have students complete **Workbook 4 pages 46–47, Multilevel Activity Book 4 pages 81–82**, and the corresponding **Unit 7 Exercises** on the **Multilevel Grammar Exercises CD-ROM 4.**

Unit 7 Lesson 4

Objectives	Grammar	Vocabulary	Correlations
On-, Pre-, and Higher-level: Negotiate and compromise on a budget and listen for financial-planning information	Present unreal conditional with *be* (*If I were you, I wouldn't buy that car.*)	*Negotiate, compromise,* financial-planning vocabulary For vocabulary support for pre-level students, see these **Oxford Picture Dictionary** topics: Money, The Bank	**CASAS:** 0.1.2, 0.1.5, 1.5.1, 6.0.3, 6.0.4, 6.1.1, 6.1.2, 7.4.7 **LCPs:** 49.02, 49.09, 49.16, 49.17 **SCANS:** Arithmetic/Mathematics, Listening, Money, Reading, Speaking **EFF:** Listen actively, Observe critically, Read with understanding, Use math to solve problems and communicate

Warm-up and Review

10–15 minutes (books closed)

Write *Entertainment* on the board, and elicit students' ideas for things they spend money on that fall into that category—for example, cable TV, movies, Internet, magazines, dancing, CDs, restaurants, MP3 players.

Introduction

5 minutes

1. Ask students if they think they spend a lot of money on entertainment. Point out that this is one area of the budget that people often cut when they need to save money.

2. State the objective: *Today we're going to learn to negotiate and compromise on a budget.*

1 Learn to negotiate and compromise on a budget

Presentation I

15–20 minutes

 1. Direct students to look at the picture. Ask: *Who are these people?*

2. Play the audio. Give students a minute to answer the questions. Go over the answers as a class.

Guided Practice

20–25 minutes

 1. Read the instructions aloud. Play the audio. Ask students to read along silently and listen for the answer to the question. Elicit the answer.

2. Ask students to read the conversation with a partner. Circulate and monitor pronunciation. Model and have students repeat difficult words or phrases.

3. Say and have students repeat the expressions in the *In other words* box. Elicit the placement of the expressions in the conversation. Ask volunteers to read the conversation using expressions from the box.

Communicative Practice and Application

15–20 minutes

 1. Ask students to read the instructions silently. Check comprehension of the exercise. Ask: *What are the two roles? What is the situation?* Elicit examples of what each roommate might say.

2. Set a time limit (five minutes). Ask students to act out the role-play in both roles. Ask one to three volunteer pairs to act out their conversations for the class. Tell students who are listening to note how the partners compromise.

Multilevel Strategies

For 1C, adapt the role-play to the level of your students.

•**Pre-level** Provide the beginning of the conversation for these students. *A: You know, if we shopped at a cheaper store, we'd save a lot of money. B: But I like buying fresh food _____.*

1 Learn to negotiate and compromise on a budget

A Look at the picture. Listen to the conversation. Then answer the questions below with your classmates.

1. How much do Julia and Roberto agree to spend on food? $ 250 a month
2. How much do they agree to spend on entertainment? $25 a month

B Listen and read. What do Julia and Roberto decide?

They decide that Roberto will make coffee at home and Julia will bring her own snacks.

Julia: You know, if you didn't buy coffee on the way to work, we'd save a lot of money.

Roberto: You mean quit drinking coffee?

Julia: No, but those coffee places are expensive.

Roberto: What if I made coffee at home and took it to work? And how about if you stopped buying snacks at work?

Julia: Let's compromise. I'll bring my own snacks...

Roberto: ...And I'll make my own coffee. And we'll save about $100 a month.

Julia: It's a deal!*

***Idiom note:** It's a deal = I agree; let's do it

> **In other words...**
>
> **Making suggestions**
> What if I/you +
>   (simple past verb)...?
> How about if I/you +
>   (simple past verb)...?
> How about ...?
> Let's make it ....

C Role-play a compromise with a partner. Use the example in 1B to make a new conversation.

Partner A: You and your roommate want to save money. Suggest that if your roommate stopped buying fresh fruit at Helson's, you'd save a lot of money. Explain that Helson's is an expensive grocery store. Offer a compromise. You'll buy fewer microwave meals and do more cooking. Agree with your roommate.

Partner B: Check to see if your roommate wants you to stop buying fresh fruit. Offer to buy fruit on sale and suggest that your roommate stop buying so many expensive microwave meals. Come to an agreement.

☑ Ask and answer questions about expenses in order to plan a budget   **95**

2 Learn present unreal conditionals with *be*

A Look at the picture in the chart. Is Jason's father giving him good advice?

Present unreal conditionals with *be*

What would you do?

If I were you, I'd look for a newer car.

$2,000 1998

If his father weren't here, Jason would buy the car.

Note

In formal speech with present unreal conditionals, use *were* for all people (*I, you, he, she*, etc.).
If I **were** you, I'd look for a newer car.

B Work with a partner. Use the words below and your own ideas to make a conversation.

1. the owner of a big company
   A: *What would you do if you were the owner of a big company?*
   B: *If I were the owner of a big company, I would…*

2. a millionaire

3. the president of the United States

4. the director of this school

3 Practice your pronunciation

A Listen to the sentences. Notice that the speakers pause at the commas.

1. If I were you, I wouldn't buy that car.
2. If you had the money, a newer car would probably be better.

B Circle the commas in these sentences. Say the sentences. Then listen and check the pauses.

1. If I were Jason, I'd keep looking.
2. That car is old, but it runs well.
3. If you bought an older car, it'd cost less.

4. If he bought a new car, he'd be in debt.
5. If he buys this car, he won't be in debt.
6. He can take a bus, so a car isn't necessary.

C Practice the sentences in 3A and 3B with a partner.

2 Learn present unreal conditionals with *be*

Presentation II and Guided Practice

10–15 minutes

 A 1. Introduce the new topic. *Now we're going to talk about unreal conditions using* be.

2. Read the instructions aloud. Direct students to look at the cartoon. Call on volunteers to answer the question.

3. Read the *Note* aloud. Write *If I were the president, I would _____.* on the board. Provide your own completion. Call on volunteers and ask them to complete the sentence. Write their ideas on the board in the third person. *If (Ana) were the president, she would declare a few more holidays.*

Communicative Practice

15–20 minutes

TIP For 2B, get students to go beyond the obvious answers by writing each phrase at the top of a large sheet of paper and posting the sheets around the room. Have partners circulate from phrase to phrase, adding their own conditional sentence. Tell them not to repeat any ideas. Additional phrases to use: *ten years older, in my hometown right now, the mayor of this city, the owner of a TV station, the teacher of this class.*

B 1. Have students work with a partner to complete the conversations.

2. Call on volunteers to report on what their partners said. *If (Javier) were a millionaire, he'd travel around the world.*

Multilevel Strategies

After 2B, provide conditional practice targeted to the level of your students.

•**Pre-level** Provide these students with skeleton sentences to complete. *If I _____ you, I _____ that bicycle. If I _____ more money, I _____ a nicer car. If my mother _____ here, she _____. If I _____ an artist, I _____. If I had a _____, I would _____.*

•**On- and Higher-level** Pair these students and provide each pair with a section of a newspaper. Direct them to look at the headlines and pictures and write sentences about the people in the articles. *If I were this soldier, I would be frightened. If this politician were honest, he wouldn't be in trouble.*

Call on volunteers to share their sentences with the class.

3 Practice your pronunciation

Pronunciation Extension

10–15 minutes

A 1. Write *If I were you, I'd study the vocabulary tonight* on the board. Say the sentence and ask students to repeat it. Ask them to identify the pause. Say: *Now we're going to focus on pausing when we see a comma.*

2. Play the audio. Direct students to listen for the pauses.

B 1. Tell students to read each sentence and circle the comma.

2. Play the audio. Tell students to listen for the pauses.

C Have students take turns reading the sentences with a partner. Monitor and provide feedback.

4 Focus on Listening

Listening Extension

20–25 minutes

A Read the questions aloud, and elicit answers from volunteers. Encourage students to respond to each other's ideas. After one student speaks, ask other students for their opinions. *Do you agree or disagree with what he or she said? Why?*

B Play the audio. Elicit the answers to the questions.

> **TIP**
> Use this focused listening exercise as a launching point for a discussion of credit-card debt. Ask: *Why do you think Mr. Moreno got into so much debt?* Discuss credit-card interest rates and ways that credit-card companies encourage people to go into debt—for example, offering no-interest for the first three months, offering cash loans, etc. Use credit-card advertisements for a lesson in "reading the fine print."

C 1. Direct students to read through the exercise before listening.

2. Replay the audio and have students work individually to choose the correct answers. Take a tally of responses for each item, and if students disagree on a response, replay the audio so they can check their answers.

> ### Multilevel Strategies
> After 4C, replay the conversation to challenge on- and higher-level students while allowing pre-level students to catch up.
> •**Pre-level** Have these students listen again to go over their answers.
> •**On- and Higher-level** Write these questions on the board, and tell these students to listen for the answers. *How much does Mr. Moreno spend on entertainment? How can he lower his cable bill and his phone bill? Will those changes affect his service?*

5 Real-life math

Math Extension

5–10 minutes

1. Read the story aloud. Ask volunteers to explain how they will solve the problem.

2. Give students time to read the questions and find the answers individually.

3. Have a volunteer write the problem and the solution on the board. Invite students to share any alternate method they used to solve the problem.

Evaluation

10–15 minutes

TEST YOURSELF

1. Model the role-play with a volunteer. Then switch roles.

2. Pair students. Check comprehension of the exercise by eliciting things that each partner might say.

3. Set a time limit (five minutes), and have the partners act out the role-play in both roles.

4. Circulate and monitor. Encourage pantomime and improvisation.

5. Provide feedback.

> ### Multilevel Strategies
> Target the *Test Yourself* to the level of your students.
> •**Pre-level** Provide the beginning of the conversation for these students. *A: You know, if everyone gave $20, we'd have enough for food and drinks. B: I think $20 is too much. It would be cheaper _____.*

To compress this lesson: Conduct *Real-life math* as a whole-class activity.

To extend this lesson: Provide more practice with conditionals.
1. Put students in mixed-level groups. Give each group a large sheet of paper, and tell them to write three to five *if* clauses for conditional sentences. Direct them to leave spaces for others to complete the sentences.
2. Have each group pass the paper to another group. Tell the groups to complete the sentences. Have a reporter from each group read the completed sentences aloud.

And/Or have students complete **Workbook 4 page 48** and **Multilevel Activity Book 4 page 83**.

4 Focus on listening

A Talk about the questions with your class.

1. What advice would you give a friend who wants to save money?
2. What do you think *financial planning* means?

B Listen to the conversation. Answer the questions.

1. What is Ms. Ogun's job?   She's a financial planner.
2. What is Mr. Moreno's problem?   He has too much debt.

C Listen again. Circle *a* or *b*.

1. Mr. Moreno pays _____ on his credit card each month.
   a. the total due
   b. the minimum payment

2. His total debt is about _____.
   a. $5,000
   b. $15,000

3. He spends about _____ a day for lunch.
   a. $3
   b. $5

4. If he followed Ms. Ogun's suggestions, he'd save about _____ a year.
   a. $1,000
   b. $5,000

5. Ms. Ogun thinks he should _____.
   a. get a home loan
   b. get a low-interest loan

6. Ms. Ogun also thinks that he should _____.
   a. cut up his credit cards
   b. put his cards away for one year

5 Real-life math

A Read the story and answer the question.

Veronica's paycheck is $1,050 a month after deductions. She pays $450 a month for rent, $75 a month for utilities, and $45 a month for health insurance. If she put $90 a month into a savings account, how much would she have left for other expenses? _____ $390

B Explain your answer to your classmates.

TEST YOURSELF ✔

Role-play a conversation between co-workers planning a party at work. Partner A: You want each employee to give $20 for food and drinks. Partner B: You think $20 is too much. You think it would be better if everyone brought food. Compromise and make a plan with your co-worker. Then change roles.

1 Get ready to read

A Why is it important to save money for the future? Is it easy to save? Why or why not?

B Read the definitions. Which word means *suggest*? advise

advise: (verb) to give advice, make a suggestion
equivalent: (noun) an equal amount
intimidating: (adj.) frightening, scary

C Look at the title, the chart, and the headings in the article in 2A. What do you think the article is about?

2 Read and respond

A Read the article. Who do you think this advice is good for?

SAVING: THE KEY TO REACHING YOUR GOALS

BY CECILIA OGUN

FINANCIAL PLANNING

Do you remember your grandmother talking about "saving for a rainy day?" My grandmother knew how important it was to have savings. If she were here today, she'd be a financial planner!

Financial planning means deciding how you want to use your money. It's important in today's economy, and it's the best way to afford "big-ticket" items, like a new home, a car, college tuition, and retirement.

MAKING A PLAN

Financial planning may sound intimidating, but it isn't. The first step is to make a record of your income and expenses. As a financial planner, I advise keeping track of all your expenditures[1] for a month, to see where the money is going. Next, I tell my clients to decide how much they can afford to put into savings each month. I recommend saving 10 percent of your take-home pay. One common method is to "pay" yourself first by putting money into savings as soon as you get a paycheck.

[1]expenditures: expenses, costs

Unit 7 Lesson 5

Objectives	Grammar	Vocabulary	Correlations
On-, Pre-, and Higher-level: Read about and discuss financial planning	Simple past and present perfect (*My mother taught me about saving money. I have learned to limit my spending.*)	*Advise, equivalent, intimidating, expenditures* For vocabulary support for pre-level students, see these **Oxford Picture Dictionary** topics: Money, The Bank	**CASAS:** 0.1.2, 0.1.5, 0.2.1, 1.5.1, 7.4.4 **LCPs:** 39.01, 49.02, 49.06, 49.09, 49.16 **SCANS:** Interprets and communicates information, Reading, Speaking **EFF:** Listen actively, Learn through research, Take responsibility for learning, Use information and communications technology

Warm-up and Review

10–15 minutes (books closed)

Tell students about something you are saving money for. Ask: *Are you saving for anything? What are you saving for? What are some things that people often save for?* Write their ideas on the board.

Introduction

5 minutes

1. Say: *Some of the things we want are too expensive for us to buy easily. In order to save for them, we have to have a plan.*

2. State the objective: *Today we're going to read about financial planning.*

1 Get ready to read

Presentation

15–20 minutes

A Read the questions aloud, and elicit answers from volunteers.

B Read the words and definitions. Elicit sample sentences from students using the words. Write the sentences on the board, providing help with the grammar.

Pre-Reading

C 1. Direct students to look at the title, chart, and headings. Elicit an answer to the question.

2. Discuss the expression: *Save for a rainy day.*

2 Read and respond

Guided Practice I

25–30 minutes

A 1. Ask students to read the article silently.

2. After they're finished reading, direct students to underline unfamiliar words they would like to know. Elicit the words and encourage other students to provide definitions or examples.

3. Check students' comprehension. Ask: *What are "big-ticket" items?* [things that are very expensive] *What is the first step in financial planning?* [make a record of your income and expenses.] *How much does Cecilia Ogun recommend that you save?* [ten percent of your take-home pay]

Multilevel Strategies

Adapt 2A to the level of your students.

•**Pre-level** Provide these students with a summary of the ideas in the reading. *Financial planning means deciding how to use your money. The first step is to keep track of your spending for a month. Next, decide how much you can save. Ms. Ogun recommends saving ten percent of your take-home pay. It's a good idea to save your money in a bank. The chart shows you how much you make if you save one dollar a day in a bank with 4% interest. You should try to keep three to six months' living expenses in a savings account.*

Direct these students to read the summary while other students are reading 2A.

Guided Practice II

15–20 minutes

B 1. Play the audio. Have students read along silently.

2. Elicit and discuss any additional questions about the reading.

TIP If you have access to the Internet in class, show students an online compound interest calculator. (You can find one by typing "compound interest calculator" into a search engine.) Students can plug in the current principal, annual addition, years to grow, and interest rate. The calculator will show them how much they can save over time.

C Have students work individually to complete the sentences. Write the answers on the board.

Multilevel Strategies

For 2C, work with pre-level students.

•**Pre-level** Ask these students questions about their summary while other students are completing 2C. *What's the first step to financial planning? How much should you save? Why is it better to save money in a bank? How much should you keep in the bank?* Give students time to copy the answers to 2C from the board.

3 Talk it over

Communicative Practice

15–20 minutes

1. Read the questions aloud. Set a time limit (three minutes). Have students work independently to think about the questions and write their answers in note form.

2. Elicit students' answers and encourage them to respond to each other's ideas.

TIP Discuss allowances. *Should children have to work for an allowance? Or should they get a regular age-based allowance to teach them about managing and saving money? What's a reasonable allowance for different age groups?*

Application

5–10 minutes

BRING IT TO LIFE

Read the instructions aloud. Provide students with names of magazines they might want to look through if they go to the library.

To compress this lesson: Conduct 2C as a whole-class activity.

To extend this lesson: Role-play a financial planner and customer.
1. Divide the class in half. Give half of the students *A* cards and half of them *B* cards (see page T-199). Assign a time limit for completing the first part of the activity (three minutes).
2. Tell the *A* students they are going to be financial planners, and ask them to work with a partner to write five questions that they will ask their clients about their income and spending habits.
3. Tell the *B* students that they are the clients. They make plenty of money, but they have very bad spending habits and are in debt. Direct them to write down their (imaginary) income and living expenses. Tell them to think of excuses for their bad spending habits. *I have to eat in restaurants every day—I don't know how to cook!*
4. Have the *A* students meet with *B* students and ask their questions. The *B* students should respond with the information they have invented. Tell the *A* students to give advice.
5. Ask several volunteer pairs to perform their role-plays for the class.
And/Or have students complete **Workbook 4 page 49** and the **Multilevel Activity Book 4 pages 84–85**.

HOW SAVINGS GROW

If you saved a dollar a day in a jar in your kitchen, you would have $365 in savings by the end of a year. If you saved the same money in the bank at four percent interest, you'd have $372 at the end of a year. The chart shows the difference over 30 years; it really adds up!

$1 a day for:	equals:	with 4% daily interest, it's:
1 year	$ 365	$ 372
5 years	$ 1,825	$ 2,929
10 years	$ 3,650	$ 4,487
30 years	$ 10,950	$ 21,169

SAVING FOR A RAINY DAY

Emergencies are the "rainy days" we hope will never come. It's a good idea to keep the equivalent of three to six months' living expenses in a savings account, in case of an emergency.

Planning and saving are the keys to a healthy financial future, and they are available to everyone. So take Grandma's advice, and start your savings plan today.

Source: www.pueblo.gsa.gov

B Listen and read the article again.

C Complete the sentences with words from the article.

1. In today's _____ economy _____, it's important to have a financial plan.
2. __Big ticket_____ items are expensive things that might require a loan. Two examples are ___a new home / a car_____ and ___college tuition / retirement_____.
3. Ms. Ogun recommends putting 10 percent of your ___take-home pay_____ into savings.
4. It's a good idea to save money in a bank because it will earn ___interest_____.
5. Ms. Ogun's advice is to have enough money for three to six months' ___living expenses_____ in savings.

3 Talk it over

Think about the questions. Talk about your ideas with the class.

1. How did you learn about spending and saving money when you were a child? Who do you think should teach children about money?
2. How have your feelings about money changed over the last ten years?

BRING IT TO LIFE

Use the newspaper, a magazine, or the Internet to find an article on ways to save money. Talk about your article with your classmates.

1 Grammar

A **Read the information. Which statements are true? Circle *a* or *b*.**

1. Ed would buy a car if he didn't have credit card debts.
   a. Ed has credit card debts. *(circled)*
   b. Ed doesn't have credit card debts.

2. If Joan had to pay for her checks, she would change banks.
   a. Joan has to pay for her checks.
   b. Joan doesn't have to pay for her checks. *(circled)*

3. If you didn't have an ATM card, you'd have to write a check to get cash.
   a. You have an ATM card. *(circled)*
   b. You have to write a check to get cash.

B **Complete the sentences to make present unreal conditional statements. Use the verbs in parentheses.**

1. If we __saved__ a little every month, we __would have__ money for emergencies. (save, have)
2. We __would have__ fewer disagreements if we __talked__ more about spending. (have, talk)
3. We __wouldn't have to write__ checks if we __paid__ our bills online. (not have to write, pay)
4. If I always __put__ the checkbook in the desk, it __would be__ easier to find it. (put, be)

C **Complete the questions and answers with present unreal conditionals. Use the words in parentheses.**

1. A: If __I kept__ (I/keep) a list of everything I spend, __would you do__ (you/do) it, too?

   B: Yes, I __would__.

2. A: __Would you be__ (you/be) unhappy if __we spent__ (we/spend) less on travel?

   B: No, I __wouldn't__. That's fine with me.

3. A: How __would you cut__ (you/cut) your expenses if __you wanted__ (you/want) to save money?

   B: __I wouldn't buy__ (I/not buy) things if __I didn't need__ (I not need) them.

4. A: What __would you do__ (you/do) if __you were__ (you/be) in debt?

   B: I __would get__ (get) a second job.

Unit 7 Review and expand

Objectives	Grammar	Vocabulary	Correlations
On-, Pre-, and Higher-level: Expand upon and review unit grammar and life skills	Present unreal conditionals (*If he saved every month, he would have money for emergencies.*)	Financial-planning vocabulary For vocabulary support for pre-level students, see these **Oxford Picture Dictionary** topics: Money, The Bank	**CASAS:** 0.1.2, 0.1.5, 0.2.1, 1.5.1, 7.3.1, 7.3.2, 7.3.4, 7.4.7 **LCPs:** 39.01, 49.01, 49.02, 49.16, 49.17 **SCANS:** Acquires and evaluates information, Creative thinking, Seeing things in the mind's eye **EFF:** Convey ideas in writing, Listen actively, Solve problems and make decisions

Warm-up and Review

10–15 minutes (books closed)

1. Review the *Bring It to Life* assignment from Lesson 5.

2. Have students who did the exercise discuss what they learned from their articles.

3. Encourage students who didn't do the assignment to ask questions about the articles.

Introduction and Presentation

5 minutes

1. Use the ideas students talk about in the warm-up to write imperative sentences on the board. *Cut coupons. Don't buy on impulse. Plan meals.*

2. Restate the sentences as conditional *if* clauses. *I don't cut coupons. If I cut coupons, I would save on my grocery bill. I sometimes buy things on impulse. If I didn't buy on impulse, I would be happier with the things I buy and I would save money.*

3. State the objective: *Today we're going to review the unreal conditional in order to talk about financial planning.*

1 Grammar

Guided Practice

40–45 minutes

A Have students work individually to read the sentences and circle the correct answer. Go over the answers as a class.

B Have students work individually to complete the sentences. Write the answers on the board.

C 1. Have students work with a partner. Direct them to take turns reading the completed questions and answers aloud.

2. Call on volunteer pairs to read the questions and answers for the class. Write the answers on the board.

Multilevel Strategies

For 1C seat same-level students together.

•**Pre-level** While other students are completing 1C, provide these students with skeleton sentences to complete. *1. If I had _____, I would _____. 2. If I didn't have _____, I would _____. 3. If I had _____, I wouldn't _____. 4. If I were _____, I would _____.*

•**Higher-level** After they finish 1C, ask these students to write additional questions and answers in the unreal conditional. Have volunteers write their sentences on the board.

2 Group work

Communicative Practice

20–35 minutes

 A 1. Direct students, in groups of three to four, to focus on the picture. Ask: *Who are these people?*

2. Assign roles: leader, recorder, and reporters. Explain that students work with their groups to write the conversation.

3. Check comprehension of the roles. Ask: *Who writes the conversation?* [recorder] *Who will read the conversation to the class?* [reporters] *Who helps everyone and manages the group?* [leader] *Who creates the conversation?* [everyone]

4. Set a time limit (five minutes) to complete the exercise. Circulate and answer any questions.

5. Have a reporter from each group read the group's conversation to the class.

> ### Multilevel Strategies
>
> For 2A, use mixed-level groups.
>
> •**Pre-level** Assign these students the role of reporter.
>
> •**On-level** Assign these students the role of recorder.
>
> •**Higher-level** Assign these students the role of leader.

B 1. Have students walk around the room to conduct these interviews. To get students moving, tell them to interview three new people not in their groups for 2A.

2. Set a time limit (five minutes) to complete the exercise.

3. Tell students to make a note of their classmates' answers but not to worry about writing complete sentences.

> ### Multilevel Strategies
>
> Adapt the mixer in 2B to the level of your students.
>
> •**Pre-level** Allow these students to ask and answer the questions without writing.
>
> •**Higher-level** Have these students ask two additional questions and write all answers.

C Call on individuals to report what they learned about their classmates. Encourage students to make generalizations. *Two out of four people are spenders.*

PROBLEM SOLVING

15–25 minutes

 A 1. Ask: *Do you have any friends with bad financial habits?* Tell students they will read a story about a woman who has a friend with money problems. Direct students to read Lula's story silently.

2. Ask: *What are Adele's bad habits?* [She buys expensive clothes, food, and gifts. She goes out to eat a lot.]

3. Play the audio and have students read along silently.

 B 1. Elicit answers to question 1.

2. Put students into groups of three or four. Ask each group to think of three or four possible solutions to Lula's problems and report them to the class. Ask a volunteer to write all possible solutions on the board.

3. Pair students and have them write letters giving advice to Lula. Call on volunteers to read their letters to the class.

Evaluation

30–35 minutes

To test students' understanding of the unit grammar and life skills, have them take the Unit 7 Test on the *Step Forward Test Generator CD-ROM* with *ExamView® Assessment Suite.*

> ### Learning Log
>
> To help students record and discuss their progress, use the *Learning Log* on page T-202.

To extend this review: Have students complete **Workbook 4 page 50**, **Multilevel Activity Book 4 page 86**, and the **Unit 7 Exercises** on the **Multilevel Grammar Exercises CD-ROM 4.**

2 Group work

A Work with 2–3 classmates. Write a 6–8 line conversation between the people in the picture. Share your conversation with the class.

A: *What is your financial goal for the future?*
   What would you like to do?
B: *Well, I'd like to…*
A: *OK. If I were you,…*

B Interview 3 classmates. Write their answers.

1. Are you a spender or a saver?
2. What do you think is the best way to save money?
3. If you could give everyone in this class one piece of advice about money, what would it be?

C Talk about the answers with your class.

PROBLEM SOLVING

A Listen and read about Lula.

Lula's best friend, Adele, has a money problem. Adele has a good job and she makes a good salary, but she isn't very careful with her money. For example, she likes nice clothes, and she often buys them. She always has lunch at a restaurant on workdays, and she eats dinner out several nights a week, too. When she buys groceries, she shops at an expensive supermarket because the food looks so good there. Adele is a generous person, and she often buys expensive gifts for her friends. Lula doesn't think Adele puts any money into savings, and she's worried about her. What should Lula do?

B Work with your classmates. Answer the questions.

1. What is Lula's problem? Lula is worried about Adele because Adele isn't careful with her money.
2. What would you do if you were Lula? Think of 2 or 3 solutions to her problem.
3. Write a short letter to Lula. Tell her what you think she should do.

Satisfaction Guaranteed

FOCUS ON
- shopping and purchase problems
- problems with an order
- adjectives and adverbs of degree
- ordering by phone
- consumer protection

LESSON **1** Vocabulary

1 Learn shopping vocabulary

A **Talk about the questions with your class.**

1. Where do you like to shop for the things you need? Why?
2. Have you ever bought something without going to a store?
   If so, what did you buy and how did you buy it?

B **Work with your classmates. Match the words with the pictures.**

_6_	as is	_7_	on clearance	_5_	thrift store
_4_	catalog	_3_	online store	_2_	TV shopping network
_9_	flea market	_1_	on sale	_8_	yard sale

C **Listen and check. Then read the new words with a partner.**

D **Work with a partner. Write other shopping words you know.
Check your words in a dictionary.**

✔ Identify and use shopping vocabulary; describe problems with a purchase

Unit 8 Lesson 1

Objectives	Grammar	Vocabulary	Correlations
On-level: Describe and talk about shopping and problems with purchases **Pre-level:** Identify shopping vocabulary, and describe problems with purchases **Higher-level:** Talk and write about shopping and problems with purchases	Adjectives (*It's faded.*)	Shopping and problems with purchases For vocabulary support for pre-level students, see this **Oxford Picture Dictionary** unit and topics: Clothing, A Mall, Shopping, Describing Things	**CASAS:** 0.1.2, 0.1.5, 0.2.1, 1.3.1, 7.2.3, 7.4.5 **LCPs:** 39.01, 45.01, 49.02, 49.10 **SCANS:** Listening, Participates as member of a team, Seeing things in the mind's eye **EFF:** Listen actively, Observe critically, Reflect and evaluate, Speak so others can understand

Warm-up and Review

10–15 minutes (books closed)

Elicit items that students have returned to the store. Write the items on the board. Put them into categories—for example, appliances and clothing.

Introduction

5 minutes

1. Ask volunteers to explain where they bought the items on the board and why they returned them.

2. State the objective: *Today we're going to learn words for shopping and describing problems with purchases.*

1 Learn shopping vocabulary

Presentation I

20–25 minutes

A Elicit students' answers to question 1 and 2. Write their ideas for places and ways to shop on the board.

B 1. Direct students to look at the pictures. Ask: *What's the same about all of these places?*

2. Group students and assign roles: leader, fact checker, recorder, and reporter. Explain that students work with their groups to match the words and pictures.

3. Check comprehension of the roles. Ask: *Who looks up the words in a dictionary?* [fact checker] *Who writes the numbers in the book?* [recorder] *Who tells the class your answers?* [reporter] *Who helps everyone and manages the group?* [leader]

4. Set a time limit (three minutes). As students work together, copy the wordlist onto the board.

5. Call "time." Have reporters take turns giving their answers. Write each group's answer on the board next to the word.

C 1. To prepare students for listening, say: *Now we're going to hear a consumer reporter talk about different kinds of shopping.* Ask students to listen and check their answers.

2. Have students check the wordlist on the board and then write the correct numbers in their books.

3. Pair students. Set a time limit (three minutes). Monitor pair practice to identify pronunciation issues.

4. Call "time" and work with the pronunciation of any troublesome words or phrases.

5. Replay the audio and challenge students to listen for the advantages the reporter mentions about each kind of shopping. Elicit what they heard.

D 1. Ask students to work with their partners from 1C to brainstorm a list of related words.

2. Elicit words from the class. Write them on the board. Ask students to copy them into their vocabulary notes for the unit.

Guided Practice

5–10 minutes

 E 1. Read the questions aloud. Model the exercise by having a volunteer ask you the questions.

2. Set a time limit (three minutes). Direct students to ask and answer the questions with a partner.

2 Learn to describe purchase problems

Presentation II

15–20 minutes

 A 1. Direct students to look at the picture. Elicit the names of the items in the cubbies. Introduce the new topic: *Now we're going to talk about problems with purchases.*

2. Discuss the words *defective merchandise* and *refund.* Read and have students repeat the words.

3. Ask students to work individually to complete the sentences. Call on volunteers to read the completed sentences aloud.

4. Check comprehension. Elicit examples of items that might become faded, dented, scratched, stained, or torn.

Guided Practice

10–15 minutes

 B 1. Model the conversation with a volunteer. Model it again using a different word from 2A.

2. Set a time limit (three minutes).

3. Call on volunteers to act out one of their conversations for the class.

Communicative Practice and Application

10–15 minutes

 C 1. Give students a minute to make notes of their answers to the questions.

2. Call on individuals to share their ideas with the class.

Evaluation

10–15 minutes (books closed)

TEST YOURSELF

1. Make a three-column chart on the board with the following headings: *Ways to Shop, Pricing Items, Reasons for Return.* Have students close their books and give you an example for each column.

2. Have students copy the chart into their notebooks.

3. Give students five to ten minutes to test themselves by writing the words they recall from the lesson.

4. Call "time" and have students check their spelling in a dictionary. Circulate and monitor students' progress.

5. Direct students to share their work with a partner and add additional words to their charts.

Multilevel Strategies

Target the *Test Yourself* to the level of your students.

•**Higher-level** Have these students complete the chart and then write which are their two favorite ways to shop and why.

To compress this lesson: Conduct 1B as a whole-class activity.

To extend this lesson: Role-play returning items. Put students in pairs. Ask them to role-play returning an item under the following circumstances. Write on the board: *1. The customer doesn't have a receipt. 2. The customer is trying to return the item one day past the return date. 3. The item can't be returned because it was on sale. 4. The clerk thinks the customer damaged the item.* Ask several pairs to perform their role-plays for the class. Discuss appropriate language to use in situations of conflict.

And/Or have students complete **Workbook 4 page 51** and **Multilevel Activity Book 4 pages 88–89.**

E Work with a partner. Talk about the questions. Use the words in 1B.

1. How do you like to shop? Why?
2. Which kinds of shopping have you never tried? Why or why not?
3. How can you get the best prices on clothes and household items? Explain.

2 Learn to describe purchase problems

A Look at the picture. Complete the customers' sentences below.

1. "One part of it is a lighter color. It's _____ *faded* _____."
2. "The glass has a big mark on it. It's _____ scratched _____."
3. "It's new, but it doesn't work. It's _____ defective _____."
4. "I think something hit it. It's _____ dented _____."
5. "This happened the first time I put it on. It's ___ torn _____."
6. "It looks like there's coffee on it. It's _____ stained _____."

B Work with a partner. Practice the conversation. Use the words in 2A.

A: Excuse me. I'd like to return this mirror. It's scratched.
B: Certainly. We can give you a refund.
A: On second thought, could I exchange it for another one?
B: Of course.

C Talk about the questions with your class.

1. Which items are best to buy in person? By mail? Over the phone? On the Internet? Why?
2. What are some possible problems with items you buy at yard sales, flea markets, or thrift stores? What can you do about these problems?

TEST YOURSELF ✔

Close your book. Categorize the new words in three lists: *Ways to Shop, Sale Descriptions,* and *Reasons for Returns.* Check your spelling in a dictionary. Compare your lists with a partner.

1 Read an email about problems with an order

A   **Talk about the questions with your class.**

1. Have you ever written an email about a problem with an item? If so, what did you say? What happened?
2. Look at the email in 1B. Who wrote the email? Who did she write to?

B   **Listen and read the email.**

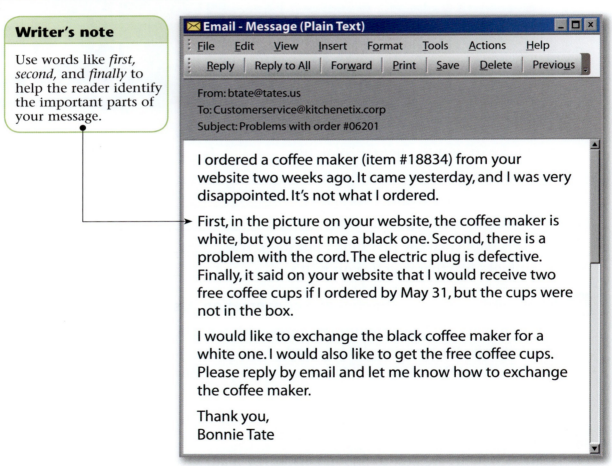

Writer's note

Use words like *first, second,* and *finally* to help the reader identify the important parts of your message.

Email - Message (Plain Text)

File   Edit   View   Insert   Format   Tools   Actions   Help

Reply | Reply to All | Forward | Print | Save | Delete | Previous

From: btate@tates.us
To: Customerservice@kitchenetix.corp
Subject: Problems with order #06201

I ordered a coffee maker (item #18834) from your website two weeks ago. It came yesterday, and I was very disappointed. It's not what I ordered.

First, in the picture on your website, the coffee maker is white, but you sent me a black one. Second, there is a problem with the cord. The electric plug is defective. Finally, it said on your website that I would receive two free coffee cups if I ordered by May 31, but the cups were not in the box.

I would like to exchange the black coffee maker for a white one. I would also like to get the free coffee cups. Please reply by email and let me know how to exchange the coffee maker.

Thank you,
Bonnie Tate

C   **Check your understanding. Work with a partner. Ask and answer the questions.**

1. Why did Bonnie Tate write the order number in the subject line?
   so the company can find her order in their system
2. What information did she give in the first sentence of her email? Why?
   She gave the item, the item number, and the place she ordered it from. She wanted to introduce the reason she's writing
3. How many problems did she write about? How did she organize the information?
   She wrote about 3 problems./ She organized the information by using First, Second, and Finally.
4. What does Bonnie want?
   She wants to exchange the black coffee maker for a white one, and she wants the free coffee cups.

Unit 8 Lesson 2

Objectives	Grammar	Vocabulary	Correlations
On- and Higher-level: Analyze, write, and edit an email about a defective item **Pre-level:** Read an email and write about a defective item	Past tense (*I ordered a coffee maker two weeks ago.*)	Problems with purchases For vocabulary support for pre-level students, see this **Oxford Picture Dictionary** unit and topics: Clothing, Shopping, A Kitchen, Electronics and Photography	**CASAS:** 0.1.2, 0.1.5, 0.2.1, 1.3.3, 1.6.3, 7.4.4 **LCPs:** 38.01, 39.01, 45.06, 49.01, 49.02, 49.13, 49.16 **SCANS:** Creative thinking, Interprets and communicates information, Reading, Writing **EFF:** Convey ideas in writing, Listen actively, Read with understanding, Reflect and evaluate

Warm-up and Review

10–15 minutes (books closed)

Show pictures of or bring in the following items: a shirt, a pair of pants, a lamp, a TV. Ask students to identify the parts of each item (sleeve, waistband, seam, electrical cord, switch, screen, etc.). Have students brainstorm the specific problems that each item might have if it's defective.

Introduction

5 minutes

1. Tell students that sometimes when we want to return something, we can just go to the store, but sometimes we need to write the manufacturer. When we order things online, we might need to send an email.

2. State the objective: *Today we'll read and write an email about a defective product.*

1 Read an email about problems with an order

Presentation

20–25 minutes

A 1. Elicit answers to questions 1 and 2.

2. Direct students to look at the picture. Ask: *What do you think she's writing about?*

B 1. Direct students to read the email silently. Check comprehension. Ask: *When did she buy the coffee maker?* [two weeks ago] *What are the problems with the coffee maker?* [wrong color, defective plug, no coffee cups]

2. Play the audio. Have students read along silently.

3. Draw students' attention to the *Writer's note*. Ask students to find the words *first, second,* and *finally* in the email.

Guided Practice I

10 minutes

C Have students work with a partner to ask and answer the questions. Call on volunteers to share their answers with the class. As students answer number 3, write the organization of the email on the board: *1. what she bought and when she bought it; 2. the problems with the item; 3. what she wants the company to do about it.*

Multilevel Strategies

Seat pre-level students together for 1C.

•**Pre-level** Work with this group. While other students are working with a partner, read the questions aloud. Help students locate the answer in the text, and elicit an answer from the group.

2 Write an email about problems with an order

Guided Practice II

20–25 minutes

A 1. Read the questions. Elicit students' answers.

2. Write the items and problems that students mention on the board.

B 1. Read the questions for each paragraph. Direct students to look back at the email in 1B. Ask them to check for how Bonnie answered each of the questions in her email. Elicit the answers.

2. Have students look at the email outline. Ask them to follow it as they write their "email" in their notebooks.

3. Check comprehension of the exercise Ask: *Whom are you writing to? What's the purpose of your email?*

Multilevel Strategies

Adapt 2B to the level of your students.

•Pre-level Provide skeleton sentences to help these students get started with their email. *I ordered a _____ a week ago. It came yesterday and I was very disappointed. First, _____.*

C 1. Lead students through the process of using the *Editing checklist*. Read the sentences aloud and answer any questions. Then ask students to check their papers.

2. Allow students a few minutes to edit their writing as necessary.

Communicative Practice

10 minutes

D 1. Read the instructions aloud. Emphasize to students that they are responding to their partners' work, not correcting it.

2. Use the email in 1B to model the exercise. *I would like to ask Bonnie if she knew anything about this company before she ordered from them. I think the company will do what she is asking because the product is defective, and she is only asking for an exchange, not a refund.*

3. Direct students to exchange papers with a partner and follow the instructions.

4. Call on volunteers to share something they liked about their partners' emails.

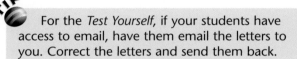 For the *Test Yourself*, if your students have access to email, have them email the letters to you. Correct the letters and send them back.

Application and Evaluation

20 minutes

TEST YOURSELF

1. Review the instructions aloud. Assign a time limit (15 minutes), and have students work independently. Give students notice when they have five minutes left.

2. Before collecting students' work, remind them to use the *Editing checklist*. Collect and correct students' writing.

Multilevel Strategies

Adapt the *Test Yourself* to the level of your students.

•Pre-level Provide skeleton sentences to help these students get started with their emails. *I ordered a _____ a week ago. It came yesterday and I was very disappointed. First _____. Second _____. I would like _____.*

To compress this lesson: Assign the *Test Yourself* for homework.

To extend this lesson: Expand the discussion to talk about services.
1. Ask these questions: *Have you ever had to call the cable, telephone, electric, or other service company? What was the problem?* Encourage students to be as specific as possible, and write their ideas on the board.
2. Have partners role-play a complaint call to a service company.

And/Or have students complete **Workbook 4 page 52** and **Multilevel Activity Book 4 page 90**.

2 Write an email about problems with an order

A Talk about the questions with your class.

1. Have you ever had problems with things that you have bought? If so, what were the problems? What did you do?

2. What information is important to include in a letter or an email about an item that is defective or incorrect?

B Write an email about one of the problems you described in 2A. Use the model in 1B and the questions below to help you.

To start: What is the email address of the company you are writing to?
What is the subject of your email?

Paragraph 1: What did you buy? When did you get it?

Paragraph 2: What were the problems with the item?

Paragraph 3: What would you like the company to do?
How can they contact you?

From:

To:

Subject:

I ordered...

C Use the checklist to edit your writing. Check (✔) the true sentences.

Editing checklist	
1. I included information that identifies the product.	
2. I explained the problems clearly.	
3. I used *first, second,* and *finally* to organize my ideas.	
4. I told the company what I want and how to contact me.	

D Exchange emails with a partner. Read and comment on your partner's work.

1. Ask a question about the problem in your partner's email.
2. Do you think the company will do what your partner is asking? Why or why not?

TEST YOURSELF ✔

Write a new email about a real or imaginary problem with a purchase you recently made.

1 Learn adjectives ending in *-ed* and *-ing*

A **Read the conversation. Does Cho like or dislike the video game? Why?** He dislikes it. It's boring.

Cho: I bought this new video game, and I'm really (disappointed) with it.

Todd: You are? Why?

Cho: Well, it was supposed to be (exciting,) but it's not. It's (boring.)

Todd: Can you return it?

Cho: Just because I don't like it? I don't think so. If you're (interested) in it, you can have it.

Todd: Uh…OK, thanks.

B **Study the chart. Circle the 2 examples of adjectives ending in *-ing* and the 2 adjectives ending in *-ed* in the conversation above.**

Adjectives ending in *-ed* and *-ing*	
Adjectives ending in *-ed*	**Adjectives ending in *-ing***
Cho was **disappointed** with the game.	The game was **disappointing**.
We were **bored** with the movie. We left after 15 minutes.	The movie was really **boring**.

Notes
• Adjectives ending in *-ed* describe a person's feelings: Cho was **disappointed** because the game wasn't good.
• Adjectives ending in *-ing* describe the cause of the feelings: Cho was unhappy because the game wasn't **exciting**.

C **Circle the correct adjective.**

1. We were really (boring /(bored)) last night, so we rented a movie and ordered a pizza.
2. The pizza wasn't very good. I was (disappointing /(disappointed)).
3. The movie was ((confusing)/ confused) at first. I couldn't understand it.
4. After about 30 minutes, though, the movie got much more ((exciting)/ excited).
5. The ending was great. It was really ((surprising)/ surprised).
6. Are you (interesting /(interested)) in seeing the movie? I think you'd like it.
7. My husband and I are usually too (tiring /(tired)) to watch movies at night.
8. But that movie sounds ((exciting)/ excited), so maybe we'll rent it on Saturday.

Unit 8 Lesson 3

Objectives	Grammar	Vocabulary	Correlations
On- and Higher-level: Use participial adjectives to complain or compliment and respond to a shopping survey **Pre-level:** Recognize participial adjectives in complaints and compliments and respond to a shopping survey	Participial adjectives (*The movie was boring. He was bored.*)	Adjectives to describe feelings and adverbs of degree For vocabulary support for pre-level students, see these **Oxford Picture Dictionary** topics: Describing Things, Everyday Conversation, Feelings	**CASAS:** 0.1.2, 0.1.5, 0.2.1, 7.4.7 **LCPs:** 49.09, 49.16, 49.17, 50.04, 50.05 **SCANS:** Interpret and communicate information, Knowing how to learn, Listening, Writing **EFF:** Convey ideas in writing, Cooperate with others, Listen actively, Read with understanding, Reflect and evaluate

Warm-up and Review

10–15 minutes (books closed)

Write *A Good Movie* and *A Bad Movie* on the board. Ask volunteers to come to the board and write adjectives that describe each kind of movie.

Introduction

5–10 minutes

1. Circle any participial adjectives that the students have written on the board. Use the adjective and its opposite to form sentences. *The movie was boring. I was bored during that movie.*

2. State the objective: *Today we're going to use adjectives ending in* –ed *and* –ing *to complain or compliment.*

1 Learn adjectives ending in -ed and -ing

Presentation I

20–25 minutes

 1. Direct students to look at the picture. Ask: *What's he holding? How does he feel?*

2. Read the question. Ask students to read the conversation silently to find the answer. Elicit the answer.

 1. Read the sentences in the chart.

2. Direct students to circle the examples of –ed/-ing adjectives in the conversation in 1A. Go over the answers as a class.

3. Ask which of the adjectives in the conversation describe the way people feel. Ask which describe causes of feelings.

4. Read the chart through sentence by sentence. Then read it again, and have students repeat after you.

5. Assess students' understanding of the charts. Write *I was surprised.* and *I was amazed.* on the board. Ask: *Do these describe feelings or causes of feelings? How would I change them to describe the thing that made me feel that way?*

Guided Practice I

15–20 minutes

Ask students to work individually to circle the correct word to complete the sentences. Ask volunteers to write the answers on the board.

TIP Seat students in mixed-level groups. Give each group a newspaper entertainment section. Tell students to look at the movie ads and circle any participial adjectives that they can find. Go over the meaning of the adjectives.

T-106

Guided Practice II

5–10 minutes

 Read each statement aloud, and ask students to raise their hands to indicate whether *a* or *b* is true.

Multilevel Strategies

After 1D, provide more practice with participial adjectives. Target the practice to the level of your students.

Write more participial adjectives on the board: *alarming, alarmed, amusing, amused, embarrassing, embarrassed, encouraging, encouraged, entertaining, entertained, exhausting, exhausted, frightening, frightened, frustrating, frustrated, overwhelming, overwhelmed, relaxing, relaxed, satisfying, satisfied, shocking, shocked, terrifying, terrified, tiring, tired*

•**Pre-level** Give these students one skeleton sentence. *I felt _____ because _____.* Ask them to complete the sentence using the following participial adjectives and their own ideas: *embarrassed, frightened, relaxed, tired,* and *satisfied.*

•**On-level** Ask these students to use five of the adjectives provided above to complete these sentences. *I felt _____ because _____. I thought the _____ was _____ because _____.*

•**Higher-level** Ask these students to write original sentences with as many of the adjectives provided as they can.

Have volunteers from all groups put their sentences on the board. Elicit whether the words are describing feelings or causes of feelings. Go over any words that no student chose to use in a sentence. Provide your own sample sentences to illustrate the meaning of those adjectives.

2 Learn adverbs of degree

Presentation II

20–25 minutes

 1. Introduce the new topic. Ask individuals if they are tired or hungry, until someone says yes. Say: *Are you very hungry or a little hungry?*

2. Say: Very *and a little* are adverbs of degree. Now we're going to look at some others. Read the sentences in the chart. Ask: *In which picture is the woman most confused? In which picture is she the least confused?*

3. Ask students to work individually to circle the correct adverb. Go over the answers as a class.

Guided Practice I

10–15 minutes

 Have students work individually to complete the sentences. Ask them to compare their ideas with a partner. Encourage the pairs to discuss each of the ideas by asking each other why?

TIP After 2B, have students write group movie reviews. Elicit the names of famous movies that many of your students have seen. Write the names on the board, and group students according to which movie they want to review. If you have students who haven't seen any of the movies, assign them to different groups, and ask them to take on the role of recorder. Have each group write a review of for its movie. Encourage students to use adverbs of degree and adjectives in their reviews. Post the reviews around the class, and have the groups circulate and read each other's reviews.

D **Get the meaning. Work with your class. Which statements are true? Circle *a* or *b*.**

1. Sam didn't like his old video games. Nothing happened in the old games.
   a. Sam was bored by the games.
   b. Sam was boring.

2. Some of the new games are difficult to play. Sam doesn't understand them.
   a. The games are confusing.
   b. Sam is confusing.

3. Sam loves the newest video game. It has lots of dangerous adventures.
   a. The new game is excited.
   b. Sam is excited.

2 Learn adverbs of degree

A **Study the chart. Circle the correct adverbs in the sentences below.**

Adverbs of degree			
I'm **a little** confused. I'm **somewhat** confused.	I'm **pretty** confused. I'm **fairly** confused.	I'm **really** confused! I'm **very** confused!	I'm **extremely** confused!

1. The customer said he was never coming back. He was (**really** / a little) annoyed.
2. Don't throw your receipts away! It's (**extremely** / fairly) important to keep them.
3. I got this book on sale for 90% off, so it was (**very** / fairly) cheap.
4. The watch is in good condition. It's only (**a little** / extremely) scratched.

B **Complete the sentences with an adverb of degree or the word *not*. Compare your ideas with a partner.**

1. I am _____ comfortable with shopping in stores in the U.S.
2. Returning items to the store is _____ easy for me.
3. Return policies and guarantees are _____ difficult for me to understand.
4. Ordering items from a catalog is _____ easy for me.
5. Shopping at yard sales and flea markets is _____ unusual for me.

3 Grammar listening

🎧 **Listen to the sentences. Circle *a* or *b*.**

1. (a.) Actually, it was a little disappointing.
   b. Actually, it was a little disappointed.

2. (a.) Not really. I was pretty confused at first.
   b. Not really. I was pretty confusing at first.

3. a. I thought it was a little bored.
   (b.) I thought it was a little boring.

4. a. They thought I was excited.
   (b.) They thought it was exciting.

5. (a.) No, I didn't. That's surprising.
   b. No, I didn't. He's surprising.

6. a. No, thanks. I'm really not interesting.
   (b.) No, thanks. I'm really not interested.

4 Practice adjectives ending in *-ed/-ing* and adverbs of degree

A **Think about each of the experiences below.**

1. a time when you did something really exciting
2. a time when you did something really interesting
3. a time when you were really bored
4. a time when you were really confused

B **Work with a group. Describe one or more of the experiences from 4A.**

I did something really exciting when I was 15. I…

C **Talk about your experiences with your classmates.**

Angela did something really exciting when she was 15. She…

TEST YOURSELF ✔

Close your book. Write 5 sentences about your experiences and about the experiences of the people in your group. Use -ed/-ing adjectives and adverbs of degree:
Klaus was really bored when…

3 Grammar listening

Guided Practice II

10–15 minutes

1. Say: *Now we're going to listen to a customer interviewer. He will ask questions about your shopping experience. You need to choose an appropriate answer.*

2. Play the audio. Direct students to listen silently without writing.

3. Replay the audio. Ask students to choose the best response for each question.

4. Call on volunteers to read the correct responses aloud.

> ### Multilevel Strategies
>
> Replay the *Grammar listening* to allow pre-level students to catch up while you challenge on- and higher-level students.
>
> •**Pre-level** Have these students listen again to choose the correct response.
>
> •**On- and Higher-level** Have these students take notes on each question. Elicit the gist of each question from a volunteer before you call on another student to read the answer.

4 Practice adjectives ending in –ed/-ing and adverbs of degree

Communicative Practice and Application

20–25 minutes

A 1. Direct students to look at the pictures. Ask: *Where are these people? How do they feel?*

2. Have students work independently to read the questions and note their answers.

B 1. Put students in groups. Ask students to take turns describing their experiences.

2. Tell them to make notes of each other's answers. Model the exercise by having a volunteer tell you about one of his or her experiences. Have the class tell you how to write the information in note form.

3. Check comprehension of the exercise. Ask: *Should you write everything your group members say?* [no] Set a time limit for the exercise (four minutes), and observe and take note of issues that arise.

C Call on volunteers to share the experiences they found the most interesting.

Evaluation

10–15 minutes (books closed)

TEST YOURSELF

Ask students to write the sentences independently. Collect and correct their writing.

> ### Multilevel Strategies
>
> Target the *Test Yourself* to the level of your students.
>
> •**Higher-level** Have these students write a paragraph in response to this prompt: *How are your experiences and your group members' experiences different or similar?*

To compress this lesson: Conduct 1C as a whole-class activity.

To extend this lesson: Have students recommend or complain about something.
1. Tell students to choose an item to recommend or complain about to their classmates. It could be a movie, a TV show, a class, a restaurant, a place to visit, an item they've purchased—anything they feel strongly about. Elicit ideas and put them on the board.
2. Give students a couple of minutes to choose an item and plan what they will say about it.
3. Assign a time limit (five minutes). Have them circulate around the room and talk to several partners.
4. Call on volunteers to share some of the "good tips" they got from their classmates.

And/Or have students complete **Workbook 4 pages 53–54, Multilevel Activity Book 4 pages 91–92**, and the corresponding **Unit 8 Exercises** on the **Multilevel Grammar Exercises CD-ROM 4**.

Unit 8 Lesson 4

Objectives	Grammar	Vocabulary	Correlations
On-, Pre-, and Higher-level: Place a catalog order over the phone and listen for information about returning a product	*So, such, such a/an + that* (*It's so expensive that we can't afford it. It's such a cheap store that you can afford anything there.*)	Shopping For vocabulary support for pre-level students, see these **Oxford Picture Dictionary** units: Clothing, Housing	**CASAS:** 0.1.2, 0.1.5, 1.3.3, 1.3.4, 6.0.3, 6.0.4, 6.2.1, 6.2.3, 6.2.5, 7.2.5 **LCPs:** 49.02, 49.09, 49.16, 51.05 **SCANS:** Arithmetic/Mathematics, Interpret and communicate information, Speaking **EFF:** Listen actively, Read with understanding, Use math to solve problems and communicate

Warm-up and Review

10–15 minutes (books closed)

Ask: *What would you be willing to buy from a catalog or online? What would you never be willing to buy from a catalog or online?* Write students' ideas on the board.

Introduction

5 minutes

1. Say: *Some companies have very convenient systems for ordering online, but with other companies, the best idea is to call to place your order.*

2. State the objective: *Today we're going to learn to place a catalog order by phone.*

1 Learn to place a catalog order by phone

Presentation I

15–20 minutes

 1. Direct students to look at the catalog. Read the instructions aloud.

2. Play the audio. Give students a minute to answer the question. Call on a volunteer for the answer.

Guided Practice

20–25 minutes

 1. Read the instructions aloud. Play the audio. Ask students to read along silently and listen for the answer to the question.

2. Ask students to read the conversation with a partner. Circulate and monitor pronunciation. Model and have students repeat difficult words or phrases.

3. Say and have students repeat the expressions in the *In other words* box. Elicit adjustments to the conversation that would allow you to use the words. Ask volunteers to read the conversation using expressions from the box.

Communicative Practice and Application

15–20 minutes

 1. Ask students to read the instructions silently. Check their comprehension of the exercise. Ask: *What are the two roles? What is the situation?* Elicit examples of what each person might say.

2. Set a time limit (five minutes). Ask students to act out the role-play in both roles. Ask one to three volunteer pairs to act out their conversations for the class. Tell students who are listening to note which expression the customer service agent uses to apologize.

Multilevel Strategies

For 1C, adapt the role-play to the level of your students.

• **Pre-level** Copy the conversation from 1B onto the board. In place of the following words, draw blanks to make a skeleton sentence that these students can use to practice their role-play: *Carry-Time Luggage, backpack, TC10-560 (x2), black (x2), brown.*

1 Learn to place a catalog order by phone

  A **Look at the catalog page. Listen to the conversations. Does the customer order the backpack in conversation 1? In conversation 2?** No, he doesn't. / No, she doesn't.

BACKPACKS

The Campus Pack 600

Holds a laptop computer!
Available in blue.
CP600-14..........**$29.99**

The Town and Country 1000

Our biggest backpack!
Available in black or brown.
TC10-560.....~~$49.99~~
$39.99

All of our products are 100% satisfaction guaranteed! Shipping and Handling: Please add 10% to your total.

B **Listen and read. What color backpack does the customer want?** black

Customer Service:	Carry-Time Luggage. Tara speaking. How may I help you?
Customer:	I'd like to place an order for a backpack, please.
Customer Service:	All right. Do you have the item number?
Customer:	Yes, I do. It's TC10-560.
Customer Service:	OK, one TC10-560. That's the Town and Country 1000 backpack.
Customer:	Yes, that's right. I'd like it in black.
Customer Service:	I'm sorry, but the black ones are sold out.*
Customer:	They're sold out?
Customer Service:	Yes, I'm afraid so. Would you be interested in brown?
Customer:	Not really, but thanks anyway.

In other words...

Apologizing
I'm sorry, (but)…
Yes, I'm afraid so.
No, I'm afraid not.
Unfortunately…

***Idiom note:** sold out = not available anymore; all gone

C **Role-play a catalog-order with a partner. Use the example in 1B to make a new conversation.**

Partner A: You're the customer. Call the Perfect Pack Company to place an order for a new suitcase. The item number is PL27-120, and you want it in red.

Partner B: You're a customer service representative at Perfect Pack. Item PL27-120 is the Perfect Suitcase 500. Apologize and explain that the red ones are sold out because they are extremely popular. Ask if the customer would be interested in black.

✔ Call and place an order over the phone   **109**

2 Learn *so...that*, *such...that*, and *such a/an...that*

A Study the chart. Complete the sentences below with *so, such,* or *such a/an*.

So...that, such...that, such a/an...that	
The prices were **so** high	
They had **such** high prices	**that** she didn't buy anything.
It was **such an** expensive store	

Notes
• Use *so, such, such a/an + that* to show a result.
• Use *so* with an adverb or an adjective.
• Use *such* or *such a/an* with an adjective + a singular count noun.

1. That backpack was _____such a_____ popular item that they don't have any more.
2. The shirt was _____so_____ small that my son couldn't wear it.
3. This is _____such a_____ busy store that it's crowded even at 9:00 in the morning.
4. That CD is _____so_____ quiet that I can't hear it.

B Work with a partner. Write sentences about Alfabuy Department Store. use *so, such,* or *such a/an.*

1. Alfabuy is cheap. _Alfabuy is so cheap that you can buy a suit for $50._
2. Alfabuy is a large store. _____
3. Alfabuy has helpful employees. _____
4. Alfabuy has a big parking lot. _____

3 Practice your pronunciation

A Listen to the sentences. Notice how the speakers link the words.

Linked consonants and vowels		
When one word ends in a consonant sound and the next word begins with a vowel, the two words are often connected, or linked, in speaking.		
I'm afraid not.	He's interested.	Thanks anyway.

B Listen. Draw a line between the linked consonants and vowels.

1. I'd like to place an order.
2. I'm sorry, but we're sold out.
3. It's a really good store.
4. It has our favorite food.

C Read the sentences in 3A and 3B with a partner.

2 Learn *so...that, such...that,* and *such a/an...that*

Presentation II and Guided Practice

10–15 minutes

A
1. Introduce the new topic by eliciting some of the *–ed/-ing* adjectives from the previous lesson. Use *so, such,* and *such as* in several sentences. _____ *was such an exciting movie that I wanted to watch it again. But the tickets were so expensive that I decided to wait for the DVD.*

2. Say: *Now we're going to learn how to use* so *and* such.

3. Tell students to read the information in the chart.

4. Check comprehension. Write *an easy test* on the board, and elicit a sentence. Change it to *easy tests,* and elicit another sentence. Write *so easy* and elicit a third sentence. Write the students' sentences on the board.

5. Have students work individually to complete the sentences. Go over the answers as a class.

Communicative Practice

15–20 minutes

B
Have students work individually to write new sentences with *such* and *so.* Ask volunteers to write their sentences on the board.

3 Practice your pronunciation

Pronunciation Extension

10–15 minutes

A
1. Write *This is such an interesting book that I can't put it down.* on the board. Say the sentence and ask students to repeat it. Draw a linking line between the *ch* and the *a* in *such as* and the *t* and the *i* in *put it.* Repeat those phrases demonstrating the link. Say: *Now we're going to focus on linking sounds.*

2. Play the audio. Direct students to listen for the linking sounds.

B
Play the audio. Have students work individually to circle the linking sounds. Go over the answers as a class.

C
Have students take turns reading the sentences with a partner. Monitor and provide feedback on pronunciation.

4 Focus on Listening

Listening Extension

20–25 minutes

A Direct students to look at the picture. Read the questions aloud. and elicit answers from volunteers.

B Play the audio. Have students work individually to answer the questions. Go over the answers with the class.

C 1. Direct students to read the sentences before listening.

2. Replay the audio and have students work individually to circle the correct answers. Take a tally of responses for each item, and if students disagree on a response, replay the audio, so they can check their answers.

Multilevel Strategies

Replay the conversation to challenge on- and higher-level students while allowing pre-level students to catch up.

•**Pre-level** Have these students listen again to go over their answers.

•**On- and Higher-level** Ask these students to listen for and write the sentence with *so…that*. [I'm so disappointed that I just want to return it.]

5 Real-life math

Math Extension

5–10 minutes

1. Read the paragraph aloud. Elicit the steps to solving the problem.

2. Give students time to read the questions and find the answers individually. Ask a volunteer to write the problem on the board. Give students time to solve it. Ask another volunteer to write the answer.

Evaluation

10–15 minutes

TEST YOURSELF

1. Model the role-play with a volunteer. Then switch roles.

2. Pair students. Check comprehension of the exercise by eliciting things the customer and the clerk might say.

3. Set a time limit (five minutes), and have the partners act out the role-play in both roles.

4. Circulate and monitor. Encourage pantomime and improvisation.

5. Provide feedback.

Multilevel Strategies

Target the *Test Yourself* to the level of your students.

•**Pre-level** Use a skeleton conversation to get these students started on their role-play. Tell them to complete the role-play with their own ideas. *Customer-Service Representative: Good morning, _____ (company name). _____ (your name) speaking. How can I help you? Customer: I'd to order a _____ (color + item). The item number is _____. CSR: I'm sorry. We don't have any _____.*

To compress this lesson: Conduct 2B as a whole-class activity.

To extend this lesson: Compare catalogs.
1. Put students in mixed-level groups. Provide each group with two catalogs from companies that sell similar items—for example, two clothing catalogs, two furniture catalogs, or two electronic store catalogs. (Alternatively, you can print catalog pages off of websites instead of using whole catalogs, or the students can compare online catalogs.)
2. Ask the groups to decide which place they would rather shop. Tell them to take item quality, prices, and return policies into account, as well as any other factors they think are important.
3. Ask a reporter from each group to explain and justify the group's decision.
And/Or have students complete **Workbook 4 page 55** and **Multilevel Activity Book 4 page 93**.

4 Focus on listening

A Look at the picture. Talk about the questions with your class.

1. How does the man feel?
2. What do you think he wants?

B Listen to the conversation. Answer the questions.

1. Who are the two people talking? Bill Seagrove, a customer, and Meg, an employee at Time Tone Electronics
2. What does Bill want? to return the watch and get a refund

C Listen again. Circle the correct words.

1. Bill ordered the watch after he saw it in (a store /(an advertisement)).
2. He's unhappy because the watch is (dented /(scratched)).
3. Bill got his order (about a week ago /(about three weeks ago)).
4. Bill wants to ((return)/ exchange) the watch.
5. Bill needs to write (the item number /(the RA number)) on the return slip.
6. The number Meg gives Bill is ((14-603-4)/ 40-703-4).

5 Real-life math

Read the story and answer the question. Explain your answer to your classmates.

Sylvia wants to order two toys for her grandchildren from a catalog. One toy costs $11.95, and the other toy costs $16.95, including tax. The company charges 10% shipping and handling on orders under $50. On orders over $50, shipping and handling is free. Sylvia wants to pay for her order by check.

What amount should Sylvia write the check for? _____ $31.79 _____

TEST YOURSELF ✔

Role-play a conversation about placing a phone order. Partner A: You're calling a company to order clothing from their catalog. Partner B: You are a customer service representative for the catalog company. You don't have the item in the color the customer wants. Then change roles.

1 Get ready to read

A What does *consumer protection* mean to you?

B Read the definitions. What do you think a *return policy* is?

issue: (verb) to send out
policy: (noun) a rule
rating: (noun) a measurement of how good something is

C Look at the cartoon in the article in 2A. What do you think
Buyer beware means?

2 Read and respond

A Read the article. Which government offices protect consumers?
the Consumer Product Safety Commission and the Federal Trade Commission

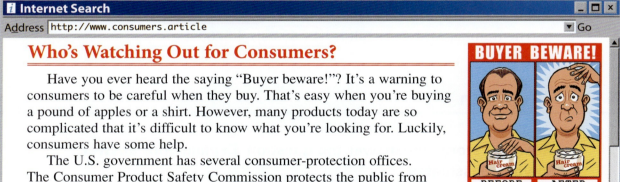

i Internet Search   _ □ ×

A̲d̲dress | http://www.consumers.article   ▼ Go

Who's Watching Out for Consumers?

BUYER BEWARE!

Have you ever heard the saying "Buyer beware!"? It's a warning to
consumers to be careful when they buy. That's easy when you're buying
a pound of apples or a shirt. However, many products today are so
complicated that it's difficult to know what you're looking for. Luckily,
consumers have some help.

BEFORE **AFTER**

The U.S. government has several consumer-protection offices.
The Consumer Product Safety Commission protects the public from
dangerous consumer products. When a product is unsafe, the CPSC may
issue a recall. A recall means that consumers can return the product and get their money back.

The Federal Trade Commission also protects consumers. The FTC monitors[1] advertising to
be sure that it is truthful. The FTC also regulates[2] product warranties and the information you
see on product labels.

Some industries have their own consumer-protection policies. The video game and movie
industries, for example, put ratings on their products so that interested parents can decide
which movies or games are OK for their children.

Private organizations protect consumers, too. Organizations like Consumers Union compare
products and then report the results to their members. These reports help consumers decide
which shampoo, insurance plan, or car to buy.

Buyers still need to beware, of course. But it's good to know that you can get help **before**
you buy a product and protection **after** you buy it.

[1]monitor: to check or watch something
[2]regulate: to control or supervise through rules or laws

☑ Interpret information about consumer protection

Unit 8 Lesson 5

Objectives	Grammar	Vocabulary	Correlations
On, Pre-, and Higher-level: Read about and discuss consumer rights	Adjective (*These earrings are beautiful.*)	*Consumer, beware, issue, policy, the public, recall, regulate* For vocabulary support for pre-level students, see this **Oxford Picture Dictionary** topic: Shopping	**CASAS:** 0.1.2, 0.1.5, 0.2.1, 1.6.2, 1.6.3, 7.4.2, 7.4.4 **LCPs:** 38.01, 39.01, 49.02, 49.04, 49.09, 49.16 **SCANS:** Applies technology to task, Creative thinking, Listening, Reading, Speaking **EFF:** Cooperate with others, Learn through research, Take responsibility for learning

Warm-up and Review

10–15 minutes (books closed)

Find out what students know about consumer protection. Ask: *What would happen if a company were selling food that made people sick? Can companies lie in their advertisements? Does the government put the PG and R ratings on movies?*

Introduction

5 minutes

1. Say: *A consumer is a person who uses a product. We are all consumers of many different products.*

2. State the objective: *Today we're going to read about and discuss consumer protection.*

1 Get ready to read

Presentation

15–20 minutes

A Read the question aloud. Elicit students' answers.

B Read the words and definitions. Elicit sample sentences from students using the words.

Pre-Reading

C 1. Direct students to look at the cartoon. Ask students to identify the items. Discuss the expression *Buyer Beware*.

2. Read the title and elicit a meaning for *watch out for*. Ask students to guess what the answer to the question in the title is going to be.

2 Read and respond

Guided Practice I

25–30 minutes

A 1. Ask students to read the article silently.

2. After students finish reading, direct them to underline unfamiliar words they would like to know. Elicit the words and encourage other students to provide definitions or examples.

3. Check students' comprehension. Ask: *How many organizations that protect consumers does the article mention?* [four] *What are they?* [Consumer Product Safety Commission, Federal Trade Commission, video game/movie industries, Consumers Union]

Multilevel Strategies

Adapt 2A to the level of your students.

•**Pre-level** Provide these students with a summary of the ideas in the reading. *There are several kinds of consumer protection in the U.S. 1. The Consumer Product Safety Commission protects the public from dangerous products. 2. The Federal Trade Commission makes sure that advertising, warranties and labels are truthful. 3. The video game and movie industries put ratings on their products so that parents know which ones are good for children. 4. The Consumers Union and other organizations compare products and report the results to their members.*

Direct these students to read the summary while other students are reading 2A.

Guided Practice II

15–20 minutes

B 1. Play the audio. Have students read along silently.

2. Elicit and discuss any additional questions about the reading.

C Have students work with a partner to ask and answer the questions. Go over the answers as a class.

Multilevel Strategies

For 2C, used mixed-level pairs. Assign each student a role: Partner A or Partner B. Partner A asks questions 2, 3, and 5; Partner B asks 1 and 4.

•**Pre-level** Assign these students the role of Partner A. Tell them to use their summaries to answer the questions.

D 1. Read the information in the chart aloud. Elicit and discuss any questions the students have about the suffix *–ful*. Say the words and have students repeat them.

2. Direct students to work individually to write the correct word to complete each sentence. Write the answers on the board.

Multilevel Strategies

After 2D, seat same-level students together for more practice with nouns and *–ful* adjectives.

•**Pre-level** Ask these students to write five original sentences using *–ful* adjectives from the chart.

•**On- and Higher-level** Have these students write six sentences, three with an adjective form and three with a noun form from the chart.

Ask volunteers from both groups to put their sentences on the board.

3 Talk it over

Communicative Practice

15–20 minutes

1. Read the question aloud. Set a time limit (three minutes). Have students work independently to think about the question and write their answers in note form.

2. Write the students' opinions and reasons for their opinions on the board.

Application

5–10 minutes

BRING IT TO LIFE

Read the instructions aloud. Tell students that they can usually find a link to a store's return policy on the home page of its website.

To compress this lesson: Conduct 2D as a whole-class activity.

To extend this lesson: Look at *Consumer Reports* or another magazine or Internet site with reviews and ratings.
1. Show students several examples of rating scales. You can find these on the website or in a monthly magazine. Choose different products—for example, a car, a television, an appliance. Then look at the different criteria used for each item.
2. Put students in groups. Give each group a page of ratings so that they can compare products. Tell them to choose one of the items to buy. Ask a reporter from each group to explain which item his/her or group chose and why.

And/Or have students complete **Workbook 4 page 56** and the **Multilevel Activity Book 4 pages 94–95**.

C Work with a partner. Ask and answer the questions.

1. What does the CPSC do?
2. What is a *product recall*?
3. What does the FTC do?
4. How does the video game industry try to help parents?
5. Where can you find ratings on products like cars and insurance policies?

D Study the chart. Complete the sentences below with the correct words.

Word Study: The suffix *-ful*

Add *-ful* to the end of some nouns to form adjectives.
Sometimes there is a spelling change: beau**ty**—beau**tiful**

Noun	Adjective		Noun	Adjective
beauty	beautiful		pain	painful
care	careful		truth	truthful
help	helpful		use	useful

---

1. This tool isn't very __useful__. I'm disappointed in it.
2. Do you think this ad is ____truthful____? It seems pretty hard to believe.
3. I burned my hand on my new stove. The burn was very ____painful____.
4. The owner's manual is very well written and clear. It was very ____helpful____.
5. Be ____careful____ when you're buying clothes on clearance. Make sure they're not torn or stained.
6. Look at her new earrings! Aren't they ____beautiful____?

3 Talk it over

Think about the questions. Talk about your ideas with the class.

Do you think the government should protect consumers, or should consumers be responsible for themselves? Why?

BRING IT TO LIFE

Visit several stores or shopping websites. Make notes about their return and exchange policies. Bring your notes to class and compare them with a group. How are they alike? How are they different? Which store or site has the most consumer-friendly policies?

1 Grammar

A Circle the correct adjectives.

1. This video is really (bored / (boring)). I'm taking it back to the library.
2. I was ((surprised) / surprising) because I usually like movies about adventure.
3. The story in this video was very (disappointed / (disappointing)).
4. After about 30 minutes, we were completely ((confused) / confusing).
5. It might be (interested / (interesting)) if you didn't have anything else to do.

B Order the sentences from the mildest to the strongest. Write 1 for the mildest sentence and 4 for the strongest.

___3___ 1. Returning a purchase to this store is really inconvenient.
___1___ 2. Returning a purchase to this store is a little inconvenient.
___4___ 3. Returning a purchase to this store is extremely inconvenient.
___2___ 4. Returning a purchase to this store is pretty inconvenient.

C Complete the sentences with *so, such,* or *such a/an.*

1. Savers City is a good store. They have ___such___ great prices that I always save money.
2. They have ___such an___ excellent guarantee that I never have a problem with returns.
3. I got this shirt there yesterday. It was ___so___ cheap that I had to buy it!
4. This sofa had ___such a___ big stain on it that they were selling it "as is" for 75% off.
5. It was ___such a___ nice color that we decided to buy it.

D Match the parts of the sentences.

___e___ 1. This website is so helpful that   a. I'm not confused anymore.
___f___ 2. It has interesting information about   b. when I save a lot of money!
___a___ 3. It was a little confusing at first, but   c. I told my friends about it.
___d___ 4. It's extremely   d. easy to use.
___c___ 5. It has such good advice that   e. I use it all the time.
___b___ 6. I get really excited   f. products and companies.

Unit 8 Review and expand

Objectives	Grammar	Vocabulary	Correlations
On-, Pre-, and Higher-level: Expand upon and review unit grammar and life skills	Participial adjectives (*It's interesting.*) Adverbs of degree (*It's really interesting.*) Sentences with *so* and *such* (*It's so interesting that I want to see it again. It's such an interesting movie that I want to see it again.*)	Shopping For vocabulary support for pre-level students, see these **Oxford Picture Dictionary** topics: Shopping, Describing Things	**CASAS:** 0.1.2, 0.1.5, 0.2.1, 4.8.1, 7.2.6, 7.3.1, 7.3.2, 7.3.4 **LCPs:** 39.01, 49.01, 49.02, 49.09, 49.13, 49.16 **SCANS:** Creative thinking, Interprets and communicates information, Problem solving, **EFF:** Convey ideas in writing, Listen actively, Solve problems and make decisions

Warm-up and Review

10–15 minutes (books closed)

1. Review the *Bring It to Life* assignment from Lesson 5.

2. Have students who did the exercise describe the return and exchange policies that they read. Have other students answer the questions about how the policies are different and which are the most consumer friendly.

Introduction and Presentation

5 minutes

1. Write on the board: *Sometimes store policies are confusing. Sometimes they are extremely confusing. Sometimes they are so confusing that it's hard to know if you can return your item or not.*

2. State the objective: *Today we're going to review the use of adjectives to talk about shopping.*

1 Grammar

Guided Practice

40–45 minutes

A Ask students to work individually to circle the correct adjective. Go over the answers as a class.

B Read the example sentence aloud. Ask students to work individually to rank the other three. Go over the answers as a class.

C Have students work individually to complete the sentences. Go over the answers as a class.

D Ask students to work with a partner to match the parts of the sentences. Call on volunteers to read the completed sentences aloud.

TIP Bring in pictures of things that students can describe with an adjective. Some possibilities are food items that look delicious, unappetizing, sour, sweet, or cold; people doing actions that look difficult, interesting, exciting, or boring; household items or clothes that look comfortable, expensive, ugly, elegant, or modern.

Seat students in mixed-level groups, and provide each group with several pictures. Have each group write sentences that use adverbs of degree, *so* or *such,* for each of its pictures. Ask groups to hold up their pictures and share their sentences with the class.

2 Group work

Communicative Practice

20–35 minutes

 1. Direct students, in groups of three to four, to focus on the picture. Ask: *How does the customer feel?*

2. Assign roles: leader, recorder, and reporters. Explain that students work with their groups to write the conversation.

3. Check comprehension of the roles. Ask: *Who writes the conversation?* [recorder] *Who will read the conversation to the class?* [reporters] *Who helps everyone and manages the group?* [leader] *Who creates the conversation?* [everyone]

4. Set a time limit (five minutes) to complete the exercise. Circulate and answer any questions.

5. Have reporters from each group read the group's conversation to the class.

Multilevel Strategies

For 2A, use mixed-level groups.

•**Pre-level** Assign these students the role of reporter.

•**On-level** Assign these students the role of recorder.

•**Higher-level** Assign these students the role of leader.

B 1. Have students walk around the room to conduct the interviews. To get students moving, tell them to interview three new people not in their groups for 2A.

2. Set a time limit (five minutes) to complete the exercise.

3. Tell students to make a note of their classmates' answers but not to worry about writing complete sentences.

Multilevel Strategies

Adapt the mixer in 2B to the level of your students.

•**Pre-level** Allow these students to ask and answer the questions without writing.

•**Higher-level** Have these students ask two additional questions and write all answers.

C Call on individuals to report what they learned about their classmates. Encourage students to make generalizations. *Three out of four students would prefer to buy shoes from a catalog.*

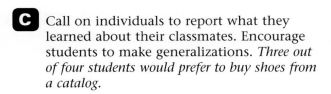
PROBLEM SOLVING

15–25 minutes

 1. Ask: *Do you ever shop at yard sales?* Tell students they will read a story about a woman who bought a vacuum cleaner at a yard sale. Direct students to read Tonya's story silently.

2. Ask: *What's wrong with the vacuum cleaner?* [It makes noise and doesn't clean well.] *How does Tonya feel?* [unhappy]

3. Play the audio and have students read along silently.

B 1. Elicit answers to question 1.

2. Put students into groups of three or four. Ask each group to think of three or four possible solutions to Tonya's problem and report them to the class. Ask a volunteer to write all possible solutions on the board.

3. Have students write letters giving advice to Tonya. Pair students and ask them to read their partners' letters. Call on volunteers to share any differences between the letter they wrote and the one they read.

Evaluation

30–35 minutes

To test students' understanding of the unit grammar and life skills, have them take the Unit 8 Test on the *Step Forward Test Generator CD-ROM* with *ExamView® Assessment Suite*.

Learning Log

To help students record and discuss their progress, use the *Learning Log* on page T-202.

To extend this review: Have students complete **Workbook 4 page 57, Multilevel Activity Book 4 page 96**, and the **Unit 8 Exercises** on the **Multilevel Grammar Exercises CD-ROM 4**.

2 Group work

A **Work with 2–3 classmates. Write a 6–8 line conversation between the people in the picture. Share your conversation with the class.**

A: *How can I help you today?*
B: *I'm having a problem with one of your products.*
A: *All right. What seems to be the problem?*
B: *Well,…*

B **Interview 3 classmates. Write their answers.**

1. What was your best shopping experience? What was your worst?
2. What shopping advice would you give someone who has just moved to your area? Why?
3. Would you prefer to buy shoes at a thrift store or from a catalog? Why?

C **Talk about the answers with your class.**

PROBLEM SOLVING

A **Listen and read about Tonya.**

Last week, Tonya's neighbors had a yard sale. Tonya doesn't know her neighbors very well, but she went to the yard sale and bought a vacuum cleaner for $25. When she got it home, however, she noticed some problems with it. It made a lot of noise, and it didn't really clean very well. Tonya knows that there are no guarantees at yard sales, but she is unhappy that her neighbors didn't tell her about the problems.

B **Work with your classmates. Answer the questions.**

1. What is Tonya's problem? Tonya bought a vacuum from her neighbors at their yard sale. The vacuum has some problems, and Tonya is unhappy that her neighbors didn't tell her.
2. What should she do? Think of 3 possible solutions for Tonya.
3. Write a short letter to Tonya. Tell her what you think she should do.

UNIT **9**

FOCUS ON
- medical histories
- making healthy changes
- forms of advice
- a doctor's visit
- health insurance

Take Care!

LESSON **1**   **Vocabulary**

1 Learn health vocabulary

A   **Talk about the questions with your class.**

1. What are some things people do to stay healthy and live a long life?
2. Who is the oldest person you have ever known? How old is he or she?

B   **Work with your classmates. Match the words with the pictures.**

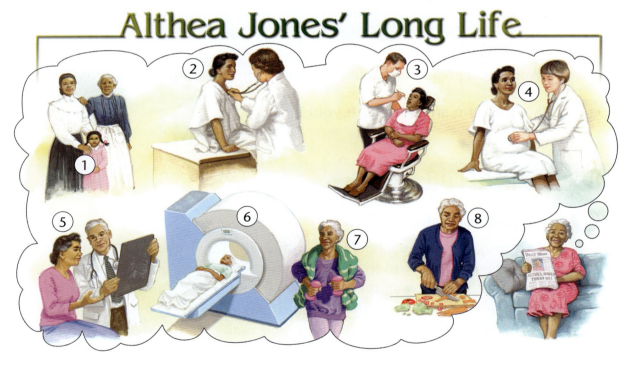

Althea Jones' Long Life

__7__ active lifestyle	__8__ good nutrition	__4__ prenatal care
__3__ dental checkups	__1__ heredity	__2__ yearly physicals
__5__ early detection	__6__ medical screenings	

C   **Listen and check. Then read the new words with a partner.**

D   **Work with a partner. Write other health history words you know.
Check your words in a dictionary.**

Unit 9 Lesson 1

Objectives	Grammar	Vocabulary	Correlations
On-level: Describe and talk about medical conditions and medical history **Pre-level:** Identify medical conditions and describe medical history **Higher-level:** Talk and write about medical history using vocabulary for medical conditions	Present tense (*Early detection saves lives.*)	Medical history For vocabulary support for pre-level students, see this **Oxford Picture Dictionary** unit: Health	**CASAS:** 0.1.2, 0.1.5, 3.5.9, 4.8.1 **LCPs:** 41.06, 49.02, 49.10 **SCANS:** Listening, Participates as member of a team, Reading, Seeing things in the mind's eye, Speaking **EFF:** Cooperate with others, Listen actively, Read with understanding, Speak so others can understand

Warm-up and Review

10–15 minutes (books closed)

Write *Illnesses* on the board, and elicit names of illnesses that students know. Write them on the board.

Introduction

5 minutes

1. Ask students which of the illnesses they think are serious. Ask which ones they would need to include on a medical history form.

2. State the objective: *Today we're going to learn how to talk about our medical history.*

1 Learn health vocabulary

Presentation I

20–25 minutes

A Write *Staying Healthy* on the board, and elicit students' answers to questions 1 and 2. Write their ideas for staying healthy.

B 1. Direct students to look at the pictures. Ask: *How old is she?*

2. Group students and assign roles: leader, fact checker, recorder, and reporter. Explain that students work with their groups to match the words and pictures.

3. Check comprehension of the roles. Ask: *Who looks up the words in a dictionary?* [fact checker] *Who writes the numbers in the book?* [recorder] *Who tells the class your answers?* [reporter] *Who helps everyone and manages the group?* [leader]

4. Set a time limit (three minutes). As students work together, copy the wordlist on the board.

5. Call "time." Have reporters take turns giving their answers. Write each group's answer on the board next to the word.

C 1. To prepare students for listening, say: *This woman's name is Althea Jones. We're going to listen to Althea talk about her secrets for a long life.* Ask students to listen and check their answers.

2. Have students correct the wordlist on the board and then write the correct numbers in their books.

3. Pair students. Set a time limit (three minutes). Monitor pair practice to identify pronunciation issues.

4. Call "time" and work with the pronunciation of any troublesome words or phrases.

D 1. Ask students to work with their partners from 1C to brainstorm a list of related words.

2. Elicit words from the class. Write them on the board. Ask students to copy them into their vocabulary notes for the unit.

Guided Practice

5–10 minutes

 1. Read the questions aloud.

2. Set a time limit (three minutes). Direct students to ask and answer the questions with a partner.

2 Learn vocabulary for medical conditions

Presentation II

15–20 minutes

 1. Direct students to look at the form on page 117. Elicit the name of the form, and ask how many students have filled out something similar. Explain that there are a lot of medical conditions or problems listed on a medical history form and that they will learn some of these conditions.

2. Ask students to work individually to circle five problems or illnesses that Althea Jones has had.

3. Call on volunteers to read the medical conditions in the chart aloud and discuss their meanings. Have students repeat the words.

4. Check comprehension. Ask: *What's a word to describe a bad headache?* [severe] *What word describes a medical condition that lasts for a very long time?* [chronic]

Guided Practice

10–15 minutes

 Have students work individually to complete the paragraph. Go over the answers as a class.

 If you have access to the Internet in class, have students look up a common illness or condition to find its symptoms. Put students in pairs, and give each pair a condition to look up—for example, diabetes, high blood pressure, the flu, arthritis, ulcer, mumps, strep throat, measles. If students are interested in a particular condition, allow them to choose. Direct partners to find the main symptoms or warning signs and to share them with the class.

Communicative Practice and Application

10–15 minutes

C Give students a minute to make notes of their answers to the questions. Call on individuals to share their ideas with the class.

Evaluation

10–15 minutes (books closed)

TEST YOURSELF

1. Pair students. Direct Partner B to close the book and listen to Partner A dictate words from 1B on page 116. Ask students to switch roles when they finish and have Partner B dictate words from 2A on page 117.

2. Direct both partners to open their books and check their spelling when they finish.

3. Circulate and monitor student work.

> ### Multilevel Strategies
>
> Target the *Test Yourself* to the level of your students.
>
> • **Pre-level** Have these students dictate five words from each page.
>
> • **Higher-level** Direct these students to write a sentence that shows the meaning of each word their partner dictates. *If you exercise regularly, you have an active lifestyle.*

To compress this lesson: Conduct 1B as a whole-class activity.

To extend this lesson: Look at a real medical history form. Find a medical history form on the Internet, and distribute copies or project a transparency of it. Ask students to identify vocabulary that they don't know. And/Or have students complete **Workbook 4 page 58** and **Multilevel Activity Book 4 pages 98–99**.

E Work with a partner. Talk about the questions. Use the words in 1B.

1. What has helped Althea Jones live a long life?
2. What did Althea Jones do when she was pregnant?
3. How does Ms. Jones try to prevent health problems?

2 Learn vocabulary for medical conditions

A Study the medical history form. Circle 5 problems Althea Jones has had.

MEDICAL HISTORY FORM

Name: Althea Jones   **Physician:** Dr. Suveena Herat

	Yes	No		Yes	No
Childhood diseases			Persistent cold (more than 2 weeks)		✓
measles	✓		**Chronic** cough (cough that does not get better)		✓
mumps		✓	High blood pressure		✓
chicken pox	✓		Heart problems or heart **disease**		✓
Recent weight gain or loss		✓	**Weakness** in arms or legs	✓	
Frequent or **severe** headaches		✓	Chest pain or other **symptoms** of heart disease		✓
Allergies to medications	✓		Family history of heart disease (Explain below.)	✓	

If yes, which medications?
I'm **allergic** to penicillin.

My mother and grandmother had heart disease.

B Work with a partner. Complete the doctor's notes with the words in 2A.

Ms. Jones is very healthy. She maintains an active lifestyle and has had regular medical screenings. There is a family history of heart _____disease_____.
(1)
However, Ms. Jones has no _____symptoms_____ of heart disease. She has some _____weakness_____ in one leg. She sometimes has headaches, but they
(2)   (3)
are mild, not _____severe_____. She sometimes coughs, but she doesn't
(4)
have a _____chronic_____ cough. It goes away with medication. She is
(5)
_____allergic_____ to penicillin.
(6)

C Talk about the questions with your class.

1. Which is more important to a person's health—heredity or lifestyle? Why?
2. What are the advantages of checkups and medical screenings?

TEST YOURSELF ✔

Partner A: Read the vocabulary words in 1B to a partner. Partner B: Close your book. Write the words. Ask your partner for help with spelling as necessary. Then change roles. Partner B: Use the words in 2A.

1 Read a personal letter about healthy changes

A Talk about the questions with your class.

1. What are some examples of changes that people make to improve their health?
2. Would you be comfortable giving health advice to a friend? To a classmate? To a family member? Why or why not?

B Listen and read the letter.

Dear Marisol,

Thank you very much for your letter. It was great to hear all your news. Wow—things have been really busy at your house!

I've been busy, too. A few months ago, I realized I was feeling tired all the time. So I decided to cut back on* sugar. I used to have a real sweet tooth, and I ate a lot of candy and sweet snacks. My plan was to cut out* sugar on weekdays.

At first, it wasn't easy. I thought, "Oh, just one candy bar won't hurt," but after a few weeks, that changed. I didn't want sweet snacks all the time. Once or twice on the weekends was enough. Since I made that change, I've felt so much better! I have more energy, and I sleep better, too. It's great!

Well, it's time for me to go to class. Please say hello to your family for me, and write again soon!

Take care,
Christina

Writer's note

Letters often start with a comment about the letter the writer is answering.

*__Idiom notes:__ cut back on = use less of
    cut out = stop using completely

C Check your understanding. Circle the correct words.

1. Christina last heard from Marisol by (letter / phone).
2. (Marisol / Christina) was feeling tired a lot.
3. Christina decided to (cut back on / cut out) sugar during the week.
4. Christina still eats (some / a lot of) sweet snacks on the weekends.
5. Eating less sugar has made Christina (have more energy / need less sleep).

Unit 9 Lesson 2

Objectives	Grammar	Vocabulary	Correlations
On- and Higher-level: Analyze, write, and edit a personal letter about healthy lifestyle changes **Pre-level:** Read a personal letter, and write about healthy lifestyle changes	Simple-past, simple-present, and present-perfect tense (*Since I cut back on sugar, I've felt much better. Now I don't want sweets all the time.*)	Healthy and unhealthy habits For vocabulary support for pre-level students, see this **Oxford Picture Dictionary** unit: Health	**CASAS:** 0.1.2, 0.1.5, 0.2.1, 3.5.9 **LCPs:** 39.01, 41.06, 49.01, 49.13, 49.16 **SCANS:** Creative thinking, Interprets and communicates information, Listening, Reading, Speaking, Writing **EFF:** Convey ideas in writing, Listen actively, Read with understanding, Reflect and evaluate

Warm-up and Review

10–15 minutes (books closed)

1. Ask: *What are some unhealthy habits that people have?* List students' ideas on the board. Ask students to quantify how much or little of something makes it unhealthy. *How much sugar and fat is unhealthy? How many cigarettes? How little exercise?*

2. Lead students in a discussion about advice, especially the cultural aspect of giving advice.

Introduction

5 minutes

1. Point out that many of the things on the board are not a problem if you do them occasionally but that doing them regularly is unhealthy.

2. State the objective: *Today we're going to read and write a personal letter about making healthy changes.*

1 Read a personal letter about healthy changes

Presentation

20–25 minutes

A Elicit answers to questions 1 and 2. Write students' ideas for healthy changes on the board next to problems they brought up during the warm-up.

B 1. Tell students to look at the greeting and read the first sentence of the letter. Ask them to guess the relationship between the writer and Marisol. Ask: *Do you think they're acquaintances? Family? Friends?*

2. Direct students to read the letter silently. Check comprehension. Ask: *What was Christina's problem?* [She felt tired all of the time.] *How did she fix it?* [She cut back on sugar.]

3. Play the audio. Have students read along silently.

4. Draw students' attention to the *Writer's note,* and point out that the first paragraph of Christina's letter is in response to the letter she received from Marisol.

Guided Practice I

10 minutes

C Have students work independently to circle the correct words. Go over the answers as a class.

Multilevel Strategies

For 1C, challenge higher-level students while working with pre-level students.

• **Higher-level** Have these students write a sentence about something they or someone they know has cut back on or cut out. Point out the use of a noun or gerund with these expressions. Remind students that they can also use *quit* or *stop* when talking about a habit and that those verbs are followed by gerunds.

2 Write a personal letter

Guided Practice II

20–25 minutes

 A 1. Read the questions. Elicit students' answers.

2. Teach the expression *to quit something cold turkey*. Ask students if (or when) quitting cold turkey is the best way to quit.

B 1. Direct students to look back at the letter in 1B. Focus students' attention on the tense changes in the letter. Ask them to look through the letter quickly and underline the verbs. Elicit the present-perfect verbs and discuss the reason for that tense choice.

2. Read the questions for Paragraph 1 aloud, and elicit some possible problems their friend might have mentioned.

3. Check comprehension of the exercise. Ask: *How will your letter begin?* [Dear _____,] *How many paragraphs will it have?* [three] *How will it end?* [Take care, or Talk to you soon,]

4. Have students work individually to write their letters.

> ### Multilevel Strategies
>
> Adapt 2B to the level of your students.
>
> • **Pre-level** Tell these students to write a one-paragraph letter, using the questions for Paragraph 2 to guide them. Ask them to close the letter by answering the question *Did making the change help you?*

 C 1. Lead students through the process of using the *Editing checklist*. Read the sentences aloud, and answer any questions. Then ask students to check their papers.

2. Allow students a few minutes to edit their writing as necessary.

Communicative Practice

10 minutes

 D 1. Read the instructions aloud. Emphasize to students that they are responding to their partners' work, not correcting it.

2. Use the letter in 1B to model the exercise. *I think it's interesting that she cut back on sweets but didn't cut them out altogether. I'd like to ask the writer if she did anything to help make it easier when she first cut back on sweets.*

3. Direct students to exchange papers with a partner and follow the instructions.

4. Call on volunteers to share some things their partners thought were interesting in their letters.

Application and Evaluation

20 minutes

 Before the *Test Yourself*, expand on the discussion of lifestyle changes. Elicit bad habits that people sometimes have—for example, gambling, disorganization, being late all the time, nail biting, forgetting things, etc. Have students work with a partner to brainstorm ways to change these habits. Call on volunteers to share their ideas with the class.

TEST YOURSELF

1. Review the instructions aloud. Assign a time limit (15 minutes), and have students work independently.

2. Before collecting students' work, remind them to use the *Editing checklist*. Collect and correct students' writing.

To compress this lesson: Assign the *Test Yourself* for homework.

To extend this lesson: Role-play a conversation about lifestyle changes.
1. Write a role-play scenario on the board. *Partner A: You haven't felt well lately. Describe your problem to your partner. Partner B: You or someone you know had a similar problem in the past. Making a change in lifestyle or diet helped eliminate the problem. Tell your partner about it. Partner A: Thank your partner for the advice.*
2. Have students practice the role-play with a partner. Call on volunteers to perform their role-play for the class.

And/Or have students complete **Workbook 4 page 59** and **Multilevel Activity Book 4 page 100**.

2 Write a personal letter

A **Talk about the questions with your class.**

1. What lifestyle changes are easy to make? What changes are difficult? Why?
2. Name two ways to break a bad habit or to start a good habit.

B **You received a letter from a friend. Write a personal letter back to your friend about a lifestyle change you have made. Use the model in 1B and the questions and suggestions below to help you.**

Paragraph 1: Respond to the news you got from your friend in his or her last letter.

Paragraph 2: Tell your friend about a problem you have had. What did you do about it? What change did you make in your life?

Paragraph 3: How did you feel about making this change at first? How do you feel about it now? Did making the change help you?

Closing: End your letter in a friendly way.

> Dear (friend's name),
>   Thank you very much for your letter. It was great to hear from you...

C **Use the checklist to edit your writing. Check (✔) the true sentences.**

Editing checklist	
1. I started with a comment about the letter I received.	
2. I wrote about a problem I had.	
3. I wrote about how making a change helped me.	
4. I indented each paragraph.	

D **Exchange letters with a partner. Read and comment on your partner's letter.**

1. Point out one idea you think is interesting.
2. Ask your partner a question about the change he or she wrote about.

TEST YOURSELF ✔

Write a new letter. Tell a friend about another change you made to improve your health, change your lifestyle, or reduce stress.

1 Learn different forms of advice

A **Look at the pictures. What advice does the doctor give each patient?**

1

You should eat more healthy food. You ought to exercise more.

He should eat more healthy food. He ought to exercise more.

2

You shouldn't stay up so late. You'd better drink less coffee.

She shouldn't stay up so late. She'd better drink less coffee.

3

You had better not go to school today.

She'd better not to go school today.

B **Study the chart. Circle the 2 sentences in 1A that give the strongest advice.**

Advice with *should*, *had better*, and *ought to*					
You	**should** **ought to**	eat more healthy food. exercise more.	You	**shouldn't**	stay up so late.
You	**had better**	drink less coffee.	You	**had better not**	go to school today.

Notes
• Use *should* and *ought to* to give advice. They mean the same thing. • In the U.S., people don't usually use *ought to* in negative statements. • Use *had better* to give strong advice or to tell someone to do something.

C **Complete the statements with *had better* or *had better not*.**

1. You _____had better_____ see a doctor. You don't look well.

2. You _____had better not_____ go to work today. You should stay home when you have a fever.

3. You _____had better_____ call in sick. Your boss needs to know that you're not coming in.

4. You need to rest. You _____had better not_____ go out until you feel better.

5. You _____had better_____ take your medicine. The doctor said that it will help you get better.

Unit 9 Lesson 3

Objectives	Grammar	Vocabulary	Correlations
On-, Pre-, and Higher-level: Use modals to give advice and listen for health advice	Advice modals (*You should eat more healthy food. You shouldn't eat so much salt. You had better drink less coffee.*)	Health ailments, conditions, health care For vocabulary support for pre-level students, see these **Oxford Picture Dictionary** topics: Symptoms and Injuries, Illnesses and Medical Conditions, Medical Care, Taking Care of Your Health	**CASAS:** 0.1.2, 0.1.5, 0.2.1, 3.5.9, 7.4.7 **LCPs:** 39.01, 41.06, 49.01, 49.02, 49.09, 49.17 **SCANS:** Creative thinking, Listening, Reading, Seeing things in the mind's eye, Speaking **EFF:** Advocate and influence, Convey ideas in writing, Speak so others can understand, Reflect and evaluate

Warm-up and Review

10–15 minutes (books closed)

1. Write *Give me some advice* on the board. Tell students that you have various problems, and elicit their advice. *I can't sleep at night. I get a lot of colds. I get a lot of stomachaches. I get out of breath easily.* Note the language you want them to use on the board: *you should, you shouldn't, you'd better, you'd better not.* If they use imperatives, write the verb.

2. Elicit how students feel when they give/get advice and when it's OK to give advice.

Introduction

5–10 minutes

1. Say: *We have a lot of different ways of giving advice. Some of them are stronger than others.*

2. State the objective: *Today we're going to learn different ways to give advice about health.*

1 Learn different forms of advice

Presentation I

20–25 minutes

 1. Direct students to look at the pictures. Elicit each patient's problem.

2. Read the questions. Ask students to read what the doctor says silently to find the answers. Call on individuals to share their answers.

 1. Demonstrate how to read the grammar chart.

2. Direct students to circle the forms of advice in 1A. Go over the answers as a class.

3. Read the chart through sentence by sentence. Then read it again, and have students repeat after you.

4. Assess students' understanding of the charts. Compare the modals in the chart to the words students used to give you advice in the warm-up. Ask students to restate their advice using modals from the chart.

Guided Practice I

15–20 minutes

 Ask students to work individually to complete the sentences. Ask volunteers to write the answers on the board.

After 1C, provide more practice with modals. Show students pictures of people with ailments, or use the ailments pictures from *The Oxford Picture Dictionary*. Call on individuals to give advice to the people in the pictures using the different modals from the chart in 1B.

D Ask students to work individually to match the sentences. Tell them to take turns reading the matched sentences with a partner. Call on volunteers to read the matching sentences aloud.

Multilevel Strategies

For 1D, seat higher-level students together.

• **Higher-level** If these students finish before the others, have them work together to develop their own matching exercise. Tell them to write three or four statements and three or four pieces of advice to match those statements. Have them write their statements and pieces of advice out of order on the board. After you have gone over the 1D responses with the class, call on pre- and on-level students to match the sentences and advice written by the higher-level students.

Guided Practice II

5–10 minutes

E Have students read each statement silently to identify the mistake. Call on volunteers to read the corrected sentences aloud.

2 Learn the differences between forms of advice

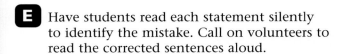

Presentation II

20–25 minutes

A 1. Introduce the new topic. Write *You should eat more vegetables.* and *You'd better eat more vegetables.* on the board. Ask students which sentence is stronger. Point out that we often use *had better* when we want to imply a negative result. *You had better eat more vegetables or you're going to get sick.*

2. Say: *Now we're going to look at other ways to give strong advice.*

3. Read the instructions and sentences in the chart aloud.

4. Call on volunteers to read their sentences aloud.

Guided Practice I

10–15 minutes

B Ask students to work individually to categorize the advice. Go over the answers as a class.

C Have students work individually to write their advice. Elicit several pieces of advice for each situation. Discuss the strength of each piece of advice.

Multilevel Strategies

After 2C, provide more practice with modals for the pre- and on-level students while you challenge the higher-level students.

Ask students to think about a mother whose first child is going off to college. Elicit advice the mother might give to her child. Direct students to put their pencils down and listen to one mother's advice. Read this paragraph aloud:

I know you'll have a lot of work to do, but you shouldn't drink too much coffee. You probably won't be eating very well, so you ought to take a vitamin every day. And you'd better not start drinking and smoking, because you have to call me every other day, and I'll know if you're up to no good!

Elicit advice that students remember from the paragraph, but don't write it on the board. Read the paragraph again. Seat students in groups, and direct them to restate the mother's advice. Emphasize that it's not important to use her exact words, just to restate the same ideas. Then read the paragraph again. Give each group a large sheet of paper, and ask students to write the mother's advice.

• **On- and pre-level** Have these students work together to write sentences restating the advice. *You shouldn't drink coffee.*

• **Higher-level** Tell these students to reconstruct as much of the paragraph as they can remember.

Put up the groups' sentences/paragraphs, and go over them as a class. Are any important ideas missing? Compare the strength of the modals students used with the original paragraph. Explain *up to no good* if students misinterpreted or ignored it.

D Match the sentences.

_c_ 1. You look very tired today.
_a_ 2. She eats a lot of sugar.
_e_ 3. Our diet isn't very healthy.
_b_ 4. We need to lose weight.
_d_ 5. She always has headaches.

a. She shouldn't eat so many candy bars.
b. We ought to exercise every day.
c. You should get more sleep.
d. She'd better see a doctor.
e. We should eat more fresh vegetables.

E Get the form. Work with your class. Correct the sentences.

1. You should to walk every day.   You should walk every day.
2. You ought talk to a doctor.   You ought to talk to a doctor.
3. You better drink a lot of water.   You'd better drink a lot of water.

2 Learn the difference between forms of advice

A Study the chart. Write 2 more examples of the strongest types of advice.

Advice and strong advice		
mild	should, ought to	You **should** eat more vegetables.
strong	had better	You'**d better** take a vacation.
stronger	must, have to, have got to	You **have to** take this medicine.

Note
Have got to is as strong as *have to* and *must,* but is less formal.

B Categorize the advice. Write *M* for mild, *S* for strong, or *SR* for stronger.

_SR_ 1. You've got to see a doctor.
_S_ 2. You'd better see a doctor.
_SR_ 3. You must see a doctor.
_M_ 4. You should see a doctor.

C Write your own advice. Use the advice words from the chart in 2A in each sentence.

should	~~ought to~~	had better	have to

1. A classmate says, "I'm sick. I have a fever."
   You say, " You ought to go home .”
2. A co-worker says, "I just cut my hand. It's bleeding."
   You say, "_____.”
3. Your teacher says, "I have a cold."
   You say, "_____.”
4. Your friend says, "I hurt my finger. I can't move it."
   You say, "_____.”

3 Grammar listening

Listen to two speakers give advice. Who gives stronger advice? Check (✔) **Speaker A** or **Speaker B**.

	Speaker A	Speaker B
1.	✔	
2.		✔
3.		✔
4.	✔	
5.		✔
6.	✔	

4 Practice *should, had better, have to,* and *must*

A Think about your answers to these questions.

1. In your opinion, what are some things people should do when they have colds?
2. What is one thing people ought to do for their health? What is one thing they should not do?
3. Imagine that a friend wants to lose weight. Talk about what he or she had better do.

B Work with a partner. Ask and answer the questions.

A: *What do you think people should do when they have colds?*
B: *I think they should rest.*

C Talk about your ideas with the class.

We think that people should rest and wash their hands when they have colds.

TEST YOURSELF ✔

Close your book. Write 5 or more sentences on how people can improve their health. Use different forms of advice.

3 Grammar listening

Guided Practice II

10–15 minutes

1. Say: *Now we're going to listen to people giving health advice. You need to decide whether Speaker A or Speaker B gives stronger advice.*

2. Play the audio. Direct students to listen silently without writing.

3. Replay the audio. Ask students to check the correct column in the chart.

4. Ask for a show of hands for each answer.

> ### Multilevel Strategies
>
> Replay the *Grammar listening* to allow pre-level students to catch up while you challenge on- and higher-level students.
>
> • **Pre-level** Have these students listen again to complete the chart.
>
> • **On- and Higher-level** Have these students listen again and write the advice words they hear.

4 Practice *should, had better, have to,* and *must*

Communicative Practice and Application

20–25 minutes

A 1. Direct students to look at the photo. Ask: *How does the woman feel? What should she do to feel better?*

2. Tell students to read the questions. Give them time to think about and note their answers.

B 1. Put students in pairs. Read and have students repeat the questions.

2. Direct students to take turns asking and answering the questions. Tell them to make notes of each other's answers. Model the exercise by asking a volunteer the first question. Have the class tell you how to write the answer in note form.

3. Check comprehension of the exercise. Ask: *Does each partner answer every question?* [yes]

4. Set a time limit (four minutes) for the exercise. Observe and take note of issues that arise.

C Discuss the students' ideas as a class. Ask students to share any interesting or unusual advice they heard from their partners.

Evaluation

10–15 minutes (books closed)

TEST YOURSELF

Ask students to write the sentences independently. Collect and correct their writing.

> ### Multilevel Strategies
>
> Target the *Test Yourself* to the level of your students.
>
> • **Pre-level** Provide these students with skeleton sentences:
>
> *When you have a cold, _____.*
>
> *When you are under a lot of stress, _____.*
>
> *When you need to lose weight, _____.*
>
> *When you have a high fever, _____.*
>
> *When you are very tired, _____.*
>
> • **Higher-level** Have these students write a paragraph in response to this prompt: *Imagine your niece or nephew is going to move away from home. What advice would give him or her?*

To compress this lesson: Conduct 1C as a whole-class activity.

To extend this lesson: Discuss mental health.

1. Write a series of statements on the board. *Occasionally, Ray feels sad for no reason. Ester often gets so frustrated that she yells at her children. Keri cries every day. Leo feels bored all of the time. He's not interested in anything.*

2. Ask students what advice they would give these people. Ask which ones they think need professional help. Tell students about local agencies that might be able to help these people.

And/Or have students complete **Workbook 4 pages 60–61, Multilevel Activity Book 4 pages 101–102,** and the corresponding **Unit 9 Exercises** on the **Multilevel Grammar Exercises CD-ROM 4.**

Unit 9 Lesson 4

Objectives	Grammar	Vocabulary	Correlations
On-, Pre-, and Higher-level: Ask and answer questions at a doctor's office, and listen for medical information	Verb + gerund or infinitive (*He quit smoking. He decided to cut back on salt.*)	*Diabetes, prevention, shot, immunization, ointment, tetanus* For vocabulary support for pre-level students, see this **Oxford Picture Dictionary** unit: Health	**CASAS:** 0.1.2, 0.1.5, 0.2.1, 3.1.3, 3.5.9, 6.0.3, 6.0.4, 6.1.1, 7.5.6 **LCPs:** 39.01, 41.03, 41.06, 49.02, 49.09, 49.16, 49.17 **SCANS:** Arithmetic/Mathematics, Seeing thing in the mind's eye, Speaking **EFF:** Cooperate with others, Listen actively, Use math to solve problems and communicate

Warm-up and Review

10–15 minutes (books closed)

Ask students how they feel about going to the doctor. *Do you go regularly or do you avoid going?* Find out if they go to an English speaking doctor or if they go to a doctor who speaks their native language.

Introduction

5 minutes

1. Point out that even if the students' regular doctor speaks their native language, there are sometimes situations where we can't choose which doctor to see—for example, in the emergency room.

2. State the objective: *Today we're going to learn to talk to the doctor and listen for medical information.*

1 Learn to ask and answer questions at a doctor's office

Presentation I

15–20 minutes

 1. Direct students to look at the pictures. Ask: *Do these patients look unhealthy?*

2. Play the audio. Give students a minute to answer the questions. Go over the answers as a class. Ask students to tell you other phrases and information they heard on the audio.

3. Model confirming advice and then replay the audio, and have students listen for the way the patients confirm their doctor's advice.

Guided Practice

20–25 minutes

 1. Read the instructions aloud. Play the audio. Ask students to read along silently and listen for the answer to the question. Elicit the answer.

2. Ask students to read the conversation with a partner. Circulate and monitor pronunciation. Model and have students repeat difficult words or phrases.

3. Say and have students repeat the expressions in the *In other words* box. Elicit the placement of the expressions in the conversation. Ask volunteers to read the conversation using expressions from the box.

Communicative Practice and Application

15–20 minutes

 1. Ask students to read the instructions silently. Check their comprehension of the exercise. Ask: *What are the two roles? What is the situation?* Elicit examples of what each person might say.

2. Set a time limit (five minutes). Ask students to act out the role-play in both roles. Ask volunteer pairs to act out their conversation for the class. Tell students who are listening to note how Partner B responds to Partner A's advice.

Multilevel Strategies

For 1C, adapt the role-play to the level of your students.

• **Pre-level** Provide the first two sentences to help these students get started on their role-play. *A: Your checkup was excellent. B: Well I've been eating better and trying to get more sleep because I'm worried about stress. A: Are you feeling stressed? B: _____.*

1 Learn to ask and answer questions at a doctor's office

A Look at the pictures. Listen to the conversations. Then answer the questions below with your classmates.

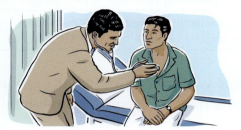 

1. What health goal does each person have? man: to live to be 100
woman: to keep healthy and in good shape
2. What does the doctor recommend? man: to eat well and get more exercise
woman: keep exercising, try to relax, cut back on salt

B Listen and read. How do you know the patient is listening carefully?
He repeats some of the doctor's words to check his understanding.

Doctor: You've lost some weight since your last checkup, Al.

Patient: Well, I'm trying to exercise more. I'm concerned about diabetes*.

Doctor: Does diabetes run in your family?

Patient: Yes. My father has it. I want to do what I can to prevent it.

Doctor: Well, keeping your weight down is an excellent first step. Cutting back on sugar can help, too.

Patient: OK. Is there anything else you'd recommend?

Doctor: Healthy eating is important. Try to get four or five servings of vegetables a day.

Patient: So I should continue exercising, cut back on sugar, and eat more vegetables.

Doctor: Yes, that's it. And it's great that you're thinking about prevention now.

> **In other words...**
>
> **Confirming advice**
> So I should…
> So I need to…
> So I'm supposed to…
> So I have to…

*diabetes = a disease that causes a person's body to have trouble controlling the amount of sugar in the blood

C Role-play a checkup with a partner. Use the example in 1B to make a new conversation.

Partner A: You're the doctor. Comment on your patient's high blood pressure. Listen to your patient and ask if high blood pressure runs in the family. Explain that cutting out salt is a good first step. Suggest cutting back on tea and coffee too. Recommend swimming or cycling.

Partner B: You're the patient. Tell your doctor that you're eating less salt because you're concerned about high blood pressure. Your mother has it. Ask the doctor for other recommendations to help you. Confirm your doctor's advice.

☑ Ask and answer questions about health issues **123**

2 Learn verbs with gerunds and infinitives

A Study the chart. Give 5 examples of an infinitive. Give 5 examples of a gerund.

Verbs with gerunds and infinitives			
Verb + gerund	quit consider	avoid feel like	He **quit smoking** ten years ago. I'd **consider joining** a gym.
Verb + infinitive	decide plan	agree need	We **decided to limit** sugar in our coffee. She's **planning to make** some changes.
Verb + gerund OR **infinitive**	start like	continue prefer	I've **started walking** to work every day. I've **started to walk** to work every day.

B Work with a partner. Complete the sentences with the infinitive or gerund form of the verbs in parentheses. Some items have two correct answers.

1. Why did he quit _____exercising_____? (exercise)
2. Which types of exercise do you like ____doing / to do____? (do)
3. What did you decide ____to change____ in your diet? (change)
4. I'm going to start ____eating / to eat____ more healthy food. (eat)

C Work with a group. Look at the picture. Give George some advice. Use the verbs in 1A.

George should quit / start…
He shouldn't continue…
He needs…

3 Practice your pronunciation

A Listen to the pronunciation of *s* and *ch* in these words. How are they different?

Pronunciation of *s*		Pronunciation of *ch*	
since	sugar	checkup	headache

B Circle the sound of the underlined letters in these words. Then listen and check.

1. in<u>s</u>urance   (s /(sh))
2. <u>s</u>erving   ((s)/ sh)
3. stoma<u>ch</u>   (ch /(k))
4. ea<u>ch</u>   ((ch)/ k)
5. <u>ch</u>ange   ((ch)/ k)
6. <u>ch</u>ronic   (ch /(k))

C Say the sentences with a partner. Then listen and check your pronunciation.

1. She should not serve sugar.
2. She has a stomachache.
3. I have to change my health insurance.
4. I shouldn't eat it. I'm sure it's sweet.

2 Learn verbs with gerunds and infinitives

Presentation II

10–15 minutes

 A 1. Introduce the new topic. *Now we're going to talk about health using verbs followed by gerunds or infinitives.*

2. Read the instructions aloud. Direct students to study the chart and answer the questions. Read and have students repeat the sentences in the chart.

Guided Practice

15–20 minutes

 B Have students work with a partner to complete the sentences. Call on volunteers to read the completed sentences aloud.

Multilevel Strategies

Seat higher-level students together for 2B.

• **Higher-level** If these students finish 2B early, provide them with this list of verbs followed by a gerund: *postpone, recommend, can't help,* and this list of verbs followed by an infinitive: *deserve, intend, refuse.* Direct them to write a sentence with each of the words. Have volunteers write their sentences on the board to share with the class.

Communicative Practice and Application

10–15 minutes

C 1. Combine pairs to make groups of four. Tell them to take turns giving George advice.

2. Set a time limit (five minutes). Call on a reporter from each group to share a piece of advice for George. Continue until the class runs out of ideas.

 TIP Provide more practice with infinitives and gerunds after 2C. Write conversation starters on the board. *1. Tell me about a time you quit doing something. 2. What do you always avoid doing? 3. Tell me about a time you considered doing something and then changed your mind. 4. What have you decided to do recently? 5. What do you plan to do this weekend? 6. Tell me about something you agreed to do recently.* Direct students to walk around the room and talk to six people. Tell them to use a different conversation starter with each person.

3 Practice your pronunciation

Pronunciation Extension

10–15 minutes

A 1. Write *I'm sure she's had that chest cold since Christmas.* on the board. Say the sentence and ask students to repeat it. Underline the *s* in *sure* and *since* and the *ch* in *chest* and *Christmas.* Say and have students repeat those words. Say: *Now we're going to focus on different pronunciations of* s *and* ch.

2. Play the audio. Direct students to listen for the pronunciation of *s* and *ch.*

3. Call on volunteers to tell you how the sounds are different.

B 1. Have students work individually to choose the correct sound for each word.

2. Play the audio and have students check their answers.

C Have students take turns saying the sentences with a partner. Play the audio and have students check their pronunciation. Call on volunteers to say the sentences for the class.

4 Focus on listening

Listening Extension

20–25 minutes

A 1. Direct students to read the poster. Elicit any questions about the vocabulary.

2. Call on volunteers to answer the questions.

B Read the questions aloud. Play the audio. Direct students to ask and answer the questions with a partner.

C 1. Direct students to read the sentences before listening.

2. Replay the audio and have students work individually to circle the correct words. Take a tally of responses for each item, and if students disagree on a response, replay the audio, so they can check their answers.

Multilevel Strategies

Replay the audio to challenge on- and higher-level students while allowing pre-level students to catch up.

• **Pre-level** Have these students listen again to go over their answers.

• **On- and Higher-level** Write questions on the board. Tell these students to write the answers. *Does Mr. Gomez need stitches? What other shot is he getting? Why does he need to go back to the doctor's office?* Ask volunteers to write the answers on the board.

5 Real-life math

Math Extension

5–10 minutes

Direct students to look at the immunization chart. Give students time to read the questions and find the answers individually. Call on volunteers for the answers.

TIP Show students a real immunization chart. You can share one from your family, or you can find one on the Internet that includes an explanation of each required immunization.

Evaluation

10–15 minutes

TEST YOURSELF

1. Model the role-play with a volunteer. Then switch roles.

2. Pair students. Check comprehension of the exercise by eliciting things that the patient and the doctor might say.

3. Set a time limit (five minutes), and have the partners act out the role-play in both roles.

4. Circulate and monitor. Encourage pantomime and improvisation.

5. Provide feedback.

Multilevel Strategies

Target the *Test Yourself* to the level of your students.

•**Pre-level** Ask these students to use this skeleton conversation: *A: Could you give me some advice about staying healthy? B: Sure. You should _____ and you ought to _____. A: So I need to _____ and _____. B: That's it.*

To compress this lesson: Conduct *Real-life math* as a whole-class activity.

To extend this lesson: Write "Ask Doctor Dora" notes.
1. Seat students in mixed-level groups. Give each group a large sheet of paper. Tell them that Dr. Dora is a newspaper columnist who gives people health advice. She can't help with emergencies, but she can give general advice about on-going problems. Have groups fold the paper in half and write a letter to Dr. Dora on the top half.
2. Direct groups to pass their papers to another group. Tell students to read the letters and write back as Dr. Dora. Point out that they can only give general recommendations, including what kind of doctor the person should see. Dr. Dora can't prescribe medicine!
3. Go over the letters with the class and discuss whether Dr. Dora gave good advice.

And/Or have students complete **Workbook 4 page 62** and **Multilevel Activity Book 4 page 103**.

4 Focus on listening

A Look at the poster. Talk about the questions with your class.

1. Have you ever had a tetanus shot? Why?
2. How do you feel about getting shots?

B Listen to the conversation. Work with a partner.
Ask and answer the questions.

1. Why is Mr. Gomez visiting the doctor? He cut his hand.
2. How does Mr. Gomez feel about getting a shot?
   He doesn't like getting them.

C Listen again. Circle the correct words.

1. Mr. Gomez cut himself when he was working in
   the (house /(garden)).
2. The doctor gives Mr. Gomez antibiotic ((ointment)/ pills) for the cut.
3. Mr. Gomez had a tetanus shot (less than 10 /(more than 20)) years ago.
4. The doctor gives Mr. Gomez (two shots /(one shot)) on this visit.
5. Mr. Gomez ((has to)/ doesn't have to) see the doctor again next week.

Prevent Tetanus Infections!

Tetanus is a serious disease. Tetanus germs live in dirt and soil. If you get a cut, check with your doctor. You might need a tetanus shot.

5 Real-life math

Read Mr. Gomez's immunization record and answer the questions.
Explain your answers to your classmates.

PERSONAL IMMUNIZATION RECORD					
Name: Ernesto Gomez		**DOB:** 6/19/50			
Immunization		**Received on:**			
Td¹ (Tetanus and Diptheria)		9/79	9/89		
Flu²					

¹Every 10 years for life
²After age 50

1. Mr. Gomez is getting a Td immunization today. When will he need one again? in ten years
2. Why does Mr. Gomez need a flu shot? Because he's over 50.

TEST YOURSELF ✔

Role-play a conversation. Partner A: Ask your friend for advice about staying healthy. Then confirm the advice. Partner B: You have a healthy lifestyle. Ask your friend questions and give advice about good health habits. Then change roles.

1 Get ready to read

A　Why is health insurance important?

B　Read the definitions. Name 3 kinds of medical specialists.

cover: (verb) to pay for
referral: (noun) a suggestion or permission to visit a doctor or get a screening
specialist: (noun) a doctor who is an expert in one kind of medicine or health care

C　Look at the title and the headings in the article in 2A. Answer the questions.

1. What are *FAQs*? Frequently Asked Questions
2. What will this article help the reader do? It will help the reader choose a health-care plan.

2 Read and respond

A　Read the article. What are two kinds of health insurance plans?
fee-for-service plans and managed-care plans

FAQs (Frequently Asked Questions) about Health Insurance

Are you trying to choose a health-care plan? These FAQs may help.

1) What kinds of health insurance are available?

There are several options. For example, in a fee-for-service plan, you can see any doctor in any part of the country. The insurance company pays part of the cost (often 80%) and you pay the rest. You pay a monthly premium for the insurance. There's also a deductible, usually about $250.

In a managed-care plan, you see a doctor from the plan's network[1] of doctors. These plans also have a monthly premium. In some plans, you don't have to pay for doctors' visits; in others, you pay a co-payment of $5 or $10 for each doctor's visit.

2) I'm confused by deductibles and co-payments. What's the difference?

Deductibles and co-payments are both amounts of money that you have to pay. A deductible is the amount you pay in a fee-for-service plan before the plan starts to pay (e.g., the first $250 of a bill). A co-payment is the amount you pay for each doctor's visit in a managed-care plan.

3) What should I think about when I choose a plan?

This is an important decision. Before you choose, compare:

Services • What medical care is covered? What isn't? Are chronic conditions and specialists covered? Does the plan have offices near your home or job?

[1]network: a group of people, things, or organizations that work together

✔ Interpret information about health insurance

Unit 9 Lesson 5

Objectives	Grammar	Vocabulary	Correlations
Pre-, On- and Higher-level: Read about and discuss health insurance	Questions with modals (*What should I look at when I'm trying to choose a health plan?*)	*Cover, referral, specialist, deductibles, co-payments, network* For vocabulary support for pre-level students, see this **Oxford Picture Dictionary** unit: Health	**CASAS:** 0.1.2, 0.1.5, 2.5.6, 3.2.3, 3.5.9, 7.4.4 **LCPs:** 38.01, 49.02, 49.06, 49.09, 49.16, 50.02 **SCANS:** Acquires and evaluates information, Applies technology to task, Knowing how to learn, Listening, Reading **EFF:** Learn through research, Listen actively, Read with understanding

Warm-up and Review

10–15 minutes (books closed)

Write *Health Insurance* on the board. Ask students to brainstorm words and phrases that they associate with this topic.

Introduction

5 minutes

1. Ask students to describe the health insurance system in their countries and say whether they think it is the same as the health insurance system in the U.S.

2. State the objective: *Today we're going to read about and discuss health insurance.*

1 Get ready to read

Presentation

15–20 minutes

A Read the question aloud. Call on volunteers to share their ideas.

B Read the words and definitions. Elicit sample sentences from students using the words. Point out that *refer* is the verb form of *referral*.

Pre-Reading

C Direct students to look at the title and the headings. Call on volunteers for the answers to the questions.

2 Read and respond

Guided Practice I

25–30 minutes

A 1. Ask students to read the article silently.

2. After they've finished reading, direct students to underline unfamiliar words they would like to know. Elicit the words and encourage other students to provide definitions or examples.

3. Check students' comprehension. Ask: *What is a fee-for-service plan?* [You can see any doctor.] *What is a co-payment?* [the amount you pay for each visit to the doctor]

Multilevel Strategies

Adapt 2A to the level of your students.

• **Pre-level** Provide these students with definitions of the important terms in the reading. *1. Fee-for-service health plan: You can see any doctor. The insurance pays part of the cost (usually 80%). There's usually a deductible (around $250). 2. Managed-care plan: You see a doctor from the plan's network of doctors. Visits are free or you pay a small co-payment. 3. Deductible: an amount you pay before the fee-for-service plan starts to pay 4. Co-payment: an amount you pay for each doctor's visit in a managed-care plan.*

Direct these students to read the definitions while other students are reading 2A.

Guided Practice II

15–20 minutes

 1. Play the audio. Have students read along silently.

2. Elicit and discuss any additional questions about the reading.

 After 2B or 2C, look at a coverage summary page from a real health insurance policy description. Have students find the deductibles and co-payments. Go over the coverage categories and discuss the vocabulary.

C 1. Have students work individually to write the numbers of the correct sections. Direct them to ask and answer the questions with a partner.

2. Elicit the answers from volunteers. Ask students what the advantages are of each kind of health plan.

Multilevel Strategies

For 2C, use mixed-level pairs. Assign each student a letter, A or B. Partner A asks questions 1 and 2. Partner B asks 3 and 4.

• **Pre-level** Assign these students the role of Partner B. Tell them to refer to their definitions to answer the questions.

• **On- and Higher-level** Assign these students the role of Partner A.

D 1. Read the information in the chart aloud. Elicit and discuss any questions the students have. Say the verbs for talking about health and illness and have students repeat them.

2. Direct students to work individually to complete the sentences. Write the answers on the board.

Multilevel Strategies

For 2D, seat same-level students together.

• **Pre-level** Direct these students to copy the words from the chart into their notebooks with a definition. Allow them to look in their dictionaries if necessary.

• **Higher-level** If these students finish before the others, ask them to write sentences using the verbs for talking about health and illness in the chart. Ask volunteers to write their sentences on the board.

3 Talk it over

Communicative Practice

15–20 minutes

1. Read the questions aloud. Set a time limit (three minutes). Have students work independently to think about the questions and write their answers in note form.

2. Call on individuals to share their ideas with the class. Ask students if there is a saying in their native language with a similar meaning.

Application

5–10 minutes

BRING IT TO LIFE

Read the directions aloud. Ask students to predict what advice they will find. Write their ideas on large sheet of paper.

To compress this lesson: Conduct 2D as a whole-class activity.

To extend this lesson: Provide additional practice with the verbs for talking about health and illness.
1. Have students write questions using the verbs for talking about health and illness. *When did you last see a doctor?*
2. Pair students and have them ask and answer the questions they wrote. Monitor and provide feedback.

And/Or have students complete **Workbook 4 page 63** and the **Multilevel Activity Book 4 pages 104–105**.

Choices • Does the plan include the doctors you want to see? Do you need a referral to see a specialist?

Costs • What would the total cost (the plan, fees, deductibles, etc.) be for you and your family?

Choosing health care, like choosing a good doctor, isn't easy. The more you know, the better your choice will be.

Adapted from: *http://www.ahrq.gov*

B Listen and read the article again.

C Write the number of the FAQ that answers these questions. Then ask and answer the questions with a partner.

___1___ 1. How are fee-for-service plans and managed-care plans different?

___2___ 2. What is a deductible?

___3___ 3. What should I look at when I am trying to choose a health plan?

___1___ 4. How much does it cost to see the doctor in a managed-care plan?

D Study the chart. Complete the sentences below.

Word Study: Verbs for talking about health and illness				
feel well/better	get sick	have { a physical / an illness	see { a doctor / a dentist	take { medicine / vitamins

1. When are you going to ___see___ the ear, nose, and throat specialist?

2. I wash my hands often because I don't want to ___get___ sick.

3. Do you ___have___ a cold? I hope you ___feel___ better soon.

4. When you ___see___ your doctor, he'll probably tell you to ___take___ vitamins.

3 Talk it over

Think about the questions. Talk about your ideas with the class.

1. Who should pay for health insurance—employers, the government, or people? Why?

2. What do you think the saying "An ounce of prevention is worth a pound of cure" means? Do you agree with the saying? Why or why not? Give examples.

BRING IT TO LIFE

Find an article on the Internet or in the library about preventing colds.
Bring your article to class and share the information in small groups.

1 Grammar

A   Circle the correct words.

1. Luz hurt her back. She (**had better** / had better not) see her doctor.
2. She (has got to / **had better not**) lift anything heavy.
3. Her doctor said she (**has to** / had better not) be careful when she exercises.
4. Her doctor also said that she (ought to / **had better not**) go back to work until she feels better.
5. She (**ought to** / had better not) call her boss.

B   Read the information. Which sentences are closest in meaning? Circle *a* or *b*.

1. You really need to brush your teeth often.
   - **a.** You must brush your teeth often.
   - b. You must not brush your teeth often.

2. It's a good idea to brush at least twice a day.
   - a. You shouldn't brush twice a day.
   - **b.** You ought to brush twice a day.

3. Too much sugar is bad for your teeth.
   - **a.** You shouldn't eat foods with a lot of sugar.
   - b. You ought to eat foods with a lot of sugar.

4. It's important to see the dentist every six months.
   - **a.** You've got to see the dentist every six months.
   - b. You shouldn't see the dentist every six months.

C   Complete the sentences with the gerund or infinitive form of the verb in parentheses. Some items have two correct answers.

1. Jean and Lars decided ____to make____ some changes in their lives. (make)
2. They considered ____joining____ a health club, but it was a little expensive. (join)
3. So they started ____riding / to ride____ their bikes for exercise. (ride)
4. They agreed ____to have____ a salad with dinner every night. (have)
5. Jean says she is going to quit ____eating____ so much meat. (eat)
6. Lars says he is going to start ____drinking / to drink____ more water and less soda. (drink)

Unit 9 Review and expand

Objectives	Grammar	Vocabulary	Correlations
On-, Pre-, and Higher-level: Expand upon and review unit grammar and life skills	Modals of advice (*You ought to exercise more.*)	Health advice and concerns For vocabulary support for pre-level students, see this **Oxford Picture Dictionary** unit: Health	**CASAS:** 0.1.2, 0.1.5, 3.5.9, 4.8.1, 7.2.6, 7.3.1, 7.3.2, 7.3.4 **LCPs:** 41.06, 49.01, 49.02, 49.03, 49.16, 49.17 **SCANS:** Creative thinking, Participates as member of a team, Problem solving, Reading **EFF:** Convey ideas in writing, Listen actively, Solve problems and make decisions

Warm-up and Review

10–15 minutes (books closed)

1. Review the *Bring It to Life* assignment from Lesson 5.

2. Have students who completed the exercise discuss what they learned.

3. Ask students who didn't complete the homework to share any cold remedies that are commonly used in their countries.

Introduction and Presentation

5 minutes

1. If students have used sentences with modals of advice during the warm-up, copy those sentences onto the board—for example, *You should wash your hands frequently.* Elicit the other modals (*ought to, had better, have to, have got to* and *must*). Write the modals on one side of the board, and elicit a sample sentence for each.

2. Elicit the negative form of each modal and a sample sentence where appropriate. Remind students that *ought to* and *have got to* are not used in the negative.

3. Point out that although *have to* and *must* have the same meaning, *don't have to* and *must not* have very different meanings. *Don't have to* means that something is not necessary—it is not used to give advice.

4. State the objective: *Today we're going to review the ways to give advice so that we can understand and give health advice in different situations.*

1 Grammar

Guided Practice

40–45 minutes

A Direct students to work individually to circle the correct words. Ask volunteers to read the completed sentences aloud.

B Read each sentence aloud. Ask students to choose the sentence that is closest in meaning. Ask for a show of hands to check their answers.

C Direct students to work individually to complete the sentences. Ask volunteers to read the completed sentences aloud.

Multilevel Strategies

Seat higher-level students together for 1A, 1B, and 1C.

• **Higher-level** Have these students complete all of the activities individually, and then compare answers with a partner. When they finish, ask them to work with a partner to write a conversation using *have got to, had better,* and *don't have to.* Ask volunteers to read their conversations for the class.

2 Group work

Communicative Practice

20–35 minutes

 1. Direct students, in groups of four, to focus on the picture. Ask: *Does the patient look healthy?*

2. Assign roles: leader, recorder, and reporters. Explain that students work with their groups to write the conversation.

3. Check comprehension of the roles. Ask: *Who writes the conversation?* [recorder] *Who will read the conversation to the class?* [reporters] *Who helps everyone and manages the group?* [leader] *Who creates the conversation?* [everyone]

4. Set a time limit (five minutes) to complete the exercise. Circulate and answer any questions.

5. Have reporters from each group read the group's conversation to the class.

Multilevel Strategies

For 2A, use mixed-level groups.

- **Pre-level** Assign these students the role of reporter.
- **On-level** Assign these students the role of recorder.
- **Higher-level** Assign these students the role of leader.

 1. Have students walk around the room to conduct the interviews. To get students moving, tell them to interview three new people not in their groups for 2A.

2. Set a time limit (five minutes) to complete the exercise.

3. Tell students to make a note of their classmates' answers but not to worry about writing complete sentences.

Multilevel Strategies

Adapt the mixer in 2B to the level of your students.

- **Pre-level** Allow these students to ask and answer the questions without writing.
- **Higher-level** Have these students ask two additional questions and write all answers.

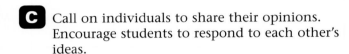 Call on individuals to share their opinions. Encourage students to respond to each other's ideas.

PROBLEM SOLVING

15–25 minutes

 1. Ask: *Do you have any friends or relatives with bad health habits?* Tell students they will read a story about a man whose sister has bad habits. Direct students to read Ivan's story silently.

2. Ask: *What are Katya's bad habits?*

3. Play the audio and have students read along silently.

B 1. Elicit answers to question 1.

2. Write *He could say* on the board, and ask volunteers to write their ideas under it. Write *He shouldn't say,* and ask volunteers to write their ideas.

3. Pair students. Have them write two lists of what Ivan should and shouldn't say.

4. Go over the lists. Have the class vote on Ivan's best course of action.

Evaluation

30–35 minutes

To test students' understanding of the unit grammar and life skills, have them take the Unit 9 Test on the *Step Forward Test Generator CD-ROM* with *ExamView® Assessment Suite.*

Learning Log

To help students record and discuss their progress, use the Learning Log on page T-202.

To extend this review: Have students complete **Workbook 4 page 64**, **Multilevel Activity Book 4 page 106**, and the **Unit 9 Exercises** on the **Multilevel Grammar Exercises CD-ROM 4.**

2 Group work

A Work with 2–3 classmates. Write a 6–8 line conversation between the people in the picture. Share your conversation with the class.

A: *You're in very good health. Do you have any health concerns?*
B: *Well, I'm worried about…*

B Interview 3 classmates. Write their answers.

1. How much should people have to pay for health care? Why?
2. Should people with healthy lifestyles pay less for health care? Why or why not?
3. If you could give everyone advice on how to prevent health problems, what would your advice be?

C Talk about the answers with your class.

PROBLEM SOLVING

A Listen and read about Ivan.

Ivan is worried about his sister, Katya. He thinks that Katya doesn't pay enough attention to her health. Ivan believes in preventing health problems, and he exercises and eats a healthy diet. Katya doesn't exercise. She eats fast-food for dinner several times a week, and she doesn't have health insurance at her job. Katya is an independent person who doesn't like it when people try to tell her what to do. Ivan wants Katya to be healthy, but he doesn't know how to help.

B Work with your classmates. Answer the questions.

1. What is Ivan's problem? Ivan is worried about his sister's health.
2. What do you think he should do? Think of 2 or 3 solutions to the problem.
3. Make two lists—a list of things Ivan could say to Katya, and a list of things he should *not* say.

Get Involved!

FOCUS ON
- community involvement and community services
- community issues
- indirect questions
- addressing community problems
- environmental issues

LESSON **1** Vocabulary

1 Learn community-involvement vocabulary

A Talk about the questions with your class.

1. What do you like about your community? What don't you like?
2. What makes a community a good place to live?

B Work with your classmates. Match the words with the pictures.

_4_	develop a plan	_5_	get approval	_6_	implement the plan
_3_	discuss the issue	_1_	identify a problem	_2_	propose a solution

C Listen and check. Then read the new words with a partner.

D Work with a partner. Write other community-involvement words you know. Check your words in a dictionary.

☑ Identify community-involvement and community-services vocabulary

Unit 10 Lesson 1

Objectives	Grammar	Vocabulary	Correlations
On-level: Talk about community involvement, and describe community services **Pre-level:** Identify community-involvement vocabulary, and describe community services **Higher-level:** Talk and write about community involvement and community services	*Should (You should develop a plan.)*	Community involvement and community services For vocabulary support for pre-level students, see this **Oxford Picture Dictionary** topics: Community Cleanup, Public Safety	**CASAS:** 0.1.2, 0.1.5, 0.2.1, 5.6.1, 7.4.5 **LCPs:** 39.01, 49.02, 49.09, 49.10 **SCANS:** Listening, Participates as member of a team, Reading, Seeing things in the mind's eye, Speaking **EFF:** Cooperate with others, Listen actively, Read with understanding, Speak so others can understand

Warm-up and Review

10–15 minutes (books closed)

Get students to start thinking about their communities. Ask: *Do you know your neighbors? What's your relationship like? What language do you speak to them? What do you have in common with your neighbors?*

Introduction

5 minutes

1. Say: *Even if we don't socialize with our neighbors, we still have a lot in common. We use the same parks and schools, drive down the same streets, and receive the same services.*

2. State the objective: *Today we're going to learn words for community involvement and community services.*

1 Learn community involvement vocabulary

Presentation I

20–25 minutes

A Elicit students' answers to question 1 and 2. Make a list of things students like and don't like about their communities.

B 1. Direct students to look at the pictures. Ask: *What was the problem in this community?*

2. Group students and assign roles: leader, fact checker, recorder, and reporter. Explain that students work with their groups to match the words and pictures.

3. Check comprehension of the roles. Ask: *Who looks up the words in a dictionary?* [fact checker] *Who writes the numbers in the book?* [recorder] *Who tells the class your answers?* [reporter] *Who helps everyone and manages the group?* [leader]

4. Set a time limit (three minutes). As students work together, copy the wordlist onto the board.

5. Call "time." Have reporters take turns giving their answers. Write each group's answer on the board next to the word.

C 1. To prepare students for listening, say: *Now you're going to listen to a man tell his friend about how to get involved.* Ask students to listen and check their answers.

2. Have students check the wordlist on the board and then write the correct numbers in their books.

3. Pair students. Set a time limit (three minutes). Monitor pair practice to identify pronunciation issues.

4. Call "time" and work with the pronunciation of any troublesome words or phrases.

5. Replay the audio and challenge students to listen for the answers to these questions: *What was the problem? What was the solution? What details did they need to work out? Who did they need to get approval from?*

D 1. Ask students to work with their partners from 1C to brainstorm a list of related words.

2. Elicit words from the class. Write them on the board. Ask students to copy them into their vocabulary notes for the unit.

Guided Practice

5–10 minutes

 E 1. Read the questions aloud. Set a time limit (three minutes). Direct students to ask and answer the questions with a partner.

2. Call "time" and elicit students' answers to number 2.

2 Learn community-services vocabulary

Presentation II

15–20 minutes

 A 1. Direct students to look at the directory of community services. Introduce the new topic. Say: *Now we're going to talk about community services.*

2. Read the instructions and the department names aloud. Ask for examples of when a person might call each department.

3. Elicit answers to the question. Ask students to justify their choices for the department that gets the most calls.

Guided Practice

10–15 minutes

 B Have students work individually to complete the sentences. Go over the answers as a class.

TIP If you have access to the Internet in class, have students visit the website for their city. Ask them to make a list of services and departments. Elicit the information and write any ideas not included in the directory in 2A on the board.

Communicative Practice and Application

10–15 minutes

 C 1. Give students a minute to make notes of their answers to the questions. Call on individuals to share their ideas with the class.

2. Ask follow-up questions: *What keeps people from getting involved in their communities? How can people be encouraged to get involved?*

Evaluation

10–15 minutes (books closed)

TEST YOURSELF

1. Make a two-column chart on the board with the headings *Community Involvement* and *Community Services*. Have students close their books and give you an example for each column.

2. Have students copy the chart into their notebooks.

3. Give students five to ten minutes to test themselves by writing the words they recall from the lesson.

4. Call "time" and have students check their spelling in a dictionary. Circulate and monitor students' progress.

5. Direct students to share their work with a partner and add additional words to their charts.

Multilevel Strategies

Target the *Test Yourself* to the level of your students.

• **Higher-level** Have these students complete the chart and then write sentences about where to go if you need a particular service. *If you are in a car accident, you can call Legal Services to get low-cost legal advice.*

To compress this lesson: Conduct 1B as a whole-class activity.

To extend this lesson: Bring a copy of the city newsletter or bulletin to class. You may be able to get one at the city website. Pass out copies of or project the front page of the newsletter. Have a class discussion about the information you find there.

And/Or have students complete **Workbook 4 page 65** and **Multilevel Activity Book 4 pages 108–109.**

E Work with a partner. Ask and answer the questions.

1. What steps should you follow to identify and solve problems in a community?
2. Who should be involved in each step? Neighbors? Community leaders?

2 Learn community-services vocabulary

A Study the community services directory. Which office do you think gets the most telephone calls? Why?

Department / Telephone Extension	Services	Department / Telephone Extension	Services
Administration x5510	mayor, council, city manager	Parks & Recreation x5514	sports, art, music programs, community centers
Child Care Services x5511	low-cost daycare	Public Safety x5515	crime prevention, fire safety
Health Services x5512	low-cost health clinics	Public Works x5516	street and lighting maintenance, building permits
Legal Services x5513	low-cost law clinics	Senior Services x5517	senior centers, lunch programs

B Work with a partner. Complete the sentences with names of the departments. Use the words in 2A.

1. Isabel wants to talk to the city manager. She'll call __Administration__.
2. A traffic light is broken on Main Street. I'll call __Public Works__.
3. Yosef wants information about community centers. He'll call __Parks & Recreation__.
4. Maria wants information on low-cost daycare. She'll call __Child Care Services__.
5. Gary wants to know how to reduce crime. He'll call __Public Safety__.
6. We want to know where the nearest low-cost health clinic is. We'll call __Health Services__.
7. Paco needs some low-cost legal help. He'll call __Legal Services__.
8. I want information on lunch programs for my grandmother. I'll call __Senior Services__.

C Talk about the questions with your class.

Which community services are the most important to you?
Which are the least important to you? Why?

TEST YOURSELF ✔

Close your book. Categorize the new words in two lists: *Community Involvement* and *Community Services*. Check your spelling in a dictionary. Compare your lists with a partner.

1 Read about a community issue

A   **Talk about the questions with your class.**

1. How do people help improve their communities?
2. Have you ever tried to solve a problem in your community, school, or workplace? If so, what was the problem? What did you do?

B   **Listen and read the letter.**

Alan Hart
1856 Arroyo St.
Edison, TX 75002

July 12, 2007

Ms. Toya Butler
County Council Member, District 3
3300 Hilltop Road
Edison, TX 75002

Dear Ms. Butler:

I am writing to ask for your help with a problem in our community. I live in the Melrose neighborhood, near the intersection of Pine and Arroyo streets.

I am very concerned about people who walk across the street at this intersection. The traffic light changes too quickly. I think we need to increase the time that the light stays red. Older people who walk with canes or walkers cannot make it across the street in time. Parents with children also have a difficult time. I have timed the light and it changes from green to yellow to red in 13 seconds. If the light stayed red for 5 more seconds, everyone would be able to cross safely.

I would like to invite you to visit our neighborhood to see the problem for yourself. Please contact me at (972) 555-1409. I look forward to hearing from you.

Sincerely,
Alan Hart
Alan Hart

Writer's note

Each paragraph of this letter has a special purpose:
1. Introduction
2. Explanation
3. Invitation

C   **Check your understanding. Work with a partner. Ask and answer the questions.**

1. How does Alan Hart start his letter? Why?   He starts with an introduction to explain why he's writing.
2. What two examples show that the problem is serious?   Older people and parents with children have difficulty crossing the street.
3. What are two things he wants?   He wants to increase the time the light stays red and to have Ms. Butler visit the neighborhood.

✔ Write a letter expressing concern about a community issue

Unit 10 Lesson 2

Objectives	Grammar	Vocabulary	Correlations
On- and Higher-level: Analyze, write, and edit a letter about a community issue **Pre-level:** Read and write a letter about a community issue	Conditional (*If the street had a speed bump, everyone would feel safer.*)	Community issues For vocabulary support for pre-level students, see these **Oxford Picture Dictionary** topics: City Streets, An Intersection, Public Safety	**CASAS:** 0.1.2, 0.1.5, 0.2.1, 0.2.3, 5.6.1, 5.6.2 **LCPs:** 39.01, 49.01, 49.03, 49.13, 49.16 **SCANS:** Interprets and communicates information, Knowing how to learn, Speaking **EFF:** Convey ideas in writing, Listen actively, Read with understanding, Solve problems and make decisions

Warm-up and Review

10–15 minutes (books closed)

Write *Community Problems* on the board, and elicit examples from students—possibilities include cracked pavement, potholes, bad lighting, trash, graffiti, old playground equipment, and undesirable businesses. Write the problems on the board.

Introduction

5 minutes

1. Ask students if they think they can do anything about these kinds of problems.

2. State the objective: *Today we're going to read and write a letter about a community issue.*

1 Read about a community issue

Presentation

20–25 minutes

A Elicit answers to questions 1 and 2. Tell students about a time when you tried to solve a problem. Explain whom you discussed the issue with, what solution you proposed, and how you developed and implemented the plan.

B 1. Direct students to read the letter silently. Check comprehension. Ask: *What's the problem?* [The traffic light changes too quickly.] *How will keeping the light green for five more seconds help?* [People will be able to cross safely.]

2. Play the audio. Have students read along silently.

3. Draw students' attention to the *Writer's note.* Relate the note to the letter. *What does Alan Hart talk about in his introduction? How does he explain? Why does he issue the invitation?*

Guided Practice I

10 minutes

C Have students work with a partner to ask and answer the questions. Ask a volunteer to write the answers on the board.

Multilevel Strategies

For 1C, challenge on- and higher-level students while allowing pre-level students to catch up.

• **On- and Higher-level** While pre-level students are finishing 1C, ask these students to come up with specific examples to explain why the problems on the board from the warm-up are serious. After you go over 1C, ask volunteers to share their ideas with the class.

2 Write a letter about a problem in the community

Guided Practice II

20–25 minutes

 A 1. Read the questions. Elicit students' answers.

2. Put the students' ideas about whom to write to on the board.

B 1. Direct students to look back at the letter in 1B. Read the questions for each paragraph, and ask students to find the answer in Alan Hart's letter.

2. Point out the letter sample, and ask students to follow it as they write their letters on their own papers.

3. Check comprehension of the exercise. Ask: *What are you writing about?* [community problems] *How many paragraphs does your letter need to be?* [three]

> ### Multilevel Strategies
>
> Adapt 2B to the level of your students.
>
> • **Pre-level** Provide these students with this skeleton letter:
>
> Dear _____,
>
> I'm writing to ask for your help with a problem in our community. I live in _____.
>
> I am very concerned because _____.
>
> I would like to invite you to visit to see the problem for yourself.
>
> Sincerely,
>
> _____

C 1. Lead students through the process of using the *Editing checklist.* Read the sentences aloud and answer any questions. Then ask students to check their papers.

2. Allow students a few minutes to edit their writing as necessary.

Communicative Practice

10 minutes

 D 1. Read the instructions aloud. Emphasize to students that they are responding to their partners' work, not correcting it.

2. Use the letter in 1B to model the exercise. *I think* Older people who walk with canes or walkers cannot make it across the street in time *is a good example. I'd like to ask the writer if he thinks there are any other solutions besides extending the light.*

3. Direct students to exchange papers with a partner and follow the instructions.

4. Call on volunteers to share some interesting things they read in their partners' letters.

Application and Evaluation

20 minutes

TEST YOURSELF

1. Review the instructions aloud. Assign a time limit (fifteen minutes), and have students work independently. Give students notice when they have five minutes left.

2. Before collecting students' work, remind them to use the *Editing checklist.* Collect and correct students' writing.

> ### Multilevel Strategies
>
> Adapt the *Test Yourself* to the level of your students.
>
> • **Pre-level** Provide these students with the same skeleton they used in 2B.

To compress this lesson: Assign the *Test Yourself* for homework.

To extend this lesson: Write *Whom should you call?* on the board.
1. Write a list of situations on the board. *The sidewalks are cracked. There's a suspicious person hanging around the neighborhood. The corner needs a crosswalk. You want your daughter to join the soccer team. A neighbor has a large amount of trash piled up in the yard.*
2. Pair students and ask them to discuss what public-service agency they would call for each situation.

And/Or have students complete **Workbook 4 page 66** and **Multilevel Activity Book 4 page 110**.

2 Write a letter about a problem in the community

A **Talk about the questions with your class.**

1. What are some things you would like to improve in your community? Why?
2. Who could you write to about these situations?

B **Write a letter about one of the problems you described in 2A. Use the model in 1B and the questions below to help you.**

To start: Write your return address, the date, and the mailing address at the top of your letter.
Write *Dear* and the title and last name of the addressee.

Paragraph 1: Why are you writing? Where is the problem?

Paragraph 2: What is the problem? What are some examples that show that the problem is serious?

Paragraph 3: What do you want the person to do? How can the person contact you?

To close: Write a closing. Sign and print your name.

(Your address)

(Receiver's name and address)

Dear _____:

I am writing to...

C **Use the checklist to edit your writing. Check (✔) the true sentences.**

Editing checklist	
1. My letter includes the name and address of the person I am writing to.	
2. I introduced the problem in the first paragraph.	
3. I explained the problem and gave examples in the second paragraph.	
4. I included my contact information in the third paragraph.	

D **Exchange letters with a partner. Read and comment on your partner's letter.**

1. Point out a good example in your partner's letter of how serious the problem is.
2. Ask a question about the problem your partner described.

TEST YOURSELF ✔

Write a new letter about a problem in the area near your school or workplace.

1 Learn indirect information questions

A Look at the letter to the editor and the editorial cartoon. What do the letter writer and the cartoonist disagree about? how the city should spend money

LETTER TO THE EDITOR

Do you know what our city's biggest problem is? We need money for schools, not for public transportation!

B Study the charts. Underline the 2 indirect questions in 1A.

INDIRECT INFORMATION QUESTIONS

Direct information question	Indirect information question
When **is** the bus **coming**?	Do you know when the bus **is coming**?
Where **do** the buses **stop**?	Could you please tell me where the buses **stop**?
What **does** the mayor **want**?	Do you have any idea what the mayor **wants**?
What **were** the issues?	Do you know what the issues **were**?
How **did** this **happen**?	Can you tell me how this **happened**?

Note
Indirect questions sound more polite than *Yes/No* or information questions.

C Match each situation with an indirect question.

You don't know...

  _b_ 1. the location of the bus stop.

  _a_ 2. the reason the bus isn't here yet.

  _d_ 3. the bus schedule.

  _c_ 4. which buses use this bus stop.

a. Do you have any idea why the bus is late?

b. Could you tell me where the bus stop is?

c. Do you know which buses stop here?

d. Can you tell me when the bus will come?

D Get the form. Work with your class. Correct the indirect questions.

1. Do you know where is the park? _Do you know where the park is?_

2. Do you know what does want the teacher? _Do you know what the teacher wants?_

3. Could you tell me where is the post office? _Could you tell me where the post office is?_

4. Can you tell me how do you get to city hall? _Can you tell me how you get to city hall?_

✔ Use and respond to indirect questions to talk about community issues

Unit 10 Lesson 3

Objectives	Grammar	Vocabulary	Correlations
On- and Higher-level: Ask and respond to indirect questions about community issues and listen for information about community services **Pre-level:** Recognize and respond to indirect questions about community issues, and listen for information about community services	Indirect questions (*Do you know what the mayor wants? Could you tell me if City Hall is open?*)	Community issues For vocabulary support for pre-level students, see this **Oxford Picture Dictionary** topics: An Intersection, Government and Military Service	**CASAS:** 0.1.2, 0.1.5, 0.2.1, 5.6.1, 7.4.5 **LCPs:** 39.01, 49.02, 49.09, 49.10 **SCANS:** Listening, Participates as member of a team, Reading, Seeing things in the mind's eye, Speaking **EFF:** Cooperate with others, Listen actively, Read with understanding, Speak so others can understand

Warm-up and Review

10–15 minutes (books closed)

Write *When, Where, What,* and *How* on the board. Ask students to come up with questions they might ask if they were calling their area's city hall or using a city service like the library. Write their ideas on the board.

Introduction

5–10 minutes

1. Ask students to provide examples of where they might ask each question. Point out that sometimes it's more formal and polite to use an indirect question. Give an example by saying one of the questions on the board as an indirect question.

2. State the objective: *Today we're going to use indirect questions to talk about community issues.*

1 Learn indirect information questions

Presentation I

20–25 minutes

A 1. Direct students to look at the cartoon. Ask: *What does the man want?*

2. Read the instructions aloud. Ask students to read the cartoon and the letter to find the answer to the question. Elicit the answer.

B 1. Read the direct and indirect questions in the chart aloud.

2. Direct students to underline the indirect questions in 1A. Go over the answers as a class.

3. Point out that the woman is using the indirect form *Can you tell me. . .* to be polite. The letter writer is using *Do you know. . .* because the question is rhetorical (the writer is going to answer the question him or herself), but *Do you know. . .* can also be used for polite questions.

4. Read and have students repeat the indirect questions. Read the *Note* aloud.

5. Assess students' understanding of the charts. Elicit indirect forms of the questions on the board from the warm-up.

Guided Practice I

15–20 minutes

C Ask students to work individually to match each situation with an indirect question. Ask volunteers to write the answers on the board.

Multilevel Strategies

For 1C, seat higher-level students together.

• **Higher-level** When these students finish 1C, have them work with a partner to write three direct questions and three corresponding indirect questions. Ask volunteers to write them on the board in two columns. Have other students match the direct and indirect questions.

D Lead students through the process of rewriting each question correctly. Ask volunteers to write the corrected versions on the board.

TIP For more practice with indirect information questions before 1E, write scrambled questions on the board. *1. know do you the library finished when will be new 2. school board you tell me where the can meets 3. you is have any the when do next idea election 4. you tell me is my please representative could who.* Ask students to unscramble them. Have volunteers write the unscrambled questions on the board. *1. Do you know when the new library will be finished? 2. Can you tell me where the school board meets? 3. Do you have any idea when the next election is? 4. Could you please tell me who my representative is?* Ask any students who finish early to write their own scrambled question and put it on the board.

E 1. Ask students to work individually to complete the indirect questions. Call on volunteers for the answers.

2. Direct students to take turns asking and answering the questions with a partner.

Multilevel Strategies

For 1E, seat pre-level students together.

• **Pre-level** Work with these students. Underline the section of each answer that needs to be used in the question. Elicit each completion before students write it in their books.

2 Learn indirect *Yes/No* questions

Presentation II and Guided Practice

30–35 minutes

A 1. Introduce the new topic. Say: *Now we're going to learn how to ask indirect* Yes/No *questions.* Elicit an example of a *Yes/No* question, and write it on the board. Show students how to rewrite it as an indirect question.

2. Read the direct and indirect questions in the chart. Ask students to work individually to complete the indirect questions. Have volunteers write the answers on the board.

Multilevel Strategies

After 2A, seat students in same-level groups. Provide each group with magazines or with pictures that show people engaged in conversation. Ask the groups to come up with questions that one person might be asking the other.

• **Pre-level** Have these students write direct questions. Before they begin writing, review present- and past-tense questions with them.

• **On- and Higher-level** Have these students write indirect questions. Tell them to be sure to include some information and some *Yes/No* questions.

Have a reporter from each group share the group's pictures and questions with the class.

E Read the answers. Then complete the indirect question.
Practice reading the questions and answers with a partner.

1. Do you know _____when the meeting is_____? (when)
   I think the meeting is at 6 p.m.

2. Do you know _where it is_____? (where)
   It's in Room A.

3. Do you have any idea _what the mayor wants to talk about_____? (what)
   I believe the mayor wants to talk about the budget.

4. Could you please tell me _what the mayor's proposal cuts_____? (what)
   The mayor's proposal cuts bus service.

5. Can you tell me _which budgets the city cut_____? (which)
   The city cut the parks, transportation, and senior services budgets.

2 Learn indirect *Yes/No* questions

A Study the charts. What word means the same as *if*? whether

Direct *Yes/No* questions	Indirect *Yes/No* questions		
Is the bus **coming?**	Can you tell me Could you tell me	**if**	the bus **is coming?**
	Do you know	**whether**	
Did they **get** approval?	Can you tell me Could you tell me	**if**	they **got** approval?
	Do you know	**whether**	

B Read the direct questions. Then complete the indirect questions.

1. Is the meeting at 5:00?
   Do you know _if the meeting is at 5:00_____?

2. Did they discuss the issue?
   Could you tell me _if/whether they discussed the issue_____?

3. Are they going to approve the budget cut?
   Do you know _if/whether they are going to approve the budget cut_____?

4. Was the mayor at the meeting?
   Do you have any idea _if/whether the mayor was at the meeting_____?

5. Did the meeting end on time?
   Can you tell me _if/whether the meeting ended on time_____?

6. Are they going to meet next month?
   Could you tell me _if/whether they are going to meet next month_____?

3 Grammar listening

Listen to the speakers. What does the person want to know? Circle *a* or *b*.

1. (a.) When is the next public works committee meeting?
   b. Where is the next public works committee meeting?

2. (a.) Why is the law clinic closed?
   b. When is the law clinic closed?

3. a. Did you talk about childcare services?
   (b.) Who do I talk to about childcare services?

4. a. Where is the nearest senior center in your city?
   (b.) Does your city have any senior centers?

5. a. What does the city manager want?
   (b.) Where did the city manager go?

6. (a.) Did the public safety committee discuss my idea?
   b. When did the public safety committee discuss my idea?

4 Practice indirect questions

A **Write at least 5 indirect questions about services in your community.**

Do you know where the senior center is?

B **Work with your classmates. Ask and answer each other's questions. Talk to at least 5 people.**

A: *Do you know where…*
B: *I'm not sure, but…*

C **Take turns writing and correcting the indirect questions on the board.**

TEST YOURSELF ✔

Close your book. Write 6 new indirect questions about services or programs at your school.

3 Grammar listening

Guided Practice II

10–15 minutes

1. Say: *Now we're going to listen to some questions about community services.*

2. Play the audio. Direct students to read along silently without writing.

3. Replay the audio. Ask students to circle the letter of the question with the same meaning.

4. Go over the answers as a class.

> ### Multilevel Strategies
> Replay the *Grammar listening* to allow pre-level students to catch up while you challenge on- and higher-level students.
> • **Pre-level** Have these students listen again to circle the letter of the correct question.
> • **On- and Higher-level** Have these students listen and write the questions they hear for numbers 2 and 4.

4 Practice indirect questions

Communicative Practice and Application

20–25 minutes

A 1. Direct students to look at the pictures. Ask them to identify the community services.

2. Give students time to read and think about the questions.

B 1. Put students in pairs, and direct them to take turns asking their indirect questions about community services from 4A. Tell them to make notes of each other's answers. Model the exercise by asking a volunteer the first question. Have the class tell you how to write the answer in note form.

2. Check comprehension of the exercise. Ask: *Should you ask direct or indirect questions?* Set a time limit for the exercise (four minutes), and observe, taking note of issues that arise.

> ### Multilevel Strategies
> Adapt 4B to the level of your students.
> • **Pre-level** Allow these students to ask direct questions.

C 1. Call on volunteers to share the questions that were answered by their partners.

2. Ask students whose questions were not answered to ask the class at large. If no one knows the answer, suggest a resource where your student might find the answer.

Evaluation

10–15 minutes (books closed)

TEST YOURSELF

Ask students to write the questions independently. Collect and correct their writing.

> ### Multilevel Strategies
> Target the *Test Yourself* to the level of your students.
> • **Pre-level** Allow these students to write direct questions.

To compress this lesson: Conduct 1C as a whole-class discussion.

To extend this lesson: Provide more practice with indirect questions.
1. Put up poster paper with a situation at the top of each sheet. *At the Supermarket, At Your Child's School, At a Restaurant, At a Park Entrance, At an Amusement Park, At a Mall Information Booth, At a Police Station, In a College Office, In an Airport, On an Airplane*
2. Put students in mixed-level groups, and assign each group to a poster. Tell them to write one indirect question they might ask in that situation. Have the groups move to a new poster. Continue until there are five questions on each poster.

And/Or have students complete **Workbook 4 pages 67–68**, **Multilevel Activity Book 4 pages 111–112**, and the corresponding **Unit 10 Exercises** on the **Multilevel Grammar Exercises CD-ROM 4**.

Unit 10 Lesson 4

Objectives	Grammar	Vocabulary	Correlations
On-, Pre-, and Higher-level: Talk about a problem in the community, and listen for directions	Statements with *wh-* and *if/whether* phrases (*I don't know where the meeting is.*)	*Public hearing, encouraged, proposals, Council Chamber* For vocabulary support for pre-level students, see this **Oxford Picture Dictionary** topics: An Intersection, The Legal System	**CASAS:** 0.1.2, 0.1.5, 1.1.3, 5.6.1, 6.0.3, 6.0.4, 6.1.2, 6.7.4, 7.4.7, 7.5.6 **LCPs:** 49.01, 49.09, 49.16, 49.17, 51.05 **SCANS:** Arithmetic/Mathematics, Seeing things in the mind's eye, Speaking **EFF:** Cooperate with others, Read with understanding, Use math to solve problems and communicate

Warm-up and Review

10–15 minutes (books closed)

Using an indirect question, ask a volunteer to give you directions to your area's city hall from school (or to the city center from school). Write the student's directions on the board. Elicit corrections and help from other students as you go.

Introduction

5 minutes

1. Say: *If you want to go to a city council meeting, or you want to inquire in person about city services, that's where you need to go.*

2. State the objective: *Today we're going to talk about a community problem and listen for directions.*

1 Learn to talk about a problem in the community

Presentation I

15–20 minutes

A Direct students to look at the notice. Read the instructions aloud. Play the audio. Give students a minute to answer the question. Call on a volunteer for the answers.

Guided Practice

20–25 minutes

B 1. Play the audio. Ask students to read along silently and listen for the answer to this question: *Why does Geraldo want to go to the public hearing?* Elicit the answer.

2. Ask students to read the conversation with a partner. Circulate and monitor pronunciation. Model and have students repeat difficult words or phrases.

3. Say and have students repeat the expressions in the *In other words* box. Elicit the placement of the expressions in the conversation. Ask volunteers to read the conversation using expressions from the box.

Communicative Practice and Application

15–20 minutes

C 1. Ask students to read the instructions silently. Check comprehension of the exercise. Ask: *What are the two roles? What is the situation?* Elicit examples of what each person might say.

2. Set a time limit (five minutes). Ask students to act out the role-play in both roles. Ask one to three volunteer pairs to act out their conversations for the class. Tell students who are listening to note how Partner B shows understanding.

Multilevel Strategies

For 1C, adapt the role-play to the level of your students.

• **Pre-level** Provide the beginning of the role-play for these students. *A: City Clerk's Office. How can I help you? B: Hi. I'm calling because I heard that the city is going to close the library. A: _____.*

1 Learn to talk about a problem in the community

 A Look at the notice. Listen to the phone calls. How do the callers feel about the plans for the apartment building and the Jobs for Teens program?

They don't agree with the plan to build the apartment building or to reduce the Summer Jobs for Teens program.

NOTICE OF PUBLIC HEARINGS

Tomas Noyes, City Clerk, City of Dawson   **November 15**

ISSUE: Plan to build an apartment building next to the 40th Street Park.
Date: Nov. 20

ISSUE: Proposal to reduce the Summer Jobs for Teens Program from 500 to 150 participants.
Date: Nov. 28

ISSUE: Proposal to close the Community Police Station in the Hilltop Apartments.
Date: Dec. 12

All hearings will take place at 7 p.m. in the Council Chamber, on the 1st floor of the Municipal Building, 440 State St. Interested residents are encouraged to attend and comment on the proposals.

 B Listen and read. How does Maria feel about the Hilltop Police Station?

She thinks it's an important service that should not be cut.

City Clerk:	City clerk's office. Can I help you?
Caller:	Hi. This is Maria Delgado. I'm calling because I heard that the city wants to close the Hilltop Police Station. Can you tell me if that's true?
City Clerk:	Yes, it is.
Caller:	Why would they do that? It's an important service.
City Clerk:	I know what you mean. Listen, there's a public hearing on the issue at 7 p.m. on December 12th, in the Council Chamber.
Caller:	Really? Hmmm… I'm not sure where that is.
City Clerk:	It's in the Municipal Building, on the third floor.
Caller:	Thanks. I'll be there. I want to put in my two cents!*

In other words…

Showing understanding

I know what you mean.
I hear what you're saying.
I understand what you're saying.

*Idiom note: put in (my) two cents = give (my) opinion

C Role-play a phone call to the city clerk's office with a partner. Use the example in 1B to make a new conversation.

Partner A: Call the city clerk because you heard that the city is planning to close the Troy Street Library. You think the library is really important. Say that you don't know where the community meeting is.

Partner B: You're the city clerk. Show your understanding to the caller. Say that there's a community meeting about the issue next Wednesday at the Troy Street Library, on the second floor.

2 Learn statements with *wh-* and *if/whether* phrases

A Study the chart and the picture. What is the man's problem?

He doesn't know where the meeting is, what it's about, or when it is.

Statements with *wh-* and *if/whether* phrases	
He doesn't know	**where** the community meeting is.
He has no idea	**what** the meeting is about.
He's not sure	**when** the meeting starts.
He can't remember	**if** the meeting starts at 7 p.m.
He forgot	**whether** the meeting starts at 7 p.m.

Note

Use a *wh-* OR an *if/whether* phrase after certain expressions to talk about things you don't know for certain.

B Work with a partner. Complete the sentences. Circle the correct words.

Ed: I want to go to the meeting, but I don't know when (does it start /(it starts)).
(1)

Mai: It's at 7:00, but I have no idea what (is it /(it's)) about.
(2)

Ed: It's about the health clinic. I'm not sure what ((the issues are)/ are the issues).
(3)

Mai: I'll bet it's about the budget. I can't remember if ((they cut)/ did they cut) it.
(4)

Ed: I don't know what (do you think /(you think)), but I think we ought to go.
(5)

C Work with a partner. Talk about the people in 2B.

A: *Ed doesn't know when the community meeting starts.*
B: *Mai has...*

3 Practice your pronunciation

A Listen to these long sentences. Notice where the speakers pause.

1. I'm calling because I heard that ∧ the city wants to close the Hilltop Police Station.
2. There's a public hearing on the issue ∧ at 7 p.m. tonight, ∧ in the Council Chamber.

B Listen and mark the pauses (∧) in these sentences.

1. Older people who walk with canes or walkers ∧ cannot make it across the street in time.
2. The council members discuss the issue ∧ to try to find a solution ∧ that works for everyone.

C Practice the sentences in 3A and 3B with a partner.

2 Learn statements with *wh-* and *if/whether* phrases

Presentation II
10–15 minutes

 1. Introduce the new topic. Write *Maria Delgado didn't know where the hearing was.* on the board. Underline *where the hearing was.* Ask: *Is this a question?* [no] Say: *Now we're going to learn statements with* wh- *and* if/whether *phrases.*

2. Read the instructions aloud. Direct students to look at the picture and the chart. Call on a volunteer to answer the question. Read the sentences in the chart aloud. Read the *Note.*

Guided Practice
15–20 minutes

B Have students work with a partner to circle the best answers to complete the conversation. Tell partners to read the conversation aloud when they finish.

2. Ask a volunteer pair to read the conversation aloud for the class.

Multilevel Strategies

For 2B, seat same-level students together.

• **Pre-level** Work with this group. Read each sentence in 2B aloud with the correct completion, and have students circle the words they hear. Then ask pairs to read the conversation aloud, switch roles, and read it again.

• **On- and Higher-level** When these students finish 2B, ask them to write the *–wh* and *if/whether* phrases in the conversation as direct questions. Have volunteers write the questions on the board. Compare the questions to the statements in the conversation.

Communicative Practice and Application
15–20 minutes

C 1. Model the exercise with a volunteer.

2. Set a time limit (five minutes). Ask students to talk about the people in 2B with several partners.

 After 2C, provide more practice with *wh-* and *if/whether* phrases. Write these skeleton sentences on the board. *I don't know _____. I don't remember _____. I'm not sure _____. I have no idea _____. I forgot _____.* Use each of the sentences to tell the class something about yourself. Then ask students to write true sentences about themselves using the expressions. Elicit sentences from volunteers.

---

3 Practice your pronunciation

Pronunciation Extension
10–15 minutes

A 1. Write *I don't know what you think, but I think we ought to go.* on the board. Say the sentence and ask students to repeat it. Ask them to identify the pause. Say: *Now we're going to focus on when to pause in long sentences.*

2. Play the audio. Direct students to listen for the pause.

3. Say and have students repeat the sentences.

B Play the audio. Direct students to listen and mark the pauses. Go over the answers as a class.

C Have students take turns saying the sentences with a partner. Monitor and provide feedback on pronunciation.

4 Focus on Listening

Listening Extension

20–25 minutes

A Read the questions aloud, and elicit answers from volunteers. Encourage students to respond to each other's ideas. After one student speaks, ask other students for their opinions. *Do you know of another reason/way?*

B Tell students that they will be listening to information about a meeting. Play the audio. Ask them to circle the correct answers.

C 1. Direct students to read the sentences before listening.

2. Replay the audio and have students work individually to complete the sentences. Take a tally of responses for each item, and if students disagree on a response, replay the audio so they can check their answers.

Multilevel Strategies

Replay the directions in 4C to challenge on- and higher-level students while allowing pre-level students to catch up.

• **Pre-level** Have these students listen again to go over their answers.

• **On- and Higher-level** Write questions on the board, and have these students listen for the answers. *Where does the bus stop? Where is the parking lot?*

5 Real-life math

Math Extension

5–10 minutes

1. Direct students to look at the pie chart. Elicit the functions of a social-services department.

2. Read the questions aloud. Give students time to read the questions and find the answers individually.

3. Call on volunteers for the answers. Ask a volunteer to explain how he or she arrived at the answer for question 2.

Evaluation

10–15 minutes

TEST YOURSELF

1. Model the role-play with a volunteer. Then switch roles.

2. Pair students. Check comprehension of the exercise by eliciting things each partner might say.

3. Set a time limit (five minutes), and have partners act out the role-play in both roles.

4. Circulate and monitor. Encourage pantomime and improvisation.

5. Provide feedback.

Multilevel Strategies

Target the *Test Yourself* to the level of your students.

• **Pre-level** Provide the beginning of the role-play for these students. *A: City Clerk's Office. How can I help you? B: Hi. I'm calling because I heard that the city is going to put up a stop sign in my neighborhood, but I think _____.*

To compress this lesson: Conduct *Real-life math* as a whole-class activity.

To extend this lesson: Have students practice giving directions.
1. Write the names of several places on your campus or in your town that students are likely to know how to get to. Write *Excuse me, can you tell me how to get to _____?* on the board.
2. Have students practice asking for and giving directions with a partner. Monitor and make a note of any problems they are having. Go over those issues with the class.
3. Alternatively, do this as a computer activity. Have students use the Internet to find directions to a community place—for example, the library, DMV, police station, or city hall. Have them print out the directions and dictate them to a partner who looked up a different place.

And/Or have students complete **Workbook 4 page 69** and **Multilevel Activity Book 4 page 113**.

4 Focus on listening

A **Talk about the questions with your class.**

1. Why do people attend community meetings and public hearings?
2. How can people get information about meetings and hearings?

B **Listen to the recorded message. Circle the correct meeting day, date, time, and location.**

1. (a.) Tuesday   b. Thursday   3. a. 7:30 p.m.   (b.) 7:00 p.m.
2. (a.) March 23   b. May 23   4. a. Room 210   (b.) Hearing Room

C **Listen again. Complete the directions with the words you hear.**

1. To get to city hall, take the _____F4_____ bus.
2. Go ____straight____ one block to Beech Street to get to the parking lot.
3. Take the elevator to the ____second____ floor.
4. Follow the signs to the __Hearing Room__.
5. It will be on your _____right_____, after Room _____210_____.

5 Real-life math

Study the pie chart of East Port's annual budget and answer the questions. Explain your answers to your classmates.

1. Which two programs together use half of the city's budget? Education and Public Safety
2. If the total city budget is one hundred million dollars, how much is the city spending on arts and recreation in a year? ____$1,000,000____

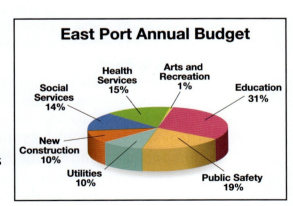

East Port Annual Budget

TEST YOURSELF ✔

Role-play a phone call about a community issue. Partner A: Call the city clerk. The city is planning to put up a stop sign at a dangerous intersection, but you think it should be a stop light. Partner B: You are the city clerk. Tell the caller about the Traffic Safety Committee meeting next week. Then change roles.

1 Get ready to read

A What are some ways that communities keep parks and open areas clean?

B Read the definitions. Which word can mean *legally take care of*? adopt

adopt: (verb) to be responsible for someone or something that isn't yours
announce: (verb) to say; make a public statement
fine: (noun) money you have to pay for breaking a law

C Look at the title of the newspaper article and the section headings in 2A. Answer the questions.

1. Which part of the newspaper do you think this article is from?
2. What do you think *dumping* means?

2 Read and respond

A Read the article. What three things can Riverview residents do to get involved?
Adopt a road, support a plan to change dumping laws, and participate in community clean-up days

Community Involvement: Something for Everyone!

What makes our city a great place to live? Is it a great location? Good neighbors? Good services? Yes—but it's also the involvement of residents in the life of the community. If you want to get involved, but don't know how you can help, here are three easy ways to get started.

Adopt-a-Road

The Riverview city council has just announced a new Adopt-a-Road program. Under this program, community groups and companies can "adopt" a section of a city or country road. The group picks up litter along the road four times a year, and in return, the group's name is posted along the road. Support the new program by adopting a road and keeping it clean.

Support our Plan to Change Dumping Laws

Our country highways and natural areas become dirty and dangerous when people dump old furniture, building materials, tires, or other trash along the road or in the river. Riverview has a law against illegal dumping, but the fine is only $50. Under the Environmental Committee's proposed new law, the fine would be raised to $500. Let your council member know that you support increased fines for illegal dumping. Make your voice heard!

Participate in Community Clean-Up Days

Four times a year, Riverview sponsors[1] Community Clean-Up Days. Residents help clean up parks, plant trees, and repair community buildings. If you aren't sure when the

[1]sponsor: to organize; support

☑ Interpret a newspaper editorial on recycling, dumping, and related issues

Unit 10 Lesson 5

Objectives	Grammar	Vocabulary	Correlations
On, Pre-, and Higher-level: Read about and discuss community involvement	Verbs and nouns (*I agree. We have an agreement.*)	*Announce, get rid of, play a part, dumping, sponsor* For vocabulary support for pre-level students, see this **Oxford Picture Dictionary** topics: Community Cleanup, Crime, Government and Military Service	**CASAS:** 0.1.2, 0.1.5, 2.5.6, 5.6.1, 5.7.1, 7.4.4 **LCPs:** 38.01, 47.03, 49.02, 49.06, 49.16 **SCANS:** Acquires and evaluates information, Applies technology to task, Knowing how to learn, Listening, Reading **EFF:** Listen actively, Read with understanding, Take responsibility for learning

Warm-up and Review

10–15 minutes (books closed)

Ask if there are any areas of your city that are dirty. Find out what students see there, and elicit their opinions about why that area is dirtier than others.

Introduction

5 minutes

1. Say: *Sometimes an area is dirty because there's nobody around who wants to take responsibility for it.*

2. State the objective: *Today we're going to read about and discuss community involvement.*

1 Get ready to read

Presentation

15–20 minutes

A Read the question aloud. Write students' ideas on the board.

B Read the words and definitions. Elicit sample sentences from students using the words. Point out that *play a part* is followed by *in*. *He played a part in getting the new law passed.*

Pre-Reading

C 1. Elicit the answers to questions 1 and 2. Ask a volunteer to explain what can be found in the editorial section of a newspaper.

2. Ask: *How much is the fine for dumping now? What do they want to raise it to?* Ask students to scan the article and raise their hands when they find the answers. When most students have their hands raised, call on volunteers.

2 Read and respond

Guided Practice I

25–30 minutes

A 1. Ask students to read the editorial silently. After they've finished reading, direct students to underline unfamiliar words they would like to know. Elicit the words and encourage other students to provide definitions or examples.

2. Check comprehension. Ask: *What is the writer mainly concerned about? How many ways of getting involved does the writer propose?*

Multilevel Strategies

Adapt 2A to the level of your students.

• **Pre-level** Provide these students with a summary of the reading. *There are three ways to get involved in cleaning up the community. 1. Adopt-a-Road. In this program, your group cleans a section of the road four times a year, and the city puts your group's name on a sign along the road. 2. People often dump large trash items by the road. The Environmental Committee wants to raise the fine for dumping to $500. Support the new law! 3. Four times a year, residents work together on Community Clean-up Days. You can volunteer to help.*

Direct these students to read the summary while other students are reading 2A.

Guided Practice II

15–20 minutes

B 1. Play the audio. Have students read along silently.

2. Elicit and discuss any additional questions about the reading.

C Direct students to ask and answer the questions with a partner. Call on volunteers for the answers.

Multilevel Strategies

For 2C, work with pre-level students.

• **Pre-level** Tell these students to refer to their summary to answer the questions.

D 1. Read the verbs in the chart aloud. Have students fill in the noun forms. Elicit and discuss any questions the students have about the *–ment* suffix. Say the nouns and have students repeat them.

2. Direct students to work individually to complete the sentences. Write the answers on the board.

Multilevel Strategies

For 2D, seat higher-level students together.

• **Higher-level** When these students finish 2D, assign or have them choose a word from the chart, and have them write sentences with the verb and the noun form. Ask them to put their sentences on the board. Have other students identify the verbs and the nouns.

3 Talk it over

Communicative Practice

15–20 minutes

Read the questions aloud. Set a time limit (three minutes). Have students work independently to think about the questions and write their answers in note form. Call on volunteers to share their ideas with the class.

Application

5–10 minutes

BRING IT TO LIFE

Read the instructions aloud. Tell students to try the city website. If it has a search engine, they can try the search terms *dump, litter, clean up,* and *Adopt-a-Highway*. Challenge them to call the city or ask a librarian to help them find the information.

To compress this lesson: Conduct 2D as a whole-class activity.

To extend this lesson: Talk about cleanliness at school.
1. As a class, brainstorm a list of cleanliness problems that often occur at schools. The list might include gum on the floor and under the tables, lunch trash thrown on the campus grounds, and graffiti. Write the ideas on the board.
2. Put students in small groups. Tell them to imagine that their children's school has these problems. They need to draw up a list of at least three proposals for the school principal.
3. Have a reporter from each group share the proposals with the class. Have a class discussion about which are the most practical proposals and which would be most effective.

And/Or have students complete **Workbook 4 page 70** and the **Multilevel Activity Book 4 pages 114–115**.

next Community Clean Up is, check the city's website at www.riverside.city. Volunteer, and get children to volunteer. You're never too young, or too old, to play an active part[2] in your community!

A great community is everyone's responsibility. Let's all get involved in making Riverview an even better place to live.

[2]to play an active part: to be involved; to participate

B Listen and read the newspaper article again.

C Check your understanding. Work with a partner. Ask and answer the questions.

1. In the Adopt-a-Road program, what does a group do? What does the group get?
2. Why is dumping a problem?
3. What solution did the Environmental Committee propose?

D Fill in the chart with nouns ending in *-ment*. Check your spelling in a dictionary. Then complete the sentences below with nouns from the chart.

> **Word Study: Changing verbs to nouns with *-ment***
>
> Add *-ment* to the end of some verbs to form nouns: *agree + ment = agreement*
>
> | Verb | Noun | Verb | Noun |
> |---|---|---|---|
> | agree | agreement | govern | government |
> | announce | announcement | involve | involvement |
> | assign | assignment | state | statement |

1. Residents have been calling ____government____ officials about the dumping problem.
2. The council agreed to a budget increase, and the mayor signed the ____agreement____.
3. They also made an ____announcement____ on TV about a new community clean-up program.
4. It said they wanted to increase residents' ____involvement____ in their communities.

3 Talk it over

Think about the questions. Talk about your ideas with the class.

Whose responsibility is it to keep a community clean? Why do you think so?

> **BRING IT TO LIFE**
> How does your area keep roads and parks clean? Use the library or the Internet to find information on clean-up or Adopt-a-Road programs in your area, or on littering and dumping laws in your area. Bring the information to class and tell your classmates about it.

1 Grammar

A **Read the direct questions. Complete the indirect questions.**

1. How do organizations adopt a road?

   Do you know _____ how organizations adopt a road _____?

2. What are the program rules?

   Can you tell me what the program rules are _____?

3. Where is the program office?

   Do you know where the program office is _____?

4. When did the program begin?

   Do you have any idea when the program began _____?

B **Complete the indirect questions with *if* or *what*.**

1. Can you tell me __if__ the senior center is open on weekends?

2. Do you know __what__ their hours are?

3. Do you have any idea __what__ services they have?

4. Do you know __if__ the services are free?

5. Can you tell me __if__ all seniors can receive services?

C **Complete the sentences. Use the questions in parentheses.**

1. I'm not sure _____ what the proposal is _____.

   (What is the proposal?)

2. I don't know which budgets they cut _____.

   (Which budgets did they cut?)

3. I have no idea if/whether the committee likes the plan _____.

   (Does the committee like the plan?)

4. I don't know if/whether residents are serving on the committee _____.

   (Are residents serving on the committee?)

D **Match the parts of the sentences.**

__c__ 1. I have no idea why   a. the budget includes money for fire trucks?

__d__ 2. I can't remember when   b. a new truck costs.

__e__ 3. Can you tell me what   c. the mayor wants a new fire truck.

__b__ 4. I'm not sure how much   d. they purchased the last fire truck.

__a__ 5. Do you know whether   e. the problem with the old truck is?

Unit 10 Review and expand

Objectives	Grammar	Vocabulary	Correlations
On-, Pre-, and Higher-level: Review and expand upon unit grammar and life skills	Indirect questions, *wh-* and *if/whether* statements (*Do you know when the meeting starts? I don't know when the meeting starts.*)	Community involvement For vocabulary support for pre-level students, see this **Oxford Picture Dictionary** unit: Community	**CASAS:** 0.1.2, 0.1.5, 4.8.1, 5.6.1, 5.7.1, 7.2.6, 7.3.1, 7.3.2, 7.3.4 **LCPs:** 47.03, 49.01, 49.02, 49.13, 49.16, 49.17 **SCANS:** Creative thinking, Participates as member of a team, Problem Solving **EFF:** Convey ideas in writing, Listen actively, Solve problems and make decisions

Warm-up and Review

10–15 minutes (books closed)

1. Review the *Bring It to Life* assignment from Lesson 5.

2. Have students who did the exercise discuss what they learned. Encourage other students to ask questions. Write the questions on the board. If no one knows the answers, assign them to different students as research.

Introduction and Presentation

5 minutes

1. Rewrite one of the questions on the board as an indirect question. Rewrite another one as a *wh-* or *if/whether* statement. Have volunteers do the same with the other questions on the board.

2. State the objective: *Today we're going to review indirect questions and statements with* wh- *and* if/whether *phrases in order to talk about community involvement.*

1 Grammar

Guided Practice

40–45 minutes

A Have students work individually to complete the indirect questions. Ask volunteers to write their answers on the board.

B Have students work individually to complete the questions with *if* or *what.* Call on volunteers to read the completed questions aloud.

C Have students work with a partner to complete the sentences. Ask volunteers to write the answers on the board. Tell the partners to take turns reading the sentences aloud.

D Have partners work together to match the parts of the sentence. Ask them to take turns reading the completed sentences aloud.

Multilevel Strategies

Use mixed-level pairs for 1C and 1D.

- **Pre-level** For 1C, tell these students to read the question to their partners. Tell them to listen and write as their partners read the completed statement. For 1D, have these students read the first part of each sentence.

- **On- and Higher-level** For 1C, direct these students to read the completed statement after their partners read the question. For 1D, have them listen to their partners read the first part of the sentence and respond with the second.

2 Group work

Communicative Practice

20–35 minutes

 A 1. Direct students, in groups of three to four, to focus on the picture. Ask: *Where are they going? Why?*

2. Assign roles: leader, recorder, and reporters. Explain that students work with their groups to write the conversation.

3. Check comprehension of the exercise. Ask: *Who writes the conversation?* [recorder] *Who will read the conversation to the class?* [reporters] *Who helps everyone and manages the group?* [leader] *Who creates the conversation?* [everyone]

4. Set a time limit (five minutes) to complete the exercise. Circulate and answer any questions. Have a reporter from each group read the group's conversation to the class.

> ### Multilevel Strategies
>
> For 2A, use mixed-level groups.
>
> • **Pre-level** Assign these students the role of reporter.
>
> • **On-level** Assign these students the role of recorder.
>
> • **Higher-level** Assign these students the role of leader.

B 1. Have students walk around the room to conduct these interviews. To get students moving, tell them to interview three new people not in their groups for 2A.

2. Set a time limit (five minutes) to complete the exercise. Tell students to make a note of their classmates' answers but not to worry about writing complete sentences.

> ### Multilevel Strategies
>
> Adapt the mixer in 2B to the level of your students.
>
> • **Pre-level** Allow these students to ask and answer the questions without writing.
>
> • **Higher-level** Have these students ask two additional questions and write all answers.

 C 1. Call on individuals to share their ideas. Elicit a list of important community services, and write them on the board.

2. Have students vote for which services should be free. Write the results on the board. Discuss how they think the free services should be paid for.

PROBLEM SOLVING

15–25 minutes

 A 1. Ask: *Are your neighbors involved with the community?* Tell students they will read a story about a woman whose neighborhood has many problems. Direct students to read Teresa's story silently.

2. Ask: *What are the problems in her neighborhood?* [trash, cracked sidewalks, broken glass, dead trees] *Does she think they can be fixed?* [yes]

3. Play the audio and have students read along silently.

B 1. Elicit answers to question 1.

2. Put students into groups of three or four. Ask each group to think of three or four possible solutions to Teresa's problems and report them to the class. Ask a volunteer to write all possible solutions on the board.

3. Ask students to write possible indirect questions Teresa could ask based on the solutions on the board. Have a volunteer from each group write one or two indirect questions on the board.

Evaluation

30–35 minutes

To test students' understanding of the unit grammar and life skills, have them take the Unit 10 Test on the *Step Forward Test Generator CD-ROM* with *ExamView® Assessment Suite*.

> ### Learning Log
>
> To help students record and discuss their progress, use the *Learning Log* on page T–203.

To extend this review: Have students complete **Workbook 4 page 71, Multilevel Activity Book 4 page 116**, and the **Unit 10 Exercises** on the **Multilevel Grammar Exercises CD-ROM 4**.

2 Group work

A Work with 2–3 classmates. Write a 6–8 line conversation between the people in the picture. Share your conversation with the class.

A: *Excuse me. Do you know where the recycling committee meeting is?*
B: *Yes, it's...*

B Interview 3 classmates. Write their answers.

1. What should people do if they are unhappy about something in their community?
2. What are the most important services a community should have for residents?
3. Which community services should be free? Which ones should residents pay for?

C Talk about the answers with your class.

PROBLEM SOLVING

A Listen and read about Teresa.

Teresa is worried about problems in her neighborhood. There's always a lot of trash in the streets, the sidewalks are cracked, and there's broken glass in the playground. The trees in the area used to be beautiful, but now they're dying because no one takes care of them. People in the neighborhood have stopped taking walks or spending time together outside, and many people don't know their neighbors.

Teresa believes that her neighborhood can solve its problems. She knows that other communities have neighborhood organizations, and she would like to start one in her area. She has a lot of questions, but she's not sure how to get more information.

B Work with your classmates. Answer the questions.

1. What is Teresa's problem? Teresa wants to start a neighborhood organization. She has a lot of questions but she's not sure how to get more information.
2. What could she do? Think of 3 or 4 possible solutions.
3. Write some indirect questions Teresa could ask.

Find It on the Net

FOCUS ON
- Internet and website vocabulary
- changes in technology
- tag questions
- offering and responding to help
- renters' rights

LESSON 1   Vocabulary

1 Learn Internet vocabulary

A Talk about the questions with your class.

1. Do you use a computer? If you do, what do you use it for?
2. What can the Internet help people do?

B Work with your classmates. Match the words with the picture.

_4_ cursor	_6_ pop-up ad	_3_ search box
_5_ links	_7_ pull-down menu	_1_ URL box
_9_ pointer	_8_ scroll bar	_2_ webpage

C Listen and check. Then read the new words with a partner.

D Work with a partner. Write other Internet words you know. Check your words in a dictionary.

Unit 11 Lesson 1

Objectives	Grammar	Vocabulary	Correlations
On-level: Talk about the Internet, and describe website information **Pre-level:** Identify Internet and website vocabulary **Higher-level:** Talk and write about the Internet and websites	Unreal conditional (*If I had a website, I would put my favorite links on it.*)	Internet and website vocabulary For vocabulary support for pre-level students, see this **Oxford Picture Dictionary** topics: Computers, The Internet	**CASAS:** 0.1.2, 0.1.5, 0.2.1, 4.8.1, 7.4.4 **LCPs:** 38.01, 39.01, 49.02, 49.10 **SCANS:** Participates as member of a team, Reading, Seeing things in the mind's eye **EFF** Cooperate with others, Listen actively, Read with understanding, Speak so others can understand, Reflect and Evaluate

Warm-up and Review

10–15 minutes (books closed)

Put a picture of a computer on the board, or indicate the parts of a real computer. Ask students to name the parts they can, and write them on the board.

Introduction

5 minutes

1. Tell students that the parts they have named are the computer's hardware but that today you're going to focus on aspects of the computer controlled by its software.

2. State the objective: *Today we're going to learn vocabulary for the Internet and websites.*

1 Learn Internet vocabulary

Presentation I

20–25 minutes

A Write *Computers* and *Internet* on the board, and elicit students' answers to questions 1 and 2. List students' ideas in the correct category.

B 1. Direct students to look at the picture. Ask: *What is this website for?*

2. Group students and assign roles: leader, fact checker, recorder, and reporter. Explain that students work with their groups to match the words and pictures.

3. Check comprehension of the roles. Ask: *Who looks up the words in a dictionary?* [fact checker] *Who writes the numbers in the book?* [recorder] *Who tells the class your answers?* [reporter] *Who helps everyone and manages the group?* [leader]

4. Set a time limit (three minutes). As students work together, copy the wordlist onto the board.

5. Call "time." Have reporters take turns giving their answers. Write each group's answer on the board next to the word.

C 1. To prepare students for listening, say: *We're going to listen to a woman explain how to use this website.* Ask students to listen and check their answers.

2. Have students check the wordlist on the board and then write the correct numbers in their books.

3. Pair students. Set a time limit (three minutes). Monitor pair practice to identify pronunciation issues.

4. Call "time" and work with the pronunciation of any troublesome words or phrases.

D 1. Ask students to work with their partners from 1C to brainstorm a list of related words.

2. Elicit words from the class. Write them on the board. Ask students to copy them into their vocabulary notes for the unit.

Guided Practice

5–10 minutes

 E 1. Read the questions aloud. Set a time limit (three minutes). Direct students to ask and answer the questions with a partner.

2. Call on volunteers for their answers to the questions.

2 Learn website vocabulary

Presentation II

15–20 minutes

 A 1. Direct students to look at the menu. Introduce the new topic: *Now we're going to look at parts of a typical website.*

2. Say and have students repeat the words in the website.

3. Ask students to work individually to match the links with the information they give.

4. Call on volunteers to read the matching links and information aloud.

5. Check comprehension. Ask: *Where can you find other websites on the same topic?* [Related Links] *Where can you find the organization's address?* [Contact Us]

TIP
Show the class your school's or your district's home page and discuss the items on the menu and what they link to. If you have no way of projecting a computer screen, print the home page out and make a transparency of it.

Guided Practice

10–15 minutes

 B 1. Model the conversation with a volunteer. Model it again using a different word from 2A.

2. Set a time limit (three minutes).

3. Call on volunteers to say one of their conversations for the class.

Communicative Practice and Application

10–15 minutes

 C 1. Give students a minute to make notes of their answers to the questions. Call on individuals to share their ideas with the class.

2. Write the students' favorite websites on the board. Share some of your favorite sites as well.

Evaluation

10–15 minutes (books closed)

TEST YOURSELF

1. Pair students. Direct Partner B to close the book and listen to Partner A dictate five words from 1B. Ask students to switch roles when they finish and have Partner B dictate five words from 2A.

2. Direct both partners to open their books and check their spelling when they finish.

3. Circulate and monitor student work.

> **Multilevel Strategies**
>
> Target the *Test Yourself* to the level of your students.
>
> • **Higher-level** Direct these students to write a sentence defining each of the words their partner dictates. *The URL box is the place you type the address of the website.*

To compress this lesson: Conduct 1B as a whole-class activity.

To extend this lesson: Make a class-annotated website list.
1. Seat students in mixed-level groups. Tell the students to compile a list of their favorite websites and write a brief description of each one. If you have students who don't use the Internet, assign them to different groups, and tell them to take the role of recorder or reporter.
2. Have a reporter from each group share the group's work with the class. Post the lists on the wall so that students can refer to them.

And/Or have students complete **Workbook 4 page 72** and **Multilevel Activity Book 4 pages 118–119**.

E Work with a partner. Talk about these questions. Use the words in 1B.

1. What parts of a webpage can you click on?
2. Where can you type or enter information on a webpage?
3. What are some things you can do with the cursor and the pointer?

2 Learn website vocabulary

A Look at the website menu. Work with your classmates. Match the links with the definitions.

___b___ 1. information about the organization

___a___ 2. the website's first page

___c___ 3. a list of questions many people have

___f___ 4. the organization's phone number or email address

___e___ 5. new information on the website topic

___d___ 6. other websites on the same topic

B Work with a partner. Practice the conversation. Use the words in 2A.

A: How do I go to the first page of the website?
B: Click on Home.
A: What happens if I click on What's New?
B: You see new information on the website topic.

C Talk about the questions with your class.

1. What are some websites that people in your class like? Why do they like them?
2. If you had a website, what would you put on it?

TEST YOURSELF ✔

Work with a partner. Partner A: Read the vocabulary words in 1B to your partner. Partner B: Close your book. Write the words. Ask your partner for help with spelling as necessary. Then change roles. Partner B: Use the words in 2A.

1 Read about changes in the use of technology

A Talk about the questions with your class.

1. Describe your computer skills. Are you an expert, an experienced user, or a beginner?
2. How has technology changed the way you get information?

B Listen and read the essay.

Writer's note

When comparing times, use time expressions to make the times clear for the reader.

Technology Then and Now

By: Pedro Sanchez

→ Ten years ago, I used technology a lot less in my daily life. I used the Internet at work, but I didn't have it at home. When I needed information from a store or a business, I used to make a phone call. Of course, I could only call during business hours. To shop, I went to a store or ordered by phone, and to get directions, I used a map. It seems funny now to think about how much time it took to get things done.

→ Today, I use the Internet at home for many of these tasks. I can get information any time. I don't have to wait for business hours. I get a lot of things done without leaving home. I've even taken an online class.

Some things haven't changed, though. I never buy shoes online because I can't try them on, and I still like paper maps better than Internet maps. When it comes to* really important information, I still use the phone. Of course, these days I usually use a cell phone to make those calls!

*Idiom note: when it comes to = when you are talking about

C Check your understanding. Write T (true), F (false), or NI (no information).

F 1. Pedro's use of technology hasn't changed much.

T 2. Ten years ago, he used a paper map to get directions.

F 3. He has had the Internet at home for more than ten years.

NI 4. He has taken an online English class.

F 5. He usually buys shoes on the Internet.

☑ Compare use of technology in the past and present

Unit 11 Lesson 2

Objectives	Grammar	Vocabulary	Correlations
On- and Higher-level: Analyze, write, and edit an essay about technology use **Pre-level:** Read an essay and write responses to questions about technology use	Contrast past and present (*Ten years ago, I didn't use the Internet. Now I use it every day.*)	Information technology For vocabulary support for pre-level students, see these **Oxford Picture Dictionary** topics: Computers, An Office	**CASAS:** 0.1.2, 0.1.5, 0.2.1, 1.4.1, 4.5.5, 4.5.6, 7.4.4, 7.4.7 **LCPs:** 38.01, 39.01, 49.13, 49.16, 49.17 **SCANS:** Knowing how to learn, Listening, Participates as member of a team, Reading, Speaking **EFF:** Convey ideas in writing, Listen actively, Read with understanding, Reflect and evaluate

Warm-up and Review

10–15 minutes (books closed)

Write these questions on the board, and call on volunteers to answer: *When is the last time you went online? What did you do or what site did you look at? Is there something you would like to do online but haven't tried yet?*

Introduction

5 minutes

1. Ask how many students were using the Internet ten years ago.

2. State the objective: *Today we're going to read and write about changes in the use of technology.*

1 Read about changes in the use of technology

Presentation

20–25 minutes

A Elicit answers to questions 1 and 2. Write students' ideas about how technology has changed their ways of getting information on the board.

B 1. Say: *Now we're going to read an essay about how use of the Internet has affected someone's life.*

2. Direct students to read the essay silently. Check comprehension. Ask: *How did Pedro use to get information from a store? Does he still use the phone?*

3. Play the audio. Have students read along silently.

4. Draw students' attention to the *Writer's note.* Elicit other time expressions: *yesterday, years ago, when I was younger.*

Guided Practice I

10 minutes

C Have students work independently to mark the statements T (true), F (false), or NI (no information). Write the answers on the board.

Multilevel Strategies

Seat pre-level students together for 1C.

• **Pre-level** While other students are working on 1C, ask these students questions about the reading. *How did the writer shop before? How did he or she get directions? How does he or she do those things now? Which things have not changed?* Give students time to copy the answers to 1C from the board.

• **On- and Higher-level** Write two column heads on the board: *Ten Years Ago* and *Now.* Direct these students to first complete 1C and write the answers on the board. When they finish, ask them to write ideas for ways that their use of technology has changed in the last ten years.

2 Write about using technology

Guided Practice II

20–25 minutes

A 1. Read the questions. Elicit students' answers.

2. Put the students ideas under the two column heads on the board (*Ten Years Ago* and *Now*). Include ways of using technology as well as kinds of technology.

B 1. Direct students to look back at the essay in 1B. Read through the questions for each paragraph, and elicit how the writer in 1B answered them.

2. Draw students' attention to the example, and ask them to follow the format as they write in their notebooks.

3. Check comprehension of the exercise. Ask: *How many paragraphs are you going to write?* [three]

4. Have students work individually to write their essays.

Multilevel Strategies

Adapt 2B to the level of your students.

• **Pre-level** Tell these students to compose their essays by writing a one-sentence answer to each question.

• **Higher-level** Tell these students to include more than one kind of technology and to provide specific examples of how they used (or use) them.

C 1. Lead students through the process of using the *Editing checklist*. Read each sentence aloud, and ask students to check their papers before moving onto the next item.

2. Allow students a few minutes to edit their writing as necessary.

Communicative Practice

10 minutes

 1. Read the instructions aloud. Emphasize to students that they are responding to their partners' work, not correcting it.

2. Use the essay in 1B to model the exercise. *I think the part about how he still prefers paper maps is interesting. I'd like to ask why.*

3. Direct students to exchange papers with a partner and follow the instructions.

4. Call on volunteers to share some interesting things they read in their partners' essays.

Application and Evaluation

20 minutes

TEST YOURSELF

1. Review the instructions aloud. Assign a time limit (15 minutes), and have students work independently. Give students notice when they have five minutes left.

2. Before collecting students' work, remind them to use the *Editing checklist*. Collect and correct students' writing.

Multilevel Strategies

Adapt the *Test Yourself* to the level of your students.

• **Pre-level** Tell these students to compose their essays by writing a one-sentence answer to each question.

To compress this lesson: Assign the *Test Yourself* for homework.

To extend this lesson: Talk about entertainment technology. Have a class discussion about how technology has changed entertainment. Ask: *How do you listen to music now? How did people listen to music ten or twenty years ago? How has watching television and movies changed? What are the advantages of the new technology? Are there any disadvantages?*

And/Or have students complete **Workbook 4 page 73** and **Multilevel Activity Book 4 page 120**.

2 Write about using technology

A **Talk about the questions with your class.**

1. Name some items in your home today that use or connect to a computer.
2. How many of these items did you have ten years ago?

B **Write about changes in your use of technology. Use the model in 1B and the questions below to help you.**

Paragraph 1: What technology did you use ten years ago?
How did you use it?

Paragraph 2: What technology do you use today?
How do you use it?

Paragraph 3: What has not changed?
What do you still do in the same way?

[Title]

Ten years ago,…

Today, I use…

Some things…

C **Use the checklist to edit your writing. Check (✔) the true sentences.**

Editing checklist	
1. My first paragraph is about a time in the past.	
2. My second paragraph is about the present.	
3. My third paragraph tells about things that haven't changed.	
4. I used time expressions to make the times clear.	

D **Exchange stories with a partner. Read and comment on your partner's work.**

1. Point out one idea you think is interesting.
2. Ask your partner a question about one of the changes he or she wrote about.

TEST YOURSELF ✔

Write a new paragraph. Compare the technology you use when you study now with the technology you used when you studied ten years ago.

1 Learn tag questions with *be*

A Read the conversation. Why does Abby go to Leo for help?

She's having trouble emailing the landlord.

Abby: Hi, Leo. You're an expert with email, <u>aren't you?</u>

Leo: Yes, I am. Why do you ask?

Abby: I'm having trouble emailing the landlord. There's no heat in my apartment.

Leo: That's terrible. The landlord is aware of the problem, <u>isn't he?</u>

Abby: No, he isn't. I want to put it in writing.

Leo: I'd be happy to help you.

B Study the charts. Underline the 2 tag questions with *be* in the conversation above.

TAG QUESTIONS AND SHORT ANSWERS WITH *BE*

Affirmative statement	Negative tag	Agreement	Disagreement
You**'re** an expert with email,	**aren't** you?	Yes, I **am**.	No, I**'m not**.
The heat **is** off,	**isn't** it?	Yes, it **is**.	No, it **isn't**.
I **was** helpful,	**wasn't** I?	Yes, you **were**.	No, you **weren't**.

Negative statement	Affirmative tag	Agreement	Disagreement
You**'re not** an expert,	**are** you?	No, I**'m not**.	Yes, I **am**.
The heat **isn't** off,	**is** it?	No, it **isn't**.	Yes, it **is**.
I **wasn't** very helpful,	**was** I?	No, you **weren't**.	Yes, you **were**.

Notes

- Use a negative tag after an affirmative statement. Negative tags are usually contracted.
  Ask a negative tag question when you think the answer will be *Yes*.
- Use an affirmative tag after a negative statement.
  Ask an affirmative tag question when you think the answer will be *No*.

C Match the parts of the questions.

   c   1. The heaters are old,

   f   2. This one isn't working very well,

   d   3. You're not calling the landlord,

   e   4. The landlord was here,

   b   5. She's writing an email,

   a   6. You weren't cold today,

a. were you?

b. isn't she?

c. aren't they?

d. are you?

e. wasn't he?

f. is it?

✔ Use tag questions to clarify assumptions

Unit 11 Lesson 3

Objectives	Grammar	Vocabulary	Correlations
On- and Higher-level: Use tag questions to ask for and clarify instructions **Pre-level:** Identify and respond to tag questions; use tag questions	Tag questions (*You live here, don't you?*)	Housing For vocabulary support for pre-level students, see this **Oxford Picture Dictionary** topics: Housing, The Internet	**CASAS:** 0.1.2, 0.1.5, 0.1.6, 0.2.1, 7.4.7, 7.5.6 **LCPs:** 39.01, 49.01, 49.09, 49.13, 49.17 **SCANS:** Listening, Reading, Speaking, Writing **EFF:** Convey ideas in writing, Listen actively, Observe critically, Read with understanding, Reflect and evaluate, Speak so others can understand

Warm-up and Review

10–15 minutes (books closed)

Write skeleton sentences and ask volunteers to complete them. *Email is _____. Computers are _____. Ten years ago, life was _____. Ten years ago, telephones were _____. Today, life isn't _____. Ten years ago computers weren't _____. Ten years ago email wasn't _____.*

Introduction

5–10 minutes

1. Ask students how many of them use email every day, how many use it every week, and how many never use it. Direct tag questions to the students who use email. *It's very convenient, isn't it? They're expensive, aren't they?*

2. State the objective: *Today we're going to use tag questions to talk about housing problems and emailing the landlord.*

1 Learn tag questions with *be*

Presentation I

20–25 minutes

A Read the instructions aloud. Ask students to read the conversation silently to find the answer. Elicit the answer.

B 1. Read the questions and answers in the chart aloud.

2. Direct students to underline the tag questions with *be* in the conversation. Elicit the answer from the class.

3. Ask: *Why didn't Abby just say,* Leo, are you an expert with email?

4. Read the tag questions in the chart, and call on volunteers to agree or disagree with you. Point out that you need to use a negative to agree with a negative tag question.

5. Assess students' understanding of the charts. Ask them to convert the statements on the board from the warm-up into tag questions. Call on volunteers to say the tag questions and tell other volunteers to agree or disagree.

Guided Practice I

15–20 minutes

C Ask students to work individually to match the tags with the first part of the questions. Call on volunteers to read the completed tag questions aloud.

Multilevel Strategies

Target 1C to the level of your students.

• **Pre-level** Direct these students to underline the verb *be* in the first part of each question. As their classmates read the completed questions aloud, point out that the tag has the same verb form as the first part of the question, but if the first part is negative, the tag is positive and vice versa.

Guided Practice II

5–10 minutes

D Have students work individually to complete the tag questions. Ask volunteers to read the completed questions aloud.

2 Learn tag questions with *do* and *did*

Presentation II

20–25 minutes

A 1. Introduce the new topic. Now we're going to learn tag questions with *do, does,* and *did.*

2. Read and have students repeat the questions and answers in the chart.

Provide practice with tag questions after 2A. Make cards with each of the tags from the charts in 1B and 2A. Put students in groups, and provide each group with a complete set of tags. Make statements and have the students in each group take turns holding up the group's tag to go with the sentence. Give groups time to discuss and make their choices before they hold up a tag. Possible statements: *You're a good student. You don't work Mondays. The FAQ is on the first page. You're not tired. He doesn't attend this class. The computer crashed. That website was interesting. He works on computers. You come to school every day. The computer isn't on. The email didn't arrive. The homework was difficult. I wasn't late today.* If students have difficulty choosing the correct tag, elicit the verb you used and write it on the board. Refer students to the charts in 1B and 2A to find the correct tag.

Guided Practice I

10–15 minutes

B Direct students to work individually to complete the tag questions. Ask volunteers to write the answers on the board.

C 1. Direct students to look at number 1. Elicit the problem with the tag question. [The verb and the tag are both affirmative.] Do the same for each of the remaining sentences, and have students rewrite the questions with the correct tag.

2. Call on volunteers to read the new tag questions aloud.

D Complete the sentences with tag questions.

1. The heater is broken, _____ isn't it _____?
2. The repairman wasn't in his shop, _was he_____?
3. It isn't working well, _is it_____?
4. The neighbors were having problems, too, _weren't they_____?
5. You're going to fix this, _aren't you_____?
6. We're not being very helpful, _are we_____?

2 Learn tag questions with *do* and *did*

A Study the charts. What punctuation mark comes before a tag? a comma

TAG QUESTIONS AND SHORT ANSWERS WITH *DO* AND *DID*

Affirmative statement	Negative tag	Agreement	Disagreement
You **live** here,	**don't** you?	Yes, I **do**.	No, I **don't**.
He **prefers** email,	**doesn't** he?	Yes, he **does**.	No, he **doesn't**.
The heat **worked** Friday,	**didn't** it?	Yes, it **did**.	No, it **didn't**.

Negative statement	Affirmative tag	Agreement	Disagreement
You **don't live** here,	**do** you?	No, I **don't**.	Yes, I **do**.
He **doesn't like** email,	**does** he?	No, he **doesn't**.	Yes, he **does**.
The heat **didn't work** Friday,	**did** it?	No, it **didn't**.	Yes, it **did**.

B Complete the questions with tags.

1. The landlord fixed this broken window, _____ didn't he _____?
2. You don't want to call him tonight, _do you_____?
3. I needed to talk to him, _didn't I_____?
4. He doesn't work on Mondays, _does he_____?
5. You didn't send him an email, _did you_____?
6. He usually fixes things right away, _doesn't he_____?

C Get the form. Work with your class. Correct the sentences.

1. You wrote this, ~~did~~ you? _____ You wrote this, didn't you? _____
2. Frank doesn't remember, ~~doesn't~~ he? _Frank doesn't remember, does he?_
3. Bonita and Barry got that email, ~~did~~ they? _Bonita and Barry got that email, didn't they?_
4. Lena uses the Internet, ~~did~~ she? _Lena uses the Internet, doesn't she?_
5. Yukio didn't work yesterday, ~~didn't~~ he? _Yukio didn't work yesterday, did he?_

3 Grammar listening

🎧 **Listen to the speakers. Choose the correct tags to complete the questions. Circle _a_ or _b_.**

1. a. aren't you?
   b. didn't you?

2. a. don't you?
   b. aren't you?

3. a. do you?
   b. did you?

4. a. is it?
   b. does it?

5. a. is she?
   b. isn't she?

6. a. doesn't it?
   b. do they?

7. a. aren't they?
   b. aren't we?

8. a. did we?
   b. didn't we?

9. a. did it?
   b. didn't it?

4 Practice tag questions

A **Choose a partner. Think about your answers to the questions, but don't check your answers yet.**

1. Where is your partner from?
2. What does your partner like to do in his or her free time?
3. How long has your partner studied English?
4. Does your partner live in a house or an apartment?
5. Can your partner use a computer?

B **Work with your partner. Ask tag questions to check your answers in 1A. Answer your partner's questions. Try to add extra information.**

A: _You're from Sri Lanka, aren't you?_
B: _Yes, I am. I came here last year._
A: _You like to cook, don't you?_
B: _No, actually, I don't. I…_

Need help?

After a short answer, people often add extra information. This helps keep the conversation going.

C **Test your classmates. Ask questions about your partner and answer your classmates' tag questions.**

A: _Where's Adil from?_
B: _He's from Thailand, isn't he?_
A: _No, he isn't. He's from Sri Lanka._

TEST YOURSELF ✔

Close your book. Think of a famous person and 6 things you think you know about him or her. Write 6 tag questions about the person. Then test your classmates' knowledge.

3 Grammar listening

Guided Practice II

10–15 minutes

1. Say: *Now we're going to listen to some statements about a class. You'll need to choose the correct tag to turn the statement into a question.*

2. Play the audio. Direct students to read along silently without writing.

3. Replay the audio. Ask students to choose the correct tag.

4. Call on volunteers for the answers.

Multilevel Strategies

Replay the *Grammar listening* to allow pre-level students to catch up while you challenge on- and higher-level students.

• **Pre-level** Have these students listen again to choose the correct tag.

• **On- and Higher-level** Have these students take notes on the questions. When you go over the answers, call on these students to reconstruct the first part of the question.

4 Practice tag questions

Communicative Practice and Application

20–25 minutes

A Direct students to read the questions. Tell students to write their answers without speaking to their partners. Encourage them to make guesses even if they have no idea.

B 1. Put students in pairs. Elicit the tag questions that students will ask their partners.

2. Read the *Need help?* box. Read the model conversation with a volunteer, and point out the extra information. Tell students that we often use tag questions to get a conversation going.

3. Direct students to ask their partners the questions. Tell them to make notes of each other's answers. Model the exercise by asking a volunteer the first question. Have the class tell you how to write the answer in note form.

4. Check comprehension of the exercise. Ask: *Are you going to ask regular questions or tag questions?* [tag] *Are you going to give a* Yes/No *answer or are you going to add information?* [add information] Set a time limit for the exercise (four minutes), and observe and take note of issues that arise.

C 1. Have the partners from 4B join with another pair. Model the exercise with two volunteers. First play the role of A, and then play the role of B to demonstrate that A asks a regular question and B responds with a tag question.

2. Set a time limit (five minutes). Monitor and provide feedback.

Evaluation

10–15 minutes (books closed)

TEST YOURSELF

1. Brainstorm names of famous people, and write them on the board.

2. Ask students to write the questions independently. Then pair students and have them ask their partners the questions they wrote.

3. Collect and correct their writing.

Multilevel Strategies

Target the *Test Yourself* to the level of your students.

• **Pre-level** Encourage these students to write tag questions with the verb *be*.

To compress this lesson: Conduct 1C as a whole-class activity.

To extend this lesson: After the *Test Yourself*, group students and have them write tag questions for each of the members of their group to confirm what they know about them. For example: They can confirm their likes or dislikes, where they are from, or other observations about their classmates.

And/Or have students complete **Workbook 4 pages 74–75, Multilevel Activity Book 4 pages 121–122**, and the corresponding **Unit 11 Exercises** on the **Multilevel Grammar Exercises CD-ROM 4**.

Unit 11 Lesson 4

Objectives	Grammar	Vocabulary	Correlations
On-, Pre-, and Higher-level: Ask for and clarify instructions about Internet use, and listen for information in a talk show interview	Use question words for clarification (*From where?*) Tag questions (*That's a good website, isn't it?*)	Internet and housing words, *premises* For vocabulary support for pre-level students, see this **Oxford Picture Dictionary** unit and topics: Housing, The Internet, Apartments	**CASAS:** 0.1.2, 0.1.5, 0.1.6, 6.0.3, 6.0.4, 6.1.2, 7.5.6 **LCPs:** 49.02, 49.09, 51.05 **SCANS:** Arithmetic/Mathematics, Listening, Seeing things in the mind's eye **EFF:** Listen actively, Observe critically, Read with understanding, Use math to solve problems and communicate

Warm-up and Review

10–15 minutes (books closed)

Display and elicit the purpose of different websites. If you don't have a means of projecting a computer screen, print and make transparencies of the home pages of different sites—for example, a search engine, a map finder, a weather page, news, a blog, an online game, and a fan site.

Introduction

5 minutes

1. Ask: *Who knows the most about computers and technology in your house?*

2. State the objective: *Today we're going to learn ways to offer and respond to help and clarify information.*

1 Learn to offer and respond to help

Presentation I

15–20 minutes

 1. Direct students to look at the picture. Ask: *Who are these people?*

2. Play the audio. Tell students to ask and answer the questions with a partner.

Guided Practice

20–25 minutes

 1. Read the instructions. Play the audio. Ask students to read along silently and listen for the answer to the question. Elicit the answer.

2. Ask students to read the conversation with a partner. Circulate and monitor pronunciation. Model and have students repeat difficult words or phrases.

3. Say and have students repeat the expressions in the *In other words* box. Elicit the placement of the expressions in the conversation. Ask volunteers to read the conversation using expressions from the box.

Communicative Practice and Application

15–20 minutes

 1. Ask students to read the instructions silently. Check their comprehension of the exercise. Ask: *What are the two roles? What is the situation?* Elicit examples of what each person might say.

2. Set a time limit (five minutes). Ask students to act out the role-play in both roles. Ask one to three volunteer pairs to act out their conversations for the class. Tell students who are listening to note how Partner A offers help.

Multilevel Strategies

For 1C, adapt the role-play to the level of your students.

• **Pre-level** Provide the beginning of the role-play for these students. *A: How are you doing with your lease? You're not still having trouble, are you? B: Yes, I am! It has a lot of difficult words. A: Why don't you try using an online dictionary? B: _____.*

1 Learn to offer and respond to help

A Look at the picture. Listen to the conversation. Then answer the questions below with your classmates.

1. What does Abby want to do?
2. What two things does Leo suggest?

Send an email to her landlord. Make it short, and send a second email tomorrow if she doesn't hear from her landlord.

B Listen and read. **What does Abby need help with?** with an Internet search on renters' rights

Leo: You're not still having trouble with your landlord, are you?

Abby: Yes, I am. He hasn't done *any* repairs. I've emailed five times!

Leo: Then it's about time* you got some help. Can I make a suggestion?

Abby: Please do.

Leo: Why don't you do an Internet search on renters' rights?

Abby: OK, but I'll need some help. Could you show me how?

Leo: Sure. Go to a search page and click in the search box. Then type *renters' rights* and our state.

Abby: Then I click *Go*, right?

Leo: Yep, that's it. Look, there are hundreds of renters' rights websites.

Abby: Great! This is really helpful. Thanks so much.

*****Idiom note:** It's about time = It's time for this to happen; it should have happened already

> **In other words...**
>
> **Offering help**
>
> Can I make a suggestion?
> Can I offer a suggestion?
> Can I suggest something?

C Role-play a conversation about help with a partner. Use the example in 1B to make a new conversation.

Partner A: Ask if your partner is still having trouble with his/her lease. Suggest using an online dictionary to look up difficult words. Help your partner go to the web page and click in the search box. Point out that you can also click on *listen* to hear the word.

Partner B: You've read your lease for a new apartment five times. It has a lot of difficult words, like *premises*. Listen to your partner's suggestions and follow his/her instructions. Check to see if you should click on *search*. Thank your partner.

☑ Ask for and clarify instructions about Internet use   **151**

2 Learn to use question words for clarification

A **Study the chart. Complete the questions below with *what* or *where*.**

Question words for clarification	
A: I need information on renters' rights. B: On **what**? A: On renters' rights.	A: Click in the search box. B: Click **where**? A: In the search box.

1. **A:** The states are on a pull-down menu.

   B: On a ___what___?

2. **A:** Type the URL in the URL box.

   B: Type the URL ___where___?

B **Work with a partner. Match each sentence with a clarification question.**

___e___ 1. Click this link first.

___a___ 2. This link. Then read the FAQs.

___f___ 3. FAQs. There are about ten questions.

___c___ 4. Ten. They're by a renters' group from Ohio.

___d___ 5. Ohio. You can email them with questions.

___b___ 6. Uh… Why don't you ask Tim to help you?

a. The what?

b. Ask Tim what?

c. From where?

d. With what?

e. Click what?

f. About how many?

C **Work with a partner. Read the sentences and questions from 2B.**

3 Practice your pronunciation

A **Listen to the questions. Notice how the speakers use falling and rising intonation.**

Falling intonation	Rising intonation
The speaker is fairly sure of the answer.	The speaker is not sure of the answer.
This is a good website, isn't it? ⬂	This is a good website, isn't it? ⬈
You don't use email often, do you? ⬂	You don't use email often, do you? ⬈

B **Listen. How sure are the speakers of their answers? Check *Fairly sure* or *Not sure*.**

	Fairly sure	Not sure
1.		✔
2.	✔	
3.	✔	

	Fairly sure	Not sure
4.		✔
5.		✔
6.	✔	

C **Practice the questions in 3A with a partner.**

2 Learn to use question words for clarification

Presentation II
10–15 minutes

A 1. Introduce the new topic. Read the conversations in the chart aloud. Point out that repeating the word before the one(s) you don't understand helps the listener know what to repeat.

2. Have students work individually to complete the questions with *what* or *who*. Go over the answers as a class.

Guided Practice
15–20 minutes

B Have students work with a partner to match the sentences with the clarification questions. Go over the answers as a class.

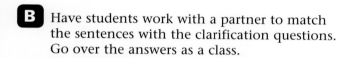TIP After 2B, practice clarification questions as a class. Make statements and mumble the endings. Call on students to ask clarification questions. *I went to the (mumble). I talked to (mumble) yesterday. I bought new (mumble). I want to go to (mumble). I'd like to (mumble).*

Communicative Practice and Application
10–15 minutes

C Model the pronunciation of the clarification questions. Ask partners to read the questions and responses aloud.

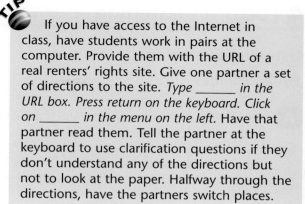TIP If you have access to the Internet in class, have students work in pairs at the computer. Provide them with the URL of a real renters' rights site. Give one partner a set of directions to the site. *Type _____ in the URL box. Press return on the keyboard. Click on _____ in the menu on the left.* Have that partner read them. Tell the partner at the keyboard to use clarification questions if they don't understand any of the directions but not to look at the paper. Halfway through the directions, have the partners switch places.

3 Practice your pronunciation

Pronunciation Extension
10–15 minutes

A 1. Write *You have the landlord's email address, don't you?* on the board. Say the question twice—once with rising and once with falling intonation. Ask students to identify which time you were not sure of the answer. Say: *Now we're going to focus on two ways to pronounce tag questions.*

2. Play the audio. Direct students to listen for the rising and falling intonation.

B 1. Play the audio and ask students to check the correct column.

2. Replay the audio. Stop after each question so that students can check their answers. Ask for a show of hands to see how many chose *fairly sure* or *not sure*. Replay any questions that caused difficulty.

C Have students practice the questions in 3A with a partner. Call on volunteers to say the questions for the class, and have the class guess whether the student is fairly sure or not sure.

4 Focus on Listening

Listening Extension

20–25 minutes

A Read the questions aloud, and elicit answers from volunteers. Encourage students to respond to each other's ideas. After one student speaks, ask other students for their opinions. *Do you agree or disagree with what he/she said? Why?*

B Play the audio. Call on volunteers to answer the questions.

C 1. Direct students to read the sentences before listening.

2. Replay the audio and have students work individually to complete the sentences. Take a tally of responses for each item, and if students disagree on a response, replay the audio so that they can check their answers.

> ## Multilevel Strategies
>
> Adapt 4C to the level of your students.
>
> • **Pre-level** Before these students listen, provide them with the answers to 4C written out of order. Have them write the words in the correct sentence as they listen. [*landlord, difficult, six, a lot of, hundreds*]

5 Real-life math

Math Extension

5–10 minutes

1. Read the problem aloud. Ask volunteers to explain how they will solve the problem.

2. Give students time to read the questions and find the answers individually.

3. Have a volunteer write the problem and the solution on the board.

Evaluation

10–15 minutes

TEST YOURSELF

1. Model the role-play with a volunteer. Then switch roles.

2. Pair students. Check comprehension of the exercise by eliciting things that each partner might say.

3. Set a time limit (five minutes), and have the partners act out the role-play in both roles.

4. Circulate and monitor. Encourage pantomime and improvisation.

5. Provide feedback.

> ## Multilevel Strategies
>
> Target the *Test Yourself* to the level of your students.
>
> • **Pre-level** Provide the beginning of the role-play for these students. *A: I want to buy renter's insurance _____, but I can't find any information about it on this website. Partner B: Can I make a suggestion? _____.*

To compress this lesson: Conduct pronunciation 3C and/or *Real-life Math* as a whole-class activity.

To extend this lesson: Have students compare websites.
1. Put students in mixed-level pairs or groups, and give each group two websites with similar functions to compare. If you don't have access to the Internet in class, print and make a transparency of the home page of each site. Give each pair (or group) two search engines, or two bookstores, or two news sites.
2. Tell students to decide which site they prefer. Ask them to consider how easy the page is to understand and navigate, how comprehensive the site looks, and its attractiveness.
3. Have reporters explain to the class which site they prefer and why.

And/Or have students complete **Workbook 4 page 76** and **Multilevel Activity Book 4 page 123**.

4 Focus on listening

A Talk about the questions with your class.

1. What are some ways that people find new homes to rent or buy?

2. In your opinion, is it a good idea to look for a home on the Internet? Why or why not?

B Listen to the interview. Answer the questions.

1. What are the people talking about?   apartmentsearch.apt

2. Which person sometimes doesn't speak clearly?   Melia

C Listen again. Complete the sentences.

1. Melia worked at an apartment rental office in _college_.

2. She learned that most people want to know about the _landlord_'s responsibilities.

3. Melia doesn't think it's _hard_ to learn to design a website.

4. It took Melia about _6_ months to design ApartmentSearch.apt.

5. Larry thinks that _a lot of_ people use Melia's site.

6. Melia says that _hundreds_ of people visit the site every day.

5 Real-life math

Look at the web page counter and answer the question. Explain your answer to your classmates.

| Visitors today: | 6 2 5 ☐ ☐ ☐ |
| Visitors last year: | 1 4 9 6 5 0 |

Today was an unusual day for ApartmentSearch.apt. The website gets about the same number of visitors, or hits, every day. Today was a very busy day. How many more hits did the site get today than it usually gets in a day? _215_ (Hint: There are 365 days in a year.)

TEST YOURSELF ✔

Role-play a conversation about using the Internet. Partner A: You want to buy renter's insurance, but you can't find information about it on your insurance company's website. Partner B: Suggest that your friend look at the website's FAQs for information about renter's insurance. Then change roles.

1 Get ready to read

A What are some issues that landlords and renters might disagree about?

B Read the definitions. What is the opposite of *routine*? not normal/unusual

check up on: (verb) to look at or visit something to determine its condition
routine: (adj.) normal; usual
tenant: (noun) a renter; a person who pays rent to live in a building

C Look at the title, headings, and pictures in the web article in 2A. Write 2 questions you think the article will answer.

2 Read and respond

A Read the article. How does the law protect renters? The law gives renters certain rights.

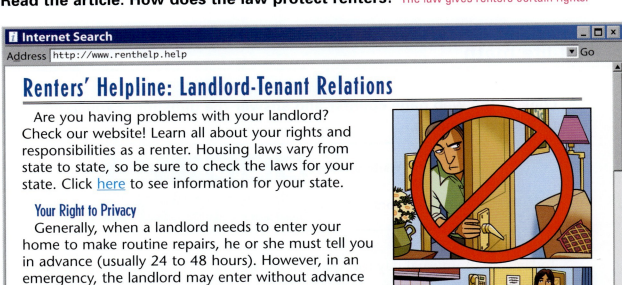

Internet Search

Address http://www.renthelp.help ▼ Go

Renters' Helpline: Landlord-Tenant Relations

Are you having problems with your landlord? Check our website! Learn all about your rights and responsibilities as a renter. Housing laws vary from state to state, so be sure to check the laws for your state. Click here to see information for your state.

Your Right to Privacy
Generally, when a landlord needs to enter your home to make routine repairs, he or she must tell you in advance (usually 24 to 48 hours). However, in an emergency, the landlord may enter without advance notice. Check your lease carefully. Local laws vary on whether a landlord may enter your home just to check up on the property.

Your Right to Home Maintenance and Repairs
Landlords are responsible for keeping their properties[1] in good condition. That includes rental units, stairways, and common areas (yards and halls). Landlords must maintain the heating and plumbing systems, supply

[1]properties: buildings or land that a person owns

 Interpret a web article on renters' rights

Unit 11 Lesson 5

Objectives	Grammar	Vocabulary	Correlations
On-, Pre-, and Higher-level: Read about and discuss renters' rights and responsibilities	*Can* (*How can the Internet help renters and landlords?*)	*Check up, reasonable, tenant, properties* For vocabulary support for pre-level students, see this **Oxford Picture Dictionary** topics: Computers, Apartments	**CASAS:** 0.1.2, 0.1.5, 1.4.1, 1.4.2, 1.4.3, 1.4.5, 2.5.6, 7.4.4, 7.4.7 **LCPs:** 38.01, 45.01, 45.07, 49.06 **SCANS:** Acquires and evaluates information, Uses computers to process information **EFF:** Listen actively, Read with understanding, Speak so others can understand, Take responsibility for learning

Warm-up and Review

10–15 minutes (books closed)

Ask your students how many of them are renters and how many are homeowners. Call on volunteers to share if they have a good relationship with their landlords. Find out if any of your students are landlords. Ask about their relationship with their tenants.

Introduction

5 minutes

1. Explain that landlords and tenants often disagree about certain issues and that most of those issues are covered by laws. Point out to students that they may find themselves in situations where it would be useful to know about renters' rights and responsibilities.

2. State the objective: *Today we're going to read about and discuss renters' rights and responsibilities.*

1 Get ready to read

Presentation

15–20 minutes

A Read the question aloud. Write students' ideas on the board.

B Read the words and definitions. Elicit sample sentences from students using the words.

Pre-Reading

C 1. Read the instructions aloud. Elicit the questions and write them on the board.

2. Have students scan the article to find the link. Ask: *What will you see on the linked page?*

2 Read and respond

Guided Practice I

25–30 minutes

A 1. Ask students to read the article silently.

2. After they've finished reading, direct students to underline unfamiliar words they would like to know. Elicit the words and encourage other students to provide definitions or examples.

3. Check students' comprehension. Ask: *When can a landlord enter your home?* [during an emergency] *Who has to keep the home clean?* [the tenant] *Why should you make a checklist of the condition of things your home?* [in case the landlord wants to keep your deposit]

Multilevel Strategies

Adapt 2A to the level of your students.

• **Pre-level** Provide these students with a summary of the ideas in the reading. *Renters' rights are different in different states, but these are true in most states: 1. Unless there is an emergency a landlord must tell you in advance if he or she is going to enter your home. 2. Landlords are responsible for keeping the property in good condition. Renters are responsible for keeping their areas clean. 3. The landlord must refund your security deposit when you move out unless you have damaged property.*

Direct students to read the summary while other students are reading 2A.

Guided Practice II

15–20 minutes

B 1. Play the audio. Have students read along silently.

2. Elicit and discuss any additional questions about the reading.

C Have students work individually to choose the best answer. Go over the answers as a class.

> ### Multilevel Strategies
>
> Target 2C to the level of your students.
>
> • **Pre-level** Tell these students to use their summaries to complete the exercise.
>
> • **Higher-level** Give these students questions to discuss with a partner when they finish 2C. *How do these laws compare to housing laws in your native country? How does the tenant/landlord relationship compare? Is the home-buying process similar or different?*

D Refer students to the questions on the board from the pre-reading. Discuss whether and how the questions were answered. If questions were not answered, discuss ways that students could find the answers.

3 Talk it over

Communicative Practice

15–20 minutes

A 1. Read the questions aloud. Set a time limit (three minutes). Have students work independently to think about the questions and write their answers in note form.

2. Call on volunteers to share their answers with the class.

> **TIP** Before students do the *Bring It to Life* assignment, have them work in groups to brainstorm a list of important questions they would want to ask before renting an apartment or buying a new home. Have each group write its questions on a large sheet of paper. Keep the questions for the follow-up to *Bring It to Life.*

Application

5–10 minutes

BRING IT TO LIFE

Read the instructions aloud. Tell students who are going to look on the Internet to try typing *home buying checklist, rental checklist,* and *apartment checklist* into a search engine.

To compress this lesson: Conduct 2C as a whole-class activity.

To extend this lesson: Discuss renters' rights and responsibilities.
1. Write a list of situations on the board. *1. There's an old car on the lawn and it's dripping grease into the ground. 2. The ceiling paint is chipping. 3. A table lamp is broken. 4. The trash is piling up by the side of the house. 5. A step in the staircase leading into the apartment building is cracked.*
2. Put students in pairs. Ask them to discuss who is probably responsible for the situation. Tell them to come up with things that the landlord or tenant might do in each case. Call on volunteers to share their ideas with the class.

And/Or have students complete **Workbook 4 page 77** and the **Multilevel Activity Book 4 pages 124–125**.

hot and cold water, and maintain working smoke detectors. Tenants are responsible for keeping their areas clean.

Your Right to Your Security Deposit

The landlord must refund your security deposit when you move out if there is no damage to the apartment. Before you move in, it's a good idea to use a checklist to note the condition of everything in the home, including plumbing, appliances, and locks. Give a copy to your landlord and keep a copy. You may need it if your landlord tries to keep some of your security deposit when you move out.

Source: *www.jud2.ct.gov*

B **Listen and read the article again.**

C **Choose the best answers. Circle *a* or *b*.**

1. What is the most important idea in the first section of the article?
   a. A landlord can enter your home at any time.
   b. A landlord can only enter your home in certain situations.

2. What is the most important idea in the last section of the article?
   a. The law protects renters' security deposits.
   b. The renter has to pay for any damage to an apartment.

3. What is the main idea of the article?
   a. Landlords have more rights than renters do.
   b. Renters have rights under the law.

D **Look at the questions you wrote in 1C. Did the article answer the questions?**

3 Talk it over

Think about the questions. Talk about your ideas with the class.

1. What are some ways that landlords and tenants can have a good relationship?
2. How can the Internet help renters and home buyers?

BRING IT TO LIFE

Use the Internet or the library to find a checklist of things to look at in choosing an apartment or a house. Bring your information to class. Compare checklists with a group. With your group, list the top ten things to ask or do when renting a home.

1 Grammar

A **Circle the correct tags.**

1. This apartment is nice, (doesn't it / (isn't it))?
2. We looked at apartments in this building last year, ((didn't we) / don't we)?
3. The building was built a long time ago, (didn't it / (wasn't it))?
4. The halls and stairways are pretty clean, ((aren't they) / are they)?
5. The landlord doesn't allow pets, (do they / (does he))?
6. You know some people who live here, (do you / (don't you))?

B **Complete the sentences with tag questions with a form of *be* or *do*.**

1. This is the same website we looked at yesterday, _____ isn't it _____?
2. The cursor moves when you move the mouse, doesn't it _____?
3. Some of these links don't work anymore, do they _____?
4. We're going to print this page, aren't we _____?
5. You didn't click on that pop-up ad, did you _____?
6. This information wasn't here the last time we checked this site, was it _____?

C **Match the sentences with the clarification questions.**

___c___ 1. I found a website with free email.   a. Is where?

___d___ 2. We could email the building supervisor.   b. Since when?

___e___ 3. We need to tell him about our sink.   c. With what?

___b___ 4. It's been broken since last week.   d. Email who?

___a___ 5. The sink is in the kitchen.   e. Our what?

D **You want to move into a new apartment. Write questions with tags for these situations.**

1. You think you have to write a letter to your current landlord.

   I have to write a letter to my current landlord, don't I?

2. You think your current landlord is going to give back your security deposit.

   My current landlord is going to give back my security deposit, isn't he?

3. You're not sure, but you think that the new building doesn't have cable TV.

   The new building doesn't have cable TV, does it?

4. You're fairly certain that the rent for the new apartment includes utilities.

   The rent for the new apartment includes utilities, doesn't it?

Unit 11 Review and expand

Objectives	Grammar	Vocabulary	Correlations
On-, Pre-, and Higher-level: Review and expand upon unit grammar and life skills	Tag questions and clarification questions (*She lives in Lakewood, doesn't she? She lives where?*)	Housing and the Internet For vocabulary support for pre-level students, see these **Oxford Picture Dictionary** topics: Computers, The Internet, Apartments	**CASAS:** 0.1.2, 0.1.5, 0.1.6, 0.2.1, 4.8.1, 7.2.6, 7.3.1, 7.3.2, 7.3.4, 7.4.7 **LCPs:** 39.01, 49.02, 49.13, 49.17 **SCANS:** Creative thinking, Interprets and communicates information **EFF:** Convey ideas in writing, Listen actively, Read with understanding, Solve problems and make decisions

Warm-up and Review

10–15 minutes (books closed)

1. Review the *Bring It to Life* assignment from Lesson 5.

2. Have students who did the exercise share their checklists with the class. Ask students who didn't do the exercise to say which items on the checklists they think are most important.

3. Ask students if, after seeing the checklists, there are any questions they would like to add to their lists of essential questions to ask a landlord or real estate agent.

Introduction and Presentation

5 minutes

1. Rewrite some of the checklist information as past- and present-tense tag questions. *You checked the water pressure, didn't you? She is looking at the emergency exits, isn't she? Listening for the traffic noise is a good idea, isn't it?*

2. Call on a volunteer to say a tag question using one of the checklist ideas. Respond to the question with a clarification question. *I should check the what?*

3. State the objective: *Today we're going to review tag questions and clarification questions to talk about housing and the Internet.*

1 Grammar

Guided Practice

40–45 minutes

A Have students work individually to circle the correct tag for each question. Go over the answers as a class.

B Have students work individually to complete the tags. Ask volunteers to write the answers on the board.

C Have students work with a partner to match each clarification question with its sentence. Tell partners to take turns reading the questions and answers. Ask volunteer pairs to read the questions and answers for the class. Provide feedback on pronunciation.

D Have students work with their partners to write the tag questions. Ask them to read the tag questions to their partners. Tell the partners to use a short answer to agree.

Multilevel Strategies

For 1C and 1D, seat same-level students together.

• **Pre-level** Give these students extra time to complete 1C. Work with them as a group to write the tag questions for 1D.

• **On- and Higher-level** When these students finish 1C and 1D, have them write original tag questions. Tell them to imagine that they are being shown around a new home. Have them write tag questions they might ask a rental or real-estate agent. *Utilities are paid for, aren't they?*

2 Group work

Communicative Practice

20–35 minutes

 1. Direct students, in groups of three to four, to focus on the picture. Ask: *What are they doing?*

2. Assign roles: leader, recorder, and reporters. Explain that students work with their groups to write the conversation.

3. Check comprehension of the roles. Ask: *Who writes the conversation?* [recorder] *Who will read the conversation to the class?* [reporters] *Who helps everyone and manages the group?* [leader] *Who creates the conversation?* [everyone]

4. Set a time limit (five minutes) to complete the exercise. Circulate and answer any questions.

5. Have reporters from each group read the group's conversations to the class.

> ### Multilevel Strategies
>
> For 2A, use mixed-level groups.
>
> • **Pre-level** Assign these students the role of reporter.
>
> • **On-level** Assign these students the role of recorder.
>
> • **Higher-level** Assign these students the role of leader.

B 1. Have students walk around the room to conduct the interviews. To get students moving, tell them to interview three new people not in their groups for 2A.

2. Set a time limit (five minutes) to complete the exercise.

3. Tell students to make a note of their classmates' answers but not to worry about writing complete sentences.

> ### Multilevel Strategies
>
> Adapt the mixer in 2B to the level of your students.
>
> • **Pre-level** Allow these students to ask and answer the questions without writing.
>
> • **Higher-level** Have these students ask two additional questions and write all answers.

C Call on individuals to report what they learned about their classmates. Encourage students to make generalizations. *Three out of four students think libraries should buy books and computers.*

PROBLEM SOLVING

15–25 minutes

 1. Ask: *Have you ever had a family member teach you a new skill? Was he or she a good teacher?* Tell students they will read a story about a man who wants to learn computer skills from his brother. Direct students to read Eric's story silently.

2. Ask: *Why is Louis not a good teacher for Eric?* [He talks quickly and he doesn't let Eric try things for himself.]

3. Play the audio and have students read along silently.

B 1. Elicit answers to question 1.

2. Put students into groups of three or four. Ask each group to think of some possible solutions to Eric's problem and report them to the class. Ask a volunteer to write all possible solutions on the board.

3. Pair students and have them write a conversation between Eric and his brother. Call on volunteer pairs to read their conversations to the class.

Evaluation

30–35 minutes

To test students' understanding of the unit grammar and life skills, have them take the Unit 11 Test on the *Step Forward Test Generator CD-ROM* with *ExamView® Assessment Suite.*

> ### Learning Log
>
> To help students record and discuss their progress, use the *Learning Log* on page T–203.

To extend this review: Have students complete **Workbook 4 page 78, Multilevel Activity Book 4 page 126,** and the **Unit 11 Exercises** on the **Multilevel Grammar Exercises CD-ROM 4.**

2 Group work

A   **Work with 2–3 classmates. Write a 6–8 line conversation between the people in the picture. Share your conversation with the class.**

A: *You're good with computers, aren't you?*
I need some help finding…
B: *I can help you…*

B   **Choose one of the questions below. Interview 3 classmates. Write their answers.**

1. Are computers and technology important to you? Why or why not?
2. Should public libraries use their budgets to buy books or to provide computers? Why?
3. Some people spend most of their time using the Internet. Is this a problem? Why or why not?

C   **Talk about the answers with your class.**

PROBLEM SOLVING

A   **Listen and read about Eric.**

Eric doesn't know how to use a computer very well. Everyone in his family is good with computers, and Eric would like to be able to use email and find information on the Internet.

Eric's brother, Louis, is a computer expert. Louis has offered to help Eric learn to use the Internet, but it's difficult for Eric to learn from his brother. Louis talks quickly, and he likes to show Eric how to do things instead of letting Eric try for himself. Eric finds it really hard to learn that way. Eric likes having his brother's help, but so far, he hasn't learned anything.

B   **Work with your classmates. Answer the questions.**

1. What is Eric's problem? It's difficult for Eric to learn how to use email and the Internet from his brother.
2. What could he do? Think of 2 or 3 solutions to Eric's problem.
3. Write a conversation between Eric and his brother.

How did I do?

FOCUS ON
• achievements and leadership
• personal goals and plans
• gerunds as objects
• giving and getting feedback
• success stories

LESSON **1** Vocabulary

1 Learn achievement vocabulary

A Talk about the questions with your class.

1. What is something you've done that you're really proud of?
2. What is something you'd like to achieve in your life?

B Work with your classmates. Match the words with the pictures.

__5__ achieve a goal   __1__ have a dream   __3__ start a business

__6__ give back to the community   __4__ overcome adversity   __2__ win a scholarship

C Listen and check. Then read the new words with a partner.

D Work with a partner. Write other achievement words you know. Check your words in a dictionary.

✔ Identify and use achievement and leadership vocabulary

Unit 12 Lesson 1

Objectives	Grammar	Vocabulary	Correlations
On-level: Describe and talk about achievements and leadership qualities **Pre-level:** Identify and describe achievements leadership qualities **Higher-level:** Talk and write about achievements and leadership qualities	Adjectives (*I am confident.*)	Achievements and leadership qualities For vocabulary support for pre-level students, see this **Oxford Picture Dictionary** topic: Life Events and Documents	**CASAS:** 0.1.2, 0.1.5, 0.2.1, 4.8.1, 7.4.5 **LCPs:** 39.01, 49.02, 49.10 **SCANS:** Participates as member of a team, Reading, Seeing things in the mind's eye **EFF** Cooperate with others, Listen actively, Observe critically, Read with understanding, Speak so others can understand, Reflect and evaluate

Warm-up and Review

10–15 minutes (books closed)

Write *Famous Person* and *Person I Know* on the board. Ask students to name people they admire, and write the names in the correct column. (For *Person I Know*, include the relationship—*my mother, my friend Joe,* etc.)

Introduction

5 minutes

1. Ask volunteers to talk about why they admire the people on the board. Say: *We usually admire people for their achievements and their qualities.*

2. State the objective: *Today we're going to talk about achievements and leadership qualities.*

1 Learn achievement vocabulary

Presentation I

20–25 minutes

A Elicit students' answers to questions 1 and 2. Write the things they are proud of on the board.

B 1. Direct students to look at the pictures. Ask: *Has he had a good life?*

2. Group students and assign roles: leader, fact checker, recorder, and reporter. Explain that students work with their groups to match the words and pictures.

3. Check comprehension of the roles. Ask: *Who looks up the words in a dictionary?* [fact checker] *Who writes the numbers in the book?* [recorder] *Who tells the class your answers?* [reporter] *Who helps everyone and manages the group?* [leader]

4. Set a time limit (three minutes). As students work together, copy the wordlist onto the board.

5. Call "time." Have reporters take turns giving their answers. Write each group's answer on the board next to the word.

C 1. To prepare students for listening, tell them: *We're going to listen to Elio Moya talk to a reporter about his life.* Ask students to listen and check their answers.

2. Have students check the wordlist on the board and then write the correct numbers in their books.

3. Pair students. Set a time limit (three minutes). Monitor pair practice to identify pronunciation issues.

4. Call "time" and work with the pronunciation of any troublesome words or phrases.

5. Replay the audio and challenge students to listen for the answers to these questions: *What were his dreams? Did he realize all of them? What happened to his shop?*

D 1. Ask students to work with their partners from 1C to brainstorm a list of related words.

2. Elicit words from the class. Write them on the board. Ask students to copy them into their vocabulary notes for the unit.

Guided Practice

5–10 minutes

 1. Read the questions and answers aloud. Set a time limit (three minutes). Direct students to ask and answer the questions with a partner.

2. Ask volunteers to share the answers with the class.

2 Learn vocabulary for leadership qualities

Presentation II

15–20 minutes

 1. Direct students to look at the checklist. Introduce the new topic. Say: *Now we're going to look at a checklist of leadership qualities. Read through it, and check the words that describe you.*

2. Say and have students repeat the words. Check comprehension. Ask: *What word means you'll try something even if it's difficult or scary?* [courageous]

Guided Practice

10–15 minutes

 1. Model the conversation with a volunteer. Take the role of Partner B.

2. Set a time limit (three minutes). Tell students to practice the conversation with a partner. Call on volunteers to say one of their conversations for the class.

> **TIP**
> After 2B, ask students to apply this vocabulary to the famous people they mentioned during the warm-up. Ask: *Which words describe _____? Why?* Encourage students to supply specific examples of how the person demonstrates the leadership quality.

Communicative Practice and Application

10–15 minutes

 1. Give students a minute to make notes of their answers to the questions. Call on individuals to share their ideas with the class.

2. When students answer question 2, encourage them to be specific about how people they know demonstrate the leadership qualities.

Evaluation

10–15 minutes (books closed)

TEST YOURSELF

1. Make a two-column chart on the board with the headings *Goals and Achievements* and *Leadership Qualities*. Have students close their books and give you an example for each column.

2. Have students copy the chart into their notebooks.

3. Give students five to ten minutes to test themselves by writing the words they recall from the lesson.

4. Call "time" and have students check their spelling in a dictionary. Circulate and monitor students' progress.

5. Direct students to share their work with a partner and add additional words to their charts.

> **Multilevel Strategies**
>
> Target the *Test Yourself* to the level of your students.
>
> • **Higher-level** Have these students complete the chart and then write an example of behavior that demonstrates each leadership quality.

To compress this lesson: Conduct 1B as a whole-class activity.

To extend this lesson: Have students write about someone they admire. Put students in mixed-level groups. Tell the group to think of someone they all admire. Direct them to work together to write a list of the person's achievements and qualities. Have a reporter from each group share the group's work with the class.

And/Or have students complete **Workbook 4 page 79** and **Multilevel Activity Book 4 pages 128–129**.

E **Work with a partner. Talk about these questions. Use the words in 1B.**

1. What things did Elio do before he achieved his goal?
2. Why do you think Elio wanted to give back to the community?

2 Learn vocabulary for leadership qualities

A **Look at the checklist. Check the words that describe you.**

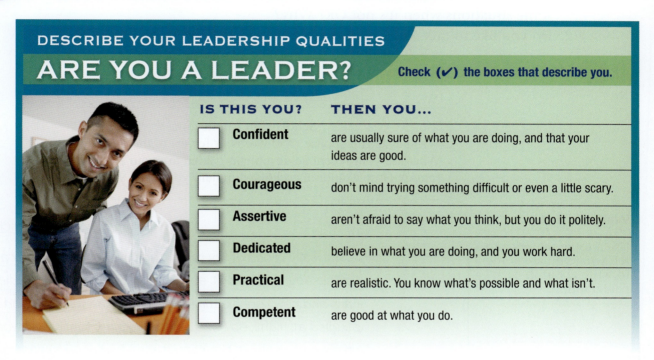

DESCRIBE YOUR LEADERSHIP QUALITIES

ARE YOU A LEADER?

Check (✔) the boxes that describe you.

IS THIS YOU?	THEN YOU...
☐ Confident	are usually sure of what you are doing, and that your ideas are good.
☐ Courageous	don't mind trying something difficult or even a little scary.
☐ Assertive	aren't afraid to say what you think, but you do it politely.
☐ Dedicated	believe in what you are doing, and you work hard.
☐ Practical	are realistic. You know what's possible and what isn't.
☐ Competent	are good at what you do.

B **Work with a partner. Practice the conversation. Use the words in 2A.**

A: *Which leadership qualities do you think you have?*
B: *Well, I'm not afraid to say what I think, so I guess I'm pretty assertive. What about you?*
A: *I'm really dedicated. I believe in what I'm doing.*

C **Talk about the questions with your class.**

1. Talk about someone you know who has achieved something important. What did the person do before he or she achieved the goal?
2. Talk about someone you know who has good leadership qualities. Which qualities does the person have? How do you know?

TEST YOURSELF ✔

Close your book. Categorize the new words in two lists: *Goals and Achievements* and *Leadership Qualities*. Check your spelling in a dictionary. Compare your lists with a partner.

1 Read an application essay

A **Talk about the questions with your class.**

1. What are some situations when it's OK to talk about your achievements? What are some situations when it's not OK? Why?
2. Do you like to talk about your plans for the future? Why or why not?

B **Listen and read the essay.**

Scholarship Application
Write a short response (150 words or fewer) to these questions:
What are your recent achievements? What are your goals for the future? How would this scholarship help you reach your goals?

Writer's note

Use a topic sentence to tell what you are going to write about in each paragraph.

Name: _Victoria Sanchez_

I'm really proud of my recent achievements. When I came to this country, I didn't speak much English, but I studied hard and now I speak English well. I worked full-time and studied at night, so I was able to help my family and work on my own goals at the same time. I had good evaluations at my job, and last year I received an Outstanding Volunteer award for my work at the City Help Center.

I have several important goals. My first goal is to get a college degree. Then I plan to go to law school. I dream about being a lawyer. I'd like to be able to help people and contribute to the community that has helped and supported me. Receiving this scholarship would give me the money I need to start my education and make my dream come true.

C **Check your understanding. Work with a partner. Ask and answer the questions.**

1. What did Victoria choose to say in her topic sentences? Why? She writes about her recent achievements and goals so she can win the scholarship.
2. Why did she list both school and non-school achievements? Answers will vary.
3. What goals did she list? get a college degree and go to law school
4. Did she answer all of the questions in the application? yes
5. How many words did she use? Was she within the limit? She used 144 words. Yes, she was in the limit.

Unit 12 Lesson 2

Objectives	Grammar	Vocabulary	Correlations
On- and Higher-level: Analyze, write, and edit an application essay in response to a prompt **Pre-level:** Read an application essay, and write a paragraph in response to a prompt	Past and present tense (*I studied hard, and now I speak very well.*)	Achievements For vocabulary support for pre-level students, see this **Oxford Picture Dictionary** topic: Life Events and Documents	**CASAS:** 0.1.2, 0.1.5, 0.2.1, 7.1.1 **LCPs:** 39.01, 49.13, 49.16 **SCANS:** Knowing how to learn, Listening, Participates as member of a team, Reading, Speaking **EFF:** Convey ideas in writing, Listen actively, Read with understanding, Reflect and evaluate

Warm-up and Review
10–15 minutes (books closed)

Ask students what they think is required to get into a four-year college or to get a college scholarship. Write their ideas on the board.

Introduction
5 minutes

1. If students mentioned *essay*, circle it on the board. If they didn't mention it, write it. Say: *Many people don't realize that a very important part of a four-year college application is the essay you write to get in. In addition, many scholarships are won because of a student's ability to write a convincing essay.*

2. State the objective: *Today we're going to read and write an application essay.*

1 Read an application essay

Presentation
20–25 minutes

A Read the questions aloud, and elicit students' answers. Point out that although many people are uncomfortable talking about their achievements, in an application essay (as well as in a resume cover letter), it's important to be able to describe them.

B 1. Read the title aloud.

2. Direct students to read the application essay silently. Check comprehension. Ask: *Did Victoria answer all of the questions?* [yes] *What's her most important goal?* [to go to college]

3. Play the audio. Have students read along silently.

4. Draw students' attention to the *Writer's note*. Ask a volunteer to read the topic sentences from both paragraphs. Point out that all the other sentences in the paragraph support the topic sentence.

Guided Practice I
10 minutes

C Have students work with a partner to answer the questions. Call on volunteers to say the answers for the class.

Multilevel Strategies

Seat pre-level students together for 1C.

• **Pre-level** While other students are working on 1C in pairs, sit with this group. Ask the questions aloud, and help these students find any difficult answers.

• **On- and Higher-level** Ask these students to note the answers as they talk to their partners.

2 Write an application essay

Guided Practice II
20–25 minutes

 1. Read the questions. Elicit students' answers.

2. List students' ideas for question 2 on the board.

 1. Direct students to look back at the essay in 1B. Read the questions for paragraph 1 and paragraph 2 aloud. Ask students to identify how Victoria answered the questions.

2. Tell students to follow the essay outline as they write their essay in their notebooks.

3. Check comprehension of the exercise. Ask: *How many paragraphs are you going to write?*

4. Have students work individually to write their essays.

Multilevel Strategies

Adapt 2B to the level of your students.

• **Pre-level** Tell these students to compose their essays by writing a one-sentence answer to each question.

C 1. Lead students through the process of using the *Editing checklist*. Read each sentence aloud, and ask students to check their papers before moving onto the next item.

2. Allow students a few minutes to edit their writing as necessary.

TIP Call the admissions counselor at a university in your area to get a recommendation for a scholarship search website. These sites provide services that allow students, ages 13 and up, to complete a profile and then get a list of scholarships for which they might be eligible. The list includes all of the necessary application information. Such sites can be an excellent source of higher-education funding, but students should not use them unless they are recommended by a reputable source.

Communicative Practice
10 minutes

 1. Read the instructions aloud. Emphasize to students that they are responding to their partners' work, not correcting it.

2. Use the essay in 1B to model the exercise. *I think the part about receiving the Outstanding Volunteer Award might help her get the scholarship. I'd like to ask the writer about what she did at the City Help Center and what her job was.*

3. Direct students to exchange papers with a partner and follow the instructions.

4. Call on volunteers to share some interesting things they read in their partners' essays.

Application and Evaluation
20 minutes

TEST YOURSELF

1. Review the instructions aloud. Assign a time limit (15 minutes), and have students work independently. Give students notice when they have five minutes left.

2. Before collecting students' work, remind them to use the *Editing checklist*. Collect and correct students' writing.

Multilevel Strategies

Adapt the *Test Yourself* to the level of your students.

• **Pre-level** Tell these students to compose their essays by writing a one-sentence answer to each question in 2B using their partners' information instead of their own.

To compress this lesson: Assign the *Test Yourself* for homework.

To extend this lesson: Have students talk about their partners' achievements. After 2D, have each pair join with another pair. Tell each student to tell the new group about his or her partner's achievements.

And/Or have students complete **Workbook 4 page 80** and **Multilevel Activity Book 4 page 130**.

2 Write an application essay

A **Talk about the questions with your class.**

1. Why do people usually apply for scholarships?
2. What kinds of achievements help people get scholarships and other awards?

B **Write a short essay about your achievements and goals for a scholarship application. Use the model in 1B and the questions below to help you.**

Paragraph 1: How do you feel about your recent achievements? (your topic sentence)
What are your recent achievements?
What did you do to achieve these things?

Paragraph 2: How many goals do you have for the future? (your topic sentence)
What are your goals and plans for the future?
How will this scholarship help you reach your goals?

Scholarship Application
Write a short response (150 words or fewer) to these questions:
What are your recent achievements? What are your goals for the future? How would this scholarship help you achieve your goals?

Name: _____

I'm really proud of my recent achievements…

I have several goals for the future…

C **Use the checklist to edit your writing. Check (✔) the true sentences.**

Editing checklist	
1. My topic sentences tell what I am going to write about.	
2. In the first paragraph, I wrote about my achievements.	
3. In the second paragraph, I wrote about my goals.	
4. My essay is not more than 150 words.	

D **Exchange essays with a partner. Read and comment on your partner's work.**

1. Point out one sentence that you think will help your partner get a scholarship.
2. Ask your partner about his or her achievements and goals.

TEST YOURSELF ✔

Write a new essay to recommend your partner for a scholarship. Talk about your partner's achievements and goals and why your partner should receive the scholarship.

1 Learn to use gerunds after prepositions

A Read the performance review. What is Kim Tran's job title? Desk Clerk

S&S hotels — PERFORMANCE REVIEW

Name Kim Tran   Title Desk Clerk   Reviewing Manager M. Perez

Period of Review 9/06 - 9/07   Date of Review 10/15/07

Rating Codes: E = excellent   S = satisfactory   NI = needs improvement

Responsibility	Rating	Comments
Greets hotel guests, answers questions and requests	E	Ms. Tran does a good job of (welcoming) guests. She cares about (helping) people.
Records information accurately	S	She checks information after (recording) it.
Takes phone messages	NI	She needs to work on (taking) messages.

B Study the chart. Circle the 4 examples of gerunds after prepositions in 1A.

GERUNDS AFTER PREPOSITIONS

Preposition + gerund
She does a good job **of welcoming** guests.
She knows a lot **about managing** the front desk.
Instead **of getting** a promotion, she got a raise.
She needs to work **on taking** messages.

Notes
• Gerunds are used after prepositions like *about, at, for, in, of,* and *to*. • Gerunds are also used after verb phrases with prepositions: She cares about **helping** people.

C Complete the sentences in Kim's review. Use gerunds.

Kim does a good job of _____greeting_____ guests and _____asking_____ them about
                          1. greet   2. ask

their stay when they check out. Before _____calling_____ me about problems, she tries
                                       3. call

to solve them herself. Kim often works late hours without _____complaining_____. Instead of
                                                              4. complain

_____sitting_____ down when the desk isn't busy, she helps out by _____looking_____ for
5. sit   6. look

extra work to do. Her work contributes to _____making_____ the hotel more welcoming for
                                            7. make

our guests.

Unit 12 Lesson 3

Objectives	Grammar	Vocabulary	Correlations
On-, Pre-, and Higher-level: Use gerunds after prepositions to interpret evaluations and feedback	Gerunds after prepositions (*She knows a lot about working the front desk.*)	Employment words, *performance review* For vocabulary support for pre-level students, see this **Oxford Picture Dictionary** unit and topic: Work, A Hotel	**CASAS:** 0.1.2, 0.1.5, 0.2.1, 0.2.4, 7.4.7 **LCPs:** 39.01, 49.03, 49.09, 49.13, 49.17, 50.06 **SCANS:** Listening, Reading, Speaking, Writing **EFF:** Convey ideas in writing, Listen actively, Observe critically, Read with understanding, Reflect and evaluate, Speak so others can understand

Warm-up and Review

10–15 minutes (books closed)

Ask: *What are you good at?* Write students' answers on the board. Ask: *What do you know a lot about?* Write the answers on the board. If a student supplies a simple verb, change it to a gerund.

Introduction

5–10 minutes

1. Circle any gerunds that are on the board. Say: *We use this form here because* good at *and* know about *have prepositions at the end.*

2. State the objective: *Today we're going to use gerunds after prepositions to evaluate and give feedback.*

1 Learn to use gerunds after prepositions

Presentation I

20–25 minutes

A Read the instructions. Discuss the meaning of *performance review*. Ask students to read the performance review silently to find the answer to the question. Elicit the answer.

B 1. Read the sentences in the chart aloud.

2. Direct students to circle the examples of gerunds after prepositions in 1A. Go over the answers as a class.

3. Read the *Notes* aloud.

4. Assess students' understanding of the charts. Write these sentence skeletons on the board: *We talked about _____. She's an expert at _____. I thanked him for _____. They succeeded in _____. We bought lunch instead of _____. I'm used to _____.* Tell students to complete the sentences with *make* (in gerund form). Elicit their ideas and write them on the board.

Guided Practice I

15–20 minutes

C Ask students to work individually to complete the paragraph. Ask volunteers to write the answers on the board.

Multilevel Strategies

After 1C, seat students in same-level pairs.

• **Pre-level** Tell these students to complete these sentences about their partner: *She/He is good at _____. She/He knows a lot about _____. She/He cares about _____. She/He is looking forward to _____.*

• **On- and Higher-level** Have these students write five sentences about their partners using any preposition + gerund combination.

Guided Practice II

5–10 minutes

D Ask students to work individually to match the sentence parts. Have volunteers read the complete sentences aloud.

> ### Multilevel Strategies
>
> Adapt 1D to the level of your students.
>
> **Pre-level** Work with this group. Read each sentence beginning aloud, and have students match the correct ending before moving on to the next item.

2 Learn gerunds after *be* + adjective + preposition

Presentation II

20–25 minutes

A 1. Introduce the new topic. Say: *Now we're going to look at more gerunds after prepositions, this time with adjectives.*

2. Read the instructions. Read the sentences in the chart aloud, and elicit the answer to the question.

3. Read the *Note.*

Guided Practice I

10–15 minutes

B 1. Read and have students repeat the list of adjectives + prepositions.

2. Have students work individually to complete the sentences. Ask partners to take turns reading the questions and answers. Have volunteer pairs read the conversations aloud.

> ### Multilevel Strategies
>
> For 2B and 2C, use mixed-level pairs.
>
> • **Pre-level** For 2B, have these students complete as many of the sentences as they can. Tell them to check with their partners for the answers they don't know.
>
> For 2C, encourage these students to write short answers to the questions. Have them ask their partners the questions and listen to the answers before they answer the questions themselves.
>
> • **On- and Higher-level** For 2B, ask these students to assist their partners before they read the conversations aloud.
>
> For 2C, tell these students to answer the questions first to provide a model for their partners.

C Ask students to work individually to write their answers to the questions. Have them ask and answer the questions with a partner.

> ### Multilevel Strategies
>
> After 2C, provide more practice with gerunds after prepositions. Target the practice to the level of your students.
>
> • **Pre-level** Give these students scrambled sentences. When they finish unscrambling them, ask them to write the sentences on the board. *1. new learning not afraid he's of things.* [He's not afraid of learning new things.] *2. class interested taking they're another in* [They're interested in taking another class.] *3. a lot furniture about building knows he* [He knows a lot about building furniture.] *4. trying best believes she in her* [She believes in trying her best.] *5. nervous I front about in am of class the speaking* [I am nervous about speaking in front of the class.]
>
> • **On-level** Ask these students to write a new conversation using the expressions in the box in 2B. Ask volunteer pairs to read their conversations aloud for the class.
>
> • **Higher-level** Ask these students to write a new conversation using these adjective or verb + preposition phrases followed by a gerund: *thank you for _____, sorry about _____, worried about _____, believe in _____, plan on _____.* Ask volunteer pairs to read their conversations aloud for the class.

D Match the parts of the sentences.

  _b_ 1. Kim cares about   a. helping employees.

  _c_ 2. She sometimes worries about   b. doing her job well.

  _a_ 3. The hotel managers believe in   c. remembering people's names.

  _d_ 4. Kim looks forward to   d. learning more about the hotel business.

2 Learn gerunds after *be* + adjective + preposition

A Study the chart. What verb is used in all of these sentences? be

Be + adjective + preposition + gerund
The manager **is responsible for evaluating** Kim's work.
Kim **was happy about getting** a raise.
The guests **were interested in hearing** about the hotel's services.

Note
Certain adjectives are almost always followed by a preposition. For example, *interested* is usually followed by *in*: She's interested in taking a management class.

B Look at the adjectives + prepositions in the box. Complete the sentences. Then compare answers with a partner.

nervous about   tired of   ~~good at~~   proud of   interested in

1. **A:** Is your boss _____good at_____ giving helpful feedback?

   B: No. My boss marks everyone "Needs Improvement."

2. **A:** I'm really _____nervous about_____ being evaluated next week.
   Reviews make my stomach hurt.

   B: Don't worry. Your boss is only _____interested in_____ helping you.
   That's what feedback is for.

3. **A:** Aren't you _____tired of_____ doing the same work every day?

   B: Not really. I'm _____proud of_____ being good at what I do.

C Write your answers. Then ask and answer the questions with a partner.

1. What are you interested in learning?

2. What are you afraid of doing?

3. What do you believe in doing?

3 Grammar listening

🎧 **Listen to the people talk about Michael. Choose the sentences with the same meaning. Circle *a* or *b*.**

1. **a.** He might try a new career.
   b. He tried a new career.

2. a. He's tired all the time.
   b. He doesn't like his job.

3. **a.** He'll start a new business.
   b. He'll stay with the company.

4. a. He's spent his money.
   b. He's saved his money.

5. a. His job makes him nervous.
   b. The change makes him nervous.

6. **a.** He'll make a decision.
   b. He's made a decision.

4 Practice gerunds after prepositions

A **Think about your answers to these questions.**

1. What are you good at doing?
2. What is one thing you have been thinking about doing but have never done?
3. What is one thing you are tired of doing every day?
4. What are you planning on doing in the future?
5. What's one change you plan on making in the next five years?

B **Work with a partner. Ask and answer the questions.**

A: *What are you good at doing?*
B: *Well, I'm pretty good at…*

C **Talk about your partner with the class.**

Ernestine is good at…

TEST YOURSELF ✔

Close your book. Write 6 sentences about yourself and your partner.
Use the information from 4A and 4B. Use a gerund after a preposition
in each sentence.

3 Grammar listening

Guided Practice II

10–15 minutes

1. Say: *Now we're going to listen to some sentences about a man named Michael. Michael is thinking about his goals.*

2. Play the audio. Direct students to read along silently without writing.

3. Replay the audio. Ask students to circle the letter of the sentence with the same meaning.

4. Go over the answers as a class.

> ### Multilevel Strategies
>
> Replay the *Grammar listening* to allow pre-level students to catch up while you challenge on- and higher-level students.
>
> • **Pre-level** Have these students listen again to choose the sentence with the same meaning.
>
> • **On- and Higher-level** Have these students listen again and write the preposition + gerund combination that they hear.

4 Practice gerunds after prepositions

Communicative Practice and Application

20–25 minutes

A 1. Direct students to look at the photos. Ask what each person is doing. Ask which activity looks more interesting.

2. Read the questions aloud. Ask students to think about and note their answers.

B 1. Put students in pairs, and have them ask their partners the questions. Tell them to make notes of each other's answers. Model the exercise by asking a volunteer the first question. Have the class tell you how to write the answer in note form. Encourage students to give complete (not one- or two-word) answers.

3. Check comprehension of the exercise. Ask: *Are you giving short answers or having a conversation?* [having a conversation] Set a time limit for the exercise (four minutes), and observe and take note of issues that arise.

C Call on individuals to share some interesting things they learned about their partners.

Evaluation

10–15 minutes (books closed)

TEST YOURSELF

Ask students to write the sentence independently. Collect and correct their writing.

> ### Multilevel Strategies
>
> Target the *Test Yourself* to the level of your students.
>
> • **Pre-level** Provide skeleton sentences for these students to complete. _____ (partner's name) *is good at* _____. _____ (partner's name) *is tired of* _____. _____ (partner's name) *is thinking about* _____. _____ (partner's name) *is planning on* _____ *in the summer.*
>
> • **Higher-level** Have these students write a paragraph in response to this question and the accompanying instructions: *What are some similarities and differences between you and your partner? Use at least three preposition + gerund combinations in your paragraph.*

To compress this lesson: Conduct 1C as a whole-class discussion.

To extend this lesson: Use preposition + gerund combinations to describe job skills Ask students what occupations they think are interesting, and write them on the board. Put students in pairs. Have them talk with their partners about what people in each profession are good at, what they know a lot about, what they are probably interested in, and what they probably get tired of doing. Call on volunteers to share their ideas with the class.

And/Or have students complete **Workbook 4 pages 81–82, Multilevel Activity Book 4 pages 131–132,** and the corresponding **Unit 12 Exercises** on the **Multilevel Grammar Exercises CD-ROM 4.**

Unit 12 Lesson 4

Objectives	Grammar	Vocabulary	Correlations
On-, Pre-, and Higher-level: Respond to positive feedback and criticism in a performance review	Suggestions with gerunds (*I suggest taking the training.*)	Work, Feelings For vocabulary support for pre-level students, see this **Oxford Picture Dictionary** unit: Work	**CASAS:** 0.1.2, 0.1.5, 4.4.4, 6.0.3, 6.0.4, 6.2.3, 6.4.2, 6.4.3, 6.7.4, 7.5.6 **LCPs:** 49.02, 49.09, 49.16, 51.05 **SCANS:** Arithmetic/Mathematics, Listening, Seeing things in the mind's eye **EFF:** Listen actively, Observe critically, Read with understanding, Use math to solve problems and communicate

Warm-up and Review

10–15 minutes (books closed)

Put adjectives from the previous lesson on the board: *nervous, tired, good, worried, proud, interested, afraid, responsible, happy.* Elicit the prepositions to go with the adjectives; then elicit a sentence using the combination with a gerund.

Introduction

5 minutes

1. Ask students if they've ever had a performance review. Ask: *Would you be nervous about going through one?*

2. State the objective: *Today we'll learn to ask and answer questions in a performance review and listen for feedback from the boss.*

1 Learn to participate in a performance review

Presentation I

15–20 minutes

A Read the questions aloud. Play the audio. Give students a minute to ask and answer the questions with a partner. Go over the answers as a class.

Guided Practice

20–25 minutes

B 1. Read the instructions aloud. Play the audio. Ask students to read along silently and listen for the answer to the question. Elicit the answer.

2. Ask students to read the conversation with a partner. Circulate and monitor pronunciation. Model and have students repeat difficult words or phrases.

3. Say and have students repeat the expressions in the *In other words* box. Elicit the placement of the expressions in the conversation. Ask volunteers to read the conversation using expressions from the box.

4. Go over the *Idiom note*. Elicit other ways to use *deal with*—for example, deal with a situation, deal with customers, deal with problems.

Communicative Practice and Application

15–20 minutes

C 1. Ask students to read the instructions silently. Check their comprehension of the exercise. Ask: *What are the two roles? What is the situation?* Elicit examples of what the manager and the employee might say.

2. Set a time limit (five minutes). Ask students to act out the role-play in both roles. Ask one to three volunteer pairs to act out their conversations for the class. Tell students who are listening to note how the employee responds to feedback.

Multilevel Strategies

For 1C, adapt the role-play to the level of your students.

• **Pre-level** Give these students the beginning of the role-play. *A: You've done a great job this year. B: Thank you. A: You've done a great job of keeping the store neat and handling money. B: Thanks for saying so. A: However, _____.*

T-165

1 Learn to participate in a performance review

 **A** Look at the picture. Listen to the conversation. Then answer the questions below with your classmates.

1. What positive feedback does Kim hear?
2. What negative feedback does she hear?

She's done a great job of helping out the chef and learned a lot about working in a restaurant kitchen. She's often late for work.

 **B** Listen and read. What does Kim's supervisor want her to do?

He wants her to improve the way she deals with phone messages.

A: Well, Kim, you've done pretty well this past year.

B: Thank you.

A: You've done a great job of helping guests, and you've started making suggestions, too. I really value that.

B: I appreciate your saying so.

A: I'd like to see some improvement, though, in the way you deal with* phone messages. Sometimes your co-workers can't understand the phone messages you write.

B: Oh, I'm sorry. I didn't know there was a problem. Can you tell me what I need to do?

A: I'd suggest asking the caller about anything you don't understand.

B: I see. I'll try to do better.

A: That would be great.

Idiom note: deal with = take care of

In other words...

Responding to feedback

I appreciate your saying so.

I didn't know there was a problem.

Thanks for saying so.

I didn't realize anything was wrong.

C Role-play a performance review with a partner. Use the example in 1B to make a new conversation.

Partner A: You're the manager of a clothing store. Go over your employee's performance review. Your employee keeps the store neat and handles money well. You'd like to see some improvement in his or her customer service. Sometimes the employee avoids talking to customers. Tell your employee to offer to help customers when they walk in the door.

Partner B: You're an employee at a clothing store. Listen and respond to the manager's positive feedback. Listen to the manager's negative feedback and ask for advice. Promise to do better.

2 Learn polite requests and suggestions with gerunds

A Study the chart. What two phrases can you use to make polite requests and suggestions in question form?

Polite requests and suggestions with gerunds
I would suggest delivering messages right away.
I'd recommend taking a training class.
May I suggest getting an earlier bus?
Would you mind telling me a little more about the opportunity?

B Work with a partner. Write polite requests or suggestions. Use each polite expression in 2A once.

1. Can I give you some advice? Apply for a management position.

   May I suggest applying for a management position?

2. Give me some more information.

   Would you mind giving me some more information?

3. Think about your long-term goals.

   I would recommend/suggest thinking about your long-term goals.

4. Make a plan to reach your goals.

   I would recommend/suggest making a plan to reach your goals.

C Work with a partner. Read the actions in the box. Which things should you avoid doing at a performance review? Which would you recommend doing?

argue   listen carefully   talk a lot   criticize co-workers   ask for suggestions

I'd avoid arguing with my supervisor. I'd recommend...

3 Practice your pronunciation

A Listen to the sentences. Notice how the words are grouped. (∧ = pause)

1. I'd suggest asking the caller ∧ about anything you don't understand.
2. I was able to help my family ∧ and work on my own goals ∧ at the same time.

B Listen and mark (∧) the pauses in these sentences.

1. I'd like to see some changes ∧ in the way you deal with phone messages.
2. Is a training class for cooks ∧ something you'd be interested in?
3. She helps out her co-workers ∧ by looking for extra work to do.
4. I've learned a lot about working in a restaurant kitchen ∧ since I got this job.

C Practice the sentences in 3A and 3B with a partner.

2 Learn polite requests and suggestions with gerunds

Presentation II

10–15 minutes

A 1. Introduce the new topic. *Now we're going to make polite requests and suggestions with gerunds.*

2. Read the instructions aloud. Read the sentences in the chart aloud, and elicit the answer to the question.

3. Read the sentences again and have students repeat them.

4. Check comprehension. Write a series of common commands on the board. *Bring a pencil to school. Listen to the teacher. Come to class on time. Take notes.* Call on students to turn the commands into polite requests and suggestions using gerunds.

Guided Practice

15–20 minutes

B Have students work individually to turn the commands into polite requests and suggestions. Have volunteers write their sentences on the board.

> ### Multilevel Strategies
>
> Adapt 2B to the level of your students.
> • **Pre-level** Provide these students with sentence skeletons. *2. Would you mind _____. 3. I would suggest _____. 4. I'd recommend _____.*

Communicative Practice and Application

10–15 minutes

C 1. Read and have students repeat the words in the box. Read the sample sentence aloud.

2. Set a time limit (five minutes). Ask students to work with their partners to talk about which things they would avoid and which they would recommend. Call on volunteers to share their answers.

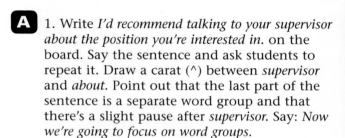

After 2C, provide more practice with *avoid* and *recommend*. Tell students they have a friend who is just beginning to learn English. Ask them to use *avoid* and *recommend* to give advice about how to make the language-learning process go smoothly. Elicit their advice.

3 Practice your pronunciation

Pronunciation Extension

10–15 minutes

A 1. Write *I'd recommend talking to your supervisor about the position you're interested in.* on the board. Say the sentence and ask students to repeat it. Draw a carat (^) between *supervisor* and *about*. Point out that the last part of the sentence is a separate word group and that there's a slight pause after *supervisor*. Say: *Now we're going to focus on word groups.*

2. Play the audio. Direct students to listen for the pauses. Have students repeat the sentences.

B Play the audio. Ask students to mark the pauses. Go over the answers as a class.

C Have students work with a partner to practice saying the sentences in 3A and 3B.

For further practice with requests and suggestions, read this story to your class: *You are a server in a restaurant. One of your co-workers is a waitress named Nancy. She's very nice and you'd like her to keep her job, but the boss is not happy with her, and sometimes her habits make your job more difficult. Listen to this information about Nancy; then write some suggestions for her: Nancy usually arrives at work just at the moment her shift is supposed to start, but she's out of uniform. She goes into the bathroom to change into her uniform and ends up starting her shift ten minutes late. She's very friendly and sometimes she gets so interested in talking to one customer that she forgets about her other customers. She doesn't work very efficiently. She does one thing at a time. For example: She takes one order, gives it to the kitchen, and then comes back to take another order.*

Repeat the information about Nancy. Have students work with a partner to write their advice. Call on volunteers to share their sentences.

4 Focus on Listening

Listening Extension

20–25 minutes

A Read the questions aloud, and elicit answers from volunteers. Write their ideas on the board.

B Say: *Now we're going to listen to a manager giving positive feedback and criticism to an employee.* Direct students to listen to the audio and mark the correct column in the chart. Go over the answers as a class.

C Direct students to read the sentences before listening. Replay the audio and have students work individually to choose the best response. Go over the answers as a class. Take a tally of responses for each item and if students disagree on a response, replay the audio, so they can check their answers.

Multilevel Strategies

Replay the audio to challenge on- and higher-level students while allowing pre-level students to catch up.

• **Pre-level** Have these students listen again to go over their answers.

• **On- and Higher-level** Ask these students to make quick notes about what the manager says. Elicit what the manager said before you go over each response.

5 Real-life math

Math Extension

5–10 minutes

1. Read the instructions and the question. Ask two volunteers to count the number of students, and write it on the board.

2. Tell students that although everyone wants all three of the choices, for the purpose of this survey, they need to choose only the most important one. Ask for a show of hands for each choice. Have volunteers count the raised hands. Write the numbers on the board.

3. Have a volunteer explain how to figure the percentages. Write the problems on the board. Give students time to solve them. Then call on volunteers for the answers.

Evaluation

10–15 minutes

TEST YOURSELF

1. Model the role-play with a volunteer. Then switch roles.

2. Pair students. Check comprehension of the exercise by eliciting things the teacher and the student might say.

3. Set a time limit (five minutes), and have the partners act out the role-play in both roles.

4. Circulate and monitor. Encourage pantomime and improvisation.

5. Provide feedback.

Multilevel Strategies

Target the *Test Yourself* to the level of your students.

• **Pre-level** Give these students a skeleton to help them get started on the role-play. *Teacher: You've done a great job this year. Student: Thank you. T: You've done a great job of _____. B: Thanks for saying so. A: However, _____.*

To compress this lesson: Conduct 2B as a whole-class activity.

To extend this lesson: Make a compliment envelope with gerunds. Put students in large groups of eight or ten. Provide each person with an envelope and the same number of slips of paper as they have partners. Tell students to write something nice about one of their group members on each slip of paper. Encourage them to start their sentences with *(Name), you're very good at _____.* Or *I appreciate your _____.* Or *Thank you for _____.* Or *You do a good job of _____.* Have everyone put the slips of paper in the appropriate group member's envelope. Tell students to take the compliments home, read them, and smile.

And/Or have students complete **Workbook 4 page 83** and **Multilevel Activity Book 4 page 133**.

4 Focus on listening

A Talk about the questions with your class.

1. What are three things an employer can say to give positive feedback?
2. What are three ways an employer can introduce negative feedback?

B Listen to the speakers. Do the managers use positive feedback or negative feedback with the employees? Check (✔) *Positive feedback* or *Negative feedback*.

	Positive feedback	Negative feedback		Positive feedback	Negative feedback
1.		✔	4.	✔	
2.	✔		5.		✔
3.		✔	6.	✔	

C Listen again. Choose the best response. Circle *a* or *b*.

1. a. Thank you. I will.
   b. I'm really sorry.

2. a. Thanks. That's good to hear.
   b. I didn't know anything was wrong.

3. a. I appreciate your saying so.
   b. I'll try to do better.

4. a. I'm sorry, but I can't.
   b. I'm sorry.

5. a. Yes, I do.
   b. I didn't know there was a problem.

6. a. I didn't know anything was wrong.
   b. That's wonderful. Thank you.

5 Real-life math

A Survey the class. Ask the following question.

Are you most interested in having a career that you love, making a lot of money, or having a lot of free time?

B Write the totals for each response on the board. Figure out the percentage for each answer. Then make a pie chart to show your classmates' opinions.

There are 20 students in our class. Five students are most interested in making a lot of money. That's 25%.

TEST YOURSELF ✔

Role-play a classroom conversation. Partner A: You're an ESL teacher. Talk to a student. Tell the student two things he or she does well and one thing that needs work. Partner B: Listen and respond to the teacher's feedback. Then change roles.

1 Get ready to read

A Do you think there are jobs that only men, or only women, should do? Explain your answer.

B Read the definitions. What is one traditional thing that you do?

eventually: (adv.) after a long time
gradually: (adv.) slowly
tradition: (noun) something people in a culture have done for a long time

C Look at the title and the picture in the newspaper article in 2A. Write a question you think the article will answer.

2 Read and respond

A Read the article. What has Ms. Sugimoto achieved? She's the only female sushi chef in the restaurant where she works.

Eri Sugimoto's Story

Historically and traditionally, making sushi, the Japanese rice-and-raw-fish favorite, has always been a man's world. Some people believed that women's hands were too warm to make sushi. Today, however, the number of female sushi chefs in the U.S., and in Japan, is gradually starting to rise.

When Eri Sugimoto was in her early 20s, she worked as a cook at a restaurant in Tokyo, cooking home-style Japanese food. Over time, she became interested in learning to make sushi. "I have always wanted to work with raw fish because I love to eat it," said Ms. Sugimoto. However, she knew of only one sushi chef who was a woman.

She asked a friend who owned several sushi restaurants if she could apprentice[1] with one of his chefs. "I had to beg him to let me clean the restaurant," Ms. Sugimoto said. He said "yes," so she mopped floors, waited on tables, and learned to make sushi. She bought fish with her own money and practiced making sushi for hours at home. It took her a year just to make the rice correctly. Eventually, she learned to make fifty kinds of sushi, but she had to practice for two years before being allowed to serve her sushi to customers.

In 2000, Ms. Sugimoto finally began working at a sushi restaurant in New York City. She became the restaurant's only female sushi chef. The restaurant's owner said, "It's time to break tradition. Why not women chefs?"

Ms. Sugimoto's achievement has opened the door for others to reach their dreams.

[1] apprentice: learn a skill from an expert by working for him or her

Copyright © 2002 by the New York Times Co. Adapted from "She Has a Knife and She Knows How to Use It" by Elaine Louie, originally published June 5, 2002, by the New York Times

Unit 12 Lesson 5

Objectives	Grammar	Vocabulary	Correlations
On-, Pre-, and Higher-level: Read about and discuss a personal achievement	Past tense (*She worked as a cook at a restaurant in Tokyo.*)	*Eventually, gradually, tradition, apprentice* For vocabulary support for pre-level students, see this **Oxford Picture Dictionary** topic and unit: Life Events and Documents, Work	**CASAS:** 0.1.2, 0.1.5, 2.5.6, 7.2.2, 7.4.4 **LCPs:** 38.01, 49.06 **SCANS:** Acquires and evaluates information, Uses computers to process information **EFF:** Listen actively, Read with understanding, Speak so others can understand, Take responsibility for learning

Warm-up and Review

10–15 minutes (books closed)

Write *Women's Jobs* and *Men's Jobs* on the board. Ask volunteers to write in each column the jobs that are traditionally done by men and traditionally done by women.

Introduction

5 minutes

1. Ask students which of the jobs on the board they think are most interesting. Point out there can be many barriers in the way for a woman doing a traditionally male job or a man doing a traditionally female job. This can create more work for the person breaking the tradition.

2. State the objective: *Today we're going to read about and discuss this kind of personal achievement.*

1 Get ready to read

Presentation

15–20 minutes

A Read the question aloud. Find out if there are any of the jobs on the board that students think should never be done by the other sex. Elicit their reasons.

B Read the instructions and elicit an answer to the question. Read the words and definitions. Elicit sample sentences from students using the words.

Pre-Reading

C Direct students to look at the title and picture. Elicit the questions they think the story will answer, and write them on the board. Have students scan the article for the footnote. Read the definition and have students repeat the word *apprentice*. Ask if they know anyone who apprenticed in an occupation.

2 Read and respond

Guided Practice I

25–30 minutes

A 1. Ask students to read the article silently. After they've finished reading, direct students to underline unfamiliar words they would like to know. Elicit the words and encourage other students to provide definitions or examples.

2. Check comprehension. Ask: *How many female sushi chefs did Ms. Sugimoto know of? How long did she have to practice before she was allowed to serve her sushi to customers?*

Multilevel Strategies

Adapt 2A to the level of your students.

• **Pre-level** Provide these students with a summary of the reading. *Eri Sugimoto wanted to be a sushi chef, a job which was traditionally done only by men. In her 20s, she worked in a restaurant. She became interested in making sushi. She apprenticed with a sushi chef in exchange for cleaning a restaurant. She practiced making sushi for two years before she was allowed to serve sushi to customers. Now she is a sushi chef in New York.*

Direct students to read the summary while other students are reading 2A.

Guided Practice II

15–20 minutes

B 1. Play the audio. Have students read along silently.

2. Elicit and discuss any additional questions about the reading.

C Read the instructions and the first event aloud. Have students work individually to put the rest of the events in order. Go over the answers as a class.

Multilevel Strategies

For 2C, work with pre-level students.

• **Pre-level** Have these students refer to their summary to put the events in order.

D 1. Read the chart aloud. Elicit and discuss any questions the students have about compound adjectives. Say the words and have students repeat them.

2. Direct students to work individually to complete the sentences. Write the answers on the board.

Multilevel Strategies

For 2D, seat higher-level students together.

• **Higher-level** If these students finish early, ask them to think of other compound words (with or without hyphens) and make a list. Get them started with *newspaper, handbag, and sailboat.*

3 Talk it over

Communicative Practice

15–20 minutes

1. Read the questions aloud. Set a time limit (three minutes). Have students work independently to think about the questions, and write their answers in note form.

2. Elicit students answers to the questions. As a class, make a list of positive and negative aspects of the "good old days."

Application

5–10 minutes

BRING IT TO LIFE

Read the instructions aloud. Ask the class to brainstorm names of people they might want to look up. Write the names on the board. Tell students that if they are going to search the Internet, they should type the person's name plus *short biography* into a search engine. (Otherwise they are apt to get biographies that are many pages long.) Sometimes using an image search engine can also yield a short biography.

To compress this lesson: Conduct 2D as a whole-class activity.

To extend this lesson: After the class brainstorms the names of people to look up for their *Bring It to Life* assignment, have students talk about what they already know about the people.
1. Have students tell a partner, *I'm going to look up _____.* Direct the partner to ask questions about the person. Have students talk to several partners.
2. Tell students to make a note of the questions they couldn't answer. They can search for those answers in the biography.
And/Or have students complete **Workbook 4 page 84** and the **Multilevel Activity Book 4 pages 134–135.**

B Listen and read the article again.

C In what order did these events happen in Ms. Sugimoto's life? Number the events from 1 (first) to 5 (last).

___4___ 1. She served sushi to customers.

___2___ 2. She became interested in making sushi.

___5___ 3. She became a sushi chef at a restaurant in New York.

___3___ 4. She apprenticed with a sushi chef.

___1___ 5. She worked at a restaurant in Tokyo.

D Study the chart. Complete the sentences below with compound adjectives from the chart.

> **Word Study: Using hyphens to make compound adjectives**
>
> Sometimes two or more words are joined together by a hyphen (-) to show that they make one compund adjective.
>
> | Words | Compound Adjective |
> |---|---|
> | home style | home-style restaurant |
> | long term | long-term plans |
> | real life | real-life math |
> | sushi making | sushi-making class |

1. Ms. Sugimoto's __long-term__ goal was to learn to make sushi.
2. She was the only __sushi-making__ apprentice who was a woman.
3. Before that, she had worked in a restaurant doing __home-style__ cooking.
4. Today, hers is a __real-life__ success story.

3 Talk it over

Think about the questions. Talk about your ideas with the class.

1. How can the success of a person like Ms. Sugimoto help other people?
2. People often use the phrase "the good old days" to say that life was better in the past. What do you think about "the good old days"? Were they better? Why or why not?

BRING IT TO LIFE

Use the public library or the Internet to find an article with a short biography (life story) of an interesting person. Bring the biography to class and talk about the person's achievements with your group.

1 Grammar

A **Complete the sentences. Use the gerund form or the simple present of the verbs in parentheses.**

1. Alfredo doesn't believe in _____talking_____ about his achievements. He never _____talks_____ about them. (talk)

2. He _____volunteers_____ at the Literacy Center. He got an award for _____volunteering_____ to help people learn to read. (volunteer)

3. He never _____sits_____ down for long. He stays busy instead of _____sitting_____ on the couch and watching TV. (sit)

4. Alfredo cares about _____helping_____ people. He always _____helps_____ me. (help)

B **Complete the sentences with adjectives from the box.**

good	interested	nervous	proud	~~responsible~~	tired

1. At work, I'm _responsible_ for taking care of the youngest children.

2. At first, I wasn't very _____good_____ at talking to the parents.

3. Sometimes I think my family is _____tired_____ of hearing me talk about the children.

4. I'm happy with my work. I am _____proud_____ of doing a good job with the children.

5. I'm _____nervous_____ about getting my first performance review tomorrow. I'm _interested_ in hearing the director's feedback.

C **Complete the email. Use the verbs in parentheses.**

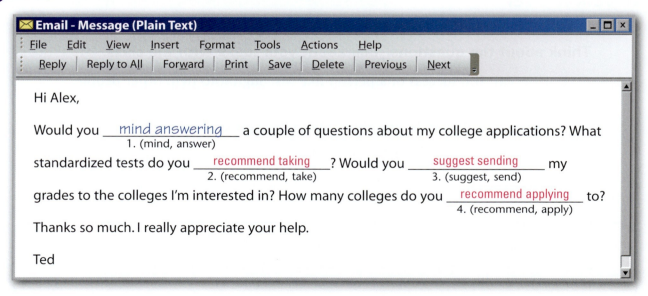

Email - Message (Plain Text)

File Edit View Insert Format Tools Actions Help

Reply Reply to All Forward Print Save Delete Previous Next

Hi Alex,

Would you ___mind answering___ a couple of questions about my college applications? What
      1. (mind, answer)

standardized tests do you ___recommend taking___? Would you ___suggest sending___ my
      2. (recommend, take)   3. (suggest, send)

grades to the colleges I'm interested in? How many colleges do you ___recommend applying___ to?
         4. (recommend, apply)

Thanks so much. I really appreciate your help.

Ted

Unit 12 Review and expand

Objectives	Grammar	Vocabulary	Correlations
On-, Pre-, and Higher-level: Review and expand upon unit grammar and life skills	Gerunds after verbs and prepositions (*I suggest studying more often. He's worried about losing his job.*)	Accomplishments and work For vocabulary support for pre-level students, see these **Oxford Picture Dictionary** topic and unit: Life Events and Documents, Work	**CASAS:** 0.1.2, 0.1.5, 0.2.1, 4.8.1, 7.1.1, 7.2.6, 7.3.1, 7.3.2, 7.3.4, 7.5.6 **LCPs:** 39.01, 49.02, 49.13, 49.16 **SCANS:** Creative thinking, Interprets and communicates information **EFF:** Convey ideas in writing, Listen actively, Read with understanding, Solve problems and make decisions

Warm-up and Review

10–15 minutes (books closed)

1. Review the *Bring It to Life* assignment from Lesson 5.

2. Have students who did the exercise discuss what they learned. Encourage students who didn't do the assignment to ask questions about the people their classmates looked up.

Introduction and Presentation

5 minutes

1. Use the information about the people students looked up to write sentences with gerunds. *(Maria) cared about helping people. (Lee) believed in standing up for the rights of others.*

2. State the objective: *Today we're going to review gerunds after verbs and gerunds after prepositions to talk about achievements and goals.*

1 Grammar

Guided Practice

40–45 minutes

A 1. Go over the first sentence together. Remind students about the third-person *s*.

2. Have students work individually to complete the sentences. Go over the answers as a class.

B 1. Read and have students repeat the words in the box.

2. Have students work individually to complete the sentences. Go over the answers as a class.

C Have students work individually to complete the email. Ask a volunteer to read the completed email aloud for the class.

Multilevel Strategies

For 1C, seat same-level students together.

• **Pre-level** Work with this group to complete the paragraph. Elicit the answers from the group. Have everyone write the answers before moving on to the next sentence. When you finish, ask students to take turns reading the letter aloud with a partner.

• **On- and Higher-level** While you are working with pre-level students, ask these students to finish 1C and then write another letter. Tell them to write a letter to you asking for advice about how to improve their English. Encourage them to use at least three gerund constructions in their letters. Ask volunteers to read their letters aloud for the class. Give your advice in response.

---

2 Group work

Communicative Practice

20–35 minutes

 1. Direct students, in groups of four, to focus on the picture. Ask: *Who are these people? Where are they?*

2. Assign roles: leader, recorder, and reporters. Explain that students work with their groups to write the conversation.

3. Check comprehension of the roles. Ask: *Who writes the conversation?* [recorder] *Who will read the conversation to the class?* [reporters] *Who helps everyone and manages the group?* [leader] *Who creates the conversation?* [everyone]

4. Set a time limit (five minutes) to complete the exercise. Circulate and answer any questions.

5. Have reporters from each group read the group's conversation to the class.

> ### Multilevel Strategies
>
> For 2A, use mixed-level groups.
>
> • **Pre-level** Assign these students the role of reporter.
>
> • **On-level** Assign these students the role of recorder.
>
> • **Higher-level** Assign these students the role of leader.

 1. Have students walk around the room to conduct these interviews. To get students moving, tell them to interview three new people not in their groups for 2A.

2. Set a time limit (five minutes) to complete the exercise. Tell students to make a note of their classmates' answers but not to worry about writing complete sentences.

> ### Multilevel Strategies
>
> Adapt the mixer in 2B to the level of your students.
>
> • **Pre-level** Allow these students to ask and answer the questions without writing.
>
> • **Higher-level** Have these students ask two additional questions and write all answers.

 Call on individuals to report what they heard from their classmates. Ask them to share their classmate's achievements.

PROBLEM SOLVING

15–25 minutes

 1. Ask: *Are you working on your goals right now?* Tell students they will read a story about a man who has achieved many of his goals and now has a new one. Direct students to read Jafari's story silently.

2. Ask: *Why wasn't life easy when Jafari first came to the U.S.? What has he achieved?*

3. Play the audio and have students read along silently.

 1. Elicit answers to question 1.

2. Put students into groups of three or four. Ask each group to think of three or four possible solutions to Jafari's problem and report them to the class. Ask a volunteer to write all possible solutions on the board.

3. Have students write letters giving advice to Jafari. Pair students and ask them to read their partners' letters. Call on volunteers to share any differences between the letter they wrote and the one they read.

Evaluation

30–35 minutes

To test students' understanding of the unit grammar and life skills, have them take the Unit 12 Test on the *Step Forward Test Generator CD-ROM* with *ExamView® Assessment Suite*.

> ### Learning Log
>
> To help students record and discuss their progress, use the *Learning Log* on page T–203.

To extend this review: Have students complete **Workbook 4 page 85, Multilevel Activity Book 4 page 136**, and the **Unit 12 Exercises** on the **Multilevel Grammar Exercises CD-ROM 4.**

2 Group work

A Work with 2–3 classmates. Write a 6–8 line conversation between the people in the picture. Share your conversation with the class.

A: *You've done very well over the last six months.*
B: *Thank you…*

B Interview 3 classmates. Write their answers.

1. Name someone you think is really successful. What has that person achieved?
2. What is one achievement of yours that your classmates probably don't know about?
3. Name one leadership quality that you would like to work on developing. Why did you choose this quality?

C Talk about the answers with your class.

PROBLEM SOLVING

A Listen and read about Jafari.

When Jafari immigrated to the U.S. ten years ago, he had a lot of dreams. Life wasn't easy at first. He worked two jobs and didn't have much time to work on his goals. But over time, things got easier. Jafari was able to go to college, find a good job, and finally buy a house for his family.

Today, Jafari owns his own business and is proud of everything he's accomplished. Now that he has a little more free time, he's interested in giving something back to the community. He'd like to be involved in something that would really make his community a better place to live, but he doesn't know where to start.

B Work with your classmates. Answer the questions.

1. What is Jafari's problem? Jafari wants to make his community a better place to live, but he doesn't know where to start.
2. What should he do? Think of 2 or 3 possible solutions for Jafari.
3. Write a short letter to Jafari. Tell him what you think he should do.

LISTENING SCRIPT

UNIT 1: It Takes All Kinds!

Pg. 4   Lesson 1—Exercise 1C

W = Woman, N = Narrator
1. W: My new class is great. There are some
        really interesting people in it. Let me
        tell you something about them. That's
        Omar. He likes to talk, and he likes words.
        If you don't know what a word means,
        just ask Omar! He's a verbal person.
    N: verbal
2. W: Fatima's good with numbers, and she's good
        at solving problems. She wants to teach
        math someday. She's very mathematical.
    N: mathematical
3. W: Now that's Ari. On the weekends, he goes
        canoeing or climbs mountains. He loves
        going to new places and trying new things.
        He's adventurous.
    N: adventurous
4. W: Nora likes spending time with people.
        She's so friendly; everyone likes her.
        I'd definitely say she's social.
    N: social
5. W: That's Ariana. She paints pictures. She loves
        to work with her hands. She's very artistic.
    N: artistic
6. W: That's Carlos. He plays the guitar and
        the piano. He's really musical.
    N: musical
7. W: Eric likes to run, play basketball, and
        swim. If it's a sport, he likes it. He plays
        soccer on the weekends. He's athletic.
    N: athletic
8. W: And that's me. I don't talk a lot in class,
        but I really like listening to what other
        people say. I guess I'm pretty quiet.
    N: quiet

Pg. 10   Lesson 3—Exercise 3

1. Eric is a lot like his brother, Tom. He looks
    like him. They both have black eyes and
    dark hair. And they like the same things.
2. Omar reads a book every week. Then he
    writes a report about it. He also makes lists of
    the new words he learns when he reads.
3. Ariana doesn't have a car. She doesn't really need
    one. But she wants a new bicycle. She believes
    that bicycles are good for the environment.
4. Nora and her sister go to the community
    center every Saturday. They swim in the
    pool there and talk with their friends.
5. Ari, the adventurous one, climbs mountains and
    travels to far-away places. He does something
    new every time he takes a vacation.
6. Some people think that I'm not very social, but
    that's not true. I may seem unfriendly, but I really
    like people. I also like to be alone sometimes.
    My friends understand that about me.

Pg. 11   Lesson 4—Exercise 1A

W = Woman, M = Man
1. W: I think our school is great.
        What's your opinion?
    M: Well, I think the teachers are great
        and the campus is nice, but my classes
        always have too many students.
    W: Really? Do you prefer smaller classes?
    M: Yes, I love small classes! I think they're
        better for students.
    W: Maybe you're right, but in a large class
        you can meet lots of people. I like that.
2. M: I think teachers should get more money.
    W: That may be so, but their job seems easy.
    M: Easy? Really? Why do you say that?
    W: Because they just talk to students all
        day. That's not very difficult.
    M: I'm not sure I agree. I think
        teaching is hard work.

Pg. 13   Lesson 4—Exercise 4B

T = Talk show host, K= Dr. Kwang, H = Mr. Holt
T: Our guests today are Dr. Violet Kwang, from the
    Center for Education, and Mr. Fred Holt, from Hills
    County Public Schools. Welcome to you both.
K: Thank you.
H: Thanks.
T: Let's start with a general question. What would you
    say is the biggest problem facing our schools today?
K: Well, for me, it's a problem of staffing. We
    simply don't have enough good teachers.
H: I would have to agree. We need to get more
    college graduates to become teachers.
T: And how can we do that?
K: By paying teachers higher salaries and
    giving them better benefits.
H: I agree totally.
K: And with more teachers, we could have
    smaller classes. Right now, there are too
    many students in most classes.
H: But then we'd need more schools—
    or at least more classrooms.
K: We need to build new schools.
    There's no question about that.
H: I'm not sure I agree. Where is the money
    for new schools going to come from?
K: From taxes. We need just a small
    increase in state taxes.
H: I have to disagree on that one, too.
    Nobody wants higher taxes.
T: OK. Well, what about safety in our
    schools? Are things getting any better?
H: We think so. And we hope to install
    security cameras in every high school
    next year. That should help a lot.
K: Security cameras? That doesn't sound
    like a very good idea. The money you're
    going to spend on cameras needs to go
    toward new books and computers.
H: I agree that we need books and computers,
    but safety is important, too.

T: Well, we're out of time. Thank you both for being here. See you next time on *The Education Show*. Bye!

UNIT 2: Keeping Current

Pg. 18 Lesson 1—Exercise 1C

W = Wanda, S = Stan, N = Narrator
1. W: Good morning, Stan. Hey, did you see the *Times* this morning? There was a great article about the meeting of world leaders on the front page.
   N: front page
2. S: Uh…, well, I don't have much time in the morning.
   W: Hmmm, that's too bad. It's interesting to find out people's opinions of the news and politics. At least you should take the time to read the editorial page.
   N: editorial page
3. S: OK, OK, Wanda! Sometimes I read more of the paper. When I was looking for a job and a good used car, I always checked the classified ads.
   N: classified ads
4. S: And come to think of it, I've learned a lot about things around the home, exercising, and healthy eating in the lifestyle section.
   N: lifestyle section
5. W: Well, yes, the newspaper is useful for that kind of thing, too. If I want to see movie or a TV show, I look at the entertainment section.
   N: entertainment section
6. S: Yes, and any time I miss a baseball or football game on TV, I read the sports section.
   N: sports section
   W: Still Stan—it's a newspaper—you should take a look at the news once in a while.
   S: OK, Wanda, OK… (sound of crinkling newspaper) Happy now?

Pg. 24 Lesson 3—Exercise 3

1. Our car was hit by a tree.
2. The information was given to the reporter by the neighbors.
3. The teenagers' parents were called by the police.
4. The fire was caused by an electrical problem.

Pg. 25 Lesson 4—Exercise 1A

W = Woman, M = Man
W: Did you hear about the protest downtown?
M: No. What was it about?
W: The city wanted to prohibit food carts on the street. You know, those carts that sell sodas and snacks downtown. The protesters tied themselves to the carts.
M: The city wanted to limit the carts?
W: No, not limit, they wanted to *prohibit* them. They didn't want *any* carts in the city. The protesters were very upset.
M: I can understand that. We need to support small businesses—and the food is good and cheap. So were the carts prohibited?
W: No. To make a long story short, the protesters won. The carts were allowed to stay.

Pg. 27 Lesson 4—Exercise 4B

Thousands of people were told to leave their homes today in Florida towns along the Gulf Coast. Weather forecasters predict Hurricane Timothy will reach the coast sometime Wednesday. Local residents must leave their homes by noon today. Several schools in neighboring towns were opened for the residents to stay in. Food and water are being brought in. The hurricane is expected to bring strong winds and heavy rain. Because of the dangerous conditions, news reporters, including myself, were also asked to leave by local officials. From the Florida Gulf Coast, this is Ron Avery, reporting live for Channel 4 News.

UNIT 3: Going Places

Pg. 32 Lesson 1—Exercise 1C

W1 = Woman 1, M1 = Man 1, N = Narrator, O = Operator, M2 = Man 2, W2 = Woman 2, B = Bus Driver, D = Dispatch Operator, W3 = Woman 3, M3 = Man 3
1. W1: Gary, what's that sound? Look at the smoke coming out from the hood.
   M1: Oh no! I can't believe this. Another problem with this car? We don't have time to have a breakdown.
   N: have a breakdown
2. W1: Turn on the hazard lights—we need to warn other drivers.
   M1: I already did. I know it's important to turn on the hazard lights.
   N: turn on the hazard lights
3. W1: I'll call the auto club. They'll help us.
   O: Thank you for calling All City Auto Club. May I help you?
   W1: My husband didn't want to call you, but I did… our engine was smoking, and now we're on the side of the road, across from the city mall. I told my husband we had to call the auto club.
   N: call the auto club
4. O: OK. If the smoke is gone, he can raise the hood of the car.
   W1: If there's no more smoke, the operator says to raise the hood of the car.
   N: raise the hood
5. M2: Oh, great! We've got a flat tire.
   W2: We're miles from a gas station. This is a terrible place to have a flat tire.
   N: have a flat tire
6. W2: Honey, do you need help changing the tire?
   M2: I'm OK. Just keep the kids away. It's not that hard to change a tire.
   N: change a tire
7. B: Oh, this is bad. The bus breaks down on my first day of work. OK, first thing to do is use these safety triangles…gotta warn the other drivers. Geez, this is a big bus. I've got to use a lot of safety triangles.
   N: use a safety triangle

8. B: Dispatch? This is driver 719. My bus broke down at Cedar and King. Can you send a tow truck right away?

   D: No problem. We'll send a tow truck.

   N: send a tow truck

9. W3: That's it. I have to walk... Excuse me, I can't wait for the bus, and I need to get directions to the library from here. Can you help me?

   M3: I'm not from this area, but I believe you go straight on this street for two blocks, then turn left. The library should be on your right. I hope...

   W3: Thanks. And don't worry about it. If I get lost, I can call my roommate to get directions.

   N: get directions

Pg. 38   Lesson 3—Exercise 3

W1 = Woman 1, M1 = Man 1, M2 = Man 2,
W2 = Woman 2, M3 = Man 3, W3 = Woman 3,
M4 = Man 4, W4 = Woman 4, W5 = Woman 5,
M5 = Man 5, M6 = Man 6, M7 = Man 7,
W6 = Woman 6, W7 = Woman 7, M8 = Man 8,
M9 = Man 9, W8 = Woman 8

1. W1: Hi, David. What's up?
   M1: I'm lost!
2. M2: Hi, Patricia. Is everything OK?
   W2: No, it isn't. I have a flat tire.
3. M3: Hi, Gina. How are you?
   W3: Not so good. My car broke down. I'm waiting for a tow truck.
4. M4: Hi Donna. It's Sam. I'm with Joe.
   W4: It's late. Where are you guys?
   M4: We're stuck in traffic.
5. W5: Do you want to drive with me?
   M5: No. I'm taking the bus.
   M6: Yeah. I'm taking the bus, too.
6. M7: Cindy, why don't you call your sister? She can help.
   W6: I don't have a cell phone.
7. W7: Hi, Hank. What's going on?
   M8: I'm not going to class today. My car's out of gas.
8. M9: Do you need anything else for your trip, Maria?
   W8: I need a map.

Pg. 39   Lesson 4—Exercise 1A

M = Man, A = Artie, W = Woman, R = Rhonda

1. M: Hey, Artie. I'm thinking about going to San Francisco next month. I have a long weekend and I've never been there before.

   A: Have you already booked your ticket?

   M: No, but my cousin said to look for a ticket on the Internet. Do you have any website suggestions?

   A: I'd check out Southair if I were you.

   M: Is it hard to find information on the website?

   A: Nah—it's really easy. And I bet they'll have the cheapest prices.

   M: Thanks!

2. W: Rhonda, I'm traveling to Atlanta next month, but I don't know anything about the city.

   R: Do you have your hotel reservation?

   W: Not yet. I don't know any motels in that city. Can you give me a recommendation?

R: You could stay in a Motel 22. They're all over the U.S. They probably have a motel in Atlanta.

W: Is it hard to find out?

R: No, it's easy. Just call their 800 number and make a reservation.

W: That's a great idea. Thanks for your help.

R: My pleasure.

Pg. 41   Lesson 4—Exercise 4B

Welcome to the Motel 22 automated message system. Please listen to the following choices. To make a room reservation at one of our 120 motels around the country, please press one. To locate the Motel 22 nearest you, please press 2 and enter your zip code. To inquire about reserving 15 or more rooms for a conference, wedding, or other large event, please press 3. For employment information, please press 4. For all other inquiries, please call 1-800-555-5252. To hear this message again, please press the pound key. Thank you for calling Motel 22.

UNIT 4:   Get the Job

Pg. 46   Lesson 1—Exercise 1C

W = Woman, N = Narrator

W: If you're thinking about your future, one of the things you really should do is visit the career center. It's a great place.

1. W: I'm starting a medical-technician training class next week. I needed help to pay for my classes, so I applied for financial aid. If money for training or college is a problem for you, you should apply for financial aid.

   N: apply for financial aid

2. W: A career counselor can help you apply for jobs or practice for an interview. I recommend that everyone see the career counselor at the center.

   N: see a career counselor

3. W: Our career center has a classroom upstairs. It's really convenient to take a training class at the center.

   N: take a training class

4. W: The career center posts new jobs on the job board every week. That's how my sister found her job. It definitely pays to look at job listings.

   N: look at job listings

5. W: And I always use the resource center. They have a lot of books about finding a good job and planning for a career. It's easy to use the resource center.

   N: use the resource center

6. W: In the resource center, you can take an interest inventory on the computer. This computer program matches your interests to different types of jobs. You'll learn a lot about yourself if you take an interest inventory.

   N: take an interest inventory

Pg. 52   Lesson 3—Exercise 3

Coming to live in the U.S. meant a lot of big changes in my life. Everything here was different. Before I came here, I had never lived in a small town; I had always lived in a big city. Now, I live in a small town, and I love it.

In my home country, I spoke English, so that's not different. I studied French in school, but since there are a lot of Spanish-speaking people in my neighborhood in the U.S., now I study Spanish.

And I have different goals now. Before I came to the U.S., I had always wanted to be a businessman. Now, I want to be a teacher.

Pg. 53 Lesson 4—Exercise 1A

I = Interviewer, J1 = Job Applicant 1 (Ms. Jones), J2 = Job Applicant 2 (Ms. Adams)
1. I: Tell me about your experience, Ms. Jones.
   J1: You mean work experience?
   I: Yes.
   J1: Well, I've never really had a job.
   I: I see. How about training?
   J1: You mean like job training?
   I: Yes.
   J1: No. I haven't had that, either.
   I: Well, thank you, Ms. Jones.
2. I: Tell me about your experience, Ms. Adams.
   J2: Do you mean work experience?
   I: Yes.
   J2: Well, I've worked in a restaurant for the last two years.
   I: I see. How about training?
   J2: Is that job training?
   I: Yes.
   J2: Well, let's see. I took a class in restaurant cooking at the college. And I've always loved cooking for my family.
   I: I see. That's good. You have a lot of the skills we're looking for.
   J2: Thank you.

Pg. 55 Lesson 4—Exercise 4B

H = Hanna, L = Liz
H: I'm working on my resume, and I have some questions. Could you help me out with a couple of things?
L: Sure. I'd be happy to. What's the problem?
H: Well, I'm taking a training class at the college, but I haven't finished yet. How do I write that?
L: Just write the month you started the class *to present*. That shows you haven't finished yet.
H: Uh-huh. I took an ESL class, too. Should I include that?
L: Yes, definitely. When did you finish?
H: Last year.
L: OK, then just write the school, the place, the name of the class, and the year.
H: And what about high school? I graduated from high school in my country.
L: I think you should include that, too. Write *high school diploma*, and the year you received it.
H: Great. I've already finished the employment history, so I think I'm done. Thanks for your help.
L: My pleasure. Now you just have to type it neatly, and then check it—twice.

UNIT 5: Safe and Sound

Pg. 60 Lesson 1—Exercise 1C

W = Woman, N = Narrator
1. W: We work with a lot of hazardous materials. Because these materials are so dangerous, we store them in this locked area. Only trained employees have the key to get in the restricted area.
   N: restricted area
2. W: We lock up the chemicals that give off poisonous fumes. Use those chemicals only in the open air. It's dangerous to breathe in poisonous fumes.
   N: poisonous fumes
3. W: We also keep flammable liquids here. Those are liquids that could catch fire easily. Of course, there's no smoking near flammable liquids.
   N: flammable liquids
4. W: There are also radioactive materials in the area. You should make sure you don't open any containers with the *radioactive materials* symbol.
   N: radioactive materials
5. W: Containers with corrosive chemicals are stored here, too. These chemicals can burn your skin if you touch them, so be careful if you work with corrosive chemicals.
   N: corrosive chemicals
6. W: Look at that fan. It has a frayed cord. An electrical fire can be caused by a frayed cord.
   N: frayed cord
7. W: There's a broken ladder over there. We need to put a sign on it. No one should ever use a broken ladder.
   N: broken ladder
8. W: Do you see that yellow warning sign? Always put one out if there's water on the floor. We always need to warn people when there's a slippery floor.
   N: slippery floor

Pg. 66 Lesson 3—Exercise 3

1. There's an electrical fire. We've got to call 911.
2. The reporter said a tornado is heading our way. We must evacuate the area.
3. The tornado might come close to the school. The children have got to go to the basement.
4. There's a major hurricane coming. Residents must leave the area.
5. Last year, there were three big storms, but it wasn't necessary for people to leave the area.
6. To prepare for the storm, it was necessary for most people to buy emergency supplies.

Pg. 67 Lesson 4—Exercise 1A

W = Woman, J = Mr. Jenks, M = Man
1. W: Excuse me, Mr. Jenks. I want to report a problem in the basement.
   J: OK. What's wrong?
   W: There are some flammable chemicals too close to the furnace.
   J: You're right. We shouldn't have put

them there. I'll get someone to move
them. Thanks for letting me know.
W: No problem.
2. M: Excuse me, Mr. Jenks. I noticed a problem in
the basement.
J: Really? What is it?
M: There's a spill near the oil containers.
J: Thanks for bringing this to my attention.
I'll call maintenance.

Pg. 69   Lesson 4—Exercise 4B

W = Wally, A = Amelia
W: People talk a lot about the most dangerous
jobs. But you don't hear much about the
jobs that are the safest. Which jobs do you
think are the safest? Let's go to Amelia Holt
for a story on jobs that will keep you safe.
A: Thanks, Wally. When you think of safe jobs
you might think of jobs in education, like
teachers and librarians. And it's true that these
jobs are pretty safe compared to many others.
For example, in one year people working in
educational services had an injury rate of just
2,440. Compare this with over 10,000 injuries
for workers in the hospitality industry, places
like hotels and other vacation facilities. But the
safest workers in the United States work in the
telecommunications industry. They have only
150 injuries and illnesses for every 10,000 workers.
The computer industry is also very safe, with just
220 injuries or illnesses for every 10,000 workers.
The reason for this may be that these people work
in a very clean environment. They also wear
protective clothing and work slowly and carefully.
For other safe jobs, think about scientists with
only 400 injuries or illnesses per 10,000 and
veterinarians with just 680. Maybe those dogs
and cats aren't that dangerous after all!

UNIT 6:   Getting Ahead

Pg. 74   Lesson 1—Exercise 1C

W = Woman, N = Narrator
W: Good interpersonal skills are important
in every part of my life.
1. W: I like my job, and I like my boss. He's
friendly, and he likes to hear new ideas. He
likes it when people make suggestions.
N: make suggestions
2. W: He listens carefully. If he doesn't
understand what you mean, he'll
always ask for clarification.
N: ask for clarification
3. W: I volunteer at the community parks,
and people often tell me, "You're a
good team player." I know that means
they like the way I work in a group. It's
important to be able to work on a team.
N: work on a team
4. W: When I help out at the community parks,
I look for ways to make our work easier. I like
to solve problems.
N: solve problems
5. W: I'm a mother, too, and of course my children
disagree sometimes. I try to help my kids

calm down, and I try not to get angry. It's
important to know how to manage conflict.
N: manage conflict
6. W: I always ask my kids to help find a solution
when there's a problem between them. That's
how I help them resolve disagreements.
N: resolve disagreements
7. W: I'm a student, too—I'm learning to paint.
My teacher is great. When I ask him to look
at my work, he always gives feedback.
N: give feedback
8. W: When my art teacher gives me feedback, I try
to respond. I let him know that I will follow
his suggestions when I respond to his feedback.
N: respond to feedback
W: I think these interpersonal skills are
really important, and I try to use them
every day no matter where I am.

Pg. 80   Lesson 3—Exercise 3A

W1 = Woman 1, M1 = Man 1, M2 = Man 2,
W2 = Woman 2
1. W1: What kind of people do you need?
M1: We're looking for people that
can manage conflict.
2. M2: Why are you changing your security systems?
W2: We need systems that are reliable.
3. M1: How was the new employee's evaluation?
W1: She got an evaluation which was very positive.
4. W2: What kind of people does the company need?
M1: We're hiring people who work well on a team.
5. W1: What is the most important personal quality
for this job?
M1: The person that gets the job must be reliable.
6. W2: Who are you going to interview?
M1: We'll interview the applicants who have the
right experience.

Pg. 81   Lesson 4—Exercise 1A

M1 = Man 1, Ma = Marta, M2 = Man 2, J = Jamal
1. M1: Hey, Marta. What's wrong?
Ma: There's a problem with my schedule.
Who do I talk to about it?
M1: The warehouse manager. She's the
person who takes care of schedules.
Ma: Oh yeah. She's the one whose office is
upstairs. Do I need an appointment?
M1: Nope. Just go to her office. That's the way
it works.
Ma: OK. Thanks for the help. I'll see you later.
2. M2: What's the matter, Jamal?
J: I don't understand this benefits memo.
What should I do about it?
M2: You need to talk to someone in
the human resources office.
J: Do I go to the manager?
M2: No, no. Mr. Gupta, the benefits
officer, sent that memo. See him.
J: Mr. Gupta? Who's he?
M2: He's the man whose office is next
to Accounting. You've got to make
an appointment with him.
J: I'll do that. Thanks for your help.
M2: No problem.

Pg. 83 Lesson 4—Exercise 4B

You have reached Martinez Electronics. Please listen to the menu of options, and then dial the extension you need. You may dial the extension at any time.

1. If you are interested in buying a new or used computer, please dial our sales and service department at extension 111.
2. If you are calling about a computer repair, please dial our customer service department at extension 222.
3. If you are a business customer, please dial our business services department at extension 417.
4. To be connected to the warehouse, please dial extension 700.
5. For employee issues, including payroll, please dial the human resources office at extension 389.
6. For all other questions, please call our main office at extension 555.

UNIT 7: Buy Now, Pay Later

Pg. 88 Lesson 1—Exercise 1C

R = Roberto, J = Julia, N = Narrator

R: Julia and I have been renting our apartment for 6 years. Lately, we've been talking about buying a house. We know it won't be easy, but we want to try.

1. R: First, we made a list of all our assets: everything we own, including our bank accounts and our car. We have about $5,000 in assets.
   N: assets
2. J: Next, we made a list of our debts. Debts are the things we owe money on like the loans we have and the money we owe on our credit card. We have about $4,000 in debts.
   N: debts
3. R: We have an insurance policy on the things in our apartment. If there's a fire, for example, the insurance will help us replace our things. If we buy a house, we have to get a different insurance policy.
   N: insurance policy
4. J: Next, we went to State Bank to get information about a home loan. We have to borrow the money to buy a house. We got this brochure about getting a home loan.
   N: home loan
5. R: We've also been thinking about getting a new car. To buy a new car, we would need to get an auto loan, so we also picked up a brochure about getting an auto loan.
   N: auto loan
6. J: They make it look pretty easy and their interest rates are only 3.3 percent, depending on the kind of loan you get. We will decide based on the interest rate.
   N: interest rate
   R: Now we're going to look at how we're spending the rest of our money. We may need to cut our spending to afford a house. But it's worth it!

Pg. 94 Lesson 3—Exercise 3

1. If I had a credit card, I wouldn't have to carry cash.
2. If I didn't use my credit card, I would spend less money.

3. I love movies. I would rent a movie every night if I didn't have to study.
4. Not me. If I didn't have to study, I would save my money and get some sleep!

Pg. 95 Lesson 4—Exercise 1A

R = Roberto, J = Julia

1. R: Where does the money go? We'll never be able to afford a house!
   J: Sure we will. There are plenty of ways we can cut back on our spending.
   R: Well, that sounds good, but how do we do it?
   J: Well, for example, right now we spend about $300 a month on food. I bet we could cut that to $200 if we compared prices more carefully.
   R: Hmmm… Let's compromise. How about if we made it $250? Then we'd still be able to buy fresh fruit and vegetables— those are a little more expensive.
   J: OK. It's a deal.
2. J: What do you think we should spend on entertainment? $50 a month?
   R: I think that's too high. How about $20? We could rent about 5 movies a month for $20.
   J: Let's compromise. $25, and we get the videos from the library. They're cheaper there.
   R: Good idea. Even if we were millionaires, I'd still love the library.

Pg. 97 Lesson 4—Exercise 4B

O = Ms. Ogun, M = Mr. Moreno

O: Good morning, Mr. Moreno. I'm Ms. Ogun. How are you today?

M: I'm fine, but I'm afraid my finances need a little help. I decided I needed to see a financial planner, and a friend recommended you.

O: Wonderful. So tell me what's going on.

M: Well, the main problem is my debt. I thought that if I made the minimum payment on my credit card each month, I'd be OK. But the total keeps growing.

O: Yes, credit cards can be a problem if you're not careful. Tell me, what's your total debt?

M: About $5,000.

O: OK. Let's look at your monthly expenses and see where you can save.

M: Here's a list I've made. I spend about $400 a month on food. That includes about $5 a day for lunch at work. My car costs me about $250. And then I spend about $75 a month on entertainment, including cable TV. My phone bill is pretty high, too. I call my family in Honduras a lot.

O: Well, first I think you should start taking your lunch to work. If you did, you'd save at least $3 a day. You should also look for a better calling plan. You could probably save $20 a month that way. And how much do you think you'd save if you got a different cable plan?

M: At least $20 a month… You know, these are all good ideas, but it doesn't sound like I'd save that much.

O: Actually, all together you'd save almost $1,000 a year. And if you got a low-interest loan and paid off your credit-card debt with it, your monthly payments would go down and you'd save even more.

M: That's a great idea. Thanks.

O: You're welcome. Oh, and one more thing. If I were you, I'd put my credit cards away and stop using them for a year.

UNIT 8: Satisfaction Guaranteed

Pg. 102   Lesson 1—Exercise 1C

E = Vince Elko, N = Narrator

E: Good evening, viewers! I'm Vince Elko, your consumer reporter. How do you like to shop? Do you like big stores, small stores, brand new malls, or little neighborhood stores? Or would you rather not go to a store at all? Here's a look at some of the most popular ways to shop today.

1. E: The first rule of smart shopping is to look for items on sale. Today I was watching TV, and I saw this fantastic cookware on sale. The original price was $199.95, but today only they were offering the cookware on sale for $89.95. That's a savings of $110! It pays to shop when things are on sale.

   N: on sale

2. E: Of course, I was watching a TV shopping network. There are lots of shopping possibilities on TV. You see the items on TV and buy them by calling the TV shopping network.

   N: TV shopping network

3. M: Another option is an online store. You can choose items on the store's website and place an order without talking to anyone. You can shop 24 hours a day if you go to an online store.

   N: online store

4. E: Catalogs are another really convenient way to shop. You can call the company to order what you want, and they send the items to you. You can also mail in your catalog order—it just takes a little longer. If you like to shop by phone (or by mail), it's great to use a catalog.

   N: catalog

5. E: You can save money if you shop at thrift stores. These stores carry used items, things people don't want anymore. You can get clothes and furniture at really good prices if you shop at a thrift store.

   N: thrift store

6. E: You have to pay attention, though, because thrift store items are sold "as is." For example, this arm chair is being sold "as is" for $10. It has a broken arm and the fabric is torn. You won't pay much for this chair, but you can't complain about it or return it because you've bought it "as is."

   N: as is

7. E: Another great way to save when you shop is to look for items "on clearance." These items are put on sale for a very low price. For example, this old dresser has been in the thrift store for two years. The store owners wanted to sell it quickly, so they put it on clearance for only $25.

   N: on clearance

8. E: You can also shop at yard sales if you like saving money. Families sell things they don't need anymore—usually at really good prices—at a yard sale.

   N: yard sale

9. E: Then there are flea markets. These are usually outdoors, and sellers have clothes, toys, tools— just about anything you might need. You can find really interesting things at a flea market.

   N: flea market

   E: There are a lot of choices out there, consumers. Remember, it's your money, so spend it carefully. This is Vince Elko, for consumer news.

Pg. 108   Lesson 3—Exercise 3

1. Thank you for shopping at our new store today. How was your shopping experience?
2. Hmmm…Well, was it easy to find the things you wanted?
3. What did you think of the food department?
4. Oh, that's too bad. Well, what did your children think about our kids' play area?
5. Did you know that we have free babysitting while you shop?
6. I'd like to give you this application for a store credit card.

Pg. 109   Lesson 4—Exercise 1A

T = Tara, C1 = Customer 1, C2 = Customer 2

1. T: Carry-Time Luggage. Tara speaking. How may I help you?

   C1: Yes, I'm interested in ordering a blue backpack.

   T: All right. Do you have the item number?

   C1: Yes, I do. It's CP 600–14—the blue one.

   T: CP 600–14? I'm sorry, sir, but that model is sold out.

   C1: They're sold out?

   T: Yes, I'm afraid so. They're all gone. Would you be interested in brown?

   C1: No, thanks. I really wanted that one.

   T: I understand.

2. T: Carry-Time Luggage. This is Tara. May I help you?

   C2: Yes, I'd like to order backpack TC 10–560. Is it still on sale?

   T: I'm afraid not. The sale ended last week.

   C2: Oh, that's disappointing.

   T: The backpack is still available, but at the regular price.

   C2: Well, I'll think about it and maybe I'll call you back.

   T: Certainly, ma'am. And have a good day.

Pg. 111   Lesson 4—Exercise 4B

M = Meg, S = Bill Seagrove

M: Time Tone Electronics. Meg speaking. How can I help you?

S: Hi. My name is Bill Seagrove. I'm calling about a problem with a watch I ordered from you. I'm very unhappy with it.

M: OK, sir. What's wrong?

S: Well, the ad said that it would look like new for 10 years, and the glass is already scratched.

M: I'm sorry. When did you receive it?

S: I've had it for three weeks. I'm so disappointed that I just want to return it.

M: I understand. Would you like another one?
S: No, thanks. I'd just like to get a refund. What do I need to do?
M: Let me look up your order so I can give you an RA number.
S: What's that?
M: It stands for *Return Authorization*. You just need to write the RA number on your return slip and then send it to us… Your number is 14-603-4.
S: OK. Thanks for your help.

UNIT 9: Take Care!

Pg. 116 Lesson 1—Exercise 1C

J = Althea Jones, N = Narrator
J: My name is Althea Jones. I turned 101 years old yesterday! A reporter interviewed me for the newspaper. Everyone wants to know my secrets for a long life.
1. J: Heredity is one of the reasons for my long life. My great-grandmother was 94 years old when I was born. In fact, most of the women in my family have had long lives. I'm grateful for that kind of heredity.
N: heredity
2. J: I have seen the doctor for a checkup every year. My doctor says it's important to have yearly physicals.
N: yearly physicals
3. J: Since I was young, I have seen the dentist every six months. I still have all my teeth! That's because I get regular dental checkups.
N: dental checkups
4. J: I had five children. All of my babies were healthy and strong. When I was pregnant, I saw a doctor every month for prenatal care.
N: prenatal care
5. J: I have always looked for small health problems early so they don't become big problems later on. One key to staying healthy is early detection.
N: early detection
6. J: I have medical tests done every year to make sure that I don't have any big health problems. My doctor can see if a problem is starting with these medical screenings.
N: medical screenings
7. J: I have also been active. I loved to swim, and I played tennis until I was in my 80s. I don't watch TV, and I take a walk every day. I still have an active lifestyle.
N: active lifestyle
8. J: I don't eat a lot of meat, and I have fresh vegetables every day. I've always believed in good nutrition.
N: good nutrition
J: I hope everyone reads my advice about leading a healthier life and preventing health problems. I'd like you to live to be 101, too!

Pg. 122 Lesson 3—Exercise 3

1A. You've got to start taking better care of your teeth.
1B. You should start taking a little better care of your teeth.
2A. You ought to make an appointment to see the dentist soon.
2B. You have to make an appointment to see the dentist soon.
3A. You should choose a pediatrician even before your baby is born.
3B. You must choose a pediatrician for your baby before your baby is born.
4A. You'd better ask your doctor to recommend a good pediatrician.
4B. You should ask your doctor to recommend a good pediatrician.
5A. You shouldn't wait too long before you call the doctor.
5B. You'd better not wait too long before you call the doctor.
6A. You've got to get medical screenings if your doctor thinks they're important.
6B. You'd better get medical screenings if your doctor thinks they're important.

Pg. 123 Lesson 4—Exercise 1A

D = Doctor, P1 = Patient 1, P2 = Patient 2
1. D: Have you made any changes in your lifestyle since the last time I saw you?
P1: I'm trying to pay more attention to good nutrition. I want to live to be 100.
D: That's a great idea. What changes have you made in your diet?
P1: Well, I'm eating more dark green vegetables and more fruit.
D: That sounds good. You might want to try to get more exercise, too.
P1: I knew you were going to say that! I don't like running, though.
D: You could try swimming or an aerobics class at the gym.
P1: So I need to eat well and get more exercise.
D: That's right. And get regular checkups, of course.
2. D: Do you have any health concerns you'd like to talk about?
P2: Yes, I do. My family has a history of heart trouble, so I'm trying to keep myself healthy and in good shape. Last week, I started to take an exercise class.
D: That sounds like a good idea. What about your diet?
P2: Yeah… I'm cutting out fatty foods. No more donuts for me!
D: That's smart. Cutting back on salt would be good too. What about stress?
P2: Now, that's a problem. I need to relax more.
D: Well, exercise helps, and you could try spending more time doing the things you enjoy.
P2: So I'm supposed to keep exercising, try to relax, and cut back on salt.
D: Right. Those are great steps to take.

Pg. 124 Lesson 4—Exercise 3B

1. insurance
2. serving
3. stomach
4. each
5. change
6. chronic

D = Doctor, G = Mr. Gomez
D: So, Mr. Gomez, you cut your hand working
in your garden. It doesn't look too bad. I'll
clean it up and put a bandage on it.
G: I don't need stitches?
D: Not this time. You'll have to keep the cut clean.
I'll give you an antibiotic ointment to put on it.
G: Will I need a prescription for antibiotic pills?
D: No, you just need the ointment. By the way,
when was the last time you had a tetanus shot?
G: I can't remember. I don't think I've
had one in at least 20 years.
D: Well, you'll need to have a tetanus shot.
Actually, since you're over 50 years old,
you should consider having a flu shot, too.
It's a good idea at this time of year.
G: Two shots in one day? I really
don't like getting shots.
D: Well, let's see… You'll need to come back in a week
so I can take a look at your hand again. I can give
you the flu shot then. Call me if you have any
problems, and don't forget to make an appointment
for next week. I'll have the flu vaccine ready.
G: Great…

UNIT 10: Get Involved

Pg. 130 Lesson 1—Exercise 1C

M1 = Man 1, M2 = Man 2, N = Narrator
   M1: Riverview is a great city to live in. But there are
        some things I think could be better. I'm just
        one person; is there really anything I can do?
1. M2: Sure there is. Last year, for example, a group
        of us identified a problem. We were sick of
        seeing all the garbage in that empty lot on
        the corner. It really was a problem because
        the garbage attracted a lot of rats. That
        was the first step — identify a problem.
   N: identify a problem
2. M2: We stood in that lot and tried to think of
        ways to make it a good community resource.
        Maribel proposed a great solution—a new
        playground. You can't just talk about the
        problem. You have to propose a solution.
   N: propose a solution
3. M2: After that, we formed a committee to
        talk about what we wanted to do. We
        came up with a lot of good ideas once
        we started to discuss the issue.
   N: discuss the issue
4. M2: We talked about budgets and the
        kind of equipment we wanted. We
        knew we had to develop a plan.
   N: develop a plan
5. M2: Of course, we couldn't just start to build
        a playground on city property without
        permission. We needed to get approval
        and we needed money! So we took our
        plan to the city council to get approval.
   N: get approval
6. M2: Then the real work started. We agreed that
        the community would work together to build

the playground. It was a lot of fun and a
lot of hard work to implement the plan.
   N: implement the plan
M1: That sounds like the kind of thing I could
        get involved in. I guess you're right; one
        person really can make a difference!

Pg. 136 Lesson 3—Exercise 3

1. Could you tell me when the next public
   works committee meeting is?
2. Do you know why the law clinic is closed?
3. Could you tell me who I talk to
   about child care services?
4. Do you know if your city has any senior centers?
5. Do you have any idea where the city manager went?
6. Can you tell me if the public safety
   committee discussed my idea yet?

Pg. 137 Lesson 4—Exercise 1A

C = Clerk, O = Geraldo Ochoa, M = Olive Martin
1. C: City Clerk's office. Can I help you?
   O: Hi. This is Geraldo Ochoa. I'm calling because I
      heard that they want to build apartments near
      the park. Can you tell me if that's the case?
   C: Yes, it is.
   O: Why would they do that? It's a beautiful park.
   C: I hear what you're saying. You know,
      there's a meeting about it next Tuesday,
      at 7 p.m., in the Council Chamber.
   O: Hmmm… I can't remember where that is.
   C: It's in the Municipal Building, at 440 State Street.
   O: I'll try to be there.
2. C: City Clerk's office. How may I direct your call?
   M: Hi. This is Olive Martin. I'm calling because I
      understand that the mayor wants to cut the
      Summer Jobs for Teens program. Is that true?
   C: Yes, that's right. There is a budget cut planned.
   M: Why would the mayor cut that program?
      It's really important to the community.
   C: I know what you mean. If you're
      interested, there's going to be a public
      hearing on it at 7 p.m., in the Council
      Chamber, on November 28th.
   M: Really? I'd like to go, but I'm
      not sure when that is.
   C: It's on Thursday night.
   M: Great. I'll be there. Thanks.

Pg. 139 Lesson 4—Exercise 4B

A public hearing on the annual budget for the city of
East Port will be held Tuesday, March 23, at 7 p.m., at
city hall. The hearing is open to the public.

City hall is located at 1400 Washington Street. To get
to city hall, take the F4 bus to 14th Street. The bus
stops in front of city hall.

Parking is available in the public parking lot on 15th
Street. Go straight one block to Beech Street, and turn
right into the lot.

The hearing will be held in the Hearing Room. Take the
elevator or the stairs to the second floor.

Follow the signs to the Hearing Room. It will be on
your right, after Room 210.

UNIT 11: Find It on the Net

Pg. 144 Lesson 1—Exercise 1C

W = Woman, N = Narrator
- W: I've been trying to find a new apartment in Chicago, and it isn't easy. But I found this great website that really helps.
1. W: Type www.rentalhomes.rent in the URL box. The address of the website or webpage always goes in the URL box.
- N: URL box
2. W: OK, now we're on the webpage. The site is called rentalhomes.rent and it's free. When you go to this website, you start on this webpage.
- N: webpage
3. W: You can search quickly through all the information on the website to find the kind of apartment or house you want. So for example, you can type *one-bedroom* in the search box.
- N: search box
4. W: To start typing in the box, click in the box. You'll see a flashing line that goes on and off. That's the cursor. You can start typing when you see the cursor.
- N: cursor
5. W: Over here on the left, there are links for information about finding a roommate or a mover, renting a truck—things like that. To get more information, you can click on the links.
- N: links
6. W: Watch out for pop-up ads. They're advertisements, usually trying to sell you something. I hate them. You can click on the *X* at the top of the ad to close a pop-up ad.
- N: pop-up ad
7. W: The site has apartments all over the country. To tell the site which state you want to look at, you use a pull-down menu.
- N: pull-down menu
8. W: Over on the right, you can use the scroll bar to scroll down the menu to find a state. To see the last state, move down the box in the scroll bar.
- N: scroll bar
9. W: See that little white arrow on the page? That's the pointer. Point it to the state you want and click. Sometimes instead of an arrow, you'll see a little hand. That's also the pointer.
- N: pointer
- W: Well, that's how it works. And I found a great apartment! Isn't the Internet amazing?

Pg. 150 Lesson 3—Exercise 3

1. You're from a big city,...
2. You speak several languages,...
3. You didn't go to school here last year,...
4. This isn't your first English class,...
5. Ms. Coolidge is the computer teacher,...
6. Her students don't like to leave her class,...
7. They're making webpages,...
8. We wanted to take her class,...
9. It didn't take a lot of time to learn to use the Internet,...

Pg. 151 Lesson 4—Exercise 1A

A = Abby, L = Leo
- A: Leo, you're still going to help me send an email, aren't you?
- L: Yes, of course, Abby. First double click on the mail icon—that's the envelope on your menu bar.
- A: Double click?
- L: That means put your pointer on the icon and click twice quickly. That opens your email program. Now click on *new* in the menu.
- A: Like this?
- L: Yes, that's good. Now, see the blank email? Click in the *To* window and type in the landlord's email address. Then click in the *Subject* window and type *Repairs for Apartment 105*. Now you're ready to write. Just click here and start.
- A: So, I click here and start typing?
- L: Yes, but can I suggest something?
- A: Sure.
- L: Make the email short. State the problem and what you want the landlord to do. Ask him to call you as soon as he gets the email.
- A: That's a great idea.

- A: OK, I've typed in the address and the subject. Now I can send it, can't I?
- L: Yep. Click on the send button, and that's it.
- A: Click on the what?
- L: The *send* button, up there at the top left.
- A: Oh, OK. There we go.
- L: Can I make another suggestion?
- A: Well sure. Please do.
- L: If you don't hear back from the landlord today, send another email tomorrow.
- A: That's a good idea. I need to get my heat turned on.

Pg. 152 Lesson 4—Exercise 3B

1. You know how to do this, don't you? (rising intonation in tag question)
2. You don't know how to do this, do you? (falling intonation in tag question)
3. That was a good suggestion, wasn't it? (falling intonation in tag question)
4. We looked at this website last week, didn't we? (rising intonation in tag question)
5. You're going with me, aren't you? (rising intonation in tag question)
6. He's an expert with technology, isn't he? (falling intonation in tag question)

Pg. 153 Lesson 4—Exercise 4B

L = Larry, talk show host, P = Melia Pappas
- L: Our guest today is Melia Pappas, founder of the apartment finder website ApartmentSearch.apt. Welcome, Melia.
- P: Thanks, Larry.
- L: Tell us how you got started in the website business.
- P: Well, I worked at an apartment rental office when I was in...
- L: Sorry. When you were where?
- P: In college. I learned a lot about the questions people ask when they're looking for apartments.

L: What is the most common question people ask?

P: Most people want to know what the landlord's responsibilities are. For example, does he have to fix things like the heat and the plumbing? Anyway, then a couple of years ago, I took a class on making your own website, and I loved it.

L: It's hard to learn to design a website, isn't it?

P: No, it isn't. It's pretty easy, but it does take a lot of time. It took me about six months to design ApartmentSearch.apt.

L: Sorry. About how long?

P: About six months. It was a big project.

L: I can imagine. A lot of people use your site, don't they?…

P: They sure do. We get… of visitors every day.

L: You get how many?

P: Hundreds. People like being able to look for an apartment or a house without going outside.

L: All right. Thanks, Melia Pappas, for being our guest today. Come back and talk with us again soon.

P: I will, Larry. Thank you for having me.

UNIT 12: How did I do?

Pg. 158 Lesson 1—Exercise 1C

K = Katie, newspaper reporter, M = Elio Moya

K: Thanks for letting me interview you, Mr. Moya. The school paper wants a story on your achievements.

M: No problem, Katie. It's a pleasure to be interviewed by someone from my old high school. In fact, I thought we'd look at a few pictures from those days.

1. K: OK, tell me about this one, Mr. Moya. I see that you're sitting on the couch with a newspaper.

   M: I'm not just sitting. I'm dreaming. I had a dream of being in politics even when I was in high school. My teachers supported me. Everyone needs to have a dream.

   N: have a dream.

2. K: What's this picture—what's in the letter?

   M: Oh, this was when I won my scholarship. A community organization paid for my books, my college tuition, all my costs. You have to study and work very hard to win a scholarship.

   N: win a scholarship

3. K: Is this a picture of your father?

   M: No, that's me in front of my electronics store. I had always wanted to open a business, and when I started my business, I was very excited. It's exciting and a little frightening to start a business.

   N: start a business

4. K: This is a sad picture. Your store didn't burn down, did it?

   M: Yes, it did. But adversity is part of life, so I just went out and rebuilt my store. If you want to succeed, you have to be prepared to overcome adversity.

   N: overcome adversity

5. K: You were really happy when this picture was taken, weren't you?

   M: Happy? I was ecstatic! This was the day I lived my dream. I had become the mayor. It was a long road, but I managed to achieve my goal.

   N: achieve a goal

6. K: I remember this picture. It was in the newspaper last week.

   M: Yes, last week I was able to help out the local little league baseball team. These days my dream is to give back to the community that has given so much to me. I would not be where I am without the support the community gave me. It's time for me to give back to the community.

   N: give back to the community

   K: Thanks, Mr. Moya. I have all the information I need for my story.

   M: You're welcome, Katie. I look forward to reading about your achievements someday.

Pg. 164 Lesson 3 Grammar—Exercise 3

M1 = Man 1, W1 = Woman 1, M2 = Man 2, M3 = Man 3, W2 = Woman 2, W3 = Woman 3

1. M1: Michael is thinking about making a career change.

2. W1: He's tired of being a waiter, and he wants to be his own boss.

3. M2: He's planning on leaving the restaurant business and starting his own company.

4. M3: He's been saving his money instead of spending it.

5. W2: Michael is nervous about making such a big change.

6. W3: He'll talk to a small business counselor before making a final decision.

Pg. 165 Lesson 4—Exercise 1A

M = Manager, K = Kim

M: You've done very well over the past six months, Kim. You're doing a great job of helping out the hotel staff, and you've learned a lot about working in a hotel.

K: Thank you for saying so.

M: In fact, I'd like to suggest taking a training class for hotel workers. Is that something you'd be interested in doing?

K: Yes, I would, very much.

M: Good. I'll take care of signing you up for the class.

K: Thank you very much.

M: There is something you need to work on, though.

K: Oh? I didn't realize anything was wrong.

M: Well, I've noticed that you're often late for work, and that makes things difficult for everyone in the hotel.

K: I understand. I'll try to do better. I'll start taking an earlier bus.

M: That would be great.

Pg. 167 Lesson 4—Exercise 4B

1. You need to begin thinking about taking more responsibility.

2. I appreciate the fact that you really care about doing a good job.

3. You must work on getting here on time.

4. Would you mind changing to the day shift? We need someone with your skills.

5. You need to start checking with the shift manager before taking a break.

6. You're doing a great job. I'm going to recommend giving you a raise.

GRAMMAR CHARTS

ACTION VERBS IN THE SIMPLE PRESENT

Statements	
I	work.
You	
He	works.
She	
It	
We	work.
You	
They	

Negative statements		
I	don't	work.
You		
He	doesn't	
She		
It		
We	don't	
You		
They		

Note
Most verbs describe actions. These verbs are called action verbs.

ACTION VERBS IN THE PRESENT CONTINUOUS

Affirmative statements	
I'm	working.
You're	
He's	
She's	
It's	
We're	
You're	
They're	

Negative statements	
I'm	not working.
You're	
He's	
She's	
It's	
We're	
You're	
They're	

NON-ACTION VERBS

Some non-action verbs		
be	like	see
believe	love	smell
dislike	mean	sound
forget	need	taste
hate	own	think
have	possess	understand
hear	remember	want
know		

Note
Use non-action verbs to describe feelings, knowledge, beliefs, and the senses. Non-action verbs are usually not used in the present continuous.

TYPES OF QUESTIONS

Yes/No questions and answers
A: Do you agree?
B: Yes, I do. OR No, I don't.

Information questions and answers
A: Who agrees with you?
B: Everyone agrees with me.

Or questions and answers
A: Do they agree or disagree?
B: They agree.

Direct information questions
When will the meeting start?
Where is the meeting?
What does the mayor want?
What are the issues?
How did you find the meeting?
Why did the mayor call the meeting?

Indirect information questions
Do you know when the meeting will start?
Could you please tell me where the meeting is?
Do you know what the mayor wants?
Do you have any idea what the issues are?
Can you tell me how you found the meeting?
Do you know why the mayor called the meeting?

Note
Indirect questions sound more polite than *Yes/No* or direct information questions.

Yes/No question with *if* or *whether*

Direct	Indirect		
Did they discuss the issue?	Can you tell me	if whether	they discussed the issue?
	Could you tell me		
	Do you know		

Tag questions and short answers with *be*

Affirmative statement	Negative tag	Agreement	Disagreement
You're good with email,	aren't you?	Yes, I am.	No, I'm not.
The landlord was here,	wasn't he?	Yes, he was.	No, he wasn't.
The heaters are old,	aren't they?	Yes, they are.	No, they're not.

Negative statement	Affirmative tag	Agreement	Disagreement
You're not good with email,	are you?	No, I'm not.	Yes, I am.
The landlord wasn't here,	was he?	No, he wasn't.	Yes, he was.
She isn't writing an email,	is she?	No, she isn't.	Yes, she is.

Notes
• Use a negative tag after an affirmative statement. Negative tags are usually contracted. Ask a negative tag question when you expect the answer to be "Yes."
• Use an affirmative tag after a negative statement. Ask an affirmative tag question when you expect the answer to be "No."

Tag questions and short answers with *do* and *did*

Affirmative statement	Negative tag	Agreement	Disagreement
The landlord fixed it,	didn't he?	Yes, he did.	No, he didn't.
The heat works today,	doesn't it?	Yes, it does.	No, it doesn't.
They sent emails,	didn't they?	Yes, they did.	No, they didn't.

Negative statement	Affirmative tag	Agreement	Disagreement
The landlord didn't fix it,	did he?	No, he didn't.	Yes, he did.
The heat doesn't work today,	does it?	No, it doesn't.	Yes, it does.
They didn't send emails,	did they?	No, they didn't.	Yes, they did.

THE PAST PASSIVE

The past passive			Notes
I	was		• The past passive uses the verbs *was/were* + the past participle. Lunch was served.
You	were		• We usually use the active voice in English. Sara served lunch.
He		taken to the hospital.	• The passive voice directs the action toward the subject.
She	was		• The active voice directs the action toward an object.
It			• In English, use the passive voice when we do not know who performed the action, when it is not important who performed the action, or when it is clear who performed the action.
We			
You	were		
They			

Yes/No questions and short answers
A: Were they taken to the hospital?
B: Yes, they were. OR **B:** No, they weren't.

Information questions and answers
A: Where were they taken?
B: They were taken to City Hospital.

REFLEXIVE PRONOUNS

Subject pronouns	Reflexive pronouns	Notes
I	myself	• Reflexive pronouns end with *–self* or *–selves*.
you	yourself	• Use a reflexive pronoun when the subject and object of the sentence refer to the same person, people, or thing. She saw herself on TV.
he	himself	
she	herself	
it	itself	• Use *by* + reflexive pronoun to say that someone or something is alone or does something without help from others. I watched TV by myself.
we	ourselves	
you	yourselves	
they	themselves	

REPORTED SPEECH

Quoted speech statements	
I	
You	
He	
She	said, "Stop."
It	
We	
You	
They	

Reported speech statements	
I	
You	
He	
She	said (that) I should stop.
It	
We	
You	
They	

Reported speech with instructions	
I	
You	
He	
She	told me to stop.
It	
We	
You	
They	

Notes

- Use reported speech to tell what someone has said or written.
- Use *said* to report a person's words.
- For quoted speech in the simple present, the reported speech is in the simple past.
- For quoted speech in the present continuous, the reported speech is in the past continuous.

Reported speech with *told* + noun or pronoun	
I	
You	
He	
She	told me (that) I should stop.
It	
We	
You	
They	

Notes

- Use an infinitive (*to* + verb or *not to* + verb) to report an instruction.
- Use *told* to report on who heard the words. Use a noun (someone's name) or an object pronoun (*me, you, her, him, us, you, them*) after *told*.

THE PAST PERFECT

Affirmative statements

I		
You		
He		
She	had worked	the day before the party.
It		
We		
You		
They		

Negative statements

I		
You		
He		
She	hadn't worked	the day before the party.
It		
We		
You		
They		

Notes

- Use *had/had not* + past participle to form the past perfect.
- Use the past perfect to show that an event happened before another event in the past. The past perfect shows the earlier event:

  When Ms. Porter interviewed Luis, she had prepared some questions.

  = First Ms. Porter prepared some questions. Then she interviewed Luis.

Yes/No questions

	I		
	you		
	he		
Had	she	worked	the day before the party?
	it		
	we		
	you		
	they		

Answers

	I				I	
	you				you	
	he				he	
Yes,	she	had.	No,		she	hadn't.
	it				it	
	we				we	
	you				you	
	they				they	

Information questions

	I		
	you		
	he		
How many days had	she	worked	before the party?
	it		
	we		
	you		
	they		

Answers

I	
You	
He	
She	had worked one day before the party.
It	
We	
You	
They	

NECESSITY

Present				Past				Note
I	have to			I				There are no past forms of *must* or *have got to* to express necessity. Use *had to* instead.
You	must			You				
He	has to			He				
She	has got to	stop.		She	had to	stop.		
It	must			It				
We	have to			We				
You	have got to			You				
They	must			They				

PAST OF *SHOULD*

Affirmative statements			Negative statements		
I			I		
You			You		
He			He		
She	should have	stopped.	She	shouldn't have	stopped.
It			It		
We			We		
You			You		
They			They		

ADJECTIVE CLAUSES

Main clause	Adjective clause after main clause		Note
I like working with people	who / that	work hard.	Use adjective clauses to give more information about a noun in the main clause of the sentence.
I can solve problems	that / which	happen in my job.	

Main clause
Adjective clause inside main clause

The supervisor	who / that	hired me	likes my work.
The work	which / that	I do	is done well.

Main clause	Adjective clause with *whose*
I am the employee	whose paycheck was lost.
They are the people	whose children we saw.

Note

Adjective clauses with *whose* to show who something belongs to.

Main clause	Adjective clause with *wh-* or *if/whether*
I'm not sure	when the meeting starts.
She doesn't know	where the meeting will be held.
They have no idea	what the meeting is about.
I can't remember	if they're going to discuss the issue.
He wonders	whether they'll discuss the budget.

Note

Use a *wh-* or *if/whether* clause after certain expressions to talk about things you don't know for certain.

PRESENT UNREAL CONDITIONAL

Statements

If clause	Main clause
If I worked hard,	I could get a better job.
If she got a better job,	she would have more money.
If they had more money,	they could live more comfortable lives.

Notes

- Use unreal conditionals to talk about unreal, untrue, or impossible situations.
- In unreal conditionals, the *if* clause can also come after the main clause: She would have more money if she got a better job.

Yes/No questions and short answers

A: Would you work if you didn't need the money?
B: No, I wouldn't.
A: If she wanted a better job, would she go to college?
B: Yes, she would.
A: If they had a car, would they drive to work?
B: Yes, they would.

Information questions and answers

A: Where would you work if you could work anywhere?
B: I would work at the college.
A: If you could have any car, what car would you have?
B: I would have a small car.

Note

Don't use contracted forms (*I'd, you'd, she'd, he'd, we'd, you'd, they'd*) in affirmative short answers.

Statements with *be*

If clause	Main clause
If I were you,	I would ask for help.

Note

In formal speech with present unreal conditions, use were for all people (*if I were…, if you were…, if he were…, if she were…, if they were…*).

ADVERBS OF DEGREE

Least ◄─────────────────────────────────────► Most or greatest			
I am a little tired.	I am pretty tired.	I am really tired.	I am extremely tired.
I am somewhat tired.	I am fairly tired.	I am very tired.	

SO, SUCH, AND THAT

So...that, such...that, and *such a/an...that*		Notes
The store is so popular	that it is always crowded.	• Use *so, such, such a/an + that* to show a result.
The store has such low prices		• Use *so* with an adverb or an adjective.
It is such a small store		• Use *such* or *such a/an* with an adjective + a singular count noun.

ADVICE

Advice and strong advice

mild ↑	You	should shouldn't ought to	stay home today.
strong		had better had better not	
strongest ↓		have to have got to must	

Notes

• Use *should* and *ought to* to give advice. They mean the same thing.
• In the U. S., people don't usually use *ought to* in a negative statement.
• Use *had better* to give strong advice or to tell someone to do something.
• *Have got to* is as strong as *have to* and *must*, but is less formal.

Confirming advice

So I	should stay home today.
	need to stay home today.
	am supposed to stay home today.
	have to stay home today.

GERUNDS AND INFINITIVES

Verb + gerund

She avoids exercising.
He quit exercising.
I'd consider exercising.
They feel like exercising.
I started exercising.
He'll continue exercising.
She likes exercising.
They prefer exercising.

Verb + infinitive

She decided to exercise.
He agrees to exercise.
I plan to exercise.
They need to exercise.
I started to exercise.
He'll continue to exercise.
She likes to exercise.
They prefer to exercise.

Preposition + gerund

She does a good job of solving problems.
She knows a lot about answering the phone.
She is good at taking phone messages.
She got a promotion instead of getting a raise.

Notes

- Gerunds are used after prepositions like *about, at, for, in,* instead *of,* and *to.*
- Gerunds are also used after verb phrases with prepositions:
  She cares about helping people.

Be + adjective + preposition + gerund

She is interested in learning about the review.
They are proud of getting raises.
We are famous for taking management classes.
I am happy about going to the class.

Note

Certain adjectives are almost always followed by a preposition.
She is interested in helping people.

Polite requests and suggestions with gerunds

I would suggest applying for a management position.
May I recommend training to help you reach your goals?
Would you mind asking for more training?

PREFIXES, SUFFIXES, AND ENDINGS

The suffix -less

harmless = not harmful
speechless = unable to speak
wireless = without a wire

Note

Add –less to some nouns to form adjectives.
–less usually means "without" or "not".

The suffixes –er and -ee

Verb	Noun	Noun
employ	employer	employee
train	trainer	trainee
pay	payer	payee

Notes

- The suffix –er indicates the person who performs an action.
- The suffix –ee indicates the person who receives the result of the action.
  A trainer trains a trainee.

The suffix -ous

Noun	Adjective
caution	cautious
danger	dangerous
hazard	hazardous

Note

Add –ous to some nouns to form adjectives. Note that spelling might change; for example, *caution—cautious*.

The suffixes –ed and -ing

disappointed	disappointing
interested	interesting
confused	confusing

Notes

- Adjectives ending in –ed describe a person's feelings. He was bored.
- Adjectives ending in –ing describe the cause of the feelings. The game was boring.

The suffix -ful

Noun	Adjective
help	helpful
care	careful
beauty	beautiful

Note

Add –ful to some nouns to form adjectives. Note that spelling might change; for example, *beauty—beautiful*.

The suffix -ment

Verb	Noun
agree	agreement
announce	announcement
assign	assignment

Note

Add –ment to some verbs to form nouns.

Prefixes for negative forms of adjectives

Adjective	Negative form
responsible	irresponsible
flexible	inflexible
reliable	unreliable
honest	dishonest

Note

Add the prefixes *dis-*, *in-*, *ir-*, and *un-* to some adjectives to make negative forms.

VOCABULARY LIST

A

a little 107
about us 145
accessible 42
account for 70
achieve a goal 158
active lifestyle 116
adopt 140
adventurous 4
advise 98
agree 11
agreement 141
allergic 117
announce 140
applicant 53
application essay 160
apply for
    financial aid 46
apprentice 168
artistic 4
as is 102
ask for clarification 74
assertive 159
asset 88
assign 141
athletic 4
auditory learner 5
auto loan 88
automated message 34
average 13
avoid isolated areas 61

B

be alert 61
beautiful 113
beauty 113
believe 9
blizzard 62
bored 106
boring 106
broken ladder 60
budget 89

C

call the auto club 32
care 113
career 47
careful 113
catalog 102
cause 22
caution 71
cautious 71
change a tire 32

check up on 154
child care services 131
chronic 117
city clerk's office 137
classified ads 18
close 22
college entrance
    exam 14
community 130
competent 159
compromise 95
computer technician 69
concentrate 14
confident 159
confused 107
confusing 107
consider 124
consumer 112
consumer-
    protection 112
contact us 145
co-payment 126
corrosive chemicals 60
courageous 159
cover 126
cover letter 48
creative 8
current event 19
cursor 144
customers 78
cut back on 118
cut out 118

D

danger 71
dangerous 70
deal with 165
debt 88
decide 124
dedicated 159
deductible 126
defective 103
dental checkup 116
dented 103
develop a plan 130
diabetes 123
disagree 11
disappointed 106
disappointing 106
discuss the issue 130
disease 117
dishonest 85
dislike 9

diverse 84
does excellent work 77
drop 28
drought 62
dump 140

E

early detection 116
editorial page 18
emergency plan 62
emphasis 84
employ 57
employee 57
Employee of
    the month 76
employer 57
entertainment
    section 18
enthusiastic 84
equivalent 98
essay 90
evacuate 66
evaluation 75
eventually 168
excited 107
expenditure 98
experience 53
extremely 107

F

faded 103
fairly 107
FAQs 125
fee-for-service plan 126
fell well/better 127
field 56
figure 28
financial aid 56
fine 140
fixed expenses 89
flammable liquids 60
flea market 102
flexible 75
flood 62
forget 9
frayed cords 60
front page 18

G

get approval 130
get directions 32
get in touch with 42
get sick 127

give back to
the community 158
give feedback 74
gives 110% 77
goes beyond
the call of duty 77
goes the extra mile 77
good nutrition 116
govern 141
gradually 168
graduate 84
graffiti 20

H
had better 120
had to 65
harmless 43
hate 9
have a breakdown 32
have a dream 158
have a flat tire 32
have a physical 127
have an illness 127
have got to 64
have to 64
hazard 71
hazardous 71
headline 19
health services 131
hear 9
help 113
helpful 113
heredity 116
hold 34
home 145
home loan 88
honest 75
hotel worker 69
Human Resources 82
hurricane 27

I
identify a problem 130
I'll bet 39
immunization 125
implement the plan 130
include 9
income 89
increase 42
independent 75
inflexible 85
injury 70
insurance policy 88

interest 99
interest rate 88
interested 168
Internet 144
internship 47
interpersonal skills 74
interview 50
interviewer 53
intimidating 98
inventory 56
involve 141
irresponsible 85
issue 112
it's a deal 95
it's about time 151

J-K
jobs skills workshop 47
keep track of 70
kinesthetic learner 5

L
landlord 148
leadership qualities 159
learning style 5
legal services 131
lifestyle section 18
links 144
locked out of the car 33
look at job listings 46
lost 33
love 9

M
make 8
make suggestion 74
manage conflict 74
manageable 14
managed-care plan 126
mathematical 4
medical screening 116
memo 76
miscellaneous 89
mobility 42
mortgage payment 89
musical 4
must 64

N
need 9
negative feedback 165
net pay 83
network 126

news 18
news story 20

O
on clearance 102
on sale 102
online 28
online course 47
online store 102
on-the-job training 47
opinion 11
ought to 120
out of gas 33
overcome adversity 158
own 9

P-Q
paint 8
paramedics 22
parks and recreation 131
pay 57
pay off 84
payee 57
payer 57
persistent 117
personal letter 118
personal qualities 75
plan 124
play a part 140
pointer 144
poisonous fumes 60
policy 112
poll 28
pop-up ad 144
positive feedback 165
possess 9
practical 159
premium 89
prenatal care 116
prepare 64
pretty 107
prevent accidents 61
product 112
prohibit 25
property 154
propose a solution 130
protest 25
protestors 25
public hearing 139
public safety 131
public works 131
pull-down menu 144

put in (my)
two cents 137
quiet 4
quit 124

R
radioactive material 60
raise the hood 32
rating 112
really 107
reasonable 154
recall 112
recommendation 76
referral 126
regularly 28
regulate 112
related links 145
reliable 75
remember 9
renters' rights 151
report 67
report suspicious
activities 61
resolve disagreements 74
respond to feedback 74
responsible 75
restricted area 60
resume 55

S
safety hazard 67
save 98
savings 98
scholarship 56
scientist 69
scratched 103
scroll bar 144
search box 144
security deposit 155
see a career
counselor 46
see a dentist 127
see a doctor 127
seem 9
self-study course 47
send a tow truck 32
senior services 131
severe 117
shipping and
handling 111
should 120
should have 68
situation 43

skill 78
slippery floor 60
smell 9
social 4
sold out 109
solve problems 74
somewhat 107
sound 9
specialist 126
speechless 43
sponsor 140
sports section 18
sprain 70
stained 103
start 124
start a business 158
state 141
strain 70
strategy 14
stressed 123
stuck in traffic 33
student 3
studious 3
studiously 3
study 3
supplies 64
symptom 117

T
take 22
take a training class 46
take an interest
inventory 46
take care of it 67
take medicine 127
take vitamins 127
taste 9
teacher 69
technology 146
telecommunications
worker 69
tenant 154
test anxiety 14
tetanus shot 125
thrift store 102
to make a long
story short 25
tolerant 75
top story 19
torn 103
tornado 62
tradition 168
traffic report 19

train 57
trainee 57
trainer 57
training 47
travel 32
travel emergency 32
truth 113
truthful 113
turn on the
hazard lights 32
TV shopping
network 102

U
understand 9
unreliable 85
URL box 144
use a safety triangle 32
use the resource
center 46
useless 43
utility 89

V
variable expenses 89
variety 56
verbal 4
very 107
visual learner 5
vocational class 47

W-Y
watch 8
weakness 117
weather emergency 62
weather forecast 19
webpage 144
website 39
what's new 145
when it comes to 146
win a scholarship 158
wireless 42
write 8
yard sale 102
yearly physical 116

INDEX

ACADEMIC SKILLS

Grammar

Adjectives, 78, 79, 80, 82, 106, 108, 169
Adjective clause, 78, 79, 80, 82
    whose, 82
Adjective endings, 106, 108
    -ed, 106, 108
    -ing, 106, 108
Adverbs of degree, 107, 108
Changing verbs to nouns, 141
    -ment, 141
Clarification questions, 152
Forms of advice, 120, 121
    had better, 120
    have got to, 121
    have to, 121
    must, 121
    ought to, 120
    should, 120
Gerunds
    after prepositions, 162, 164
    be+adjective+preposition+gerund, 163
Indirect information questions, 134, 135, 136
    if, 135
    whether, 135
Necessity, 64, 65, 66
    have got to, 64
    have to, 64
    must, 64
Necessity in the past, 65
Past passive, 22, 23, 24
Past perfect, 50, 51, 52, 54, 68
    affirmative and negative statements, 50, 51, 52
    questions, 51
Prefixes, 85
    dis-, 85
    in-, 85
    ir-, 85
    un-, 85
Present perfect, 54
Prohibition, 64, 66
    must not, 64, 66
Pronouns, 26
    reflexive, 26
Reported speech, 36, 37, 38
    +noun or pronoun, 37
should have, 68
Simple past, 54
so...that, 110
Statements with wh- and if/whether, 138
such a/an...that, 110
such...that, 110
Suffixes, 43, 57, 113
    -ee, 57
    -er, 57
    -ful, 113
    -less, 43
Tag questions, 148, 149
    be, 148
    did, 149
    do, 149
Unreal conditional statements, 92, 93, 94, 96
    be, 96
    questions, 93
Verbs, 2, 8, 9, 10, 124, 127, 141
    action, 8, 10
    changing verbs to nouns, 141
    gerunds, 124
    health and illness, 127
    infinitives, 124
    nonaction, 9, 10
    tenses, 2
Word families, 3

Graphs, Charts, Maps

13, 28, 69, 71, 99, 139

Listening

Accidents, 71
Achievements, 158
Action and non-action verbs, 10
Adjective clauses, 80
Adjectives ending in -ing and -ed, 108
Apartment, finding an 153
Asking for information, 81
Automated messages, 41, 139
Automated phone menus, 83
Career planning, 46, 57
Cell phones, 43
Community involvement, 130, 141
Community problems, 137
Consumer protection, 113
Current events, 25
Expressing opinions about education, 11
Gerunds, 164
Getting to know your classmates, 2
Have to, 66
Health, 116
Health insurance, 127
Indirect information questions, 136
Internet, 144
Interpersonal skills, 74
Interview questions, 53
News stories, 27
Newspapers, 18
Past passive, 24
Past perfect, 52
Personal finance and banking, 88
Personalities and talents, 4
Positive feedback and criticism, 167
Present unreal conditionals, 94
Renters' rights, 154
Reported speech, 38
Reporting unsafe conditions, 67
Returning merchandise, 111
Safe jobs, 69
Safety hazards and warnings, 60
Saving money, 99
School conditions, 13

Shopping, 102
Should, had better, have to, must, ought to, 122
Skills training, 85
Tag questions, 150
Test anxiety, 15
The news, 29
Training classes, 55
Travel emergencies, 32
Visiting the doctor, 125
Women in the workplace, 169

Math

Addition, 41, 55, 97, 111, 125, 139
Average, 13
Circle graphs, 69
Decimals, 41, 111
Multiplication, 41, 111
Percentages, 139, 167
Subtraction, 27, 83, 97, 153

Problem Solving

Analyzing and negotiating, 17
Budgeting, 45
Communicating learning needs, 157
Confronting health issues, 129
Creating a positive work environment, 87
Determining how to handle problems with neighbors, 115
Financial planning, 101
Giving back to the community, 171
Organizing neighborhood clean-ups, 143
Planning for the future, 59
Reporting unsafe working conditions, 73
Understanding the news, 31

Pronunciation

Intonation, 54, 152
    rising intonation, 54, 152
    falling intonation, 152
Linked consonants and vowels, 110
Ough, 68
Pausing, 96, 138, 166
    at commas, 96
S or z sounds, 40
S and *ch* sounds, 124
T, 12
Using stress to clarify meaning, 26
Yes and *No,* 82

Reading

Accidents, 70, 71
Application essays, 160
Doctor's offices, 123
Career planning, 56, 57
Catalog orders by phone, 109
Cell phones, 42, 43
Community involvement, 140, 141
Community issues, 132
Consumer protection, 112, 113
Cover letters, 48
Emails, 104
Emergency preparation, 62
Health insurance, 126, 127
Interviews, 50

Money, 90
Learning styles, 6
Negotiating, 95
News stories, 20, 22
Offering and responding to help, 151
Performance reviews, 165
Personal letters, 118
Preparing for earthquakes, 64
Recommendations, 76
Renters' rights, 154, 155
Saving money, 98, 99
Skills training, 84, 85
Technology, 146
Test anxiety, 14, 15
The news, 28, 29
Using a phone, 34
Web articles, 154
Women in the workplace, 168, 169

Speaking

Achievements, 158, 159, 160, 169
Doctor's offices, 123
Career planning, 46
Catalog orders by phone, 109
Cell phones, 43
Community involvement, 130, 141
Community issues, 132
Consumer protection, 113
Current events, 25, 29
Describing computer skills, 146
Email problems, 104
Emergency plans, 63
Emergency preparation, 62
Expressing opinions about education, 11
Getting to know your classmates, 2
Health, 116
Health insurance, 127
Improving health, 118
Internet, 144
Interpersonal skills, 74
Learning to ask for information, 81
Learning styles, 5, 6, 7
Making travel plans, 39
Negotiating, 95
News stories, 20, 21
Newspapers, 18, 19
Offering and responding to help, 151
Participating in a performance review, 165
Personal finance and banking, 88
Personalities and talents, 4
Recommendations, 77
Renters' rights, 155
Reporting unsafe conditions, 67
Responding to interview questions, 53
Safety hazards and warnings, 60, 71
Saving money, 99
Shopping, 102
Skills, 57
Talking about a problem in the community, 137
Technology, 147
Tests, 15
Travel emergencies, 32
Using the phone, 35

Writing

Achievements, 158
Career planning, 46
Community involvement, 130
Community problems, 133
Cover letters, 49
Emails, 105
Emergency plans, 63
Getting to know your classmates, 2
Health, 116
Internet, 144
Interpersonal skills, 74
Learning styles, 7
Money, 91
Newspapers, 18
News stories, 21
Personal finance and banking, 88
Personal letters, 119
Personalities and talents, 4
Phone experience, 35
Problems, 133
Recommendations, 77
Safety hazards and warnings, 60
Shopping, 102
Technology, 147
Travel emergencies, 32
Using the phone, 35

CIVICS

Advocacy, 130, 131, 132, 133, 136, 137, 139
Banking, 88, 89
Consumer complaints, 103, 104, 105, 112, 113, 115
Educational training, 46, 47
Emergencies, 32, 33, 62, 63, 73
Employment resources, 46, 48, 49, 53, 55, 56, 57, 59,
    159, 160, 161, 165
Environment, 140, 141
Health care, 116, 117, 118, 119, 123, 125, 127, 129
    Health insurance, 126, 127
    Housing, 154, 155
    Insurance, 153
    Safety measures, 60, 61, 67, 69, 70, 71
    Volunteering, 130, 131, 140

LIFE SKILLS

Consumer Education

Catalog orders by phone, 109
Consumer protection, 112
Personal finance and budgeting, 88, 89, 95
Purchasing problems, 103
Returning merchandise, 111
Saving money, 98, 99
Shopping, 102

Environment and the World

Adopt-a-Road programs, 140
Current events, 27, 29
News stories, 18, 21

Government and Community Resources

Community involvement, 130, 140, 141
Community services, 131
Health insurance, 127

Health and Nutrition

Health insurance, 126, 127
Health, 116
Healthy changes, 118, 119
Medical conditions, 117

Interpersonal Communication

Interpersonal skills, 74
Learning styles, 6, 7, 15
Personal qualities, 75

Safety and Security

Health insurance, 127
Safety hazards and warnings, 60, 61

Transportation and Safety

Travel emergencies, 32
Travel plans, 39
Travel problems, 33

TOPICS

Buy Now, Pay Later, 88-101
Find It on the Net, 144-157
Get Involved!, 130-143
Get the Job, 46-59
Getting Ahead, 74-87
Going Places, 32-45
How did I do?, 158-171
It Takes All Kinds!, 4-17
Keeping Current, 18-31
Safe and Sound, 60-73
Satisfaction Guaranteed, 102-115
Take Care, 116-129
The First Step, 2-3

WORKFORCE SKILLS

Maintaining Employment

Achievements, 158, 159
Internet, 144, 145
Interpersonal skills, 74
Leadership qualities, 159
Performance review, 165
Skills training, 84

Obtaining Employment

Application statement, 161
Career planning, 46, 47
Cover letter, 48, 49
Interpersonal skills, 74
Personal qualities, 75
Recommendations, 76, 77
Responding to interview questions, 53
Skills training, 84

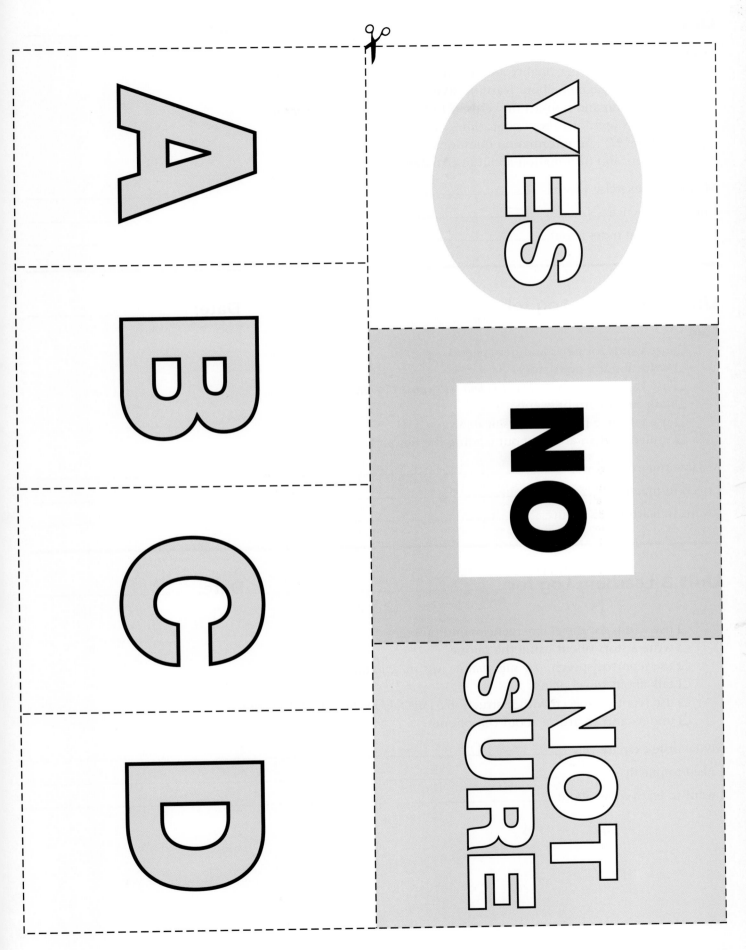

A

B

C

D

YES

NO

NOT SURE

Unit 1 Learning Log for _____ Date: _____
(name)

I can

- ❏ use words for personality and learning styles.
- ❏ write a paragraph about learning styles.
- ❏ use action and non-action verbs. *(I like books. I'm reading right now.)*
- ❏ express opinions about education.
- ❏ ask *Yes/No* and information questions.
- ❏ understand information about test anxiety.

My favorite exercise was _____.

I need to practice _____.

I want to learn more about _____.

Unit 2 Learning Log for _____ Date: _____
(name)

I can

- ❏ use words for news and newspapers.
- ❏ write about a news story.
- ❏ use the past passive. *(The accident was caused by the fog.)*
- ❏ talk about current events.
- ❏ use reflexive pronouns. *(I saw myself on TV.)*
- ❏ understand an article about reading the news.

My favorite exercise was _____.

I need to practice _____.

I want to learn more about _____.

Unit 3 Learning Log for _____ Date: _____
(name)

I can

- ❏ use words for travel emergencies and problems.
- ❏ write a story about using the phone.
- ❏ use reported speech. *(He said that he was stuck in traffic.)*
- ❏ talk about travel plans.
- ❏ use reported speech with instructions. *(She told me to look at the map.)*
- ❏ understand an article about cell phones.

My favorite exercise was _____.

I need to practice _____.

I want to learn more about _____.

Unit 4 Learning Log for _____ Date: _____
(name)

I can

- ❑ use words for career planning.
- ❑ write a cover letter.
- ❑ use the past perfect. *(I had worked in an office before I applied here.)*
- ❑ answer interview questions.
- ❑ use the simple past, the past perfect, and the present perfect. *(I've worked here since 2004. I hadn't worked in an office before. I worked in a restaurant.)*
- ❑ understand an article about career planning.

My favorite exercise was _____.

I need to practice _____.

I want to learn more about _____.

Unit 5 Learning Log for _____ Date: _____
(name)

I can

- ❑ use words for safety hazards and safety precautions.
- ❑ write an emergency plan.
- ❑ use words for necessity and prohibition. *(We have to prepare for earthquakes. You must not take the elevator during a fire.)*
- ❑ report unsafe conditions.
- ❑ use the past of *should*. *(He should have unplugged the cord.)*
- ❑ understand an article about accidents and injuries.

My favorite exercise was _____.

I need to practice _____.

I want to learn more about _____.

Unit 6 Learning Log for _____ Date: _____
(name)

I can

- ❑ use words for interpersonal skills and personal qualities.
- ❑ write a recommendation.
- ❑ use adjective clauses. *(She remembers the customers that sit at her tables.)*
- ❑ ask for information at work.
- ❑ use adjective clauses with *whose*. *(This is the employee whose paycheck was lost.)*
- ❑ understand an article about skills training.

My favorite exercise was _____.

I need to practice _____.

I want to learn more about _____.

Unit 7 Learning Log for _____ Date: _____
(name)

I can

- ❏ use words for personal finance and banking.
- ❏ write an essay about money.
- ❏ use present unreal conditional. *(If I had enough money, I would travel.)*
- ❏ negotiate a budget.
- ❏ use present unreal conditional with *be*. *(If I were you, I'd open an account.)*
- ❏ understand an article about financial planning.

My favorite exercise was _____.

I need to practice _____.

I want to learn more about _____.

Unit 8 Learning Log for _____ Date: _____
(name)

I can

- ❏ use words for shopping and purchase problems.
- ❏ write an email about problems with an order.
- ❏ use *-ed/-ing* adjectives and adverbs of degree. *(I'm really interested in this item.)*
- ❏ place a catalog order by phone.
- ❏ use *so...that, such...that,* and *such a/an...that. (The prices were so high that I didn't buy anything.)*
- ❏ understand an article about consumer rights.

My favorite exercise was _____.

I need to practice _____.

I want to learn more about _____.

Unit 9 Learning Log for _____ Date: _____
(name)

I can

- ❏ use words for health and medical conditions.
- ❏ write a personal letter.
- ❏ give different forms of advice. *(You should eat more vegetables. You had better call the doctor.)*
- ❏ ask and answer questions in a doctor's office.
- ❏ use verbs with gerunds and infinitives. *(He quit smoking. We plan to go on a diet.)*
- ❏ understand an article about health insurance.

My favorite exercise was _____.

I need to practice _____.

I want to learn more about _____.

# Unit 10 Learning Log for _____ Date: _____
_(name)

I can
- ❏ use words for community involvement and community services.
- ❏ write a letter about a community issue.
- ❏ use indirect information questions. *(Do you know when the bus is coming?)*
- ❏ talk about a problem in the community.
- ❏ use statements with *wh-* and *if/whether*. *(He's not sure when the meeting starts.)*
- ❏ understand an article about community involvement.

My favorite exercise was _____.

I need to practice _____.

I want to learn more about _____.

# Unit 11 Learning Log for _____ Date: _____
_(name)

I can
- ❏ use words for web sites and the Internet.
- ❏ write a story about using technology.
- ❏ use tag questions. *(You have a website, don't you?)*
- ❏ offer and respond to help.
- ❏ use question words for clarification. *(You want what?)*
- ❏ understand an article about renters' rights and responsibilities.

My favorite exercise was _____.

I need to practice _____.

I want to learn more about _____.

# Unit 12 Learning Log for _____ Date: _____
_(name)

I can
- ❏ use words for achievement and leadership qualities.
- ❏ write an application essay.
- ❏ use gerunds after prepositions. *(I know about managing a front desk.)*
- ❏ respond to positive feedback and criticism.
- ❏ make polite requests and suggestions with gerunds. *(I would suggest making a reservation.)*
- ❏ understand an article about a personal achievement.

My favorite exercise was _____.

I need to practice _____.

I want to learn more about _____.

MULTILEVEL CLASSROOM TROUBLESHOOTING TIPS

Instructional Challenge	Try this	Read this
Exercises seem to run too long and students go off task.	1. Set time limits for most exercises. An inexpensive digital timer will keep track of the time and allow you to focus on monitoring your learners' progress. You can always give a time extension, if needed. 2. Assign timekeepers in each group, and have them be accountable for managing the time limits.	Donna Moss, "Teaching for Communicative Competence: Interaction in the ESOL Classroom," *Focus on Basics,* http://www.ncsall.net/index.php?id=739 (2006)
There are so many different needs in my classroom, I just don't have time to teach to them all.	1. Use a corners activity to help learners identify shared goals, resulting in more realistic expectations for the group. (See the *Step Forward Professional Development Program* for more information on corners activities.) 2. Encourage learners to identify what they have to do to meet their learning goals. Having learners complete open-ended statements, such as *Good students* _____, creates a forum for a class discussion of the learners' responsibilities in the learning process.	Lenore Balliro, "Ideas for a Multilevel Class," *Focus on Basics,* http://www.ncsall.net/index.php?id=443 (2006)
I'm worried that assigning pre-level learners tasks that are different from the higher-level learners stigmatizes them.	Provide three levels of the same task, and have your learners identify which one they want to tackle. Most pre-level learners appreciate being given tasks that match their abilities in the same way that higher-level learners appreciate being given tasks that match their abilities.	Betsy Parish, *Teaching Adult ESL: A Practical Introduction* (New York: McGraw Hill, 2004), 195.
Students in groups finish tasks at different times and often start speaking in their first language.	1. Supply a follow-up task for every exercise. Often a writing task makes a good follow-up. (See the *Multilevel Strategies* throughout this book.) 2. Create a set of self-access materials that students can work on while they wait for other groups to complete the main task—for example, magazine pictures with writing prompts, level-appropriate readings with comprehension questions, grammar worksheets from the *Step Forward Multilevel Grammar Exercises CD-ROM 4, Step Forward Workbook 4,* etc.	Jill Bell, *Teaching Multilevel Classes in ESL,* (San Diego: Dominie Press, 1991), 134–146.
I like the high energy of group interaction, but it's hard to get the groups' attention once they've been engaged in group work.	1. Establish a quiet signal such as a bell, harmonica, train whistle, or music to bring the groups back into "whole-class" mode. 2. Give group leaders the job of getting the group quiet once the group timekeeper calls "time."	Peter Papas, "Managing Small Group Learning," *Designs for Learning,* http://www.edteck.com/blocks/2_pages/small.htm (2006).